Encyclopedia
of the
OCCULT

RIDER

Encyclopedia
of the
OCCULT

A guide to every aspect of
occult lore, belief, and practice

FRED GETTINGS

RIDER

London Melbourne Auckland Johannesburg

Copyright © Fred Gettings 1986

Pictures provided by
Charles Walker of Images Colour Library, Leeds

First published by Rider & Co. Ltd,
an imprint of Century Hutchinson Ltd,
Brookmount House, 62–65 Chandos Place,
Covent Garden, London WC2N 4NW

Century Hutchinson Publishing Group
(Australia) Pty Ltd, 16–22 Church Street,
Hawthorn, Melbourne, Victoria 3122

Century Hutchinson Group (NZ) Ltd,
32–34 View Road, PO Box 40–086, Glenfield,
Auckland 10

Century Hutchinson Group (SA) Pty Ltd,
PO Box 337, Bergvlei 2012, South Africa

Set by Wyvern Typesetting Ltd, Bristol
Printed and bound in Great Britain by
Butler and Tanner Ltd, Frome

British Library Cataloguing in Publication Data
Encyclopaedia of the occult: a guide
to every aspect of occult lore,
belief and practice.
1. Occult sciences—Dictionaries
133'.03'21   BF1407
ISBN 0 7126 1262 9

Introduction

The text of this dictionary has been designed as an easy reference to the more frequently encountered terms used in occult circles. Towards this end I have marshalled some 2000 terms and constructed around them a series of relatively long entries covering the more familiar terms. By means of these it has been possible to introduce many related (if less familiar) terms within a meaningful context. For example, within the longish entry on the important occult concept of the 'subtle body', I introduce several pagan and Christian occult terms, such as the 'Augoeides', the 'Astroeides', the 'Helioedes', the 'aetherial body', the 'perfect body', the 'resurrectional body', and so on. Some of these terms, thus set in context, are then examined more briefly in the relevant entries under their own names. Within this framework, I have included what I hope will be the major terms used in alchemy, astrology, demonology, Qabbalism, Theosophy and witchcraft, as well as some of the more useful terms from psychic science. I have listed only the most important (or, shall we say, the most notorious) of the demons and the most exalted of the angels.

The modern view of occultism is somewhat confused. The Latin word *occulta* actually meant 'things hidden', and within the present climate of thought (which is rooted in a sort of instinctive Neo-Platonism) almost everything has the feeling, if not the appearance, of being 'hidden'. In other words, almost everything could be defined in occult terms, for each thing evinces a secret life of its own, from the financial cycles of the Stock Exchange (linked perhaps with the nine-year cycles of the asteroids or the Uranus cycles?) to the autumnal fall of a leaf (at the cold touch of Ahriman, perhaps, or as the air chariot of a Nenuphar?). It is all a question of vision – of how we adjust the inner eye to the outer world and the outer eye to the inner world. Whatever our vision, however, we all have certain prejudices as to what occult terms lie within certain categories – we instinctively know what is occult and what is not. After all, we do have the two words 'exoteric' and 'esoteric', and it is only occult specialists who begin to see the latter in the former, as the marvellous truth slowly dawns, that all the world (even the shadows of the world) is bathed in light and the exoteric is really esoteric.

In the popular imagination the prejudices are strongly marked and the word 'occult' is generally taken to include areas of study which its theoreticians and practitioners would deny belong to the occult realm at all. Among these we might list astrology, for example, or the Chinese system of the *I Ching*, and so on. In view of the popular notion of occultism, however, I have included many terms which fall into these areas, in the confidence that those who consult the book for information will probably consider such subjects to fall well within the occult domain. An astrologer may be surprised to find his subject described as one of the black arts – as happened in a book by Cavendish★ – so he may also be surprised to find such terms in a dictionary of this kind. In spite of all that has been written on the fire philosophers, there are still some materialists around who insist that there is really nothing occult about alchemy. Such people see alchemists as the prototypes of modern scientists who lacked modern tools and vision and yet, in spite of all, somehow managed to lay the foundations for that 'objective' research into matter which is the obsession (and I use this word advisedly) of the modern world. Such people might well define the salamander as being a species of newt, yet, however they see the race of salamanders, the truth is that these people are wrong and the true alchemy was ever an occult pursuit. Again, the genuine occultist may be offended to find terms from the so-called psychic sciences (which he will almost certainly look at askance) included in a book which deals with his own subject.

Some who take their subject to be of an entirely non-occultist bias may be astonished to find terms for this subject defined or mentioned in the following text. A case in point might be the Chinese divinatory system of the *I Ching* text (*The Book of Changes* as it is called by those who have no idea as to what 'changes' meant to the Chinese). In the

★ Throughout this text, for all references to authors or authorities see the Bibliography, page 254.

eyes of the psychologist Jung the *I Ching* was not regarded as an occult text at all, yet the fact is that Jung appears to have misunderstood certain of the Chinese traditions concerning this text, which (in the eyes of those scholars who wrote commentaries on it many centuries ago) had nothing to do with 'synchronicity' and everything to do with the consultation of spirits – in a word, with 'daimonomancy' – which makes it a fair inclusion in any dictionary of occultism.

Specialists in occult realms, therefore, may be surprised by what they find in this text. Yet my overriding aim has been to present to the layman, the nonspecialist, a fairly comprehensive overview of the terms which he himself will probably consider to be rightfully occult. Such terms are given even in cases in which I myself am convinced that a term is not 'occult' at all, but belongs rather to romantic fiction. An example of this might well be Bulwer-Lytton's Vril, which he romanticized from Keely, and which took grip of the late-Victorian imagination. Not only the Victorian imagination, of course, but the modern popular imagination, which still sees in Bulwer-Lytton's Vril a sort of augury of the devastating power of the atom bomb or of nuclear fission, and of the worse things which are still to come. Few who know or use the term doubt for one moment that it is Theosophical, and that it was a power linked with the lost continent of Atlantis. Yet this is far from being the case – the word is not Theosophical (although it was discussed by Blavatsky, who gave the correct equivalent name), nor is it linked with Atlantis, but with an imaginary subterranean culture in the brain of Bulwer-Lytton! Such a term, although strictly no more occult than many of the words invented for us in an aura of gnomish Middle English by Tolkien, must be included in a book of this kind.

Those who are more specialist and perhaps more aware of the actual confines of occultism in its ancient connection with the Mysteries may have need of this book only in regard to certain specialist words. In some cases, therefore, they will be disappointed. However, I take comfort in the fact that such individuals (more likely than not) will be aware of the vastness and complexity of the occult terminologies: they are probably as aware as I am that a book which pretended to deal with all the occult terms in even European literature would be unmanageable. For every term I have included in the following text, I have had to reject at least twenty. A comprehensive book of European occult terms would probably finish up being somewhat like the early Chinese encyclopedias, which were of such bulk that their owners had to carry them around on bullock carts. Fortunately there are one or two highly specialist texts which border on our chosen subject, and in the case of little-used terms I would warmly recommend a reader to consult these. For example, one who finds himself in the invidious position of treading his way through the maze of orientalizing terms, which entered the stream of occultism by way of Theosophy, will probably find Hoult a useful guide. Again, one who is looking into the sophisticated occultism or anthroposophy of Steiner will best be guided by the specialized treatment of Arenson. In reference to the history and terminology of witchcraft, one might do no better than consult Robbins, for example, or, in relation to Paracelsian alchemical terms, Dorneus. A list of reliable sources would not be endless, but it would be wearisome for the general reader.

On the other hand, if accuracy of definition is sought, the many popular books of occult terminologies on the market are perhaps best avoided. Spence is out of date, and Fodor, while specializing mainly in the psychic sciences, is unreliable in many details. Leo's encyclopedia of astrology is something of a joke even among nonspecialists. Stebbing is occasionally useful, but somewhat partisan in his definitions. The search for accuracy of definition, or conciseness of information, is best conducted without the aid of the popular commentators (or, indeed, even the academic specialists); wherever possible, one should go directly to primary sources. Rather than consult even Hoult, it is more informative (and certainly more entertaining) to wade through Blavatsky's masterpieces by way of the useful index to *The Secret Doctrine* compiled by her seemingly indefatigable devotees in Adya in 1893. Similarly, rather than consulting Arenson, one might be better served by spending some years reading through the lectures and books of Steiner. The circumlocutions of Waite and the unavailable Dorneus are best avoided for the circumlocutions of Paracelsus himself. In occultism it is really only the initiates who speak with assurance and clarity. The fact is that, behind the back of any occult lexicographer or commentator, the mixed-company shades of Paracelsus, Boehme, Blavatsky, Leadbeater, Steiner, Gurdjieff, Ouspensky and Bailey (to name only the masters) smile in quiet amusement. Perhaps they even grimace in anguish or despair?

In occultism the first letter of the alphabet is given the numerical value of 1. It is said that the form of the modern A was derived from a hieroglyphic for an eagle and that the Hebraic form Aleph was derived from the head of an ox. This latter supposed origin explains why the A is sometimes linked with the zodiacal sign Taurus. Although the letter alpha in the Greek sequence was originally regarded as a sign of bad augury during sacrifices, it was adopted in early Christian art as the symbol of the past, so that the alpha and omega were placed on either side of the Christ symbol to indicate Christ's dominion over the past and the future. The twelfth-century Joachim di Fiore wrote of it as a holy letter because he saw the form as triangular, hence associated with the number 3, the Trinity. As a matter of fact he also saw the last letter of the Greek alphabet, the omega ω as holy, for it was a 3 arising from 2, the pair of crescents supposedly joined by a dot ᘓᘐ. See also HANSA.

Aanroo   One of the three levels of the Egyptian AMENTI, a wheat field, which was the occult symbol for the harvesting of KARMA in the afterlife.

Abaddon   The name of a demon said to be the 'Angel' of the Bottomless Pit (as mentioned in Revelation, 9, 11). The name is said to be from the Hebrew word *abad* ('he perished') and is sometimes confused wrongly with *abaton*, which is really the Greek equivalent of a 'no-go area' or a place difficult to reach.

Abaris   The dart of Abaris is said to be a magical arrow given to the mythical Greek sage Abaris by the god Apollo. This dart or arrow had the power to make its bearer invisible, to cure diseases and to permit access to knowledge of the future; in addition it was said to give the power of translocation. The dart is a symbol of initiation knowledge: Abaris is supposed to have given it to Pythagoras (when it became the wand of Pythagoras) so that what previously belonged to the world of myth

incarnated into the realm of man. Some authorities link this wand with the CADUCEUS.

Abba Amona   An occult term meaning 'father–mother' and applied to the two higher SEPHIROTH, CHOKMAH and BINAH, completed as a ternary by KETHER.

Abbamsi   A Sanskrit term for the four orders of beings, which are the gods, the demons, the PITRIS and men.

Abdals   A Mohammedan word for 'initiates', whose real identity is known only to God, through whom the civilized life of the world continues.

Abhasa   A Sanskrit name for a PHANTOM.

Abhijna   The name given to the occult power (supernatural gifts) of Buddhahood; significantly the word is derived from the Sanskrit for 'remembrance'. In southern Buddhism there are several *abhijna*: the ability to take any form at will; hearing and seeing at any distance; the ability to read the thoughts of men (and the cosmos); the knowledge of man's history and present state.

Abiegnus mons A Latin name (*Monte Abiegno* is the normal form) often used on Rosicrucian documents. Westcott, who calls it a 'mystic name', links it with the esoteric idea of Mount Meru, the fabled Olympus of the ancients, the omphalos of the world, the Land of Bliss.

Abigor The name of a demon, conjured mainly for his ability to foretell the future and to give military advice and assistance.

Abiri One of the Greek names for the KABIRI.

Abracadabra A Qabbalistic charm, perhaps originally derived from the initials of the Hebraic words *Ab, Ben* and *ruach aCadesch* ('Father, Son and Holy Spirit').

Abrasax Sometimes Abraxas, a mystical word, probably of Gnostic origin, said to mark 365 attributes (a number expressed gematrically (see

Figure 1 *Abrasax, a design on a Gnostic gem (third century* BC)

GEMATRIA) within the name) and to be linked with solar cycle. The image associated with the word (found on Gnostic gems, as in Figure 1) is that of a cock-headed man bearing a shield and whip. The being was eventually demoted to demonic form and his image frequently carved on gems or stones for amuletic purposes. Sometimes amulets are called 'abraxas stones', even when they do not bear the image of the demon god.

Abyss In Qabbalism Abyss relates to the Masak Mavdil, a place of failures, a cleft between the Sephiroth CHESED and DAATH. Grey calls this cleft 'the Divine dustbin', after pointing to the tradition that God had made three previous creations prior to the present one, and, being unsatisfied with these, he swept them into the Abyss. From a point of view of Western occultism there is a link between the Abyss and that personification called DWELLER ON THE THRESHOLD. The Abyss is also linked with that curious theological concept of Hell, though the occult systems do not regard this, or indeed anything in the created world, as a state infinitely projected in time (see, however, ABADDON). As with all the areas designated in the SEPHIROTHIC TREE, this sewerage system exists within everyone; and there is a lesson to be learned from the occult tradition (which so contradicts many of the teachings of modern psychology) that the inner human abyss, where rejected failures of this and previous incarnations lie, should not be disturbed without considerable inner disciplines and occult knowledge.

Acadine Fountain A magical fountain in Sicily mentioned by Diodorus Siculus as being used to test writings. Literature would be thrown into its waters as test of authorship – if genuine the tablets would float, if spurious they would sink.

Acquisitio 'Gain', one of the sixteen figures of GEOMANCY.

Actinobolism The term appears to have been used in astrology in connection with the theory of ASPECTS, in which it was believed that planets projected rays of influence down to the earth (the etymology of the word suggesting the idea of 'throwing out beams'); Ptolemy uses the word in this sense. The term has been used to denote the idea of spirits (or even materialities) shooting forth from some source such as the sun. In more recent times occultists have adapted the word to techniques of HYPNOSIS, and it is used at times to denote forms of divination involving trance, such as SCRYING.

Acvini The Sanskrit name for sidereal ARIES, as used especially in Hindu astrology and predictive techniques.

Adam In the first chapter of Genesis Adam is the name given to the male–female created by God; esoterically, this duality was called the 'twin', and in Greek *didumoi*. But see also ADAM KADMON and ADAMIC.

Adam Kadmon The Hebraic (Qabbalistic) name for archetypal man, the spiritual perfection of present humanity, sometimes translated in popular occultism as 'heavenly man' (the 'one who has not sinned'), which relates on the microcosmic level to the higher TERNARY in man.

Adamastor The name given to a supposed spirit of the stormy Cape of Good Hope, which prophesies disaster for those seeking to make a voyage beyond the Cape to India.

Adamic A name given by occultists to the first of the seven ROOT RACES – the first type of humanity to live on the earth. It is said that the Adamic race was not able to live in the material body of flesh; they had only ASTRAL forms and possessed only the faculty of hearing. See FIRST RACE.

Adech An alchemical term explained by Sendivogius as denoting the 'interior and invisible man' and probably relating to the formative force of mental ideation or image making.

Adept Literally 'one who is skilled'; in occultism, however, one who is skilled in esoteric wisdom. The word is sometimes used as being synonymous with INITIATE and is said to be from the participle of the Latin *adipisci*, meaning 'one who has attained'. It is said that within the realm of secret alchemical lore there are always eleven adepts.

Adityas A Sanskrit name for the seven planetary gods.

Adjuration A formula of command in the conjuring of evil spirits; the demon is adjured in the name of the Christian God to obey the orders of the magician. See CEREMONIAL MAGIC.

Admetos The name given to one of the HYPOTHETICAL PLANETS.

Adnachiel The ruling Angel of zodiacal Sagittarius.

Adonai Malakh See MALKUTH.

Adonis The name given to one of the HYPOTHETICAL PLANETS.

Adrammelech Sometimes a name given to a demon in relatively modern grimoires, but historically a Babylonian god to whom infants were sacrificed.

Adversary See AHRIMAN.

Adytum The 'sanctum', originally the Greek name for the holiest sanctum in a temple, but used in occultism to denote the holiest part of any initiation centre.

Aeradi A name given to corporeal spirits of the air – the SYLPHS – when seen by clairvoyant vision.

Aeromancy A term, from the Greek *aer* (atmosphere) and *manteia* (divination), applied to fortune-telling from atmospheric conditions, such as air currents, winds or cloud formations. Some early authorities describe aeromancy as the art of predicting from spectres which appear in the air (see, for example, AERADI); it was once widely believed that spirits could manifest only by wrapping themselves in a 'clothing' of air. By the seventeenth century the word 'aeromancy' was also being used for weather forecasting. See also AUSTROMANCY.

Aeshma A name given to the hairy or furry demon of Persian demonology which was said to rule over cruelty and devastation. The term is from the Persian name for a demon of earthly desire called Aeshma Deva, which passed into Western occultism as ASMODEUS.

Aether A Greek term for the 'divine luminiferous substance which pervades the whole universe' (Blavatsky's words) and a name given by early alchemists to the QUINTESSENCE. The term was probably coined to contrast with the Latin *aer* (air), which properly belongs to the earth. In popular occultism the term is much misunderstood, often being confused with the ASTRAL LIGHT, which is really a manifestation of the Aether. Technically, however, Aether is the name given to the third principle of the cosmic septenary, the lowest being the Earth, the second being the Astral Light (see also AKASHA). This ancient Aether is not to be confused with the ether of the modern physicists. It is, however, almost certainly directly related to the ETHERIC of the occultists. The Chaldean *aith-ur*, meaning 'solar fire', is sometimes given as the etymological source for 'aether'.

Aethereum See ANIMAL MAGNETISM and MACROCOSM.

Aetherial body See SUBTLE BODY.

Aethnici An alchemical term for SALAMANDERS, though Sendivogius described them as 'spiritual men burning in the fire, which appear in diverse forms and shapes, as fiery flames, firebrands, etc.' See also AETNEAN.

Aethrobacy A Greek term for LEVITATION.

Aetites A magical stone, mentioned often in medieval treatises on gems), said to be found in the neck or stomach of an eagle – hence its variant name, 'aquilaeus'. It was thought to ensure safe birth.

Aetnean A name given by alchemists to one of their forms of fire (but see in this connection FIRE ELEMENT and GRADES OF FIRE). The Aetnaei are the SALAMANDERS.

Affliction Generally, a planet is said to be 'in affliction' with another when it is in unfavourable aspect with it; the planet receiving the aspect is said to be 'afflicted'. However, the term may also be used of the conjuction of planets with certain degrees of the zodiac, as, for example, when the degree is marked by a malevolent fixed star, which then 'afflicts' the planet. In a popular or even poetic sense a person may be 'afflicted' by an evil star or even by his entire horoscope.

Afrit In the demonology of Modhammedanism the name given to a class of gigantic and fearsome demons.

Agaliarept Name of a demon said by the GRAND GRIMOIRE to be commander of the Second Legion in Hades. He has the power of discovering and revealing the hidden secrets of courts and council chambers throughout the world.

Agares One of the seventy-two SPIRITS OF SOLOMON. He is said to appear in the form of a sage riding on a crocodile.

Agatana yene A Sanskrit-derived term used by certain occultists to denote the OBSESSION of a medium by an elementary.

Agate The stone agate, sometimes called the 'achates' and said to be named after the river in Sicily, where it is still found, is said to have the power to turn the possessor invisible, and to protect his person in battle. The stone was consequently widely used in the art of TALISMANS. For a curious use of this stone, see AXINOMANCY.

Agathion A name given to an invisible FAMILIAR, which may enclose itself in a bottle or a talisman to attain its own (or its owner's) will.

Agathodaemon A Greek word for 'good spirit'. In some occult texts it is also said to be a flying dragon (but see INITIATION). In specialist use among the Ophites the Agathodaemon was the Good Lord, the Logos. See also AGOTHODEMON.

Age of Aquarius See AGES, EPOCHS, PLATONIC YEAR and PRECESSION.

Age of Jupiter See AGE OF SATURN.

Age of Pisces See AGES, EPOCHS, PLATONIC YEAR and PRECESSION.

Age of Saturn A term derived from the poetic historicism of Virgil. He divides the historical period of mankind into two ages – that of Saturn and that of Jupiter, the former corresponding to the Golden Age, familiar to us from the description of Hesiod. The age of Jupiter is merely a later age, one of expansion, yet involved with a reform of those darker elements developed towards the end of the preceding age. Some call the age of man and woman before thirty-five years 'the age of Jupiter', and after that year 'the age of Saturn'.

Ages   There are several different systems of ages in astrology. Most often the term is applied to the so-called zodiacal ages, the epochs, which are said to arise due to the phenomenon of the PRECESSION of the equinoxes. The entire period of this precession is an age of 25,920 years, which is divided into twelve subperiods, of 2160 years' duration, allocated to each of the twelve signs of the zodiac (see PLATONIC YEAR). There is little agreement among astrologers as to when the twelve epochs begin and end; some schools insist that we are now well into the age of Aquarius, others that we are in the age of Pisces and will so remain for another century or so, while yet others claim that we are in the age of Capricorn. It is, of course, a question of which coordinates and philosophical outlooks are adopted. An important astrological tradition linked with ages is that concerned with the periodicities during which the Archangels have rule over the destiny of the world and shape human history (see SECUNDADEIAN BEINGS). In personal astrology a great deal of attention is placed on the crisis points linked with specific ages (or years) such as twenty-eight, thirty-five and fifty-six, when major changes are to be expected (see CLIMACTERICS). There is also another system of personal ages linked with the sequence of the planets, which are allocated periods of rule over the growing human (see SEVEN AGES).

Ages of man   See CLIMACTERICS and SEVEN AGES.

Agiel   The name of the Intelligency of Saturn.

Agla   A Qabbalistic term used in talismanic magic and derived, some say, from the Hebrew *Atha gibor leolam Adonai* ('Thou art mighty for ever, O Lord'), which is replete with numerological significance (see NOTARICON). Stones and talismans bearing this and related phrases or abbreviations are sometimes called 'aglas'.

Agneyastra   A Sanskrit word, mentioned in early Indian epics, for the fiery missiles or magic weapons used by the developed races of ATLANTIS. See AGNI-RATHA.

Agni-ratha   A word meaning 'fiery vehicles', sometimes described as 'flying machines', said to have been used in ancient ATLANTIS. See also AGNEYASTRA.

Agnoia   In the simplistic division of the human being, the Greek term *agnoia* (sometimes *anoia*) was used to denote the irrational or lower soul, which should be controlled by the higher 'neotic' soul (see NOUS).

Agra-sandhani   The Sanskrit name for the recorders who read out the judgement of the newly deceased from the living records of his previous life. See also LIPIKA.

Agnishwattas   A Sanskrit term meaning 'one who has been sweetened by fire' and used for a class of solar PITRIS or ancestors of mankind. (For the lunar Pitris, see BARHISHADS.)

Agothodemon   A term derived from Ptolemy for the ELEVENTH HOUSE, properly 'Agathodaemon', from the Greek toast *Agathou daimonos* ('To the good daemon'), the Greek DAIMON being a higher spirit.

Ahankara   A Sanskrit word from the root *kri* ('to make'), relating to the egoistical principle in man, the personality born of that ignorance which separates the 'I' from the universal.

Ah-hi   The name given in Blavatsky's *The Secret Doctrine* to the DHYAN-CHOHANS.

Ahih   See KETHER.

Ahriman   A modern occultist term used to denote the dark god Angra Mainyu (said by some to mean 'negative thought') of the Zoroastrian dualism. Ahriman is the Prince of Darkness, the Prince of Lies, who works against the light-filled creativity of ORMUZD. He is sometimes called Druj, seemingly derived from a Zoroastrian term for 'deceit'. Occultists recognize Ahriman as the Satanas of the Gospels, the great Adversary who tempts through the sensual and earthly, and who seeks to pull man down into a complexity of arid intellectualism, lacking in spirituality and richness of soul life. In modern occultism he is opposed by LUCIFER. See also DAIMONIARCHON.

Ahura Mazda   See ORMUZD.

Aiel According to grimoires, this is the name given to the governor of zodiacal Aries; he is said to rule Sunday. See ZODIACAL SPIRITS.

Aigokeros Greek name, meaning 'horned creature', used to denote the sign and constellation CAPRICORN.

Ain The Hebraic term for 'the negatively existent' (Westcott's phrase) – the quiescent and passive deity. The Ain Soph is the deity without limit, in reality the God who has no likeness with any formed thing. Blavatsky supports this notion that the word 'ain' in this context means 'nothing' (which is etymologically incorrect), and claims that the Ain Soph is the No-Thing, the Nameless. See SEPHIROTHIC TREE, in which the progression is from the quiescent Ain Soph down to the lowest reaches of the human world. See also KETHER.

Ain Soph See AIN.

Aini Sometimes Aym, one of the seventy-two SPIRITS OF SOLOMON. He is said to appear with three heads – one of a snake, one of a cat, and the third of a man. He is mounted on a viper.

Air element In alchemy air is not the mixture of gases of modern science but (in the words of Philalethes) 'a certain miraculous hermaphrodite, the cement of two worlds, and a medley of extremes. It is the sea of things invisible. . . .' In general occult use the Air element is the communicative quality in the created world. In astrology the Air element finds expression in the zodiac through the three signs Gemini, Libra and Aquarius (see AIR TRIPLICITY). It is the element most deeply associated with thinking and with volatility. Philalethes wrote that the Air element is 'the envelope of the life of our sensitive spirit', by which he meant that the human being swims in the world of thought as though swimming in a sea. See also SANGUINE.

Air signs In astrology these are the zodiacal signs Gemini, Libra and Aquarius.

Air triplicity In astrology this is the generic term for the three signs linked with the AIR ELEMENT, manifesting different aspects of the Sanguine temperament – Gemini, Libra and Aquarius. Air is all-pervasive, a palpable link between the inner world of man (lungs) and the outer environment. It is this tendency towards unification of the individual with the whole which is manifest in each of the signs of the Air triplicity.

Aishim See YESOD.

Aja The Sanskrit term meaning 'unborn' and used of the gods, who are regarded as uncreated, having existed from all time.

Ajna The oriental name for the Brow or Frontal CHAKRA, located between the eyes. It is sometimes called the Third Eye. Occultists claim that the vision of this Third Eye is not fully developed in ordinary people, that when its energies and potentials are awakened it enables the human to see clearly on the astral plane (see ASTRAL). It is described by occultists as having ninety-six spokes, although it is often symbolized as consisting of two lobes or semicircles, one being of a rose-yellow, the other of a blue-purple colour.

Avalon, who was the most learned occultist in the field of oriental chakric centres, called the Third Eye the Juanachaksha.

Aka The shadow body or spiritual power in KAHUNA magic. According to the Kahuna system, man has three *aka* bodies, each one invisible to ordinary sight and each contributing different faculties and energies to his being. Invisible *aka* threads are said to connect man to every object or person he touches. The tradition that such *aka* threads may be activated for magical (beneficient or evil) purposes, regardless of the passage of time elapsing since the formation of such threads, is the basis for much of the praxes of Kahuna magic.

Akasa See AKASHA.

Akasha Sometimes Akasa, Akasia or Akashya, from the Sanskrit meaning 'luminous', and sometimes used in modern occultism as an equivalent of the ancient AETHER; it is called the 'Soniferous Ether'. In modern theosophical use it relates to the QUINTESSENCE, that luminous fifth element (invisible to ordinary sight) which was seen as binding together in union or pact the other four elements. Blavatsky writes of it as being 'cosmically a radiant, cool, diathermous plastic matter, creative in its physical nature. . . .' An important related term derived from the Sanskrit (but of entirely European occult use) is the so-called Akashic Chronicles (sometimes the Akashic Records) which are the historical records of all world events and personal experiences of all thoughts and deeds which have taken place on the earth. These are indelibly imprinted upon the Akasha and may under normal circumstances be read only by adepts or initiates. In medieval occultism the Akasha was sometimes called the 'Luminous Waters' or even the 'Mercurial Waters'; in modern occultism it is sometimes called the 'Akashic Tableau' or the 'Cosmic Memory'. The spiritual beings who are said to inscribe these records on the Akasha are called LIPIKA. See also MAGNESIA.

Akashic Chronicles See AKASHA.

Al See EL.

Alastor In ancient Roman demonology a name given to the evil genius of a house, but in earlier times the word in Greek meant something like 'avenging god'.

Alaya A Sanskrit word meaning 'indissoluble' and used to denote the universal soul. It is sometimes said to be the equivalent of the ANIMA MUNDI, sometimes the Over-Soul of Emerson (see SECRET DOCTRINE).

Alberich The personalized name for the king of the dwarfs in Scandinavian mythology, popularized in the *Nieblungenlied* of Wagner as the thief of the magic ring of gold.

Albus 'White', the name given to one of the sixteen figures of GEOMANCY.

Alcahest Sometimes 'alkahest', a name used in ALCHEMY for the Universal Solvent.

Alchemical Mercury The term 'Mercury' is often used in esoteric and occult circles in a sense which does not refer to the purely astrological conception of MERCURY. This alchemical Mercury is really the hermetic Mercury, which figures in alchemical treatises under a variety of spagyric names. In the hermetic tradition which informs exoteric astrology Mercury is cold and moist, and therefore 'aqueous'; it is therefore the Permanent Water, the vitalizing spirit of the body, and is linked with what the medieval occultists would call the *Ens veneni*, the approximate equivalent of the modern ETHERIC. In this capacity Mercury has been given many names suggestive of potent liquidity – Blessed Water, Virtuous Water, Philosopher's Vinegar, Dew of Heaven, Virgin's Milk, and so on. It is sometimes

said that the whole alchemical art depends upon a true understanding of the nature of this Mercury, which is directly linked with the QUINTESSENCE. Alchemical Mercury is sometimes used of the Mercurius in the THREE PRINCIPLES. See also MAGNESIA.

Alchemilla A plant of the rose family, apparently so called because alchemists are supposed to have collected the dew of its leaves as a stage in the preparation of the elixir or stone. It is sometimes called 'lady's mantle' and is said to have been dedicated to the Virgin Mary. As with so many alchemical terms, however, the word is a blind: the first stage of the preparation of MAGNESIA is said to be blood red, the second transparent, of celestial and transcendent brightness ('a pure virgin' as Sendivogius calls it), and in the third stage a crystal. The second stage is sometimes called the *Lac virginis* and Dew of the Virgin.

Alchemy The origin of the word is obscure, in spite of much learned controversy; probably it is from the Arabian *al kimia*, the last word being an equivalent of the Greek *chemeia* which in turn seems to have meant something like 'the Egyptian art'. The word was apparently first used in the second century AD. The earliest extant document (probably by Zosimus the Panopolite, of about 400 AD) already appears to be esoteric, suggesting the idea of a Universal Solvent by which bodies may be reduced to their homogeneous substance, the pure gold or *summa materia*. The solvent, sometimes called the *Menstruum universale*, is the equivalent of the LAPIS PHILOSOPHORUM. Blavatsky insists that alchemy is properly studied under three distinct aspects – the cosmic, human and terrestrial – each reflections of the THREE PRINCIPLES of Salt, Mercury and Sulphur. She emphasizes that the exoteric aspect of alchemy (the transmutation of gross metals into gold) has always had an esoteric side – the transmutation of the base quaternary into the divine trinity of man (see TERNARY). Sendivogius, no stranger to the esoteric nature of the true art, defines his 'Alchymia' quite simply as 'the separation of that which is impure from a purer substance'; the progression in this spiritual undertaking is perhaps most clearly seen in the alchemical term 'GRADES OF FIRE', which had been mistaken for different forms of heating by the uninitiated.

A short quotation from an anonymous text of 1725, noted by Spence, shows the extent to which the alchemical literature may be regarded as alle-gorical of the human soul's path; as a strictly chemical operation it also serves to indicate some of the terms used in alchemy. It is essentially a text designed to set out the proper construction of the PHILOSOPHER'S STONE. 'Modern philosophers [that is, alchemists] have extracted from the interior of mercury a fiery spirit, mineral, veg-etable and multiplicative, in a humid concavity in which is found the primitive mercury or the universal quintessence. In the midst of this spirit resides the spiritual fluid [which] is the Mercury of the Philosophers, which is not solid like a metal, nor soft like quicksilver, but between the two.' Instruction follows on how to make the liquor known as the 'Vinegar of the Sages', which is allowed to putrefy.

This is the first operation of the Grand Work. For the second operation; take in the name of God one part of gold and two parts of the spiritual water, charged with the sal-ammoniac, mix this noble confection in a vase of crystal of the shape of an egg: warm over a soft but continuous fire, and the fiery water will dissolve little by little the gold; this forms a liquor which is called by the sages 'Chaos' containing the elementary qualities – cold, dryness, heat and humidity. Allow this composi-tion to putrefy until it becomes black; this blackness is known as the 'crow's head', and the 'darkness of the sages', and makes known to the artist that he is on the right track. It was also known as the 'black earth'. It must be boiled once more in a vase as white as snow: this stage of the work is called the 'swan', and from it arises the white liquor, which is divided into two parts – one white for the manufacture of silver, the other red for the manufacture of gold. Now you have accom-plished the work, and you possess the Philosopher's Stone. In these diverse operations, one finds many by-products; among these is the 'green lion' which is also called 'azoph', and which draws gold from the more ignoble elements; the 'red lion' which converts the metal into gold; the 'head of the crow', called also the 'black veil of the ship of Theseus', which appearing forty days before the end of the operation predicts its success.

In the famous treatise called *The Ripley Scroll* there are twelve stages or gates in the transmu-tation of the base metal. These were later linked with the twelve signs of the zodiac: calcination, dissolution, separation, conjunction, putrefac-tion, congelation, cibation, sublimation, fermen-tation, exaltation, multiplication and projection. See, however, PROJECTION.

See also ALCHEMICAL MERCURY, FIRE ELE-MENT and CONJUNCTION.

Alcohol Sometimes 'alcol' or 'alcool', in alchemy 'a most subtil powder of any thing', as Sendivogius says, although even he later in the same text gives 'Alcool Vini' as 'Spirit of Wine rectified'.

Alcyone In mythology Alcyone was the wife of Ceyx, who was drowned while on his way to consult an oracle; on hearing the news she threw herself into the sea. Both husband and wife changed into kingfishers. It is also the name of a fixed star of third magnitude, the brightest of the Pleiades, set in the shoulder of constellation Taurus. Early astronomers regarded it as a sort of central sun to the universe. Alcyone was also the name given by Leadbeater to the youthful Krishnamurti.

Aldinach A demon said to control the power of tempests, hailstorms and earthquakes.

Alecto The name of one of the three Furies of Greek mythology. She is said to have hair made from the entwined bodies of snakes. The alec-torian stone which is sometimes linked with her name is actually derived from the same root which gave us ALECTROMANCY and is a stone used by the talisman makers, said to be found in the stomach of cocks; when worn as an amulet or talisman, it brings strength, courage and wealth.

Alectorian Stone See ALECTO.

Alectromancy Sometimes 'alectryomancy' or 'alectormancy', a word derived from the Greek *alectruon* (cock) and *manteia* (divination). The name is applied to a method of divination in which a cock or hen is placed in a circle of grain, around which are placed the letters of the alphabet. The areas in which the bird pecks the seeds or grain will indicate letters, which are then reassembled to make words said to give predictive response to questions. Sometimes, when a simple yes or no is required to a question, only two piles of grain are presented to the bird; the direction in which it moves is taken as marking the response (usually left means no and right means yes). Another related form of divination is based on the angle or direction in which a dying bird will flutter after having had its throat cut.

Aleuromancy A term derived from the Greek *aleuron* (flour) and *manteia* (divination) and applied to a method of predicting the future by means of meal, flour, barley or wheat. There were several ways in which grains might be used, from GEO-MANCY to ALECTROMANCY, but the most frequently used was that of flushing out a bowl containing water and flour so as to leave chance patterns of wet flour on the sides of the bowl – the shapes of these were interpreted prophetically. See also ALPHITOMANCY.

Algol Fixed star (binary), the Beta of Perseus, set in the head of the Gorgon Medusa. It is said to be the most evil of all stars and is sometimes called the Demon Star.

Alkahest The name given by Paracelsus to the sought-after universal solvent of alchemy.

Allocen Sometimes Alocer, Allocer or Alloien, one of the seventy-two SPIRITS OF SOLOMON. He is said to appear as a warrior with a lion's face.

Almadel Name given to an early treatise on theurgia, associated with the famous GRIMOIRE, the *Key of Solomon*. See LEMEGETON.

Almuten Term derived from Arabian astrology, signifying the most influential or important planet in a horoscope chart.

Alocer See ALLOCEN.

Alomancy More usually 'Halomancy', a term derived from the Greek *halo* (salt) and *manteia* (divination) and used to denote a method of predicting the future by means of salt, probably linked with reading random patterns as in ALEUROMANCY.

Alopecy An obscure term linked with the ability to charm (in a magical sense) an enemy.

Alphitomancy A term applied from the Greek *alphitomantis* (a diviner by means of barley meal) and applied to a method of determining the guilt of a person by feeding him or her with a specially prepared barley loaf. Indigestion is supposed to indicate guilt.

Alruna-wife The name given to the household goddesses in ancient Germanic lore.

Amaimon Sometimes Maimon or Maymon, the demon king of the eastern regions of Hell.

Amanasa A Sanskrit word meaning 'mindless' and applied to certain early human races. Blavatsky says that the word is also used of certain Hindu gods.

Amandinus See MAGIC STONES.

Ambient Originally a name used of the Ambient Sphere (the Tenth Sphere), which in the Ptolemaic cosmoconception was visualized as moving all the other spheres with it. The term is now sometimes applied to the heavens in general.

Ambriel The name given in certain GRIMOIRES and methods of ceremonial magic to the governor of the zodiacal sign Gemini, although some associate the spirit with Mars.

Amduscias One of the seventy-two SPIRITS OF SOLOMON. He is said to appear in the form of a unicorn (see Figure 2).

Amen Some occultists derive the term 'Amen' from the Egyptian word for the hidden god

Figure 2 *Amduscias, demon of Hell (after de Plancy)*

Amun and give it the meaning 'concealed'. See also KETHER.

Amenti An Egyptian term properly translated as meaning 'the postmortem state', often incorrectly translated in popular occultism as 'Hell'. Esoterically it is the dwelling of the hidden god Amun – hidden, of course, only from the eyes of living men. Amenti is the Ker-neter, the Abode of the Gods, the Land of Ghosts, the Western Land. There are said to be fourteen parts in Amenti, the ones which have entered the terminologies of Western occultism being Aanroo, Neter-xer and Otamer-xers. Two of the gates of Amenti are Amh and Rustu.

Amh The gate of exit (towards reincarnation) of the Egyptian AMENTI.

Amianthus The name given by alchemists to a stone 'not burned in the fire', which is also called SALAMANDER.

Amissio 'Loss', the name given to one of the sixteen figures of GEOMANCY.

Amniomancy Divination by means of the birth caul.

Amon One of the seventy-two SPIRITS OF SOLOMON. He is said to appear in the shape of a wolf, with a serpent's head and/or tail.

Amoymon One of the names of the king of the eastern part of Hades.

Amrita A Sanskrit name for the ambrosial drink of the gods. See RAHU.

Amshaspends Sometimes the Amesha Spentas, the six angelic beings attendant upon Ahura Mazda (see ORMUZD) and his first creation. They are the Zoroastrian prototypes of the SECUNDADEIAN BEINGS.

Amulet The word was probably derived from the Latin *amuletum* ('a preservative against illness'). The difference between an amulet and a talisman is often confused in modern times, but originally an amulet contained an image, whereas a talisman contained a sigil or seal. The specialist in EVIL EYE, Elworthy, insists that amulets were designed to deflect the evil eyebeams of a magician or sorcerer by means of either laughter, envy or dread; the most common form was that appeal-

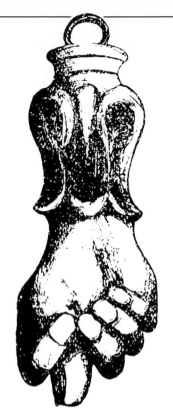

Figure 3 *This hand pendant was one of the most frequently used amulets against the evil eye (after Elworthy)*

ing to dread, and so to this end monstrous images or the sigils of demons were hung around the neck to deflect the evil eye. Amuletic images of the Medusa (usually called Gorgoneions), or of chimerical beings (usually called Chimerae) or of ALECTO (alectorian stones) were favoured. Phallic images, sometimes called *Turpicula res* or *Scaeva*, were also hung around the neck, to deflect the evil eye. The phallic significance and magical properties of the image survive in the hand gesture (itself said to be the equivalent of an amulet) which presents the thumb protruding between the middle and index fingers of the closed fist (Figure 3). The Italian word *grillo* ('grasshopper', itself a notable carrier of the evil eye) has given rise to the term 'grylli' which is applied to a grotesque form of amulet which is really a charm (Figure 4). The various forms of cross, the tau and ankh being the most common along with the related fylfot (Old English), swastika (Sanskrit) or gammadion (derived from the gamma of ancient Greek), served as amulets. Figure 5 represents a necklace of CHARMS, many of which

Figure 4   *A design for an amulet consisting of an 'evil' grasshopper and a goat*

Figure 5   *A necklace strung with a variety of amulets (after Elworthy)*

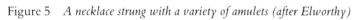

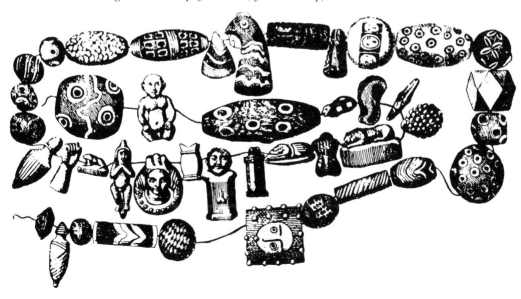

are designed to combat the evil eye. Important amulets were also made from MAGIC SQUARES which incorporated planetary forces.

It was argued from relatively early times that just as there were amulets which were storehouses of beneficial energies, so there were amulets which might be constructed by diabolic means to induce evil into the world. It was rarely doubted that a 'beneficient' charm might be just as efficacious for good as an 'evil' charm for bad, and the distinction between the two was carefully codified. The set of seven rules given in the MALLEUS MALEFICARUM of 1486 insist that a charm may be good and efficacious if it contains (1) no trace of demonic pact either in form or intention, (2) no unknown (diabolic?) names, (3) no untruth, (4) no ritual other than the signing or marking of the cross (sphragis), (5) no particular beliefs relating to the manner of writing the charm or of wearing it in amuletic form, (6) only accurately quoted biblical phrases, and (7) the avowed assurance that any efficacy stemmed only from the will of God. The majority of charms incorporated into amulets were of this orthodox kind. Diabolic amulets were often made in direct opposition to the septenary rule set out above, more or less in imitation of pagan practices.

A whole theory of amuletic praxes was developed around the relationship between specially prepared MAGICAL STONES (see GAMALEI) with corresponding planetary and zodiacal VIRTUES.

Amy   One of the seventy-two SPIRITS OF SOLOMON. He is said to appear in the form of a flame.

Ana   A Chaldean word meaning 'invisible heaven' or 'ASTRAL LIGHT'. Blavatsky suggests that the word relates to the Chaldean word 'Mav' (the name of a daughter of the goddess Ana) which is linked with many European names for the sea.

Anachithidus   See MAGICAL STONES.

Anael   The name given to the archangel associated with the sphere and planet of Venus.

Anahata   The Sanskrit name for the heart CHAKRA, situated over the heart.

Anana   The name given by the Polynesian KAHUNA magicians to their DEATH PRAYER.

Anarazel   A demon charged with the guardianship of buried treasures.

Anaretic   Term derived from the Greek, meaning 'destroyer', and used in astrology to denote the planet (sometimes a degree) which is for one reason or another regarded as the destroyer of life in a particular horoscope chart.

Ancient Moon   Another term for Old Moon (see MOON PERIOD).

Ancient Saturn   Another term for Old Saturn (see SATURN PERIOD).

Ancient Sun   Another term for Old Sun (see SUN PERIOD).

Andras   One of the seventy-two SPIRITS OF SOLOMON. He is said to appear with the body of an angel and the head of a raven, riding a wolf.

Andrealphus   One of the seventy-two SPIRITS OF SOLOMON. He is said to appear in the form of a peacock.

Androgyne   The term means 'having characteristics of both sexes', but in an astrological context this sense is often limited in application to MERCURY, the androgynous planet, which is said to participate in both the feminine and masculine natures.

Androgyne Mercury   See HOD.

Androgyne Ray   A term used to denote the first differentiated ray of humanity – the ADAM KADMON and the ADAM of the first chapter of Genesis.

Andromalius   One of the seventy-two SPIRITS OF SOLOMON. He is said to appear in human form, though in his hand is a snake.

Angaraka   Sanskrit term meaning 'fire star', relating to the planet Mars.

Angelical Stone   The stone used for SCRYING by John Dee, which was supposed by him to have been a gift of Raphael and Gabriel.

Angels   Name given to the Ninth Hierarchy of incorporeal spiritual beings above the realm of man (see SPIRITUAL HIERARCHIES). It is usual to derive the name from the Greek for 'messenger', but Davison traces it to the Sanskrit *angiras* ('divine spirit') by way of the Persian *angaros* ('courier'). While the word applies to a specific rank of the hierarchies, it is also used in a general sense of all nine levels, with resultant confusion – for example, the so-called Angels of the Zodiac are actually ARCHANGELS. According to the esoteric tradition, the Ninth Hierarchy is charged with the guidance of individuals through incarnation after incarnation: thus angels are concerned with the individual. While such guardian angels are of necessity sexless, they are said to take on the sexuality opposite that of the person whom they guard, to correspond to the archetypes of anima and animus. The order of the levels of hierarchies, from the list provided by Dionysius the Areopagite, is set out in Table 1. See also PLANETARY ANGELS, SECUNDADEIAN BEINGS and ZODIACAL ANGELS.

Table 1

Rank	Sphere	Greek name	Latinized name
Ninth	Moon	Angeloi	
Eighth	Mercury	Archangeloi	
Seventh	Venus	Archai	Principates or Principalities
Sixth	Sun	Exsusiai	Potestates or Powers
Fifth	Mars	Dynamis	Virtues or Virtutes
Fourth	Jupiter	Kyriotetes	Dominions or Dominations
Third	Saturn	Trones	Thrones
Second	Fixed Stars	Seraphim (Hebraic name)	
First	Zodiac	Cherubim (Hebraic name)	

Angra Mainyu   See AHRIMAN.

Aniadus   A term derived from Paracelsus, which appears to be the equivalent of the stellar VIRTUE 'from which we receive celestial influences by the medium of fantasy and imagination'. Sendivogius says that it is the 'celestial body' of man. See also ANIDA.

Anida   Term used by certain alchemists to signify the VIRTUE in things, sometimes called (as, for example, by Sendivogius) the 'astral virtue' or the 'celestial virtue'. Although etymologically linked with ANIADUS, it appears to be the equivalent of the ILECH.

Figure 6   *A seventeenth-century personification of* Anima mundi *among the planetary spheres (after Fludd)*

Anima mundi   The Latin term for the feminine Soul of the World, relating to the enveloping divine essence which vitalizes all beings. As Blavatsky writes, it is 'the essence of seven planes of sentience, consciousness and differentiation, moral and physical.' It is said to be of an 'igneous, ethereal nature' in the world of form, but entirely spiritual in higher realms. The higher element of the human being is said to be derived from the *Anima mundi*, which is itself an emanation of a higher spiritual realm. In occult imagery the *Anima mundi* is often pictured in the form of a naked woman, surrounded by the spheres, in which are embedded the planets; one of the most famous images is that given by Fludd in the seventeenth century (Figure 6).

Animal magnetism   The Austrian doctor F. A. Mesmer was convinced that there was an influence or force related to ordinary physical magnetism, but of an organic nature, which he called 'animal magnetism' – 'so universal and so continuous that it cannot suffer void, subtle beyond comparison and susceptible to receive,

19

propagate and communicate every impression of movement.' The healing practices built around his theories came to be called 'mesmerism', which was later associated directly with HYPNOSIS. Although he did not know it, Mesmer was merely giving a name to a force long recognized by occultists under different names – the Mumia of Paracelsus, and the Aetherium of the alchemists. Mesmer's hypothesis that this force linked together in a union the various physical bodies of the cosmos lay behind his exploration of its therapeutic value, and it was towards this end that he harnessed what he called the 'universal fluid'.

Animal soul   Although this term is sometimes used in modern occultism in connection with the GROUP SOUL, in earlier esotericism it was used for the lower nature, the lower soul (sometimes the Astral Body) of man (see TERNARY). In modern Theosophical literature, the Kama-rupa is the Sanskrit equivalent of this lower soul, sometimes loosely called the 'desired soul'.

Ankh   The name of an Egyptian symbol ⚲ said to represent the life forces and used in amuletic form as a protection against barrenness. It is said (without much real showing) to be the origin for the modern sigil for VENUS. More certain is the fact that it was adopted by the early Christians as one of the symbols for the cross, presumably because of its basic tau formation ⊤ and its link with the Egyptian Ru ◯ which means among other things 'mouth', 'birth', 'uterus', and was inevitably linked with speech, and thus with the descended Word of the Logos. As Massey has shown, in esoteric symbolism, the circle (derived from the Ru) and the cross were originally quite inseparable.

Annedotus   A Greek name for the men-fishes or dragon-men, one of whom was named Oannes (or Annedotus) who, according to the Chaldeans, introduced civilization to the world. See also INITIATION.

Annulus Platonicus   See CHAIN OF BEING. Distinguish from ANNUS PLATONICUS.

Annus platonicus   The Latin equivalent for PLATONIC YEAR.

Anoia   A Greek term (meaning approximately 'folly') explained by modern occultists as being used of the lower soul (see TERNARY) when it

becomes too deeply enmeshed in the delusions of the material plane.

Anontagius   An alchemical name for the PHILOSOPHER'S STONE.

Ansa   See HANSA.

Ansata   See TAU.

Antahkarana   Sometimes *Antaskarana*, a Sanskrit word sometimes translated in popular occultism as 'bridge' or 'interior sense organs', but really pointing to the centre through which the lower part of man (the so-called lower TERNARY) has contact with the higher being of man. Blavatsky called it the 'imaginary bridge between the divine and human egos'.

Antaskarana   See ANTAHKARANA.

Anthera   A name given by Paracelsus to an extract from the hyacinth flower which is said to have a significant resistant effect to certain influences of the sign Scorpio.

Anthos   According to Sendivogius, an alchemical term for the ELIXIR. Paracelsus reminds us that it is the old name for the rosemary flower and says that alchemists used it to denote their QUINTESSENCE.

Anthropomancy   A term derived from the Greek *anthropos* (man) and *manteia* (divination) and applied to an ancient method of foretelling the future from the raising of dead men or from the movements of the entrails of dead or dying men. See, however, NECROMANCY and SPLANCHNOMANCY.

Anthroposophus   The nickname of Thomas Vaughan, who in the middle of the seventeenth century was rector of St Bridget's in Brecknockshire. It is taken from his book on the afterlife, *Anthroposophia Teomagica*', published in 1650.

Antichrist   The name of a demonic being who, it is said, will precede in time the second coming of Christ – a concept derived from such biblical texts as Relevation, 13. Many humans have been saddled with this demonic appellation, from Nero to Napoleon, and some of the popes have been so called by the antipapists.

Antichthon Term of Greek origin, used to denote the 'anti-earth', the 'second earth' which was supposed to lie on the opposite side of the sun to our own earth, where it revolved invisible to man.

Anti-earth See ANTICHTHON.

Antipathy In astrology planets may be said to be in antipathy to each other under certain circumstances, most usually when they are in difficult or inharmonious aspect.

Antiscion In astrology the antiscion of a planet is the degree equidistant to that planet on the opposite side of the Cancer–Capricorn axis of a birth chart, the line falling through the first degrees of these signs (Figure 7). It is a sort of mirror image of a planetary position or nodal point.

Anunit Chaldean name for Venus as the morning star, the LUCIFER of European astrology.

Anunnaki A Chaldean term for 'spirits (or angels) of the earth', somtimes (wrongly) said to mean ELEMENTALS.

Figure 7 *Antiscion: the Cancer–Capricorn axis is marked CN–CP, the planetary position is marked P, and the antiscion of the planet is A*

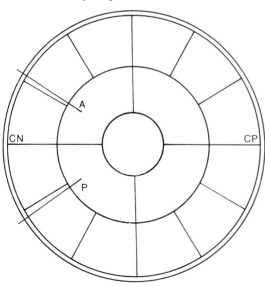

Anupadaka Sometimes *anupadada* or *anupapa-duka*, a Sanskrit word meaning 'parentless' or 'self-created' and applied to the divine incarnation of an AVATAR who is born into the world without parents. See GATI.

Aour A curious Chaldean term, according to some occultists, explained as the synthesis of the OD and the OB, life and death.

Apantomancy The name given to the method of making divinations from seemingly chance meetings with objects, animals and human beings.

Apap The Egyptian equivalent of the Greek Apophis, the symbolic serpent of evil; it is an avatar of Typhon. Occultists explain Apophis as a symbol of the physical body, as the lower part of man which must be overcome – in a word, it is the 'old serpent'.

Apheta In astrology a term applied to a planet, or to a nodal point in a horoscope, which sustains the life of the native.

Aphetic places In Graeco-Roman astrology the aphetic places were those areas in a horoscope chart which were said to maintain or enhance life.

Apocalyptic star An esoteric term used by Paracelsus for the one 'personal' star which 'exists higher than all the rest'. He probably had in mind the triune star beyond the Ego, the higher TERNARY of modern esotericism.

Apocrypha A Greek word meaning 'hidden' or 'esoteric'.

Apollo The name of this Roman god is frequently used as a synonym for the SUN in late medieval texts. The fixed star Castor (see GEMINI) was also called Apollo by Ptolemy, a name adopted by many later astrologers. The Greek equivalent, 'Helios', was also used in a similar dual way.

Apollon Name given to one of the HYPOTHETICAL PLANETS.

Apollyon The Greek equivalent of ABADDON, popularized in modern literature through Bunyan's *Pilgrim's Progress*.

Apophis   See APAP.

Aporrheta   Greek word relating to the esoteric instructions revealed to initiates during ceremonies in the Egyptian and Grecian Mysteries.

Apotelesmatic   A term used as almost synonymous with genethliacal (see GENETHLIA-CAL ASTROLOGY). It appeas to have been derived from the Greek *apotelesma* ('the sum' or 'completion'), perhaps with reference to the completing or casting of a horoscope. In a nonspecialist sense the word is applied to the casting of horoscopes of all kinds, well beyond the limits of natal astrology.

Apparitions   In an occult sense any abnormal or supranormal appearance on the material plane. A ghost may manifest as an apparition.

Apport   An object (such as a piece of jewellery, money, fruit or flowers, even live animals) which materializes (as though from nowhere) in the presence of a medium. The production of apports, or 'apporting', is one of the most frequent manifestations in SEANCE rooms. See also PRECIPITATION.

Apsaras   A Sanskrit word sometimes wrongly translated as 'undines'. The Apsaras were spiritual beings, the Daughters of Pleasure, rejected as legitimate wives by both the Suras and the Asuras. Blavatsky says that the same name is used of certain occult 'sleep-producing' aquatic plants and of 'inferior forces of nature'.

Aqua permanens   'Permanent water' does not do justice to this alchemical term, since it is clearly a reference to an astral force in that it is also called the 'Sperm of the World', the 'catholic magnesia' (see, therefore, MAGNESIA), which suggests that it is something like the supercelestial source of imagination, the ANIADUS.

Aquarius   The eleventh sign of the zodiac. It corresponds as a zodiacal sign neither in location nor extent with the constellation of the same name, which is associated with the Hebraic letter Nun and the TAROT arcanum of 'Temperance' (through similarity of imagery, no doubt). The myth of the origin of the asterism Aquarius is linked with Ganymedes, who was carried to

Figure 8   *A fifteenth-century woodcut showing the constellation Aquarius (after Hyginus)*

heaven by an eagle, to become cupbearer to Jupiter. The modern sigil for zodiacal Aquarius ♒ is said by some to represent the flow of water, especially that of the Nile, and this sign (for all that it is an air sign) has from the earliest days of astrology been associated with water. However, the stream of water which is contained in the urn of the Aquarian image is ultimately derived from a stream of stars (Figure 8) and is said to represent spiritual knowledge, the 'Celestial Waters' of the ancients, which has different names in different occult systems – it is the ANIADUS of alchemical hermeticism, the AQUA PERMANENS of alchemy, the ETHERIC of modern esotericism (see WATER ELEMENT). Some astrologers prefer to interpret the sigil as representative of the invisible waves of occult FOHAT. Aquarius is of the AIR ELEMENT and of the Fixed Quality, its influence being erratic, refined, artistic, tenacious, perverse, intuitive, independent, original, friendly, humanitarian, progressive, persistent, inventive, creative, tolerant, fond of science and literature, discreet and optimistic – in a word, all the qualities which may be associated with an Air type working with a view to establish freedom for self and others. In excess the Aquarian tends to be something of a crank, an opportunist, a rebel, with both an unsympathetic and an irresponsible attitude to life. According to the majority of modern astrologers, Aquarius is ruled by the planet URANUS, although before this planet was discovered in the eighteenth century the sign was ruled by SATURN.

Aquaster A term derived from Paracelsian occultism and used to denote the archetype of all that is watery, all that is capable of receiving impressions (see, however, AQUA PERMANENS). Sendivogius defines it as a sort of apparition, a 'Vision . . . which truly is not, but only in appearance.'

Aquila The Latin for EAGLE, used in alchemical texts to denote (among other things) Sal Ammoniac because of its lightness. The *Aquila philosophorum* or 'Alchemical Eagle' is the name given to a metal reduced to its first matter, also called 'Mercury of Metals'. Aquila is also the name of a constellation.

Arabian points A name for the PARS of astrology.

Araboth The seventh of the seven heavens of the Qabbalistic system, said to be ruled by CASSIEL.

Arahat A Pali term with many variant spellings (including *arhat*), meaning 'worthy', and used to denote the human who, having subdued the lower nature in himself, has entered the highest path of initiation. Such an *arahat* is no longer subject to the laws of rebirth. (See also ADEPT.)

Aralim In Qabbalism the name given to the Valiant Ones (sometimes taken as the equivalent to the THRONES) who work as the containers of wisdom, or act as the matrices which lend form to wisdom, in the world of YETZIRAH.

Arapadhatu In occidental esotericism, the region of formlessness.

Arariel The name of an angel said to have charge of the waters of the earth, and accordingly invoked by fishermen. Raphael is the Archangel who has dominion over water, however.

Araritha The Anglicized form of a Hebrew word of seven letters, giving by process of NOTARICON a numerological value of 813, of great mystical significance.

Arasa Maram A Sanskrit name for the Hindu equivalent of the Tree of Knowledge.

Aratron The name given to one of the superior DEMONS, corresponding to the sphere of the planet Saturn. The demon is said to have the ability to petrify living organisms, to transform coal into treasure, and to possess the power to give men command over the subterranean spirits. The magician conjures Aratron in order to learn the secrets of matter – such as alchemy, medical arts and so on – as well as learning how to make his physical body invisible.

Arbatel A name given to a ritual of transcendental magic (see GRIMOIRES) probably named after an instructing angelic agency and published under the title *De Magia Veterum* (1575). The text lists the good and evil spirits, as well as the distribution of their powers. See also SPIRITS OF SOLOMON.

Arcane knowledge See ESOTERICISM.

Arcanum In general the term means anything hidden, the plural 'arcana' being applied to all the esoteric wisdom of occult lore. Paracelsus adopts the word for specialist astrological and alchemical use, to denote 'the secret incorporeal virtue behind or within natural forms'; it is therefore a synonym for both ILECH and VIRTUE. The word is also used to denote any one of the twenty-two picture cards (the Major Arcana) of the TAROT pack.

Archaeus A term derived from the Greek, meaning 'the ancient', and used in Qabbalistic and occult texts as relating to the oldest manifest deity. It is sometimes named as the spiritual principle which animates all substances. Paracelsus uses the term (sometimes Archeus) in quite a different sense to denote the invisible spirit of things: it is the 'Universal Agent specialised in each individual'. In the words of Sendivogius, it is that spirit which 'is separated from bodies, is exalted, and ascends, the universal occult Nature, Operator, and Physician in all things.'

Archai Name given to the spiritual beings of the sphere of Venus. The word appears to have been used in this sense by Dionysius the Areopagite (see ANGELS). The Archai are said to guide the motion of time itself, and in some esoteric systems they are indeed called the 'Spirits of the Revolution of Time'. Steiner calls them 'Spirits of Personality' but, for other names, see SPIRITUAL HIERARCHIES. Sometimes the Archai are called 'Principalities', an attempt to Latinize the Greek word (see LORDS OF MIND and SECUNDADEIAN BEINGS).

Archangels Name given to the incorporeal beings of the Eighth Hierarchy, according to Dionysius the Areopagite (see ANGELS), the beings of the sphere of Mercury. Steiner calls them 'Fire-Spirits'. The Archangels are said to guide the spiritual destiny of groups of people, of nations, rather than individuals (which is the tutelary role of Angels); this probably explains why the Archangels are often pictured as carrying formalized models of cities in their arms. In Western occultism the most important of the named Archangels are MICHAEL, GABRIEL, RAPHAEL and URIEL. The traditional rulerships of the four Archangels and their equivalent ancient images are given in Table 2. See also DHYAN-CHOHANS.

Table 2

Archangel	Season	Element	Ancient prototype	Planet
Raphael	Spring	Air	Forces of healing	Mercury
Uriel	Summer	Earth	Forces of thought	Earth
Michael	Autumn	Fire	Forces of movement	Sun
Gabriel	Winter	Water	Forces of nourishment	Moon

Uriel is said to work with the united forces of the planetary system, supported by the powers of the fixed stars. The rulership of three of these four beings is linked with that of the ages (see SECUNDADEIAN BEINGS).

Archangels of the planets Sometimes called by the generic term ANGELS, these spiritual beings were originally charged with the regulation of the SPHERES, rather than with the planets themselves, although this distinction is now virtually lost. The most frequently used names

and planetary spheres are given in Table 3, but see also ARCHANGELS OF THE SEPHIROTH, PLANETARY SPIRITS and SEPHIROTHIC TREE.

Table 3

Gabriel	Moon	Samael	Mars
Raphael	Mercury	Zadkiel	Jupiter
Anael	Venus	Cassiel	Saturn
Michael	Sun		

Archangels of the Sephiroth The occult and Qabbalistic tradition has preserved several lists of names of the Archangels who have rule over the ten SEPHIROTH in the Tree of Life, which is linked with various astrological correspondences. These Archangels are opposed by their Adversaries (Table 4).

Table 4

Sephira	Meaning	Archangel	Adversary	Sphere
Kether	Crown	Metatron	Thaumiel	Primum mobile
Chokmah	Wisdom	Raziel	Chaigidiel	Zodiac
Binah	Understanding	Zaphkiel	Sathariel	Saturn
Chesed	Compassion	Zadkiel	Gamchicoth	Jupiter
Geburah	Severity	Camael	Golleb	Mars
Tiphereth	Beauty	Michael	Togarni	Sun
Netzach	Victory	Hamiel	Harab Serap	Venus
Hod	Splendour	Raphael	Samael	Mercury
Yesod	Foundation	Gabriel	Gamaliel	Moon
Malkuth	Kingdom	Metatron	Lilith	Man and elements

Archangels of the zodiac The astrological tradition has preserved many lists of ANGELS, archangels and spirits, which are said to be specifically in control of the twelve signs of the zodiac. Unfortunately, few of these lists agree, either in names or rulership, but those in Table 5 are usually given in popular occult texts. The overall ruler of the zodiac is sometimes named as Maslem, but in the esoteric view the zodiac falls under the Cherubim or Seraphim. See also SEPHIROTHIC TREE.

Table 5

AR	Malshidael, Aiel	LB	Zuriel, Jael, Joel
TA	Asmodei, Tual	SC	Barchiel, Sozol
GE	Ambriel	SG	Adnachiel, Ayil
CN	Muriel, Manuel, Cael	CP	Hamael, Semakiel, Casujoiah
LE	Vercheil, Ol, Voel	AQ	Cambiel, Ausiel
VG	Hamaliel	PI	Barchiel, Varchiel, Pasiel

Archiatius The supreme life force in physical nature, approximately the equivalent of the ETHERIC.

Archons In occultism a Greek term adapted to mean the primordial planetary beings or spirits. In the Gnostic cosmoconception the name of the spiritual hierarchies responsible for the creation of the material world.

Ares One of the ancient Greek names for Mars. Paracelsus used the same term to denote the formative power which creates differences (*differentia*) among species.

Argha A Chaldean term usually translated as meaning the 'womb of nature' (the 'ark') and hence the crescent moon, as well as a vessel for religious offerings.

Arian A term frequently misused for ARIETAN. Properly it is applied to a follower of the 'heretical' Alexandrian Arius. See also ARYAN.

Ariel The personalized name of a spirit said by Heywood (*Hierarchie of the Blessed Angels*, 1635) to be one of the spirits of the waters; but Shakespeare, who popularized the name in *The Tempest*, makes Ariel a sylph or air spirit. In the play he is first enslaved by the witch Sycorax and then becomes the tormented plaything of her son Caliban; he is finally liberated by the magician Prospero.

Aries The first sign of the zodiac. It corresponds as a sign neither in location nor extent with the constellation of the same name, which in mythology is linked with the ram of the Golden Fleece, sacrificed to Jupiter, and carried away by Jason and his Argonauts. This asterism of Aries is linked in Qabbalism with the Hebraic letter He and with the TAROT arcanum of 'The Pope'. The modern sigil for Aries ♈ is said to be a vestigial drawing of the horns of the ram, but some esoteric astrologers prefer to explain the sigil as a primitive diagram of the implosion and explosion of spirit in and out of the material body. Aries is of the FIRE ELEMENT, of the Cardinal quality, and its influence is outgoing, pioneering, self-reliant, idealistic, enthusiastic and exaggerative. There is a strong element of selfishness in the Arietan type, who tends to be insensitive to the needs of others. This outgoing nature of Aries is expressed in many key words, such as, initiatory, freedom loving, active, resourceful, aggressive, impulsive, inspirational, courageous, spontaneous, audacious – in a word, all those qualities which may be associated with a Fire nature expressing itself with unbridled confidence. In excess the Arietan nature has an underlying destructive nature, the key words being overbearing, dictatorial, resentful, sarcastic, jealous, coarse, argumentative, violent, uncontrolled, impatient and egotistical. Aries is ruled by the planet Mars – indeed, in the ancient tradition by POSITIVE MARS, as opposed to NEGATIVE MARS which has rule over Scorpio.

Arietan Pertaining to the sign or constellation of ARIES; the construction is from the Latin genitive *Arietis*.

Arioch The personalized name of one of the fallen angels in Milton's *Paradise Lost*, derived ultimately from the Hebrew meaning 'fierce lion', the name of a man in Daniel 2, 14.

Ariolater A diviner (sometimes called 'ariolist' or 'ariolus') – one who foretells the future from omens. The term is said to be from the Sanskrit *hira* ('entrails'), but some occultists trace its origin to the Latin *ara* ('altar'). See also HARUSPEX.

Ariolus See ARIOLATER.

Aristotelian principles See PRINCIPLES.

Arithmancy A variant term for ARITHMOMANCY.

Arithmomancy A term from the Greek *arithmos* (number) and *manteia* (divination), relating to divination by numbers; esoterically it is concerned with the science of correspondences between gods, men and numbers, as taught by Pythagoras.

Armomancy A term said to be used of the method of inspecting the shoulders of potential sacrificial victims to see if they were suitable for such offering. It is scarcely a method of prediction (as would be required by the Greek *manteia*) and the entire word is suspect.

Aromal planets Name given by nineteenth-century astrologers, mainly working within the framework of Theosophy, to a large group of planets said to orbit within our solar system although invisible to normal sight.

Artificial elemental See ELEMENTAL.

Artificial gamalei See GAMALEI.

Arundhati Sanskrit term for Venus as the Morning Star LUCIFER.

Arupa A Sanskrit term meaning 'formless' and used in Western occultism to denote those beings dwelling in forms of an entirely non-physical kind. The arupic world is in this sense the equivalent of the spiritual world (see ARUPA-LOKA). The arupic forms may, however, be seen by special clairvoyant vision.

Arupa-loka A Sanskrit term meaning 'formless world' and adopted into Western occultism to mean the 'spiritual world' or 'spiritual realm' in which being is of a non-physical kind.

Arupic In Western occultism, sometimes the equivalent of 'spiritual', but see ARUPA.

Aryan In an astrological context this term is sometimes used in error for ARIETAN (see also ARIAN). The word 'Aryan' is, of course, properly applied to a member of a supposed race which made use of a particular form of language, the Indo-European language, but see FIFTH RACE.

Asana A Sanskrit word used to denote one of a series of postures adopted (mainly) by those practising HATHA-YOGA. See also YOGA.

Asat Sanskrit term meaning approximately 'unreal' and often taken as referring to the unevolved or unmanifested nature of PARABRAHMAM and contrasted with SAT. By a curious transposition of meaning, in modern Western occultism Asat also points to that which is above Sat, which is 'more real than real'.

Ascendant The term is properly applied to the degree of zodiac arising on the eastern horizon of a figure, or indeed to the degree of zodiac arising over the eastern horizon. This degree was originally called the *horoscopos* in Greek astrology, from which the modern word HOROSCOPE is derived.

Ascending arc See LUMINOUS ARC.

Ashtoreth The goddess of fertility among the Phoenicians, the equivalent of the Babylonian ISHTAR. See ASTAROTH.

Asiras A Sanskrit term meaning 'headless', supposedly used to denote ELEMENTALS without heads. The first two of the ROOT RACES are sometimes called by this name, although they had neither physical heads nor bodies.

Aski-kataski The short form for a mystical phrase 'Aski-kataski-haix-tetrax-damnameneus-aision', recorded by Kircher with the translation 'Darkness, Light, Earth, Sun and Truth', supposedly engraved upon the belt of Ephesian Diana. The words are recorded as powerful demonifuges and used on AMULETS and SEALS.

Asmoday One of the seventy-two SPIRITS OF SOLOMON. He is said to appear as a king with three heads, one of a ram, another of a bull and the third human; he rides a dragon. But see ASMODEUS

Asmodeus A demon who figures in the Book of Tobit (Apochrypha) as the personal tormentor of Tobias's wife-to-be. The Hebraic name *Ashmedai* (Destroyer) was probably from the Persian *Aesham-dev*, the demon of concupiscence. The three-headed monster of Asmodeus imaged by Collin de Plancy as the 'destroyer demon' (Figure 9) suggests a demonizing of the Christian TETRAMORPH. In his list of DEMONIC SINS Binsfeld associated Asmodeus with power of the deadly sin of lechery. In *The Testament of Solomon* Asmodeus reveals himself as the demon pledged

Figure 9   *Asmodeus, demon of Hell (after de Plancy)*

Table 6

Type	Aspect name	Degrees	General meaning in horoscope
Major	Opposition	180	Tension
Major	Trine	120	Expansion
Major	Square	90	Difficult, but energizing
Major	Conjunction	0	Intensifies planets involved
Minor	Quincunx	150	Strain
Minor	Sesquiquadrate	135	Difficult (less than square)
Minor	Semi-square	45	Difficult
Minor	Sextile	60	Expansive (weaker than trine)
Minor	Semi-sextile	30	Slight strain

to plot against the newly wedded, and to 'estrange the hearts of virgins and waste away their hearts'. The 'flight of Asmodeus' is derived from literature (Le Sage, *Devil on Two Sticks*) in which Asmodeus takes one Don Cleofas for a night flight, and by magical means removes the roofs from the houses of a village to show him the secrets of what passes in private lives.

Asomatous   A Greek word meaning 'incorporeal' and applied to the angelic hosts and even to the demons, neither of which have physical bodies.

Aspects   An astrological term used to denote a large number of angular relationships between planets and other nodal points. The various angles between planets and nodal points in a chart have been invested with specific influences or powers which work through the planets concerned; thus, for example, the 'beneficient' trine aspect unites in a temporary harmony even the Moon and Saturn, which have diametrically opposed natures. The traditional forms of astrology describe nine angular relationships only, these being divided into the major aspects and the minor aspects. More specialized aspects are not included in Table 6.

Asport   A term used of a psychic phenomenon involving the disappearance of an object from a location unhindered by physical barriers such as walls and so on. Usually such a phenomenon occurs only under seance conditions, although it has been recorded during POLTERGEIST activities. See also APPORT.

Asrama   Sometimes *Ashram* or *Asram*, a Sanskrit word derived from a root meaning 'to strive' and used in Western occultism almost exclusively to denote a place, such as a school, where spiritual or religious efforts are made. The *Brahmasrama* is probably a modern compound meaning approximately 'initiation chamber'. In oriental occultism the term *asrama* is also used to denote periods of special effort in the life of a brahman of which there were four in a sequence: the student, the householder, one in monastic seclusion and *bhikshu* (religious mendicant).

Assiah   In Qabbalism this is the World of Expression, the world of our familiar material existence, which is visualized as being under the power of the planetary spirits, though within Qabbalism these include also the elemental spirits and even man himself as an incarnating spirit. The Sephiroth of the SEPHIROTHIC TREE each find themselves rooted in an incarnated sense in this lowest of the four worlds, and really it is only in the sphere of the Earth itself, called MALKUTH in Qabbalism, that Assiah is most clearly seen as a convincing projection of our senses. It is the realm where the illusory interactions of the ELEMENTS take place and where the spiritual realm is recognized only by means of SIGNATURES.

Astaroth   One of the seventy-two SPIRITS OF SOLOMON. He is said to appear in the form of an angel riding a dragon, with a snake in one hand; opinions are divided as to whether he is good or bad.

Asterism   Literally, a collection or group of stars, but the term is often applied to a configuration of such stars (see CONSTELLATION). Since the LUNAR MANSIONS are determined by star groups or identifiable fiducials, they are sometimes called 'asterisms'. The term is frequently wrongly applied to one or other of the signs of the zodiac, which are not star groups; the asterisms in relation to the zodiacal belt are shown in diagrammatic form in Figure 10.

Asteroid Scheme   A term used in some modern occultist circles in reference to an evolutionary scheme which visualized the belt of ASTEROIDS as material in a state of nascence, awaiting future development. Other occultists insist that the asteroids are fragments of a cosmic war in Heaven.

Asteroids   A term originated to denote the star-like minor planets, located at the very beginning

Figure 10   *The asterisms or constellations along a section of the zodiacal belt (from 180 degrees to 360 degrees). From left to right these are PG – Pegasus, AQ Aquarius, CP – Capricorn, SG – Sagittarius, SC – Scorpius, LB – Libra and VG – Virgo. The abstract figures traced between the major stars are traditional and do not necessarily suggest the corresponding images for the asterisms or signs*

of the nineteenth century (the first, located by Piazzi in 1801, was quickly followed by many other discoveries). Some astrologers insist that the asteroids (which are sometimes called 'planetoids') exert an influence in birth charts, but not all subscribe to this idea. See, however, HYPOTHETICAL PLANETS.

Astraea   Name of one of the ASTEROIDS. The Romans used the same word (meaning 'starry goddess') for the constellation and sign Virgo, deriving the word from the Greek story of Justice (Astraea herself) who was driven from Earth to Heaven by the wickedness of mankind.

Astragalomancy   A term derived from the Greek *astragalos* (dice or knucklebone) and *manteia* (divination) and applied to a method of telling the future from the throw of dice or bones.

Astral   The term appears to be derived from the Latin for 'star' and is sometimes applied to the stellar world as descriptive of the fabric of the heavens. Blavatsky suggests an origin from the Sythian *aist-aer* ('star'), but such an etymology should not confuse the astral with the fixed stars. In occult and astrological terminology the astral plane is contiguous in space (if not in time) with the material realm; it is the one which the spiritual part of man enters during periods of sleep and after death. The astral realm is one normally invisible to ordinary sight, yet it is the proper dwelling of the higher spiritual bodies of man (the Astral Body and Ego of modern occultism). It is significant that Paracelsus should coin his term *ens astrale* to denote the desire body or Sidereal Body of man. The realm is said to be permeated by the ASTRAL LIGHT, which is the equivalent of the ancient AKASHA, and so the Paracelsian *ens* does link with the stars; clairvoyants describe the Astral Body as consisting of light, like the stars themselves, though in continuous motion. The model of man projected in astrology is not far

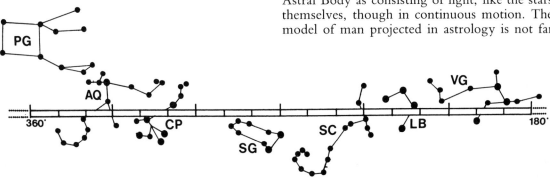

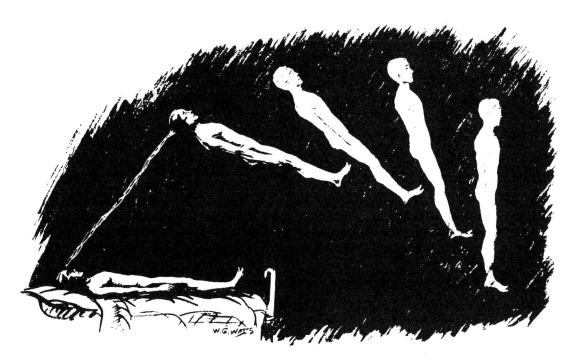

Figure 11 *A nineteenth-century visualization of how the Astral Body leaves the physical. Note the silver cord connecting the two*

removed from such occultist cosmoconceptions, and inevitably the link between the world of fixed stars and the astral has found expression in several terms, such as Sidereal Body, which make it the seat of the sensations through which planetary influences work upon man (but see also ASTRAL BODY). The ASTRUM of the alchemists relates to the old conception of hidden astral virtues, which are in turn said to proceed from the stars.

Astral Body   A name given to the Desire Body of men and animals – the spiritual seat of the emotional life. For possible etymologies, see ASTRAL. The ancients called the Astral Body the Sidereal Body or the *Ens astrale*. The function of the human astral body is threefold: to make sensation of the physical possible; to serve as a bridge between mind and physical matter; and to develop an independent vehicle of consciousness and activity. Steiner calls the Astral Body the 'Soul-Body' and the 'Sentient Body' (in the German, *Seelenleib* and *Empfindungsleib* respectively). The Astral Body is said by occultists and clairvoyants to be of a fine, highly luminous and vibrating nature, flooded with colours of inde-

scribable beauty, although the size, delicacy, rates of vibration and colour ultimately depend upon the evolutionary level of the human being it interpenetrates and informs. It is normally something like an ordinary physical body in shape, though enclosed in a largish ovoid or aura which permeates the human body. The somewhat materialistic images originated in the nineteenth century to illustrate the clairvoyant vision of the Astral Body depict it as virtually a light-filled equivalent of its attendant physical shape, but the fact is that the normal conditions of time and space do not apply to such a spiritual body as this, so that descriptions of it in terms of the material world are merely (at best) analogous.

The Astral Body is seen by clairvoyants as having an independent existence on the astral plane during periods when the physical body is asleep or when a person consciously indulges in ASTRAL TRAVEL. During such periods of conscious travel and during ordinary sleep (or in the case of an imposed trance), it is quite natural for the Astral Body to leave the physical and ETHERIC BODY behind and to lead an independent existence on its proper plane of being; it is then said to be connected to the lower plane by means of the astral cord or silver cord visible between the sleeping body and the first projection of the Astral Body in Figure 11. This

29

idea of body-free travel points to the fact – so important to occult teaching – that man may so develop his Astral Body to a point where it may become the vehicle for unbroken consciousness even during periods of sleep; the developed astrality of man is called BUDHI. Much of the so-called occult phenomena such as astral travel and certain forms of CLAIRVOYANCE are connected with the unconscious use of the Astral Body on the higher plane of being; while such activity is unconscious or atavistic in ordinary people or untrained mediums, it is quite conscious for those who have been initiated.

The Astral Body is sometimes called the Phantom Body in popular occultism. Some occultists also insist that the Astral Body is the realm in which Jupiter has direct relation to the breathing and the blood, and where Mars and Venus relate to the sensations and the passions.

After death, the consciousness principle of the Ego eventually withdraws from the Astral Body, which then dissolves back into its constituent starry world (see also ASTRAL LIGHT).

The Astral Body of Western occultism is the LINGA SARIRA of oriental occultism.

Astral cord   See ASTRAL BODY and SILVER CORD.

Astral death   See SECOND DEATH.

Astral double   The name sometimes given to the ASTRAL BODY when seen by clairvoyant means, as, for example, depicted in Figure 11. In popular thought this astral double is called a 'ghost', as it is sometimes seen (even by the non-clairvoyant) shortly after the death of a person. Distinguish, however, ETHERIC DOUBLE.

Astral image   A name used for an appearance on the earth plane of a spirit, ghost or picture originated in the ASTRAL.

Astral Light   A name for the invisible and diaphanous region around our earth, which corresponds to the Astral Body of man and is regarded by some as the cosmic memory of the AETHER. Levi has called it the 'Great Serpent' and the 'Great Dragon', but earlier occultists called it the 'Sidereal Light'. It is visible even (at times) to untrained clairvoyant vision.

Astral plane   See ASTRAL.

Astral projection   See PROJECTION.

Astral quintessence   See AZOTH.

Astral soul   A name used in modern occult circles to denote the lower MANAS.

Astral travel   A term used to denote the conscious experience of the Ego, with its heightened perceptions, during a period of sleep. During sleep all human beings leave behind their physical bodies and indulge in what might be called astral travel (imperfectly remembered in dreams), but the true form of astral travel is done consciously. See also PROJECTION and KESHARA.

Astro-alchemist   A person who combines the practice of astrology with alchemy. Many of the esoteric operations of alchemy involve the casting of charts to determine propitious moments and the careful consideration of planetary hours. This is probably a blind for certain praxes of esoteric techniques of meditation in which the individual seeks to open himself up to the cosmos (that is, the starry world).

Astro-alchemy   A term derived to denote the astrology linked with the late medieval form of alchemy. This consisted mainly of a prolix terminology that made use of astrological words and concepts in a way which recognized the occult philosophical basis of the art. The literature of such occultists as Boehme, Dee, Trithemius and Welling is representative of this approach to both alchemy and astrology.

Astro-archaeology   A term coined in modern times to designate the quasi-archaeological theory which relates the design, location and orientation of megalithic monuments to the celestial phenomena observed during the long period of their construction.

Astro-cartography   In astrology the name given to a modern system of horoscope chart extrapolation involving the imposition of the four angular positions of the ten planets of the natal chart on a world map, in order to determine geographic power zones which will correspond to potentials within the person for whom the chart was cast.

Astro-chronology   Relating to the chronology of heavenly bodies – for example, to the timing of CYCLES.

Astro-diagnosis Medical diagnosis, either from a natal chart or from a horoscope chart set up for the time of illness.

Astroeides See SUBTLE BODY.

Astrognosy Knowledge of the stars and, by extension, of the planets.

Astrolatry Worship of the stars as divine beings.

Astrological age A name wrongly given to a period usually supposed to be of 2160 years' duration, but see PRECESSION.

Astrology The study of the relationship between the macrocosm and the microcosm, which (in materialistic terms) is often defined as the study of the influence of the celestial bodies on the Earth and its inhabitants. Popular astrology is concerned with the reading of a horoscope chart cast for the moment of birth – in some cases complex methods of progressing the planets of the natal chart enable the astrologer to predict the future for the person for whom the chart was cast (technically called the 'native'). The chart is interpreted in terms of the influence of the zodiacal signs (see ZODIAC) and the various different powers which the PLANETS possess in these signs. In some cases the influence of fixed stars is also taken into account when these fall upon important points within the chart. A variety of different house systems (see HOUSES) is linked with interpreting the directions in the native's life in which planetary and other influences will manifest themselves. The planetary effects are not considered only in terms of zodiacal placing (on the basis that Mars in Leo is different from Mars in Cancer, for example), but also in terms of the angles which they may or may not hold to each other; this realm of astrology is the study of ASPECTS.

Astrology appears to be one of the most ancient of the surviving occult sciences, and vast evidence of a highly sophisticated system in Babylonian and Egyptian cultures has survived, although the lore appears to have been well guarded by the ancient Mystery schools. Oral tradition, as well as the development of astrological lore in ancient times, suggests an origin older than even Babylon and Egypt, as recent findings in the realm of ASTRO-ARCHAEOLOGY have indicated. There are many different forms of astrology, although in popular terms the most important of these is GENETHLIACAL ASTROLOGY, which deals with the casting and interpreting of horoscopes for individual humans; this does not appear to have been practised (save for kings as representatives of the state) much before the fourth century BC.

Two important forms (which to some extent overlap) are esoteric astrology and exoteric astrology. The former tends to deal with the individual incarnation in spiritual terms, to see the world populated by spiritual entities and to treat astrological doctrine as a sort of philosophical machine. Exoteric astrology is the most widely practised and is usually the only one known to the average practitioner: it tends to be involved with personal readings and horoscopic data, and with the predicting of events and experiences in the life of individuals. Attached to the esoteric astrological traditions in the present time are a large number of (often syncretic) teachings concerning the spiritual nature of man, as well as a corpus of traditions dealing with the hidden meanings of the signs, sigils, glyphs and symbols by which the horoscope may be understood as an esoteric diagram. Such esoteric forms are not always confined to the study of the events of a lifetime, but may be directed towards the study of prenatal, preconceptional and postmortem experiences, as well as to the study of the karmic consequences operative between lifetimes. In exoteric astrology the most important distinctive forms are ASTRO-METEOROLOGY, HORARY ASTROLOGY and SYNASTRY.

Astro-magical Relating to divination from the stars and planets.

Astro-mental image See THOUGHT FORMS.

Astro-meteorology A term used of that branch of astrology concerned with the predicting of weather and telluric conditions, such as earthquakes and volcanic eruptions. An alternative name for this study is meteorological astrology.

Astronomancy A term wrongly used as synonymous with ASTROLOGY; it is, in fact, a word used to denote a method of divination from the fixed stars.

Astronomos According to Blavatsky, a title given to the initiate in the seventh degree of the reception of the Mysteries. See INITIATION.

Astro-orientation   A term coined to designate the scarcely explored realm of art history and architecture, relating to FOUNDATION CHARTS and the orientation and design of buildings.

Astro-palmistry   A clumsy neologism used to designate the modern study of the relationships between astrology and palmistry. It has been taken for granted from very early times that the human hand is a physical model of the zodiac, although most of the early texts on the subject tend to establish links between the planets (rather than the zodiac itself) and parts of the hand.

Astrosophic geography   Term used by some modern astrologers to denote the now defunct practice of siting buildings and cities in accordance with astrological principles, aimed at reflecting the heavenly patterns in the earth's geography.

Astrosophy   A name given to a modern form of astrology based on indications of the nature of the celestial world set out by Steiner.

Astrosos   A medieval term to denote someone born under an evil star.

Astrum   A secret regenerative principle, almost the ancient equivalent of the ETHERIC of modern occultism. The astrum contains within itself all created things, and may be abstracted by alchemical processes from these things – it is the quintessence of things, the binding principle of life. This term is usually restricted to alchemy, but is also associated with the ancient astrological doctrine of VIRTUE.

Asura Mazda   Sometimes Ahura Mazda, Mazdeo or simply Mazda (but see ORMUZD). This particular orthography, of 'Asura', is generally avoided by occultists because of confusion with ASURAS.

Asuras   A term derived from the Sanskrit and in popular occult lore applied to a class of powerful demons, although in esotericism it is taught that these beings are highly spiritual, if not specifically concerned with the evolution of the earth. Technically the word means 'not a god', but in the old Rig-Veda they are visualized as being on the demonic, as well as the creative and harmonious, side of evolution. Eventually, however, they were considered as being the enemies of the Suras or gods. They are described as the demons or satanic powers who dwell in the 'no place' of ATALA. The Sanskrit term *asura-maya* means approximately 'black magic'. In modern esotericism they are the rebels in cosmic mythology.

Asuric   Sanskrit term often translated as meaning 'demonic'. See ASURAS.

Atala   Sanskrit term meaning approximately 'no place' and applied to the place of spiritual death. It is the realm in which the ASURAS and other demons dwell. Blavatsky records that the same name was 'contemptuously' used by the earliest pioneers of the FIFTH RACE to the lost ATLANTIS.

Atalia   One of several names given to the sky dragon who was believed by the ancients to swallow the luminaries and thus cause what we now call eclipses. The idea of such a lunar dragon survives in the astrological notion of the DRAGON'S HEAD and the DRAGON'S TAIL.

Atata   In Buddhist demonology an exclamation of anguish beyond articulation, which resounds throughout Hell.

Athanor   In exoteric lore the furnace of the alchemists, but in esotericism the astral fluid which they use. In esoteric ALCHEMY it denotes the complete human being, who is the furnace which makes transmutation possible.

Atlantean   The name given to the FOURTH RACE which established a vast and enduring civilization in an area of land now referred to as ATLANTIS. This civilization attained to a high level of cultural life, and it is taught in most occult systems that the knowledge of initiation preserved in the post-Atlantean Mystery centres was derived from teachers and initiates who survived the final catastrophe which met the surviving land area of Poseidonis.

Atlantidae   A term sometimes used in occult texts in reference to the ancestors of the Egyptians, who were taught by those who continued the Mystery wisdom of ATLANTIS.

Atlantis   The name given to a vast continent, and to the many civilizations which flourished on it, prior to the development of the Indus and Tibetan, Turanian-Iranian and Egypto-Babylonian cultures. The continental mass of Atlantis covered approximately the site of the present Atlantic ocean, into which the land mass eventually sank (parts of northern Scotland are described as remnants of the eastern reaches of the sunken mass). The civilization was undermined by the practice of black magic, and a catastrophe of 200,000 BC reduced the land mass and split it into two islands called Ruta and Daitya. For a vast age the Atlantean civilization flourished again, but eventually it fell into particularly vicious praxes of black magic, until floods and earthquakes destroyed the two continental masses of Ruta and Daitya (in 26,000 BC), leaving an island later called Poseidonis. The last flooding of Poseidonis, often referred to as the 'Atlantean deluge' by those unfamiliar with the history of Atlantis, was in 9564 BC.

Working from the records of the Akashic Chronicles (see AKASHA), Scott-Elliott has left a detailed account of the history of Atlantis. Ruled by divine kings, the social and spiritual conditions appear to have been planned for the benefit of all social levels; sculpture was the greatest of the Atlantean arts, and architecture was on a massive scale, the temples being even vaster than those of the later Egyptians. The language was agglutinative and of a universal nature. The Atlanteans participated in the INDIVIDUALIZATION of animals by methods of domestication, and it is said by certain occultists that if they had succeeded in fulfilling their obligations in this respect there would now be no carnivores. Few Atlanteans had attained to the power of abstract thought of the kind which characterizes our own civilization, and their personal advances stemmed mainly from development of innate psychic faculties.

Atma The divine MONAD, the highest of the seven principles in man – the highest spirit. Sometimes wrongly defined as the 'highest soul'.

Atma-bhu A Sanskrit term meaning 'existing as a soul'.

Atma-vidya A Sanskrit term meaning 'soul knowledge', and applied to the highest form of spiritual knowledge.

Atmabodha A Sanskrit term meaning 'self-knowledge'.

Atman See ATMA.

Atout See TAROT.

Atropos See FATAE.

Atziluth The name given to the World of Origins in the Qabbalistic SEPHIROTHIC TREE; it is approximately the equivalent of the mental world of European occultism. Atziluth is ruled and administered by a number of so-called God-aspects, through whom spiritual realities begin to take upon themselves the first manifestations of form. The Qabbalist Gray pictures these God-aspects as being rays of light, focusing from the single light of God in the Atziluthic plane for specific purposes.

Augoeides A Greek term meaning approximately 'luminous being' or 'form of splendour', and usually explained in popular occultism as relating to the higher EGO of man or the CAUSAL BODY. However, as Mead has shown, the word was misunderstood and mistranslated by Bulwer-Lytton, and the error arising from this has been perpetuated in occult lore (see, therefore, SUBTLE BODY). Blavatsky describes the Augoeides as the 'luminous divine radiation of the Ego which, when incarnated, is but its shadow.' See also AURIC EGG.

Augur A soothsayer or diviner. Originally the term 'augur' was applied to the priest or religious official who interpreted omens from the flight, song and feeding of birds (etymologically connected with the Latin *avis*, 'bird'). The 'augurista' was in medieval times one who read into futurity.

Aum See OM.

Aura The name given to a subtle emanation seen by clairvoyants around objects or around human beings, animals, plants, and so on. The quality of the aura appears to differ with the quality of the object itself, and the interesting thing is that not all clairvoyants describe the auras of similar objects or people in the same way. In the classification adhered to by the Theosophical school of thought there were several forms of aura – the health aura, the so-called karmic aura, the vital aura, the character aura and the spiritual aura.

The work of Leadbeater, who, for all his misreading of the Akashic Chronicles, seems to have been a clairvoyant of a very high order, has described in a fairly systematic way the auric colours associated with such things as human emotions, although these seem to relate not only to the aura itself but to THOUGHT FORMS.

Auraric See AZOTH.

Auric Egg In the esoteric tradition the term 'Auric Egg' is used to denote the CAUSAL BODY of man, the AUGOEIDES of the ancient Greeks. The later medieval astrological systems associated this egg with the sphere of Jupiter, though this has not passed into the correspondences drawn by modern esotericists. Sometimes the Auric Egg is symbolized in the form of a *vesica piscis*, framed by the tropical zodiac, as, for example, in the famous melothesic man in the miniature by the Limbourg brothers, painted for the Duc de Berri. See, however, SUBTLE BODY.

Auriel The name given to the Archangel of the North, the being who maintains the fertility of the earth and the formative nature of the metals and liquids within the earth's crust. He is sometimes called Uriel.

Ausiel According to certain grimoires, the name given to the governor of zodiacal Aquarius. The name is not to be confused with Auriel, which is an alternative for Uriel. See ZODIACAL SPIRITS.

Austral virtue See BOREAL VIRTUE.

Austromancy Divination by means of winds and from 'imaginations' seen in the wind-blown clouds.

Automatic writing Writing executed by an amanuensis without conscious participation in the formulation of the ideas set down. Very often such writing is done by a medium in a state of TRANCE, in which case the writing is said to be done 'under control'. In other cases the amanuensis is conscious, yet makes the effort to keep his or her mind reasonably empty to permit the overlooking spirit (the 'control') to work through his or her body without hindrance. Automatic writing is a sort of temporary and agreed OBSESSION, in the psychic sense of the word. A large corpus of modern *occulta* has been produced by means of automatic writing, but this (which is rarely of a high literary quality) must be distinguished from that body of work written under the inspiration of masters (the so-called MAHATMAS) or disincarnate spirits with the conscious participation of the amanuensis. The important writings of Bailey appear to have been produced in this way. See SLATE WRITING.

Autoscope A term suggested by Barrett to denote any mechanical means by which communication from the spiritual world may be established and maintained. The PLANCHETTE of seance rooms is an autoscope. The term has also been used in a different sense by Jung to denote methods designed to concentrate the attention of an individual in such a way as to establish free access to the subconscious levels. The formal pattern of the TAROT is such an autoscope.

Autozoon A name derived from Gnostic and Neo-Platonic sources for the image of the TETRAMORPH. The etymology of this Greek term is linked with that of the ZODIAC.

Avatar From the Sanskrit word *avatara*, which means 'descent', and used to denote a god who has descended, by way of an incarnation, into either mortal or animal form. The parentless avatar is called the *anupadaka*.

Avidya A Sanskrit term meaning 'ignorance', although it really applies to that ignorance which arises out of the hypnotism induced by the illusion of the sensory world.

Avitchi A Sanskrit term meaning 'endless hell'. It is said to be the final one of the eight hells, where 'culprits die and are reborn without interruption' – this, says Blavatsky, is because Avitchi is another name for Myalba (our earth) and also a state to which some soulless men are condemned on this physical plane. In popular occultism Avitchi is sometimes said to the 'Theosophic hell'; one presumes that no joke is intended.

Axinomancy A term derived from the Greek *axine* (axe) and *manteia* (divination) and applied to an obscure form of divination from the heating of an axehead in the embers of a fire. Another method recorded among the ancient Greeks is that of placing an AGATE stone on a red-hot axe; its motion is taken to indicate the identity of someone guilty of a crime. The term also covers other methods of prediction, or answering questions, by means of an axe.

Ayanamsa A term derived from the Sanskrit (itself meaning something like 'precession') to denote the difference in degrees for any given point in time between the fiducial of the tropical zodiac (usually the beginning of Aries) and the sidereal zodiac, the putative first degree of the asterism of Aries.

Ayil According to certain grimoires, this is the name given to the governor of zodiacal Sagittarius. See also ZODIACAL ANGELS.

Ayin A Hebraic term meaning 'nothing'. See AIN.

Azazel Milton calls the standard bearer of rebellious angels by this name (*Paradise Lost*, I, 534), but in Mohammedan demonology Azazel is a DJINN; when he is commanded with all the other angels to worship Adam, he refuses on the grounds that a son of smokeless fire (that is, an angel) should not bend to a son of dust. It is said that as a result of this disobedience he was cast from heaven and his name was changed to EBLIS.

Azoc The alchemists' MERCURY by means of which a medicine was perfected which was believed to cure all known diseases. See AZOTH.

Azoph See ALCHEMY.

Azoth One of the many names used in ALCHEMY to denote an aspect of Mercury. It is the creative principle in nature and may be extracted by alchemical means for therapeutic purposes. It is sometimes said to be the PHILOSOPHER'S STONE, and in this sense it has many alternative names, such as Astral Quintessence, Flying Salve, Ethelia, Auraric and so on. It is evidently closely linked with the medieval QUINTESSENCE. Cornell writes of the Azoth as 'the luminous, brilliant and fiery colouring in the Spinal Canal, seen by clairvoyants', a reminder that the etheric is absorbed into the lower spinal region. Blavatsky presents another level of meaning when she ponits out that the word 'Azoth' or 'Azot' was a medieval symbol for the alpha and omega (beginning and end), for the word combined the first and last letters of the Greek alphabet (alpha and omega), the Latin alphabet (A and Z) and the Hebrew alphabet (Aleph and Tau).

Azrael One of the names for the Angel of Death.

B

The ancient symbol for the second letter of the alphabet, derived from the Hebraic Beth, which is itself said to derive from a drawing of a house or an enclosure. It is thus associated with the idea of stone (such as might be used for building). In the occult view of sound meanings the B is linked with enclosing or embracing. This in turn postulates 'something embraced', pointing to the duality, or 2, which follows the singular of the letter A. In the sound B the 1 falls into the confusion of choice, of duality. See therefore TWO.

Baal One of the seventy-two SPIRITS OF SOLOMON. He is said to appear sometimes with a human head, sometimes with the head of a cat or a toad, and sometimes with all three. See BAEL.

Baalberith Name of the demon who is the keeper of the archives in Hell.

Bacchus Name of a HYPOTHETICAL PLANET. In mythology the name of the Greek god of wine, exoterically associated with untrammelled joy and licentiousness; in esoteric circles (under his Grecian names of Dionysos or Atys) he is regarded as a solar resurrectional god who atones for sin.

Backward blessing The name given to the saying of the Lord's Prayer backwards. It is said to invoke the devil and is sometimes mentioned in accounts of the SABBAT as one of the numerous profanations.

Baddha A Sanskrit term meaning 'bound' and applied to 'conditioned' humans who have not freed themselves from the Samsaric Wheel of ITARMA.

Bael The name given (perhaps by Wierius) to the first monarch of Hell; he has three heads – one that of a cat, one that of a crab and the other human. See Figure 26, under DEMONS.

Baetl One of the seventy-two SPIRITS OF SOLOMON. He is said to appear in a form resembling a cat, or sometimes a toad. He is especially conjured by magicians anxious to become invisible.

Balam One of the seventy-two SPIRITS OF SOLOMON. He is said to appear with three heads, only one of them human, the others usually those of a ram and a bull.

Balneum Mariae Sometimes *bain marie* (French for 'Mary's bath'), a name given to a kind of double cooker used by alchemists; the inner pan is gently warmed by the water in the outer pan, which is alone in direct contact with the flames. It is said that the name is derived from the gentleness of the heat, but it is more likely that the word is derived from the image of a source of spiritual heat (that is, Jesus) being nourished by water (Mary).

Banshee One of the household spirits of certain Highland or Irish families; the creature is said to wail at the death of a family member. The word is sometimes used to denote a sort of demon, but in Nordic folklore the banshee is always benevolent. The word is supposed to be derived from the Old Irish *ben sidhe*, a woman of the fairy folk.

Baphomet A name sometimes given to a supposed demon, but almost certainly a corruption of the word 'Mohammed'. It is said (quite wrongly) that the Templars worshipped the image of Baphomet.

Baraquel One of the Grigori (angels of Jewish legend – the term being derived from the word *egregori*, meaning 'the watchers'), who instructed men in the art of astrology.

Barbason The name of a demon who has passed into exoteric history through Shakespeare, being mentioned alongside Lucifer and Amaimon in *The Merry Wives of Windsor* (II, ii). Shakespeare may have had the name from Scot, who mentions Barbas as an alias of Marbas, a demon who appears in the form of a lion.

Barbatos One of the seventy-two SPIRITS OF SOLOMON. He is said to appear in the form of a hunter with a vast retinue of troops.

Barbiel A demon (properly a daemon) associated with the sign or constellation Scorpio in medieval occult texts and in some grimoires. The early nineteenth-century drawings of this demon are quite fanciful, as are the later sigils given alongside such drawings. (See Figure 12).

Barhishads A class of lunar PITRIS.

Bara A Babylonian name for an omen reader. See OMINA

Basic chakra See MULADHARA.

Basilisk A fabulous reptile, sometimes called a COCKATRICE, said to be hatched from a cock's egg by a serpent. It is thought to kill merely by its glance. Sometimes it is represented as a lizard, but as the word is derived from the Greek *basileus* ('a king'), it almost always wears a crown (Figure 13).

Baskara An ancient name for the sun, from the Sanskrit word meaning 'life giver'.

Figure 12   *A visualization of Barbiel, surrounded by sigils said to represent this demon; most of them are imaginary, however, and have nothing to do with the demonological tradition (from an eighteenth-century demonological text)*

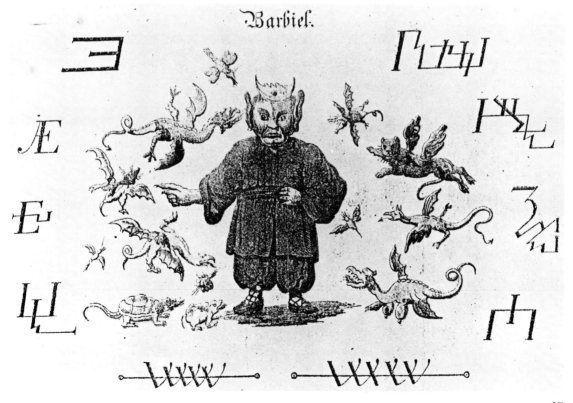

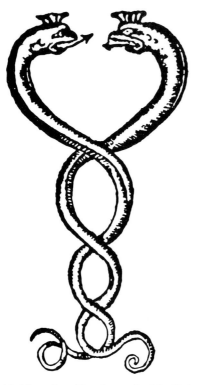

Figure 13 (above): *Two intertwined basilisks forming a caduceus (from a German woodcut, c. 1530)*

Figure 14 (below): *The Beast with seven heads and ten horns (a drawing after a medieval illustration to the biblical Revelation)*

Bath-kol The name of what is generally now regarded as a method of divination among the ancient Jews, although the word is often used as though it were the name of a god or demon. It is said that the first words uttered after the appeal to Bath-kol were taken as being oracular: the words in Hebrew meant approximately 'daughters of the voice'. Blavatsky links the word 'Bath' with the Hindu 'Vach' and points to the connection between this Hindu goddess of speech and the Word. Such a connection naturally lifts the concept of Bath-kol well out of the level of mere oracle.

Bathin One of the seventy-two SPIRITS OF SOLOMON. He is said to appear in human form, though with a serpent's tail, and rides a pale horse.

Bayemon Said in the GRIMOIRES to be the demon king of the western regions of Hell.

Beal One of the names for BERITH.

Beast The Beast or Chiva is an allegorical name given to the demonic child of SAMAEL and his consort Isheth Zenunim. It is also a name sometimes given to the creature in the hands of the image of Centaurus in constellation drawings and maps. This beast was probably the redeemed part of the asterism's horse nature – the part from which the half-man was free. See Figure 14.

Bechard A demon of the GRIMOIRES.

Beelzebub According to some, the name should be spelled 'Baalzebub' (see BAAL). Since this last word means 'Lord of the High House', it might wrongly have been taken to mean Solomon (in reference to his temple); the Jews therefore changed the name to 'Lord of the Flies'. It is said that Beelzebub was the equivalent of the Baal worshipped in Palestine and adjacent countries, and in later times a representative of the fallen gods. In Matthew, 12, 24, he is mentioned as 'Prince of the Devils' and this appellation has stuck, even though Milton has him 'next in crime' to Satan (*Paradise Lost*, I, 79).

Befor One of the occult names given to the spirit of Jupiter. See BETHOR.

Behemoth Originally Behemoth was an animal mentioned in Job, 40, 15 ff., thought to have been a hippopotamus, though the English poet Thomson (*The Seasons, c.* 1726) took it to be a rhinoceros and probably influenced William Blake in his picturing the beast as a kind of plated hippo. (See Figure 39, under GRIMOIRES.)

Bel See EL.

Beleth One of the seventy-two SPIRITS OF SOLOMON. He is said to appear as a king, but most reluctantly and always in a state of anger.

Belial A term for a devil taken from the Hebraic meaning 'worthless one', but in modern demonology he has been transformed to fit Milton's vision of the most lewd demon in Pandemonium (*Paradise Lost*, I, 490). In popular modern use the 'sons of Belial' are lawless or rebellious people. He is one of the seventy-two SPIRITS OF SOLOMON. He is said to appear as a beautiful angel drawn in a fiery chariot.

Beliar A demon, probably the same as BELIAL, and said to have control over all the evil spirits who lead man into sin, such as the demons of lust, jealousy and injustice.

Bell, book and candle After ceremonial excommunication in the Catholic Church, the ecclesiastic closes the book, throws the candle to the ground (thus extinguishing it in earth), and has the bell tolled as though for one who has died.

It is said that the book symbolizes the book of life, the candle symbolizes the (lost) soul, and the bell is technically the PASSING BELL representative in this case of the spiritual death. The rite has been wrongly linked with the EXORCISM of demons.

Bell Witch One of the most famous American spirits – sometimes called a poltergeist – who manifested in the early nineteenth century at the John Bell farmstead in Robertson County, Tennessee. It has been claimed that this 'witch' was the first spirit actually to kill a human being, for it appears that she poisoned John Bell by manipulating nostrums which he took for health reasons. Carrington and Fodor record that as early as 1828 she predicted the Civil War, the emancipation of the Negroes, the rise of the United States to a world power, and the destruction of modern civilization. It appears that she also predicted two world wars, dating the last one within four years of accuracy.

Belocolus See MAGIC STONES.

Belomancy Divination by the flight and the landing of feathered arrows. In one recorded system labels are attached to the arrows, and the advice or oracle tied to the one which travels farthest is taken as valid.

Belphegor A demon given a curious form by Collin de Plancy, but originally the Assyrian form of 'Baal-Poer' (see BAAL), who by the time the medieval demonologists took him was a devil. According to legend, Belphegor was sent from Hell by the other demons to find out if there really was such a thing on earth as married happiness. Rumour of such a thing had reached the demons, but they knew that people were not designed to live in harmony. Belphegor's experiences in the world soon convinced him that the rumour was groundless. The name of the demon reached popular consciousness through several developments of this legend (the most notable being that of John Wilson, *Belphegor, or the Marriage of the Devil*, 1691), so that in popular use the name is sometimes applied to a misanthrope or (more curiously) to a licentious person.

Benefics The planet Jupiter is often called the Greater Benefic, while Venus is called the Lesser Benefic. For the geomantic equivalent terms, see FORTUNA MAJOR and FORTUNA MINOR.

Benu An Egyptian term used of a variety of birds who were adopted as symbols of the PHOENIX, sacred to Osiris. The rech bird in particular was linked with the so-called Phoenix Cycle which was a precessional year of almost 26,000 years (see, however, PRECESSION). At a time when the cycles were exotericized from the Egyptian Mysteries the true length of the precessional periods was not understood, so that one finds Macrobius giving 660 years as the Benu Cycle, while others give 1460 years. Several other periodicities have also been linked with the benu bird (but see also HANSA).

Berith One of the seventy-two demons of the GRIMOIRE tradition, who appears mounted upon a red horse and wearing a crown of gold. He is said to be full of duplicity, but will tell the future as well as secrets of alchemy.

Bethor The name of a spirit associated with Jupiter, and conjured in the GRIMOIRES to obtain high position and great treasures. He is said to transport precious stones and to have knowledge of medicines with miraculous healing powers.

Betyles A Phoenician term, usually said to mean 'magical stones', although early writers call them 'animated stones'; they are also linked with forms of oracles. They are distinguished from ophites (serpent stones) and siderites (star stones), which were also talking stones. The physician Eusebius insisted on keeping his ophite as a sort of amulet, at times receiving from it oracles which it delivered 'in a small voice resembling a low whistling'.

Bezoar In fact a stone taken from the stomach or gallbladder of an animal, but sometimes used to denote a magic stone in a general sense. In medieval times the bezoar was supposed to be an antidote against poison.

Bhagats A Sanskrit name applied to those who exorcize evil spirits.

Bhumi A Sanskrit term for the earth.

Bhutas Sometimes *bhuts*, a Sanskrit word meaning approximately 'has-beens', and used to denote spiritual shells (ghosts), which are decaying astral bodies, the rejects of the recently deceased human.

Bi-quintile An ASPECT of 144 degrees, arising from a division of the zodiac into a two fifth arc. See QUINTILE.

Bicorn Sometimes Bycorne, a mythical creature with demonic undertones. In medieval literature it is mentioned as a beast which grows fat through living on the flesh of long-lived husbands. The equivalent 'female' version is the Chichevache.

Bifrons One of the seventy-two SPIRITS OF SOLOMON. He is said to appear in the form of a monster and to teach the conjurer the art of astrology and mathematics, as well as knowledge of herbs and stones.

Binah The third Sephirah of the Qabbalistic SEPHIROTHIC TREE. Its name means 'understanding', and it is the mother principle underlying universal existence, in spite of the traditional masculinity of the associate planet Saturn. In the lowest World of Expression (ASSIAH) it is connected with Saturn, although more with its potential for consciousness which arises from the confinements and limitations associated with this planet; it is also linked on this level with the working out of fate or KARMA. In the World of Formation (YETZIRAH) Binah is ruled by the angelic order of the Aralim, the Strong Ones, sometimes identified with the THRONES, who uphold the dictates of wisdom and lend it form. In the World of Creation (BRIAH) we find in Binah the controlling Archangel Zaphkiel, whose name is usually translated as 'beholder of God'; this spiritual being permits the vision to grow, which is a necessity for making proper choice in the world. In the World of Origins (ATZILUTH) the God-aspect is Yawe Elohim, usually translated as the 'Lord God', although properly speaking in the feminine Binah (which is sometimes described as a cosmic womb) it should be 'God the Mother'. The popular image of Binah is that of a woman emerging from the sea, and the Sephirah has actually been called the Sea.

Birth star Sometimes defined as the most powerful fixed star in conjunction with a planet or angle in a natal chart, or, failing such a conjunction, a star in close orb with such a planet or angle. However, the term is sometimes wrongly used for the Ascendant SIGN of the zodiac or for the SUN SIGN.

Birth stones Occult literature links a number of precious stones with each of the twelve signs of the zodiac; these associations are used in TALISMANIC MAGIC, and in the manufacture of AMULETS. The stones were said to transmit a specific VIRTUE (in which connection, see GAMALEI) when used to make seals. They were also sometimes worn unsealed as magnetic centres, to attract their corresponding virtues of the stars. An extensive literature, derived mainly from the Arabian-inspired medieval lore, presents very many different correspondences, and there appears to be little order or sense in some of these. Table 7 gives widely accepted correspondences from the medieval tradition.

Table 7

AR	Sardonyx	TA	Sard	GE	Topaz
CN	Chalcedony	LE	Jasper	VG	Smaragdine
LB	Beryl	SC	Amethyst	SG	Hyacinth
CP	Chrysoprase	AQ	Crystal	PI	Sapphire

The modern esoteric astrologer Thierens provides quite a different list:

Table 8

AR	Jasper	TA	Sapphire	GE	Chalcedony
CN	Emerald	LE	Sardonyx	VG	Cornelian
LB	Chrysolite	SC	Beryl	SG	Topaz
CP	Chrysoprase	AQ	Hyacinth	PI	Amethyst

Similar lists, with many varieties of correspondences, could be provided, but the above is sufficient to show that there is really no traditional system upon which one might rely. See also MAGIC STONES.

Black Age When used in an occult context the term is generally a reference to the present age. See KALI YUGA.

Black art The term is said to come from the confusion of the etymology of NECROMANCY with the Latin word *niger*, which means 'black'.

Black fire A term used by Qabbalists, meaning 'absolute wisdom', named black only because it is beyond the comprehension of ordinary intellects.

Black glance An occult term for the EVIL EYE.

Black magic The conscious exercise of evil, the perversion of WHITE MAGIC, sometimes called the LEFT-HAND PATH, the followers of which are sometimes called the BROTHERS OF THE SHADOW. The various departments of white magic are concerned with aiding the evolution of mankind; the corresponding departments of black magic are concerned with preventing the proper and natural evolution of mankind. Thus, the white magic underlying esoteric medicine is intended to ease the conflicts and disunions which exist between the physical and spiritual bodies of man; in black magic this healing process is perverted into the malpractice of poisoning, which uses the same esoteric and occult knowledge available to esoteric medicine, but with a view to creating conflict between the physical and spiritual bodies of man. The distinction, therefore, is not so much one of knowledge as of aim. The black magician always has a selfish purpose underlying his ceremonial; usually he has in mind the perversion or destruction of another entity for his own personal gain or for the gain of those whom he represents. This is one reason why blood sacrifice so frequently plays a part in the ceremonials of the black magicians, for blood is the most personal material possession of all humans, the seat and expression of the higher Ego; see, for example, the supposed rituals of the SABBAT.

The popular distinction that is drawn between white and black ceremonials – that white magic is involved with the work of the angels, whereas black magic is involved with the work of the demons – is not very far from the mark. Waite lends all the authority of his impressive scholarship to defining black magic 'with all its grim theatricals' as 'the act of exploiting lost angels with impunity'. The entries on GRIMOIRES, CONJURATIONS, WAX IMAGES, DEMONS and so on all lend support to this view.

Perhaps because of certain popular misconceptions people nowadays tend to think that the 'lost angels' and 'demons' must be somehow stupid to permit the goetic magicians to use them with impunity. However, this is far from the truth. The strict abjurations which survive even in the popular grimoires are always intended to bind demons in such a way that they may not harm the magicians conjuring them; this indeed is the main purpose behind the protective magic circles always used in such conjurations. In these dark ceremonials, as in every other thing, the demons are tricksters and liars: it is not the demons who serve, but the magicians themselves. Underlying all the dramatic externals of black magic is the sad truth that black magicians, for all they may think they are exercising their own egos (' "Do what thou wilt" is the whole of the Law,' said Crowley, misunderstanding an esoteric precept), are in reality only serving the demons. See MAGIC.

Black magicians   See BROTHERS OF THE SHADOW.

Black Mass   See SABBAT.

Blind   See OCCULT BLIND.

Bodhi   A Sanskrit term used to denote that state of contemplation in which the personalized self is merged with the eternal self.

Bodhisattva   A Sanskrit word which is frequently misused in Western occultism. Esoterically, a Bodhisattva is a human being who, through inner discipline and moral perfection, has in his higher principle attained NIRVANA. At such a stage, freed of the samsaric wheel of KARMA, he is at liberty to leave behind the earth, yet through personal choice he elects to remain on earth to work for the evolution of mankind. Through this choice he becomes a NIRMANAKAYA. See BUD-DHIC BODIES.

Body of formative forces   The name given by Steiner to the ETHERIC BODY.

Bofri   One of the names for BERITH.

Bogy   The name given to a hobgoblin, probably derived from the Scottish word 'bogle' or from 'boggart'. Some suggest that the word is from the same Welsh source as 'BUG'.

Book of Changes   See I CHING.

Book of Dyzan   One of the most remarkable sacred/occult texts of the East, extracts (from the Chinese, Tibetan and Sanskrit translations of the original Senzar) of which are used by Blavatsky as the basis for the commentaries which form the first book of her Secret Doctrine (see DYZAN). The text gives, by means of esoteric symbolism, the history of cosmic evolution. Even in translation the occultism of the text is hard to pierce: 'It must be remembered,' writes Blavatsky, 'that all these Stanzas appeal to the inner faculty rather than to the ordinary comprehension of the physical brain.'

Boreal virtue   The esotericist Fludd insisted that all things were animated by two principles, one of which he called the 'boreal virtue', which was a principle of condensation, the other of which he called the 'austral virtue', the principle of rarefaction. In modern terms these correspond to the actions of AHRIMAN and LUCIFER respectively – the centripetal and the centrifugal forces at work in the human soul and in nature.

Botis   One of the seventy-two SPIRITS OF SOLOMON. He is said to appear in the shape of a serpent.

Brahma   A Sanskrit word derived from the root *brih* (approximately 'expansion') and denoting the expansive spiritual energy-consciousness of our solar system. The 'Egg of Brahma' is indeed a term for our solar system. A 'day of Brahma' is a period of 2160 million years. A 'life of Brahma' consists of $4320 \times 72,000$ years. Distinguish from BRAHMAN.

Brahman   A Sanskrit word of the same derivation as BRAHMA, used to denote the unmanifest Logos, the male creator of the Indian pantheon. The word is sometimes given as 'Brahm', and must be distinguished from 'Brahma'.

Brahma-vidya   A Sanskrit word meaning 'knowledge of Brahma', and used to denote knowledge of esoteric teaching.

Brahmarandhra   A Sanskrit term used to denote a spot on the head (in the Crown Lotus) which is connected by the mystical subtle thread called the *sushumna* to the heart.

Braidism   See HYPNOSIS.

Briah   In the Qabbalistic SEPHIROTHIC TREE Briah is the World of Creation, the soul world of ethical and moral realities, under the tutelage of the ARCHANGELS.

Bride   Sometimes Bride of Microprosopus, the name given by Qabbalists to the Sephirah MALKUTH.

Bronze Age   A term derived from Hindu chronology and modern esoteric lore and relating to an epoch. See DWAPARA YUGA and FOUR AGES.

Brothers of the Shadow Sometimes the Dark Brothers or the Grey Brothers, terms used in modern occultism to denote those men and women who consciously choose to follow the practices and ethos of BLACK MAGIC, in what is called the LEFT-HAND PATH or the Path of Shadows. Their work, essentialy involutionary in aim, is contrary to the work of white magicians, sometimes called 'Sons of Light', who follow the pathway of evolution, self-perfection and self-sacrifice.

Broxa See ESTRIE.

Brow chakra See AJNA.

Buddha A Sanskrit term derived from the root *budh* meaning 'to perceive', 'to awaken', and used to denote a human being who has attained fully self-conscious spiritual enlightenment. A Buddha is one who has attained all that may be attained in a given series of reincarnations for an earth age and who has reached the state of enlightenment called NIRVANA.. See BUDDHIC BODIES.

Buddhi A Sanskrit term of the same derivation as BUDDHA, and is used to denote a faculty of spirit still undeveloped in ordinary man (the second of the spiritual-potential triad in contemporary man of ATMA, Buddhi and MANAS). Buddhi will develop with a transformation of the ASTRAL BODY, as a result of which man's conciousness will change. In some modern occult circles Buddhi is called 'life-spirit'.

Buddhic The Sanskrit term 'Buddha' is often applied to the Lord Gautama, the Enlightened One, from whom the Buddhism known to the Western world derives; in the oriental tradition there is more than one Buddha (see BUDDHIC BODIES). As Blavatsky pointed out long ago, the word should be written in English as 'Budhism'. The Sanskrit term *budha* is generally translated as meaning 'wisdom' and is derived from the root *budh*, 'to know or perceive' or 'to enlighten'. In modern esotericism the word 'Buddhi' is used to denote the faculty by which divine knowledge penetrates into the Ego. The Budhi or Buddhi, which is one of the human TERNARY, is the developed fruits of the astral body.

Buddhic bodies In the Westernized esoteric Buddhism special terms have been derived from oriental sources which have been incorporated into Western occultism, often in a misunderstood form. The terms especially misunderstood are the so-called Buddhic bodies, relating to the names given to the spiritual sheaths developed in Buddhahood. The following definitions of terms should clarify the issues, at least in the light of Western occultism. A Bodhisattva is a highly developed being who is not yet a perfect Buddha. When a Bodhisattva reaches a specially determined rank (sometimes called the rank of Arhat), he has the opportunity to pass into a state of bliss (called Nirvana) and dwell within the Dharmakaya body, beyond the limitations and responsibilities of earthly existence. This Dharmakaya is the body of a complete Buddha, whose consciousness is merged into the universal consciousness; it is this body (which is 'no body at all, but an ideal breath', as Blavatsky puts it) which the adept deserves, due to his own efforts and sacrifices, but which he willingly renounces in order to remain efficaciously concerned with the evolution of the earth. In freely choosing to remain responsible for humanity, in loving and invisible sacrificial service, such developed beings become Nirmanakayas. The Nirmanakaya body is an ethereal form, the developed and refined astral form unique to the Bodhisattva. This is the sheath in which the adept may dwell in between incarnations. There is a developed spiritual body or aspect of the Nirmanakya which is called the Sambhogakaya, of which one of the three additional perfections is said to be 'entire obliteration of all earthly concerns', as Blavatsky puts it. To summarize, therefore – the three Buddhic bodies are the Nirmanakaya, the Sambhogakaya and the Dharmakaya. None of these should be confused with the Buddhic in the trinity of man (see TERNARY).

Buer One of the seventy-two SPIRITS OF SOLOMON. He is said to appear as a starfish, and may be conjured only when the sun is in zodiacal Sagittarius.

Bug A now archaic name for a goblin or evil sprite, almost certainly from the Welsh word *bwg* (approximately 'ghost').

Bune One of the seventy-two SPIRITS OF SOLOMON. He is said to appear with three heads, one being human, the others being the heads of a griffin and a dog.

Buta-vidya A Sanskrit term meaning 'ghost knowledge' and used to denote the art of exorcism.

C

The third letter of the alphabet. The form of the C, which is so often linked in occult symbolism with the lunar crescent, is actually derived from the rounding-off of the Greek letter gamma, itself derived from a Phoenician image said to be a drawing of a camel. In this connection, however, see also G. For sound value, see K. For numerical value, see EIGHT.

Caasimolar Sometimes Caacrinolaas and Glasya, a grand president of Hell, supposed to bring knowledge to man and to confer invisibility through PACT. He also induces men to murder.

Cabal In popular etymology the word 'cabal' is sometimes derived from one of the ministries under Charles II of England (1670), as the initial letters of the names the ministers spelled the word (Clifford, Ashley, Buckingham, Arlington, Lauderdale). However, the word is much older than the seventeenth century, as it is from the Hebraic QABBALA.

Cabbala See QABBALA.

Cacodaemon Literally an 'evil spirit' in Greek (*kakos daimon*). Since some medieval astrologers (resting on antique terminologies) called the twelfth house of the horoscope figure 'caco-daemon', the popular interpreters of astrology have been led to the error that this house rules evil things, or the demonic element of the personality, which is far from the truth. For example, Brewer writes of the house as one 'from which only evil prognostics proceed'.

Caduceus A name given to a number of different (though ultimately related) symbolic rods, derived from the Egyptian Mystery centres, consisting of two serpents or basilisks twisted around a rod (Figure 15). It was the white wand carried by Roman heralds suing for peace and the wand of Mercury (herald of the gods, though not always

seeking peace). Some occultists claim that the serpents symbolize the healing snakes of the demi-god Aesculapius, and others claim that they refer to the two spiritual energies or healing forces which run up and down the human spine. A

Figure 15 *A caduceus in the hand of constellation Virgo (fifteenth century, after Hyginus)*

Figure 16   *A caduceus wand in the hand of Anubis–Mercury (from a third-century* AD *mosaic formerly in Thrysdus, Tunisia)*

modified form of the caduceus is used in a variety of different medical contexts in modern symbolic forms: for example, it is incorporated into the badge of the Royal Army Medical Corps, and it appears (albeit in modified form) on the main entrance doors to the Bank of England. Homer is sometimes said to refer to the caduceus as a flowered rod with three leaves, but it is possible that he is not writing of the Mystery school caduceus at all. By classical times it was called the 'wand of Hermes', and through the connection with the Mystery centres it became a symbol of the power which wakened men from sleep (and hence from death). In the calendrical mosaics of Thrysdus, the dog-headed Mercury (derived from the Egyptian Anubis) carries the caduceus (Figure 16), probably in reference to the rescue of Alcestis from Thanatos (as, for example, in the British Museum figure of Thanatos from the temple of Artemis). The sigil for Mercury is said (erroneously) to be derived from the caduceus. See also ABARIS.

Cael   In certain methods of ceremonial magic this name is given to the governor of zodiacal Cancer.

Cagaster   A term (probably) originated by Paracelsus, from the Greek *kako* ('evil') and *astron* ('star'). It is applied to that spiritual force in matter – derived from the stellar realm – which strives towards the destruction of form. It works against the ILIASTER.

Caim   One of the seventy-two SPIRITS OF SOLOMON. He is said to appear in the form of a thrush.

Calendaria Magica   The name used in medieval occultism and astrology for a series of tables setting out the correspondences, numerological connections and sigillic forms between zodiacal signs, planets, elements, celestial hierarchies and so on. The best of the surviving calendaria is that attributed to Trithemius and has influenced the associations passed into astrology by the eclecticism of Agrippa. Table 9 (p. 46) is culled from a fifteenth-century *Calendarium Naturale Magicum*: such calendaria are usually replete with magical seals, sigils, symbols and the like, and constitute one of the most fascinating realms of research into occult symbolism.

Camael   See KHAMAEL.

Caliban   The name of the deformed humanoid spawn of a devil and the witch SYCORAX in Shakespeare's *The Tempest*.

Cambion   A name given in the post-medieval period to the semi-human offspring of either an INCUBUS or a SUCCUBUS.

Cancer   The fourth sign of the zodiac. It corresponds as a zodiacal sign neither in location nor in extent with the constellation of the same name, which is linked with the TAROT arcanum 'The Moon' and associated with the Hebraic letter Tzade. The modern sigil for Cancer ♋ has been variously explained. Some see it as a vestigial drawing of the male and female seed; however, this form of the sigil is relatively modern, for it was different in medieval astrology. The image for Cancer is nowadays a crab, but in medieval astrology the sign and constellation were presented more frequently in the image of a crayfish.

Table 9

1	The one principle of all things, God, the Archetype					

2	The polarities of masculine (*agens*) and feminine (*patiens*), Sun and Moon, feeling (*cor*) and thinking (*cerebrum*)

3   The trinity of the godhead and the trinity in all things

Hierarchies	Suprema	Media	Infirma
Threefold man	Thinking (*intellectus*)	Feeling (*sensitiva*)	Body (*vegetabilia*)
Principles	Salt	Mercury	Sulphur
Elements	Fire	Air	Water

4

Elements	Fire	Air	Water	Earth
Angels	Michael	Raphael	Gabriel	Uriel
Cardinals	Oriens	Occidens	Septentrio	Meridies
Soul Powers	Intellectus	Ratio	Phantasia	Sensus
Virtues	Prudence	Justice	Temperance	Fortitude
Humours	Cholera	Sanguis	Pituita	Melancholia
Qualities	Hot	Humid	Cold	Dry

5

Elements	Water	Air	Fire	Earth	'Mixtum'
Planets	Saturn	Jupiter	Mars	Venus	Mercury

6

Celestial Hierarchies	Seraphim	Cherubim	Thrones	Dominions	Powers	Virtutes
Planets	Saturn	Jupiter	Mars	Venus	Mercury	Moon

7

Planets	Saturn	Jupiter	Mars	Sun	Venus	Mercury	Moon
Spirits	Aratron	Befor	Phalec	Och	Hagith	Ophiel	Phul
Angels	Oriphiel	Zachariel	Samuel	Michael	Anael	Raphael	Gabriel
Intelligencies	Zazel	Iophiel	Graphiel	Nachiel	Hagiel	Tiriel	Malcha
Daemons	Agiel	Hismael	Barzabel	Soreth	Kedemel	Taphit★	Hasmodai

★The full name of Taphit is Taphitartarat.

8	The Stellatum and the seven planetary spheres

9

Spheres	*Hierarchies*	*Rulers*	*Precious stones*
Primum mobile	Seraphim	Metatron	Sapphyrus
Stellatum	Cherubim	Ophaniel	Smaragdus
Saturn	Throni	Zophkiel	Carbunculus
Jupiter	Dominations	Zadkiel	Berillus
Mars	Potestates	Camael	Onix
Sun	Virtutes	Michael	Crysolithus
Venus	Principalities	Haniel	Iaspis
Mercury	Archangeli	Raphael	Topasius
Moon	Angeli	Gabriel	Sardius

10	*Primum mobile*, the zodiac (*Sphaera zodiacus*), the seven planetary spheres and the earth spheres (*Sphaerae elementaris*)

11	is regarded as having no value in the system

12	gives the associations at their richest with the twelve signs of the ZODIAC and their SIGILS, the names of the zodiacal angels (Malchidiel, Asmodel, Ambriel, Muriel, Verchiel, Hamaliel, Zuriel, Barbiel, Adnachiel, Hanael, Gabiel and Barchiel), the twelve months and the roman *numina* or gods, the twelve IMAGES of the signs, the corresponding MAGIC SQUARES and BIRTH STONES.

Cancer is of the WATER ELEMENT, of the Cardinal quality, and the influence is emotional, sensitive, imaginative, gregarious and cautious. The nature of Cancer is romantic, sociable, shrewd, domesticated, passive, strong in feelings and so on – it is, in a word, all those qualities which may be associated with a sensitive water type seeking emotional unfoldment through experiencing the material realm. In excess or when under pressure, the Cancerian nature may be described as fearful of coming out of its crablike shell, for it is timid, self-absorbed, acquisitive, vulnerable, moody, pedestrian and so on; like the other water signs, it wishes at times to withdraw from the material realm. Cancer is ruled by the Moon, marks the exaltation of Jupiter, the detriment of Saturn and the fall of Mars.

Capnomancy Divination from the movement of smoke, especially from the direction taken by the smoke from sacrificial offerings. The same term was used of divination by means of TRANCE induced by the breathing in of smoke of a specially prepared drug.

Capricorn The tenth sign of the zodiac. It corresponds neither in location nor in extent with the constellation CAPRICORNUS, although it does carry by analogy some of the occult associations of the latter – namely, the link with the Hebraic letter Yod and with the TAROT 'Wheel of Fortune'. The modern sigil for Capricorn ♑ is said by some to be a drawing of the horns of a goat, with which the modern image is associated. However, Capricorn was never properly a goat, but a goat-fish, as the Greek term *aigokeros* itself implied; the Babylonian prototype for the image was that of a goat with a curled fishtail, and it is to this which the modern sigil refers (see the fifteenth-century image in Figure 17). Capricorn is of the EARTH ELEMENT, and of the cardinal quality, the influence being practical, industrious, prudent, persevering, diplomatic, cautious, methodical and ambitious, dependable, trustworthy, efficient, just, honest, undemonstrative, conservative, responsive, patient, systematic – in a word, all those qualities which may be associated with an earth type working with integrity to achieve some particular aim. In excess or under pressure, the Capricornian nature may be described in terms which express its underlying need for security: secretive, fearful, miserly, unsympathetic, rigid, suspicious, selfish, materialistic,

Figure 17 *Capricornus as a goat-fish (a fifteenth-century image after Hyginus)*

brooding and egotistical. Like the other Earth signs, it is subject at times to deep melancholia. Capricorn is ruled by the planet Saturn, marks the exaltation of Mars, and the fall of Jupiter.

Capricornus The tenth asterism of the constellational ZODIAC, not to be confused with the sign CAPRICORN. While the Babylonian goat-fish Capricornus points to a different mythological origin, the traditional Greek myth tells how Pan, in order to escape the pursuit of Typhon, jumped into the Nile, with the result that his upper half turned into a goat and his lower half into a fish.

Caput A term from the Latin meaning 'head'. When so isolated, in most astrological contexts it usually refers to *Caput Draconis* (DRAGON'S HEAD). In a context of fixed stars the isolated term may also refer to ALGOL, the *Caput Algol*.

'Caput' is also the name of one of the sixteen figures of GEOMANCY, the Dragon's Head.

Caput mortuum A term in general use, derived originally from alchemy where it was used to denote the residue after an alchemical operation such as distillation or sublimation. It is the 'death's head', the materiality which lacks all spiritual qualities.

Carcer 'Prison', the name of one of the sixteen figures of GEOMANCY.

Cardinality A term applied in astrology to one of the three qualities (the others being FIXITY and MUTABILITY) which acts as the mainspring of action, as the fount of energy. The four Cardinal signs (Aries, Cancer, Libra and Capricorn) are each in their own way involved with initiating action, with making a movement into the world.

Cartagra A word sometimes used as an alternative for Purgatory, meaning approximately 'affliction of souls'.

Cartomancy Divination by means of playing cards. The most popular form of such divination is by means of the TAROT.

Cassiel The name given to the Archangel of Saturn. In certain occult systems Cassiel was the Angel of Solitude and Tears. In the superficial GRIMOIRE tradition he is as a demon with batwings, seated on a dragon.

Casting The concept of 'casting' a horoscope, by which is meant calculating a nativity, is probably derived from a Middle English verb relating to calculations made by means of counters. The same word is, of course, used for the casting of SPELLS, the Old English word for 'cast' being *weorpan*, which is cognate with our modern 'weapon'.

Castor See GEMINI.

Casujoiah In certain forms of ceremonial magic this is the name given to the governor of zodiacal Capricorn.

Catholic magnesia See MAGNESIA.

Catoptromancy Divination by means of a mirror, sometimes called enoptromancy.

Cauda A term from the Latin for 'tail', which in most astrological contexts refers to *Cauda draconis*, the DRAGON'S TAIL. In a context of fixed stars the term sometimes refers to *Cauda ursae*.

'Cauda' is also the name of one of the sixteen figures of GEOMANCY.

Causal Body In esotericism the BUDDHI of the higher ternary in man is called the 'Causal Body'. In initiates (and one day in all evolved men) it is the redeemed ASTRAL BODY. Blavatsky, however, insists that Buddhi itself should not be termed the 'Causal Body', but may only be so in conjunction with the incarnating Ego. See also AURIC EGG.

Celestial hierarchies The term is from the Greek compound of *ieros* (sacred), and *archen* (rule), and refers to the chain of spiritual beings which are visualized as ranged in descending order from the realm of God to the world of man. They were given an official nomenclature by Dionysius the Areopagite, who is said to have derived them from earlier sources. This list of names and their symbolic attributes are still used by occultists, esoteric astrologers and ecclesiastical writers. Each group has its distinctive function within the spiritual realm, and since (according to the laws of sympathy) each spiritual activity finds expression in the material realm, each group may be seen manifest on the earth, as the complex Qabbalistic traditions of the SEPHIROTHIC TREE makes clear. The schema, in accordance with the theory of number magic, is presented as three groups of three.

In descending order of power and responsibility, the First Hierarchy consists of the SERAPHIM, sometimes called Spirits of Love, who are directly involved with maintaining the relationship of the solar system to the entire stellar universe, and who are often accorded rule over the Stellatum; the CHERUBIM, sometimes called Spirits of the Harmonies, said by some authorities to be responsible for ordering the planetary movements within the solar system, but often accorded rule over the realm of the ZODIAC as distinct from the fixed stars; and, finally, the THRONES, sometimes called Spirits of Will, said by some to have rule over the realm of Time itself. Esoterically, time is regarded as being operative only below the sphere of Saturn, with which the Thrones are associated; this probably explains the connection in Greek mythology between Chronos (Time) and Saturn. The Second Hierarchy consists of the DOMINIONS, in Greek the Kyriotetes, sometimes called the Spirits of Wisdom, who are said to be involved with the metamorphosis of matter, and who are linked with the sphere of Jupiter; the DYNAMIS, sometimes called the Mights, and in modern esotericism the Spirits of Movement, who are directly charged with rule over the sphere of Mars; and the Exsusiai (a Greek term), in modern esotericism Spirits of Form, sometimes also called the Elohim in Qabbalistic contexts. These are the creative beings who lend form and substance to the earth itself, and who have rule over the sphere of the Sun. The Third Hierarchy consists of the ARCHAI, sometimes called the Principalities, in the modern esotericism Spirits of Personality, who have charge over the rise and fall of the epochs of civilization and the history of the world. These beings have rule over the sphere of Venus. Then follow the ARCH-ANGELS, called by Steiner Fire-Spirits, who have rule over individual nations of the earth, and who are in charge of the sphere of Mercury. The last of the Third Hierarchy is the class of ANGELS, called in modern esotericism Sons of Life or Sons of Twilight. These have charge over the lives of individual humans (according to esoteric lore, over one individual from lifetime to lifetime). They are linked with the sphere of the Moon.

At the bottom of the celestial chain is the realm of man, which has been called the Tenth Hierarchy. Below man are the various infernal spheres of the demonic and purgatorial realms, which in some systems are a mirror-image distortion of the celestial hierarchies (see INFERNAL HIERARCHIES).

The celestial hierarchies are sometimes called the Dionysian hierarchies, even in those cases where the lists do not perfectly tally with the sequence set out by Dionysius. His practice was to number the scale of angels from 1 to 9. However, Pope Gregory I not only presented a slightly different order, but also numbered the scale from 9 to 1, giving rise to several difficulties in the medieval period. Table 10 sets out the main differences. The first column refers to the sequence and nomenclature given by Dionysius, the second to Gregory's list in his *Homilies*, 34, the third to Gregory's list in his *Moralia*, and the fourth to that preserved in the Catholic liturgy.

The celestial hierarchies are also called the Nine Orders. The modern nomenclature – in which they are usually called 'spirits' – is given in tabular form under SPIRITUAL BEINGS.

Celestial light   A name sometimes given to the AKASHA.

Centiloquium   In astrology a series of a hundred astrological aphorisms (plural 'centiloquia'), usually from the pen of one writer, but sometimes collated from a variety of sources. The most important and influential collection, to which the term usually refers, is that wrongly attributed to Ptolemy.

Centres   See CHAKRAS.

Centuries   Name applied to a series of predictions made by the French astrologer and savant Nostradamus prior to 1555 (in which year they were published under the title *Centuries*). The predictions are in seven centuries of rhymed quatrains of an obscure and enigmatical nature, which none the less appear to have accurately predicted many of the major events in European history. There is, however, an extensive controversial literature attached to the interpretation of the *Centuries*. Contrary to popular belief, the predictions were not arrived at astrologically, but by means of an obscure form of divination by means of spirits. See PYROMANCY.

Table 10

No.	Dionysius	Homilies	Moralia	Liturgy
1	Seraphim	Seraphim	Seraphim	Seraphim
2	Cherubim	Cherubim	Cherubim	Cherubim
3	Thrones	Thrones	Potestates	Virtutes
4	Kyriotetes – Dominions	Dominions	Principalities	Potestates
5	Dynamis – Virtutes	Principalities	Virtues	Principalities
6	Exsusiai – Potestates	Potestates	Dominions	Dominions
7	Archai – Principalities	Virtutes	Thrones	Thrones
8	Archangels	Archangels	Archangels	Archangels
9	Angels	Angels	Angels	Angels

Ceraunoscopy Name given to a form of divination by means of air (see AEROMANCY).

Cerberus The three-headed dog which in Roman mythology is said to be the guardian of the gate to the infernal regions. The same name is also used to denote one of the seventy-two SPIRITS OF SOLOMON, otherwise known as NABERIUS.

Ceremonial magic The process of rites and conjurations by which a magician (usually in concert with one or more assistants and normally working within the confines of an occult brotherhood) establishes communication with spiritual beings towards some specific end. The goetic forms of ceremonial magic involve the use of MAGIC SQUARES, the binding of spirits, and even the Black Mass, designed to unleash evil on the world as part of the aim of BLACK MAGIC. The theurgic forms of ceremonial magic involve the use of prayers and sometimes complex rituals designed to construct useful and harmonious thought forms which will benefit other individuals and communities. See also GRIMOIRE.

Ceres Name given to the first of the ASTEROIDS to be discovered by modern astronomers, in 1801. Sometimes the constellation Virgo (and by extension, the sign Virgo) is called Ceres as well as Demeter, which is the Greek equivalent goddess, whose Mysteries were linked with the pre-Christian image of Virgo (see SPICA).

Ceromancy Divination by means of melted wax, which is poured onto cold water to congeal. The diviner reads futurity from the curious shapes of the hardened wax.

Chaigidiel A demonic Adversary of the ARCHANGELS OF THE SEPHIROTH.

Chain In the Theosophical cosmoconception a chain is a series of seven globes. Each of the seven globes of a particular chain may be regarded as having a definite and distinct existence in space and time, although not all globes in a particular chain are visible to ordinary sight. The chain is properly called a 'planetary chain', while seven successive chains are sometimes called the 'incarnation of a chain'. See, however, GLOBE PERIOD.

Chain of Being A name given to an ancient doctrine which postulates an unfaltering order of created things, ranging sequentially from the highest spiritual levels to the lowest inanimate objects on earth. This chain, or hierarchy, of beings is visualized as stretching as it were from the Throne of God to the very centre of the earth, admitting no breaks and no Chaos. Developed as a philosophical idea by Plato, added to by Aristotle, elaborated by the Neo-Platonists, this has become a stock image underlying most philosophies and cosmoconceptions, as Lovejoy has shown. Hell alone (because it had rebelled from the order of things) was not connected to this chain, yet the vision of Dante, resting as it did upon the redemptive thesis of theology, embraced even Hell in his view of the chain.

Chain period See GLOBE PERIOD.

Chakra Sometimes 'chakram', a Sanskrit word meaning approximately 'wheel', and used to denote a series of wheel-like vortices on the ETHERIC BODY of man, at which points energies are projected from one spiritual body to another. Clairvoyants describe them as small (2-inch diameter) depressions in the bodies of spiritually undeveloped (i.e. normal) men, but as larger coruscating and blazing whirlpools (rather like small suns) in highly developed humans. They are sometimes called 'centres' or 'lotus flowers' in the

Table 11

Sanskrit name	English name	Location	Number of petals
Muladhara	Root or basic	Base of spine	4
Svadhishthana	Splenic	Over the spleen	6
Manipura	Navel or umbilical	Over the solar plexus	10
Anahata	Heart or cardiac	Over the heart	12
Vishuddha	Laryngeal or throat	In front of the throat	16
Ajna	Brow or frontal	In the space between the eyebrows	96
Sahasrara	Crown or coronal	On top of the head	960

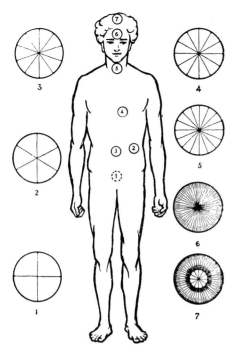

West. Modern occultism concerns itself with seven of the chakric centres, which are listed in Table 11. See Figure 18, which is based on the list given by Leadbeater, with the additional term 'SVADHISHTHANA' derived from Avalon, who also gives the term 'Jnanachaksha' for the Third Eye.

Chaldean From late classical times the word 'Chaldean' has been synonymous with 'astrologer', mainly because of the fame of the Mesopotamians as astronomers and astrologers. According to occult lore, they were first a tribe and then a caste of learned Qabbalists.

Chandra A Sanskrit term for the moon. See also SOMA.

Chaos In ALCHEMY the word used to denote the four basic elemental natures (Earth, Air, Fire and Water) when they are not organized and unified in cosmoses by the power of the QUINTESSENCE.

Characters A term used of certain symbols (sigils) used in astrological and occult texts. Many alchemical, astrological and demonological texts provide lists of such characters which are used in ceremonial magic, in the construction of AMULETS, and so on. The example sigils for the

Figure 18 (above): *The positions of the seven chakras on the human body and the number of spokes or petals in each (after Leadbeater)*

Figure 19 (below): *The characters of the planets (sixteenth century)*

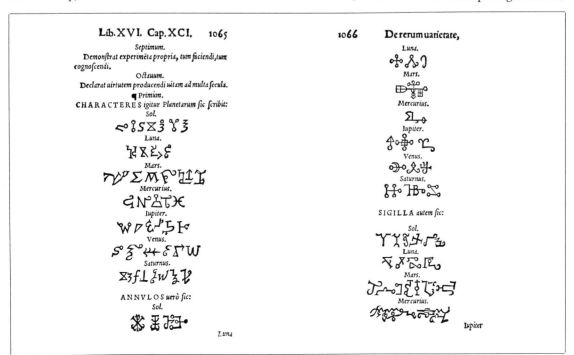

planets in Figure 19 relate to the characters used in talismanic magic – some of them are graphically derived from the corresponding geomantic figures. Paracelsus defines the characters as being drawn from the highest stars and artificially assumed by the lower realm; such are SEALS of the type so often used in the manufacture of artificial GAMALEI. It would appear that the characters were originally intended as receptacles of special VIRTUE or prophylactic value. In another context Paracelsus writes of characters as being 'words', either spoken or written, which 'produce effects which Nature itself is not able to bring about, but only magical science'.

Charm A magical formula. The etymology of the term, which is from the Latin *carmen* (song) points to the origin of charms – they were originally magical formulas intended to be sung or recited to propitiate a spirit or to bring about some desired effect. The charm is often a part of the ritual involved in making an AMULET or TALISMAN. However, the written magical charm formulas are themselves often used as amulets, so that nowadays the word 'charm' may be interchanged with the word 'amulet'. Strictly speaking, however, an amulet is preventative in action, a talisman is designed to draw to it and the wearer specific influences, while a charm is the means by which influences (for good or bad) are induced into an object or person. The philosophy underlying the use of charms arises from the belief that a sound or a picture is not merely a man-made connection between itself and the external object it depicts, but has a life of its own (a third life force) which participates in a spiritual existence.

Chart A term synonymous for HOROSCOPE in the modern sense. It probably was once cognate with 'chart' in the sense of 'map', of Greek etymology. Certainly the late medieval astrologers often referred to the horoscope figure as a map, by which they meant 'map of the heavens'.

Chasing the Moon See HUNTING THE MOON.

Chasmalim In the Qabbalistic system, the name given to the fiery beings who dwell in the World of Formation of CHESED. They are sometimes called the Hayyot.

Chaya See CHHAYA.

Chela A term introduced into Western occultism from India (sometimes 'cheta' or 'cheda'), meaning 'servant', but applied to a disciple or pupil of an adept or guru.

Chelae The word is the Greek for 'claws', and in modern astrology usually refers to the claws of the constellation SCORPIUS. In Ptolemaic astrology the word was sometimes used of the constellation Libra, which was not always distinguished from the adjacent Scorpius.

Chemical ether See ETHERIC.

Chemicograph A term used by certain spiritualist investigators for a radiograph, a photograph produced without a camera. See SPIRIT PHOTOGRAPHY.

Cherub In occultism always a reference to the CHERUBIM.

Cherubim The name (of Hebraic origin) given to the second rank of the First Hierarchy of the CELESTIAL HIERARCHIES. The singular, 'cherub', is frequently misused in modern times. The occult tradition links the Cherubim with the fixed signs of the zodiac, and they are accordingly portrayed as the TETRAMORPHS or as variously combined elements of lion, eagle, bull and human. Blavatsky points out that the word 'cherub' originally meant 'serpent' and was linked with the idea of the Serpent of Eternity. The Hebraic characters for the word are derived from an image of a serpent in a circle. Such ideas are in perfect accord with the traditional association of these beings with the circle of the zodiac. Steiner, who refers to them as Lords of Harmony, says that their prime function is that of controlling the relationships between the planets beyond our solar system. Cherubim are often depicted in Christian and occult iconography as being winged, with four faces, but traditions vary enormously as to their natures.

Chesed The fourth Sephirah of the Qabbalistic SEPHIROTHIC TREE, its name meaning 'mercy'. It is the source of all blessings in the created world, as well as the source of all exuberance and compassion. In the lowest World of Expression (ASSIAH) it is connected with Jupiter and all the compassionate, generous beneficience of this planet. In the World of Formation (YETZIRAH) it is ruled by the angelic order of the Chasmalim (the

Bright Ones) who have been described as the 'flames of fusion', in comparison with the SERAPHIM of Geburah who were the 'flames of fission'. In the World of Creation (BRIAH) the Archangel of Chesed is Zadkiel, who has the function of turning wrongs into rights. In the World of Origins (ATZILUTH) we find in Chesed the God-aspect El, a name translated all too frequently as 'God', although in reality this is the beneficient divine provider. As this fourfold chain of being implies, Chesed bestows life freely, both in a spiritual and a material sense. It is in the Sephirah GEBURAH, on the 'opposite' side of the Sephirothic Tree, that payment for such is required, and so these two Sephiroth must be considered as working together in all matters.

Chhaya A Sanskrit term meaning 'shade', and applied to the ghost or astral image of a deceased person. The Chhayaloka is the world of shades, the Sanskrit equivalent of Hades, which modern occultists call KAMALOKA.

Chichevache See BICORN.

Chidakaksam A Sanskrit name for the basis of consciousness.

Chimaera The Greek for 'she goat', but even in Greek times a monster with a goat body, head of lion and dragon's tail.

Chinese elements The Chinese distinguish five elements which, through a rich system of associations, permeate their occult, astrological and calendrical systems. The exoteric names translate as meaning Wood, Fire, Earth, Metal and Water, but the associations and correspondences established with the microcosm and macrocosm indicate that (as indeed with the European four elements) these names denote secret principles rather than materialities.

Chinese symbolic animals The rich system of associations of the Chinese Twelve Earthly Branches (linked with the zodiac) has penetrated popular astrological lore in Europe mainly through the names of the associated symbolic animals in their so-called years. These have been radically misunderstood by popular Western astrologers, who have confused the Earthly Branches with the months and with the zodiacal equivalents, and these with the sixty-year cycle of the Chinese calendar. Table 12 sets out the usual sequence given in modern Western reference books.

Table 12

Symbolic animal	Zodiacal sign	Symbolic animal	Zodiacal sign
Rat	Aries	Horse	Libra
Ox	Taurus	Sheep	Scorpio
Tiger	Gemini	Monkey	Sagittarius
Hare (Cat)	Cancer	Cock	Capricorn
Dragon	Leo	Dog	Aquarius
Snake	Virgo	Boar (Pig)	Pisces

Chioh ha Qodesh The holy living creatures of the zodiac in the Qabbalistic system (see SEPHIROTHIC TREE). See also KETHER.

Chirognomy The study of the form of the human hand as a guide to temperament and personality. See also PALMISTRY.

Chiromancy The study of the lines on the palm of the hand as a guide to temperament, personality and futurity. Properly speaking, the etymology of the word (from the Greek *cheir*, 'hand') suggests that it should be applied as the equivalent of PALMISTRY, but, through association and use, it is now linked only with the reading of the lines of the palm and hand. CHIROGNOMY is involved with the study of the form of the hand. Figure 20 sets out the traditional names of the most important lines.

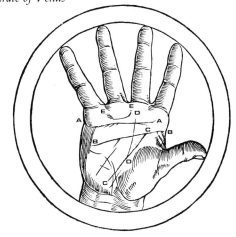

Figure 20 *Chiromancy: a hand with the major lines. AA is the Line of Heart, BB the Line of Head, CC the Line of Life, DD the Line of Saturn or Fate, EE the Girdle of Venus*

Chironomy The study of gestures as a means of conveying ideas or of expressing emotions.

Chirothesy A term used to denote the laying-on of hands for purposes of healing.

Chit A Sanskrit term, usually translated as meaning 'abstract consciousness', introduced to Western occultism by Theosophy.

Chitkala A Sanskrit term for the KUMARAS.

Chohan A Tibetan term, usually translated as meaning 'master'. See, for example, DHYAN-CHOHAN.

Chokmah A name of one of the Sephiroth in the Qabbalistic SEPHIROTHIC TREE, the word usually being translated as meaning 'wisdom'. In the realm of ASSIAH it corresponds to the zodiac; in the realm of YETZIRAH, the World of Formation, it is linked with the Auphanim (the CHERUBIM) who govern the vast cycles that lie behind the phenomena of life. In the World of Creation (BRIAH) it is under the rule of the Archangel Ratziel, who gives wisdom to all men who seek it. In the world of ATZILUTH, where the origins of all things are found, Chokmah is linked with the God-aspect of Jehovah, the YAWE of magical rites, the name which may not be spoken.

Choleric Term applied to the TEMPERAMENT linked with the element of Fire. The choleric temperament is positive, forceful, aggressive and optimistic; the faults arise from exuberance and excess, for the type becomes extravagant, proud, arrogant and lacking in sympathy or concern for others.

Chori angeli A Latin equivalent for CELESTIAL HIERARCHIES, from which the modern 'choir of angels' is derived.

Chorography A term used by astrologers to denote the linking of geographic areas to specific planets and signs. From early Roman times lists of planetary and zodiacal rulerships over places (first as geographic areas, later as cities and towns) were established within astrological tradition. Thus, England is said to be ruled by Aries (London is ruled by Gemini and the City of London by Capricorn); Scotland is said to be ruled by Cancer; Ireland by Taurus; and Wales by Capricorn. A zodiacal sign has been accorded rule over almost every country, city and town. It must be emphasized that there are many variant chorographies available, and little agreement exists among authorities as to extant chorographies and the rules for establishing these.

Christian Hermeticism See ROSICRUCIAN.

Chronocrators In general the term means 'rulers of time', which is one of the designations of the spiritual beings called THRONES. However, in astrology it is used of the planets Jupiter and Saturn. Through the interactions of their cycles these planets create successive conjunctions of a twenty-year periodicity in signs of the same element.

Cimeries One of the seventy-two SPIRITS OF SOLOMON. He is said to appear as a soldier, riding a black horse, and reveals to the conjurer the secrets of buried and lost treasures.

Circle See SEANCE.

Citra A Sanskrit name for the asterism of Libra, which is distinguished from the zodiacal TULA. Citra is also the name used for the twelfth of the Hindu lunar mansions.

Clairaudience Literally 'clear-hearing', a word used to denote the faculty of supranormal hearing. The term does not distinguish between the hearing of voices or sounds seemingly originated outside the medium and those seemingly from inside.

Clairvoyance Literally 'clear-seeing', a term used to denote the faculty of supranormal sight, covering a wide variety of different capabilities, including the ability to see into the past and the future and to experience present time by SPIRITUAL BILOCATION. The most advanced techniques of retrocognition are linked with the ability to consult the records of the AKASHA, the Akashic Chronicles. The numerous clairvoyant techniques available for the consultation of the future are touched upon under DIVINATION. Many of the techniques of clairvoyance used in seances involve TRANCE and are fundamentally involved with communication with the spirits who give, or pretend to give, knowledge of the past and future.

Clavicula Salomonis   The Latin title given to a number of different texts relating to ceremonial magic, wrongly attributed to King Solomon. The name 'key of Solomon' and its material is derived mainly from Qabbalistic sources. See GRIMOIRE.

Cledonism   A name used to denote the belief that it is possible to interpret presage from the chance words used by people when they meet together. As a divinatory method it is called cledonismantia.

Cleidomancy   Sometimes 'clidomancy', a term derived from the Greek *kleis* ('key') and *manteia* ('divination') and applied to a large number of different methods of foretelling the future through the use of a key. One method involves the writing down of a question on a key (at the time when the Sun or Moon is in Virgo) and placing the key in a Bible, which is then hung in such a way as will permit it to turn – presage is interpreted from the movement. Another method involves placing the key in a clenched fist and allowing a pregnant woman to touch one of the two proffered fists. If she touches the one in which the key is held, then it is claimed that the child will be a girl.

Cleromancy   Divination by means of dice. Sometimes the term was used to denote any method of divination involving the throwing of small objects like dice; hence the original GEO-MANCY was so called.

Clidomancy   See CLEIDOMANCY.

Climacterics   From ancient times it has been believed that certain years in the course of life are more liable to danger and/or change than others. The most important of the climacterics are the septenary years – 7, 14, 21, 28, etc. – which are associated with lunar periodicities linked by such occultists as Blavatsky and Steiner with the soul's growth. Esoterically, the full spiritual incarnation of the human does not take place until the fourth septenary (28), and some esoteric astrologers insist that properly speaking this is the beginning of life; certainly this is one of the most important of the climacterics. The important climacterics associated with Saturn usually fall in the thirtieth

and sixtieth years, when the planet transits its original position in the birth chart (just over twenty-nine years) (but see also CHRONOCRA-TORS). The climacteric period associated with the Moon's node falls on (approximately) 18 years and 2 months, and 36 years and 4 months.

Clotho   See FATAE.

Cluricaune   In Irish folklore, an elf of evil disposition; he has knowledge of hidden treasure and is the fairies' cobbler. He is the same as the leprechaun.

Cockatrice   A mythical monster, sometimes used in heraldry. It has the wings of a bird, the tail of a dragon and the head of a cock, its name being derived from the belief that it was hatched from a cock's egg by a serpent. The power of its eyes is so terrible that its glance can kill. See also BASILISK.

Cocytus   Sometimes given as the name of a demon, but in classical times the name of one of the five rivers of Hell, along whose banks the unburied would wander for a century.

Collyrie   In its occult sense a liquid application, usually made to the eyes with intent to change the vision. The word is derived from the Greek *kollerion* (poultice). Agrippa, who is followed by many occultists, uses the term very loosely (along with UNCTIONS) to explain how invisible and spiritual forces may be transferred from the magician to the subject being bewitched by means of collyries. The collyrie, or 'magic virtue', is manufactured from the subtle and invisible vapours of the blood, and these applied to the eyes of the subject will induce the same kind of vision 'as that which arises from the peculiar forces of the magician's blood'. Agrippa lists various methods of making collyries and unctions from the blood of lapwings, bats or goats, and he says that if a smooth and shining piece of steel be smeared over with a colyrie of mugwort, then it will be possible to see spirits on the surface.

Common fire   The name used in ALCHEMY for ordinary fire, to distinguish it from the FIRE ELEMENT, which is something other than incandescent gas.

Common planet   Mercury is sometimes called the 'common planet', presumably because of its ANDROGYNE nature.

Common signs Another term for the Mutable signs – Gemini, Virgo, Sagittarius and Pisces. See MUTABILITY.

Compact See PACT.

Conception chart Usually an alternative name for the prenatal chart cast for the (putative) moment of conception, by computation from the natal chart. See PRENATAL EPOCH.

Conjunctio A name given to one of the sixteen figures of GEOMANCY.

Conjunction In astrology an ASPECT maintained by two or more planets posited within the same degree of longitude. In ALCHEMY the term (usually 'conjunctio') is used to denote the act of joining the male and the female, the solar and the lunar forces, into a single harmonious whole. Figure 21 is a hermetic figure of a hermaphrodite, showing the completed work of the alchemist, in which the male (sun) and female (moon) have been united into one. The four temperaments (Phlegmatic, Sanguine, Melancholic and Choleric) are united in harmony.

Conjuration The practice of raising spirits by means of carefully formulated rituals. There are really no standard forms of conjuration, and the following notes are abstracted from a wide number of GRIMOIRES and related texts on spirit-raising, especially from versions of the *Grand Grimoire*, which contains probably the earliest printed account of the manufacture of PACTS with demons. This *Grand Grimoire* describes fairly bloody evocations, one of which is called the 'Rite of Lucifuge' and involves the decapitation of a specially garlanded virgin kid on the third day of the Moon. The skinned body must be burned to ashes and these cast towards the rising Sun; at each stage special invocations or 'prayers' are chanted (see CHARM). The magician must then prepare what is called a 'Grand Kabbalistic Circle', which in fact has nothing to do with the Qabbala: a circle is drawn with strips of the kid's skin nailed to the ground, and a triangle is marked within the circle with the aid of special marked stones. Other rituals follow, but the final outcome is the conjuration of a demon called Lucifuge Rofocale, who is then bound to the will of the magician. The text describes the rather weak entreaties of this demon to secure the soul of the magician, which is resisted with pacts and threats.

The conjuration sequence in the grimoire called HONORIUS is slightly more revolting, involving the slaughter of a black cock and the open mockery of Christian rituals more usually associated with the Black Mass, such as we find described in the witches' SABBAT.

The rites of conjuration set out in the LEMEGETON are designed to facilitate contact with one or several of seventy-two rather imposing and even hideous DEMONS (see SPIRITS OF SOLOMON). Such conjuration may be done only on certain days (usually depending upon the age of the Moon) – for example, on a Tuesday or a Saturday, commencing at midnight, with the Moon increasing in Virgo, and with the burning of aloes, resin, cedar and alum as perfume. Such astrological limitations are sufficient to preclude conjuration for as long as a year or so, since the Moon is not always increasing in Virgo on the two days allowed.

Usually special SEALS of appropriate metals must be constructed prior to conjuration, appropriate either to the demon being evoked or to the planetary hour of evocation. The magic circle must be drawn in a special form, the most suitable being that involving the triangles of the Seal of Solomon, which is a circle containing a double triangle. This seal must be drawn on a parchment of calfskin or on gold or silver, and worn upon the white clothing of the magician, alongside the engraved seal of the spirit, 'for this alone will command his obedience'. In the darker rituals the seal of Solomon is drawn in blood taken from a black cock on virgin parchment. The magician himself must have had no sexual relations for at least one month prior to the conjuration and must have obtained pardon for all sins by fasting and prayer.

The sequences of conjuration spells and evocations are complex and numerous: any delay in the appearance of the demon may be put down to the fact that the overlord demon has dispatched his minion for service elsewhere (or to the fact that the spirit is bound with chains in Hell). Appropriate invocations are designed to relieve such impediments, however. An ultimately disobedient spirit may be dispossessed of his rank and bound to the depths of the Pit until the Day of Judgement, in torment unspeakable.

Figure 22 shows one of the recommended designs for a circle (which is actually complicated

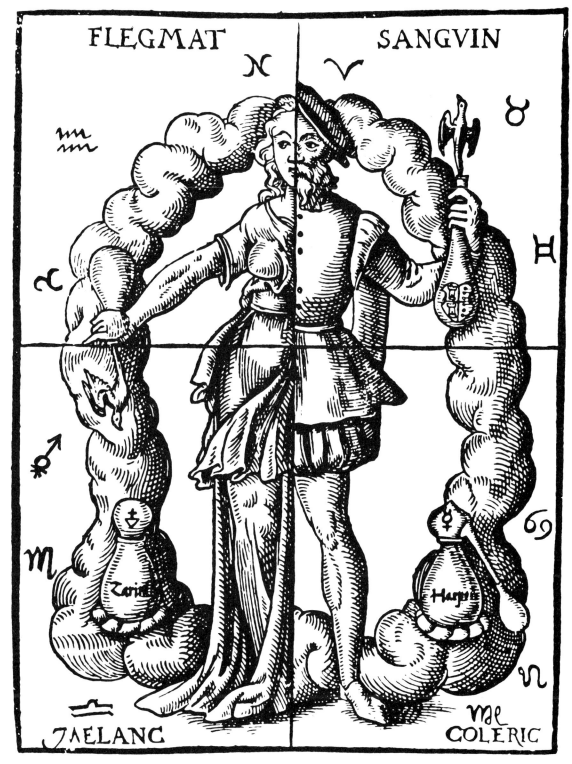

Figure 21   *The conjunction of opposites, showing the androgyne figure resulting from the union of male and female (after a woodcut of the seventeenth century)*

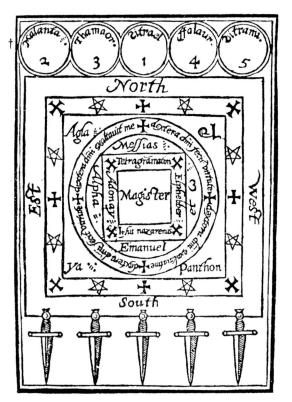

patterns, made up of much more than a circle) for the conjuration of spirits. The magician ('Magister') must stand in the protected centre, and the many conjurations and magical symbols are supposed to protect him from the loathsome and dangerous creatures which, when conjured, appear on the outside of the magical pattern. Figure 23 shows the appearance of the spirit Mephistopheles (along with many of the sigils which are used to represent this demon) as he is supposed to appear when first conjured. If the magician does not particularly like this rather horrible form, then he may command Mephistopheles to reappear in a more acceptable guise, even in human form.

Figure 22 (left): *A formal pattern designed to ensure the safety of the magician during the rite of conjuration (from Reginald Scot's* Discoverie of Witchcraft, *1665)*

Figure 23 *The image of Mephistopheles as a bear-like monster is said to be the first form of this demon immediately he is conjured. He will change this shape at the behest of the magician (from a late-eighteenth-century German demonological text)*

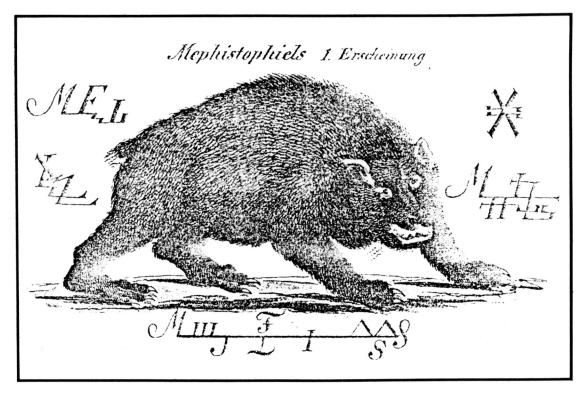

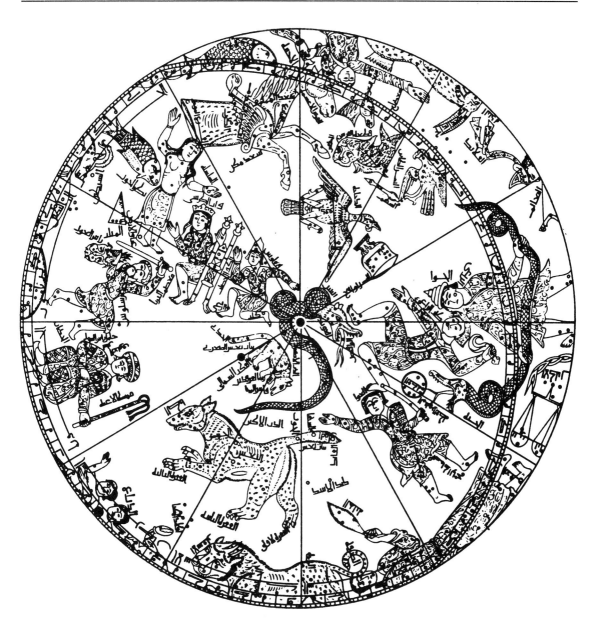

Figure 24 *An Arabian map of the northern sky showing the constellations (after a nineteenth-century engraving)*

Constellation A pattern of stars and star groups. The majority of constellations were demarcated and named in ancient times and these ancient classifications have influenced even modern astronomy (see, for example, Figure 54 under MODERN ZODIAC). Figure 24 is an Arabian constellation map in which we may recognize some of the asterisms which have survived in European astronomy and astrology. For example, to the extreme left is the front half of the flying horse Pegasus and, above the back of this,

the lower fish of Pisces. In occult and astrological circles all the major ASTERISMS have been ascribed specific influences which are regarded as being projected to the Earth, in addition to the influences cast by the FIXED STARS from which the constellations are constructed.

59

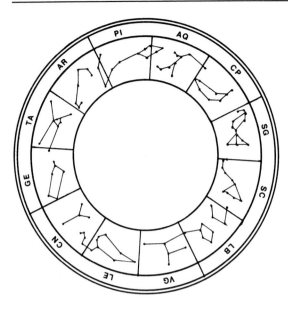

Figure 25 *A zodiac constructed from the patterns of the constellations inscribed within a framework of 30-degree arcs to show the relationship between them. Note how small the constellation of Cancer (CN) is in relation to the adjacent sign Leo (LE) or Virgo (VG) (after Powell)*

Constellational zodiac A term used of a sidereal zodiac divided into twelve unequal ASTERISMS (not signs), the boundaries or cusps of which are to some extent arbitrary and hence subject to some argument in specialist astrological circles. Figure 25 sets out a modern constellational zodiac which is contrasted with the TROPICAL ZODIAC of twelve equal-arc divisions, to give some idea of the differences involved. See ZODIAC.

Control A name given to a spiritual entity which controls a medium. Certain mediums are associated with particular (named) controls.

Coral In ancient times coral was regarded as a talismanic protection, even without the addition of pictures or sigils. It was used as a charm against whirlwinds, shipwreck and fire.

Coronal chakra See SAHASRARA.

Correspondence In its occult sense a term derived from the very earliest occult lore and used to denote the 'occult' or 'hidden' relationship between natural forms and spiritual causes, or between the microcosm and the macrocosm, which is observed acting through the 'sympathy' expressed in the CHAIN OF BEING. Swedenborg, who used the term extensively, maintained that every sublunar object is a result of the working of a spiritual cause, and claimed further that, if the nature of the correspondence between the higher and the lower is understood, then the spiritual may be read through its physical symbol. This doctrine lies at the basis of Rosicrucian meditative endeavour.

Coscinomancy Divination by means of a sieve and/or a pair of scissors or shears.

Cosmic gods A term defined by Blavatsky as 'inferior gods, those connected with the formation of matter'.

Cosmic memory A name for the Akashic Chronicles. See AKASHA.

Cosmic night A modern term derived from the Theosophical use of the Sanskrit term *pralaya*, which relates to a period of obscuration or sleep between the 'days' of creative evolution. See YUGA, where the very terms relating to 'twilight' imply a separating *pralaya* between the ages.

Cosmobiology A term coined by the Austrian doctor F. Feerhow. It has been popularized by the German astrologer Ebertin in relation to his own modernized and highly personalized astrology, which concentrates on possible correlations between the cosmos and organic life, and the effects of cosmic rhythms and stellar motions on man.

Cosmocrators A word of Greek origin meaning 'world builders'.

Creative hierarchies See TWELVE CREATIVE HIERARCHIES.

Critomancy A term derived from the Greek *krithe* ('barley corn') and *manteia* ('divination') and applied to an ancient method of divining the future from meal strewn over the bodies of sacrificed animals.

Crocodile Although exoterically the Hindu astrological equivalent of the sign Capricorn (named Makara), the crocodile is linked by Blavatsky with esoteric astrology through the fifth group of the hierarchies of spirits, who had their abode in this constellation. The crocodile appears to be a debased symbol of the dragon, the dragon of wisdom, the intelligent principle in the human being, which passes from incarnation to incarnation. Blavatsky calls the crocodile the 'great reptile of Typhon', but says that the word 'Makara' should not be translated as 'crocodile', for it is rather the equivalent of the fish-tailed goat of Capricornus. See also M.

Crown chakra   See SAHASRARA.

Crow's head   A term used in ALCHEMY to denote a process involved in the manufacture of the spagyric *Lapis*.

Crude Ilech   See ILECH.

Crux ansata   See TAU.

Cryptography   A term derived from the Greek *kriptein* ('to hide') and applied to the art of transmitting occult knowledge through SECRET SCRIPTS or through images. See also STEGANOGRAPHY.

Crystal gazing   See CRYSTALOMANCY and SCRYING.

Crystalomancy   Crystal gazing, a term used to denote a method of divination by gazing into a semi-reflectant or translucent material, such as a crystal, a precious stone, a mirror or darkened water. Almost all methods of crystalomancy involve either TRANCE, in which case the object becomes a projective autoscope, or the use of spirits. The latter technique usually involves complex operations of magical ritual, linked with astrological factors and the use of invocations and magical sigils. See also SCRYING, which is a popular form of crystalomancy.

Cupido   Name given to one of the HYPOTHETICAL PLANETS.

Cycles   In modern Theosophical occultism, which has its roots in oriental thought, the idea of cycles of vast periodicities is tied up with the 'divine years' or the four YUGAS; see, therefore, DWAPARA YUGA, KALI YUGA, KRITA YUGA and TRETA YUGA. From these oriental cycles is derived the Maya Yuga of 4,320,000 years during which all the planets are supposed to return to an original fiducial. In Western astrology this period (sometimes called the 'Great Year') was given different periodicities: Petarius, reporting from classical sources, gives 350,635 years, for example, while William of Conches gives 49,000 years. Astronomical calculations would support the vast cycle of the Maya Yuga, however. In a specialist astrological sense the theory of planetary cycles is based on the idea that each of the planetary bodies marks off periods which are reflected in human life and history.

Many of the important planetary cycles are involved with periodicities much longer than any human life and are quite rightly seen as influencing epochs of human history, changes in climate, social revolutions, wars, religious beliefs, political crises and so on. The long-term cycle most frequently referred to in popular astrological lore is that subsequent to the PRECESSION of the equinoctial point. Another important cycle is the lunar node cycle of 18 years 7 months. Among long-term cycles are those marked out by the CHRONOCRATORS (Jupiter and Saturn), those attributed to the Archangels (see SECUNDADEIAN BEINGS), as well as the first-order cycle of the superior planets. A few of the ancient cycles, which have survived in occult lore in a mutilated form (such as the SAROS CYCLE and the NAROS CYCLE), were close approximates to the synodics. The Sothic cycle, linked with the heliacal appearance of the star Sirius, was of great importance in Egyptian chronology; it is usually given as a period of 1460 years (see SOTHIS PERIOD).

D

The fourth letter of the alphabet, with the numerical value of 4 (but see FOUR), linked with the sound values of the Hebraic Daleth. The form now used is said to be derived from vestigial drawings of a doorway – an idea which is more evident in the Greek equivalent delta, which is a triangle. As a 'door into the world' it is perhaps expressed in the notion that the hieroglyphic equivalent form was that of a man's hand – the instrument of expression in the physical world. The D sound in the occult script is said to be 'incarnating', and the human hand is the incarnator of human ideas and ideals. This has led some occultists to regard the Roman use of the D as a symbol for 500 as being derived from the reincarnation cycles of 500 years (see, for example, PHOENIX), but the truth is that the form D used for 500 comes from an early (pre-Roman) symbol which is not of the same origin as the letter D itself.

Daath In the Qabbalistic system of the SEPHIROTHIC TREE Daath is the bridge by which human beings may cross the terrible ABYSS of Masak Mavdil. 'Daath' means 'knowledge', although it is of the kind gained by experience. In some occult systems Daath is wrongly described as a Sephirah. In the esoteric tradition, however, one finds that Daath was displaced to become MALKUTH. In the present time it marks the schema of redemption for man, but in some future time it will become once more a Sephirah, spiritualized by the knowledge gained in Malkuth. This is perhaps why the perfected Daath has been described as that knowledge gained in all possible ways by every possible conscious entity. See ELOAH VA DAATH.

Dactyliomancy A term derived from the Greek *daktelios* ('finger ring') and *manteia* ('divination') and applied to a number of methods of dividing the future with the aid of rings. Sometimes a ring is used as a pendulum, at other times it is dropped into a bowl of water, its position at the bottom determining the prediction or the response to a formulated question. Nèro-

man is quite wrong in linking dactyliomancy with the art of touching people or objects with the fingers in order to learn something about the future; this is really PSYCHOMETRY. However, dactyliomancy is sometimes applied to the interpretation of the patterns on fingertips, which is a branch of CHIROGNOMY.

Daemon See DAIMON and DEMONS.

Daemonomancy See DEMONOMANCY.

Dagon Sometimes Dag, the name given to the Chaldean OANNES, a man-fish, who is supposed to have taught men the arts of civilization. See ANNEDOTUS.

Daimon In this spelling, or in the variant 'daemon', the word is derived from the Greek and means almost the equivalent of 'angel' or 'genius'; it is sometimes applied to the higher being of man himself. As a term it must therefore be distinguished from 'demon' (see DEMONS). The well-known quotation from Menander, 'by every man at birth a good demon takes his stand, to initiate him in the mysteries of life', could hardly be translated with the word 'demon' in modern times. The term equivalent to 'daimon' or 'daemon' was used by the Greek astrologers to refer to an ancient PARS no longer used. In late medieval astrology the same term (as well as 'demon') was also used of spiritual beings (not the 'demon' of popular infernal lore) connected with planetary and zodiacal agencies. The word in this sense was almost certainly derived from the same Sanskrit root which gave 'DEVA', now unfortunately wrongly linked with the elemental beings but once the equivalent of the angels. See STAR DAEMON.

Daimoniarchon A name used in the HERMETIC CANON for the ruler of the demons. It is usual to distinguish between the demons of the heavens and those of the earth. The earth demons are the authors of all evil and their prince is the Devil; hence, the term 'Daimoniarchon' is another name for the Devil or Diabolos, who is to be distinguished from SATAN.

Daimonilptoi A Greek word meaning 'those possessed by demons', but applied to particular types of theomancers who offer their physical bodies as means of communicating with spirits. Such a theomancer will then give answers to questions through voices seemingly emitted from his belly or breast, although in fact remaining speechless himself. See MEDIUM.

Daitya A name of a continental island which survived the first destruction of ATLANTIS. The Daityas were also certain ASURAS in esotericism, exoterically called giants, Titans or demons.

Daivi-prakriti A Sanskrit term called in Theosophy the 'Light of the Logos', a primordial light which, when differentiated, becomes FOHAT.

Dakini The Sanskrit name usually taken to refer to female demons, vampires and evil ELEMENTALS.

Dakshina-marga See RIGHT-HAND PATH.

Dantalian One of the seventy-two SPIRITS OF SOLOMON. He is said to appear with a multitude of human faces, carrying a book.

Dark Age See KALI YUGA.

Dark Brothers See BROTHERS OF THE SHADOW.

Dark Moon See LILITH.

Dark Race A name given to the first race of man, the so-called ADAMIC. According to Blavatsky, the Akkadian *Zalmat Gaguadi*, meaning 'the dark race', is the name given to those humans who fell into generation. The Light Race (*Sarku*), as such, does not appear to have a place in modern occultism.

Darkness of sages A term used in ALCHEMY to denote a stage in the manufacture of spagyric *Lapis*.

Day of Brahma A period of 4320 million years. See KALPA.

Deale One of the *entia* of Paracelsus (see ENS). This is the spirit which most nearly accords with the triune MONAD of Theosophy. It is the incorruptible judge of the workings of the EGO, which is fragmented from it with each incarnation. It is, as the structure of the word suggests, the God in man.

Death chart A name given to a horoscope figure erected for the date or time of death, and interpreted by analogy with the natal chart of ASTROLOGY.

Death panorama A term sometimes used to denote an experience of the newly departed soul after death. It is said that when the ETHERIC BODY has finally separated itself from the physical shell (this in itself the mark of what men call death), the newly departed spirit contemplates a panoramic view of its preceding life for a period of approximately two to three days. What was before experienced sequentially, spread out in time, is now perceived as timeless (that is, in eternity) and viewed as a panoramic whole.

Death prayer This term has two different senses. First, in regard to 'praying for the dead', the death prayer is used either to help the departed soul in the spiritual abode or to request help from such souls on behalf of those still on the material plane. Secondly, the term is used to describe a special technique designed to deprive a person or persons of life. The ability to use demons or evil spirits in a way designed to facilitate the death of a living creature is one of the most terrible powers of black magicians. It is a technique widely practised by witchdoctors in primitive tribes, and is one for which the Voodoo cult in particular has gained a certain notoriety. While the death prayer finds a wide regional variety in technique, that used by the K A H U N A magicians of Polynesia, and called by them *anana* or *ana-ana*, has been studied in some depth and may be taken as representative of the general method. Magicians who indulge in such forms of black magic usually own several enslaved spirits or E L E M E N T A R S, even the disembodied souls of people who have died violently, and who (by black magical means) have been prevented from entering into the postmortem realm in the normal manner. When specially instructed such spirits may be used to hunt down human beings, provided that some personal possession of the one hunted is held by the magician himself. The spirit has the ability to follow the thread or 'scent' (called the *aka*) from such a possession to the physical body of the one hunted. The magician 'prays' to these enslaved spirits to follow the threads, to enter the body of the victim, and to devour the inner vital energies, as a result of which death rapidly follows.

Decan In general reference any 10-degree arc, but in astrology a term applied to a 10-degree arc of the zodiac, resulting in the division of the twelve signs into thirty-six equal arcs. In each of the signs these divisions are called the first, second and third decans (or decanates). See F A C E S, with which this term is sometimes confused.

Decarabia One of the seventy-two S P I R I T S O F S O L O M O N. He is said to appear in the form of a star within a pentagram, but will change this shape when so commanded.

Dee zodiac See G L A S T O N B U R Y Z O D I A C.

Degree symbols A vast astrological literature has tabulated the specific influences said to be exerted by individual degrees of the zodiac, regarded as exerting effects quite independent of occupant bodies, nodes, fixed stars and zodiacal arcs. The 'readings' or 'images' linked with such individual degrees are called 'degree symbols'.

Degrees See I N I T I A T I O N.

Delporte division See M O D E R N Z O D I A C.

Demeter Name given to one of the H Y P O T H E T I C A L P L A N E T S.

Demon See D E M O N S.

Demon star See A L G O L.

Demoniac A person possessed by an evil spirit.

Demonic sins In accordance with a well-established practice of demonologists, Binsfield published in 1589 a list of seven demons who had specific control over each of the seven deadly sins, with the powers of inducing men and women to commit these. The demons and associated sins were L U C I F E R – pride; M A M M O N – avarice; A S M O D E U S – lechery; S A T A N – anger; B E E L Z E B U B – gluttony; L E V I A T H A N – envy; B E L P H E G O R – sloth.

Demonifuge A spell or charm designed to ward off demons.

Demonize To make subject to the influence of demons. 'Demonism' is belief in the reality of demons, while a 'demonomist' is a believer in or worshipper of demons.

Demon King See M A Y M O N.

Demonocracy The rule of demons. See I N F E R N A L H I E R A R C H I E S.

Demonolater A worshipper of demons.

Demonolatry The worship of evil spirits.

Demonology The study of demons, or the study of beliefs concerning demons. One who makes such a study is called a 'demonologist' or 'demonologer', See D E M O N S.

Demonomachy The battle against demons.

Demonomagy The range of magical arts relating to D E M O N S and the C O N J U R A T I O N of demons.

Demonomancy Sometimes daemonomancy, divination with the aid of demons. It is often argued that all divinatory techniques are done with the aid of spirits, and that virtually all popular methods of foretelling the future work through the agency of low-quality demons (see, for example, SEANCE, MEDIUM and DIAKKA). The art of raising the spirits of the dead (properly the shades of the dead, see SCIOMANCY) involves the use of demons.

Demonomanie The 'foolish' belief in evil spirits.

Demons The term 'demon' is derived ultimately from the Sanskrit root *div* (to shine), through the Greek 'DAIMON' (see, however, DEVA). For very many centuries the term has been applied in Western occultism to evil spirits, which is to say, to that class of spirits conceived as working against the spiritual evolution of mankind. However, this should not disguise the fact that in terms of esoteric thought the existence of demons is seen as a necessary part of the evolution of mankind. In the light of this it is easier to understand the occult tradition which maintains that the higher beings (see ANGELS) did not so much fall into the demonic state as volunteered to live in this state as a supreme sacrifice, that man might grow. The Qabbalistic phrase

Demon est Deus inversus ('the Devil is God upside down') suggests that both classes of beings, the involutionary demons and the evolutionary angels, stem from the same source and work ultimately towards the same end. Naturally, popular occultism is not capable of embracing such a teleology and promulgates a belief in evil spirits who work against God for their own selfish purposes. The Christian view of demons is ambiguous: the idea elaborated by such early men of the Church as Justin and Tertullian is that the demons were born of the sinful intercourse of the fallen angels with women; hence, evil was created by pride and by man himself, rather than by God. However, the majority of demons found in European demonologies (and theologies, for that matter) are really pre-Christian and rooted in a dualism which is nominally rejected by the Church (see INFERNAL HIERARCHIES).

The demons of Western occultism are derived mainly from pagan sources romanticized by the Desert Fathers. Mainly they are of a hallucinatory nature, sometimes in bestial form, which can range from the composite, such as Bael (Figure 26), the organic, such as Beelzebub (Figure 27), to the anthropomorphic. Sometimes their appearance is so horrible as to throw even the

Figure 26   *Bael, demon from Hell (after de Plancy)*

Figure 27   *Beelzebub, Lord of the Flies (after de Plancy)*

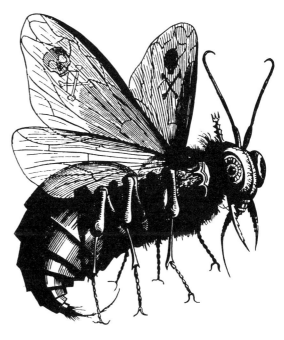

Figure 28   *A monster menacing a magician (after de Plancy, who had it in turn from Salvator Rosa)*

professional operator (the magician or conjurator) into a swoon (Figure 28), and their penetration into the earth sphere from Hell is accompanied by great commotions and foul odours. On some occasions demons will manifest as incorporeal spirits, at other times by means of POSSESSION of beasts or men. In connection with the development of the idea of demons, see also DEVIL.

Popular occultist notions of demons have been coloured by descriptions of the demonic hierarchies preserved by such writers as Psellus and Barrett. Psellus says that demons have a body and are capable of bearing the pains of hell fire; he also indicates that demons show fear of the exorcist. However, in spite of what later commentators claim, it is clear that the corporeality of demons is not the same as the corporeality of the humans. The occult tradition maintains that the physical body itself can feel nothing, for sensation is a function of the Etheric and Astral bodies, and it is widely held in occult circles that the 'bodies' of demons consist of etheric formations. The nourishment required to feed the 'etheric corporeality' is said to be derived in a variety of ways: some demons derive nourishment by inhalation, others from moisture, much as a sponge will draw in liquid from its ambient. Such demons void what Psellus calls a 'spermatic' substance.

Another ancient idea that has permeated popular occultism relates to the sexuality of demons. Psellus follows the occult tradition to the extent of teaching that demons (like the angels) are sexless, but he emphasizes that since they are rather like sponges they will take over the animal passions and sexuality of those creatures or humans they succeed in possessing – hence the male sexuality of the INCUBUS and the female sexuality of the SUCCUBUS. In contrast, the medieval demons were distinctly sexual, but it was essentially an ecclesiastical demonology which had witches 'seduced' by male demons in the SABBAT, and the Devil ejaculating cold sperm.

The demons of the Qabbalists are said to dwell in the world of matter and ASSIAH, and may take for a temporary dwelling the shells of the dead (see KLIPPOTH). The prince of the seven hells of these demons is SAMAEL, his female consort Isheth Zenunim (see also BEAST).

In a classification widely adopted in Western theology and occultism, Michael Psellus describes six different types of demon (sometimes in popular lore called 'devils'). The Aerial kind may at times be visible to men, but constantly swarm within the air around, raising winds and storms, to the consternation of mankind. His Terrestrial demons appear to be of two kinds: the first almost the equivalent of evil GNOMES, living even within the body of the earth, or in caverns; they are of a mean disposition and cause earthquakes and fires. The related Silvan demons live in woods and forests, but are also called Terrestrial; they delight in misleading travellers at night. The Aqueous demons live in rivers and lakes and are turbulent, deceitful creatures, the authors of storms and shipwrecks; when they appear to men, it is most often in the form of women, as sirens and mermaids. The Igneus are those of fire, and are said to have no dealing with men 'until the Day of Judgement'; these have been called the Lelirice. The sixth group described by Psellus are called the Heliophobes or Lucifugi because they detest the sunlight and will take on the appearance of form only at night-time. These are the most evil of the demons, as dark within as without, possessed by icy passions, with the power to kill men by touch or by breath.

Descending arc In astrology a term used to denote the degree of zodiac descending over the cusp of the seventh house. This use must be distinguished from the occult Theosophical term which is the equivalent of the shadowy arc, relating to the downward passage of life waves into the physical realms.

Descent of the soul The occult tradition insists that the act of rebirth or incarnation is preceded by a descent of the soul through the planetary spheres. It is in this descent that the incarnating spirit takes on the influences proper to his being. The tradition is widespread, under many different terms, such as 'spherical descent', the 'path of rebirth' and so on, but the hermetic texts most often quoted are those attributed to the classical texts of Macrobius and Servius, derived from commentaries on Platonic and Virgilian texts respectively. The former is linked with an Orphic tradition, the latter with an Egyptian tradition, and are accordingly dealt with under ORPHIC DESCENT OF THE SOUL and EGYPTIAN DESCENT OF THE SOUL.

Desire Body Another term for the ASTRAL BODY.

Destiny Destiny is really a sort of fore-ordained life pattern, the structure of which has been determined prior to birth by spiritual beings. In some literature it is clear that this life pattern is dimly apprehended by the person who is experiencing it; in other words, he feels as though he is in control of his own life, even though its structures are approximately determined. In other forms of literature it is clear that the person is caught up in a life structure which he distinctly feels not to be of his own making – in other words, he feels as though he is a plaything of the gods. The word 'destiny' is probably derived from the Latin verb *stare* (to stand), and thus contains within it the idea of something fixed. In classical times the concept of destiny was merged with this idea of something fixed from outside, or at least by the gods or Lords of Fate (see also FATAE). A man or woman had a 'destiny' to achieve certain things or to fail in achieving certain things, and (without application or suppli-cation to the realm of the gods) this destiny was to be regarded as immutable – it remained a sort of lot handed out by the gods, and perhaps not even deserved by the recipient. This is why the modern word 'destiny' (thoroughly debased as it is due to the romantic associations in popular literature) is not really the equivalent of KARMA, as many people suppose. Karma is really something which has been earned by the recipient through previous lives, or by undertaking (as a spiritual commit-ment) to experience certain things on the material plane with a view to changing his own inner being in connection with the needs of future rebirths. Fundamentally, the concept of destiny appears to be linked with the idea of a person having a single life, after which he must account to the gods for his achievements and failures, whereas karma is involved with the idea of a person having many incarnate lifetimes. See also FATE.

Destroying angel See GEBURAH and SAMAEL.

Deva Yuga A Sanskrit term which is approxi-mately the equivalent of the Western term 'Golden Age'. See YUGA.

Deva-yoni A Sanskrit term for an ELEMENTAL.

Figure 29 *Devas: fairies dancing (from an illustration by Shepperson to a poem by Alfred Noyes, 'How to See Fairies')*

Devachan A Sanskrit–Tibetan compound meaning approximately 'region of the gods' and corresponding fairly closely to the Christian notion of Heaven. Initiates usually have access to Devachan while in an incarnate state on earth, but ordinary people experience its bliss only long after death, after what is called the SECOND DEATH, and after the necessary experiences of KAMALOKA, when the human TERNARY is separated from the lower quaternary. In Devachan spirits experience the fulfilment of all the highest hopes of the preceding incarnation.

Devanagarai A Sanskrit term meaning 'language of the gods' and usually taken in popular occultism as reference to the written forms of the Sanskrit language. It has been argued, however, that the language of the gods has never been written down. The Devanagarai has been confused with the esoteric LANGUAGE OF THE BIRDS.

Devas A word derived from the Sanskrit root *div*, meaning 'to shine', and applied to a group of spiritual beings or gods (the 'shining ones') who are said to live on a higher plane than the human. The fact that these gods were regarded as being sometimes good and sometimes bad (from the point of view of human life) has led to the word and its derivatives having different meanings. For example, in the English language it is the root *div* which has given rise to words as different as 'deity', 'divine', 'demon' and 'devil'. In the Zoroastrian cult the devas are the malignant demons under the control of the dark AHRIMAN, working to destroy man, but in the earlier Indian religions the devas were beneficent spirits. In the Vedas we find the path of the gods in the spiritual realm is called the Devayana, from which the modern occultists have taken their own word DEVACHAN, relating to an area of Heaven. Many of the devas of Western occultism are really survivors from early cults (see, for example, AESHMA). Popular modern occultism has confused the devas (sometimes the 'devic beings') with the ELEMENTALS. As a result the term is often now used in a very wide sense to denote many different types of celestial (and infernal) beings, some of whom are virtually NATURE SPIRITS, so that in some quarters of popular occultism even ordinary fairies are now called devas (Figure 29). In Theosophical literature, however, the tendency is for the higher realms of devic beings to be denoted by the term. Thus, the devas are sometimes said to be nature spirits and sometimes the higher spiritual beings who control them. Distinguish DEVS and see also DEVIC ASCENT.

Devayana The path of the gods of Vedic philosophy. For etymology, see DEVAS.

Devic ascent A phrase used by occultists with reference to the esoteric view of evolution, as held in occult circles. The existence of the DEVAS is coterminous with human existence and is partly centred on the earth; it was at one time linked with human evolution. Occultists claim that in the middle period of evolution the life force divided into two streams. The first stream (the devic ascent, as it is called) began with a specialization of form in jewels, then rose through grasses and cereals (where roots were developed) into insect form, and then into birds. The second stream (the human ascent) began through metals, then entered mosses, shrubs and trees, finally entering into the specialized forms of animals, prior to taking a human form. The root formations which had developed in the devic ascent were interiorized in the human ascent to become the nervous system. This 'root system' underlies many of the fairytales involving trees and human beings.

Devil The word 'devil' appears to be derived ultimately from the Sanskrit root *div*, which also gave us many words of non-diabolic meaning (see DEVAS). In its strictly biblical sense (which has coloured Western occultism) the word is derived from translating the Hebraic 'Satan' into the Greek 'Diabolos', although Satan was not directly an evil or fiendish being so much as a tester of man's relationship to God. In this way the two distinct beings, Satan and Diabolos, were first confused and then later merged. 'Satanas', as a New Testament Greek word, continued to be used to denote an adversary of God, and in Revelation, 12, 9, became the 'great dragon . . . that old serpent, called the Devil and Satan. . . .' Later linguistic changes linked the Devil with 'demon', although in Greek the latter was not an evil being at all (see DAIMON) but a personal guardian spirit. The distinct demons of the Hebrews (such as the Schedim and the Seirim and even ADMODEUS) were all badly translated by the Greek 'daimon' or 'daemon', and further confusion was created. The Devil himself – the

Figure 30 *A popular image of the Devil as a goat (nineteenth century, after Eliphas Levi)*

theologically conceived supreme embodiment of evil – has taken on many related names in this babel of confusion, such as Beelzebub, Asmodeus, Abaddon, Behemoth, Belial and even LUCIFER. The classical image of the demonologists is derived from early patristic writings of the fourth century, which merged pagan elements (such as the half-bestial Pan) with a semihuman form, so what in medieval times was sometimes pictured as almost a cartoon figure of fun became a sort of hierarchic great god Pan, with cloven hooves, goat head and curiously anthropomorphized form (Figure 30). Yet in spite of this development of imagery the forms (as indeed the names) of the Devil have remained more or less legion, in that he accommodates into his single being many of the forms of the lesser devils (properly the DEMONS). See also BASILISK and INFERNAL HIERARCHIES.

Devil Card   Name given to one of the arcana of the TAROT.

Devil's mark   The name given originally to a scar, epidermal discoloration, birthmark or other surface malformation on the skin, said by witch-hunters and demonologists to have been imprinted by the Devil as a mark or seal of his possession of the person. Such malformations were called the *sigillum diaboli* ('Devil's seal'). In some early reports the Devil's mark (the *stigmata diaboli*) was sometimes confused with the witch-mark, which was properly speaking a protuberance on the body, such as a wart or a mole, regarded by witch-hunters as a supplementary teat at which familiars and demons might suck. The finding of such demon imprints as Devil's marks or witchmarks, which (in the words of Sinistrari) might have 'the likeness of a hare, sometimes like a toad's foot, sometimes a spider, a puppy, a dormouse . . . on the most secret parts of the body; with men, under the eyelids or perhaps under the armpits, or on the lips or shoulders, the anus, or elsewhere; with women . . . generally on the breasts or private parts' became an important business of the expert PRICKING which preceded much witch persecutions. Devil's marks and witchmarks were said to be insensitive to pain, and the pricking of pins into such areas was supposed to draw no blood.

Devil's picture book   Ordinary packs of playing cards are often thus called. Some people also give this name to the TAROT pack.

Devs   According to Blavatsky, the Devs were giants, sometimes associated with the gods called Danavas, who were said to live on earth before man was created. In the Zoroastrian cult the seven Devs are the equivalent of the seven OLYMPIC SPIRITS. Distinguish from DEVA.

Dhanus   A Sanskrit term of the zodiacal Sagittarius, sometimes confused with MULA.

Dharana   See YOGA.

Dharma   A Sanskrit term meaning approximately 'right union of religion, philosophy and science'. In Western occultism, a man who follows the RIGHT-HAND PATH and fulfils his duty within the bounds of his personal KARMA may be said to follow his *dharma*.

Dharmakaya   A Sanskrit term for an occult concept much misunderstood in Western occultism. It means 'glorified spiritual body' and is sometimes called the 'Vesture of Bliss'; its perfection is realized only at the very highest level of spiritual development. See BUDDHIC BODIES.

Dhyan-chohans   A Sanskrit–Tibetan compound usually translated as 'Lords of Meditation' or 'Lords of Light' and sometimes interpreted in Western occultism as denoting the equivalent of PLANETARY ANGELS (the so-called Planetary Spirits). It is likely that they are of the equivalent rank of ARCHANGELS, however. In the oriental classification the three classes of Dhyan-chohans are each divided into seven hierarchies. They are essentially the once human spiritual leaders of mankind, intimately involved in the evolution of the earth and its inhabitants.

Dhyana   A Sanskrit term used in Western occultism to denote a profound level of contemplation achieved (usually) through the practice of Yoga. It is said that a man in a state of *dhyana* consciousness is living entirely in the Buddhic part of his being (see BUDDHI). See also DHYAN-CHOHANS.

Diabolos   See DAIMONIARCHON.

Diakka   A term originated by the American spiritualist Davis in reference to a large group of 'morally deficient and affectionally unclean' spirits inhabiting a particular part of the spirit land known as SUMMERLAND. The diakka are the spirits of certain types of human beings who have passed into the Summerland after death, and who are inwardly compelled to influence, pervert and mislead those who investigate spiritualist phenomena without an adequate training.

Diaphanous Heaven   See NINTH HEAVEN.

Dido   In astrology a name given to one of the HYPOTHETICAL PLANETS.

Digestio   A term meaning approximately 'digestion', used in ALCHEMY to denote the process of dissolution which is a prerequisite for new forms to arise. It is the death which all things must periodically experience in order to find a new form for physical life.

Diksha   A Sanskrit term for 'initiation'. The *dikshit* is one initiated.

Dionysian hierarchies   See CELESTIAL HIERARCHIES.

Dioscuri   Most usually the word applies to the constellation of Gemini, but sometimes to the two stars in this asterism, Castor and Pollux.

Directions   The art of making directions, as of interpreting them, is the most important part of predictive astrology, and involves studying the future positions of planets and angles in relation to their original positions in a radical horoscope.

Direct method   See SLATE WRITING.

Divination   There are very many different forms of divination, methods of prying into the future, and (as the sound of a word connected with DEVA might suggest) the majority of these are involved with consciously or unconsciously using spirit beings, by binding them to service or by inviting them to reveal futurity through the forms of apparent chance happenings. The interesting engraving in Figure 31 illustrates two of the most popular forms of divination relating to the human body – those of palmistry and metoposcopy, divination or character reading from the form of the face or from the forehead. The engraving contains several Latin sayings from the books of well-known occultists and palmists, as well as a few references to the hand in

classical authors and the Bible. For specific forms of divination see the following entries: AEROMANCY, ALECTROMANCY, ALEUROMANCY, ALOMANCY, ALPHITOMANCY, AMNIOMANCY, ANTHROPOMANCY, APANTOMANCY, ARITHMOMANCY, ASTRAGALOMANCY, ASTRONOMANCY, AUSTROMANCY, AXINOMANCY, BELOMANCY, CAPNOMANCY, CARTOMANCY, CATOPTROMANCY, CERAUNOSCOPY, CEROMANCY, CHIROMANCY, CLEIDOMANCY, CLEROMANCY, COSCINOMANCY, CRITOMANCY, CRYSTALOMANCY, DACTYLIOMANCY, DEMONOMANCY, GYROMANCY, HIPPOMANCY, HYDROMANCY, ICHTHYOMANCY, IDOLOMANCY, KEPHALOMANCY, LECANOMANCY, LIBANOMANCY, LITHOMANCY, LOGARITHMANCY, MARGARITOMANCY, MOLYBDOMANCY, MYOMANCY, NECROMANCY, OMPHALOMANCY, ONIMANCY, ONOMANCY, ONYCHOMANCY, OPHIOMANCY, ORNITHOMANCY, PALMOSCOPY, PRESTINE LOTS, PSYCHOMANCY, PYROMANCY, RHABDOMANCY, RHAPSODOMANCY, SCIOMANCY, SORTES, SPLANCHNOMANCY, SPODOMANCY, STAREOMANCY, STERNOMANCY, STOICHEIOMANCY, STOLISOMANCY, SYCOMANCY, THEOMANCY, THERIOMANCY, XYLOMANCY.

For specific autoscopic methods of using spirits for predictive means, see GEOMANCY, I CHING and TAROT. See also PROPHECY.

Divine proportion   See GOLDEN NUMBER.

Divine year   One of the Years of the Gods in the Hindu system, regarded as being equal to 360 years of mortals. See YUGA.

Divyachakchus   A Sanskrit term meaning 'celestial eye' and used to denote the first of the six ABHIJNA – the faculty of perceiving any object in the universe, regardless of distance.

Divyasrotra   A Sanskrit term meaning 'celestial ear' and used to denote the second of the six ABHIJNA – the faculty of understanding any language or sound or any living being.

Djin   Sometimes *jinn*, an Arabian term usually translated as meaning approximately ELEMENTALS, although this can hardly be correct since the *djin* are much feared and are usually pictured as monstrous demons. It is likely that the word 'genii' comes from *djin*. See GENIUS.

Doctrine of signatures   See SIGNATURES.

Domdaniel   The fabulous dwelling place of gnomes, sprites and magicians ('Daniel' being

Figure 31   *The title page to Praetorius'* Ludicrum Chiromanticum *of 1661. This was one of the most influential collections of notes and texts on personal divination to be published in the seventeenth century*

representative of magicians in general, and 'dom' being an abbreviation of the Latin *domus*, meaning 'house') located off the coast of Tunis. It appears to be entirely a literary production, appearing first in the eighteenth century.

Dominions   Or Dominations, the name given to the first of the CELESTIAL HIERARCHIES of the second rank, sometimes called the Kyriotetes, after the nomenclature proposed by Dionysius the Areopagite. They are associated with the sphere of Jupiter. The Dominions are said by occultists to control the metamorphosis of matter, as the expression of spiritual events. Steiner calls them the Spirits of Wisdom.

Door of birth   A term used in esoteric astrology for the sign Cancer, ruled by the Archangel Gabriel. See GATE OF BIRTH.

Door of death   A term used in esoteric astrology for the sign Capricorn. See GATE OF DEATH.

Doppelgänger   A modern German word, now used in strictly non-occult circles to denote a form of DOUBLE. A double which is perceived in ordinary consciousness is usually an image of the ETHERIC DOUBLE or of the ASTRAL BODY, or (less frequently) of the SHADOW BODY. See, however, DWELLER ON THE THRESHOLD.

Double   This word is used widely in occult circles to denote a variety of different spiritual and demonic entities which certainly should not be confused. In an ordinary context the word is used to apply to the dark side of the human being, to his or her lower nature. This latter use is sometimes confused with the DOPPELGÄNGER, which in the esoteric view is directly linked with the physical body (and is therefore properly speaking a double of sorts), but which in popular use is often applied to a double which is not actually directly connected with a person – with what is in fact a human being of similar appearance. In a more specialized sense it is used to refer to the DWELLER ON THE THRESHOLD, the dark double which, under normal circumstances, remains unseen during a particular lifetime. In a far more specialized sense the word double is used to denote the ETHERIC DOUBLE, which in a sense is a spiritual replica of the physical body (though of the opposite sex to the physical). The ASTRAL

BODY is also sometimes called the 'double', and in such occult circles as this term is so used the Etheric Body is usually called the 'shadow body' or the 'shadow double'. Blavatsky also says that the term 'double image' is used among the Qabbalists to denote the Dual Ego, 'called respectively: the Higher, METATRON, and the Lower, SAMAEL. They are figured allegorically as the two inseparable companions of man through life, the one his Guardian Angel, the other his Evil Demon.'

Double Dragon   An ancient occult term for the MONAD, probably in reference to the equivalents of ATMA and BUDDHI.

Double image   An occult term, derived from Qabbalism, for what is called the 'Dual Ego' – the personification of the two aspects of each human being, called METATRON and SAMAEL, who represent respectively the good angel and the evil demon who accompany the human through each incarnation.

Dracula   The name of a VAMPIRE in the novel of that name by Bram Stoker, published in 1897. Due to the popularity of this book the term 'dracula' is often now used to denote a vampire.

Dragon   Images of dragons figure greatly in occult literature and art. Generally speaking, in the West they are regarded as being connected with evil, but in the East they are linked with wisdom. In spite of this, something of the Eastern origin of the ancient Mysteries survives in the fact that the name 'dragon', and many dragon-like attributes, are used to denote different stages of INITIATION. In non-esoteric areas, however, the dragon receives bad press: Satan is sometimes called 'dragon' or 'serpent', and a medieval version of the tempting snake of Eden is the Draconcopedes, with the body of a serpent and the face of a woman – an image derived from Egyptian art. The form of the dragon is often given to Christian images which depict AHRIMAN or his equivalent demonic agency.

In occult and astrological lore the dragon is specifically linked with the DRAGON'S HEAD and the DRAGON'S TAIL, the two points at which the path of the Moon intersects the path of the Sun, points of considerable importance both in the personal chart and in terms of cosmic phenomena; the *caput* (head) is linked with spiritual cleansing, the *cauda* ('tail') with spiritual punishment, with the release of demonic elements into the world. For certain lunar connections with the dragon, see also ATALIA.

Dragon path   See FENG-SHUI.

Dragon's Head   The north node of the Moon, the point where this body crosses the ecliptic to begin its northward journey. The term, originally *Caput draconis* in traditional astrology (although with several variants), was derived from the link made between the sphere of the Moon and the celestial dragon forces. The dragon was imagined as being curled around the Earth, in a symbol of the lunar sphere. It is said (with little evidence) that the eclipses were explained in terms of this celestial dragon swallowing the Sun and then regurgitating it. The Dragon's Head is undoubtedly a most powerful nodal point in the horoscope; some astrologers insist that when touched by directions it releases into the life of the native benefits due from karma. See ATALIA.

The term *Caput draconis* is also used to denote one of the figures of GEOMANCY.

Dragon's Tail   The south node of the Moon, the point where this body crosses the ecliptic to begin its southward journey. For the possible origin of the term, see DRAGON'S HEAD. This was the *Cauda draconis* of traditional astrology, a powerful nodal point said to carry the influence equivalent to that of Saturn. Some astrologers insist that it releases into the life of the native karmic consequences which present difficulties. See also ATALIA.

The term *Cauda draconis* is also used to denote one of the figures of GEOMANCY.

Druidic Egg   Sometimes Druid's Egg, a fabled egg hatched by serpents (see COCKATRICE) and carried in the air by their hissing. Although associated with the Gaulish and British order of Druids, a similar emblem or magical device was known in classical times.

Druids   Although synonymous with 'magicians', this name (originally applied to members of the ancient British and Gaulish priestcraft) designates a secret order concerning which almost nothing is known. The Romans tell us that the Druids were magicians, but the nature of their magic is unknown. The Romans also tell us that

they believed in the transmigration of souls (which may have been reincarnation). They are said to have conducted their cult practices in oak groves. It is probable that they were the representatives of the ancient Nordic Mysteries which were later supplanted by the Christian Mysteries. It is little more than romantic fiction to connect the historic Druids with the numerous stone circles and menhirs with which Britain is littered.

Dual Ego   See DOUBLE IMAGE and SAMAEL.

Dualism   In occult contexts a term used loosely to denote a belief which insists that the created world is the work of two forces – one striving towards good (and associated with light) and the other working towards evil (and associated with darkness). See, for example, AHRIMAN and LUCIFER.

Dumah   Qabbalistic name for the Angel of Silence, sometimes called the Angel of Death.

Dwapara Yuga   The Bronze Age of the Hindu chronology, a periodicity of 864,000 mortal years (see, however, YUGA). The period given includes the 'twilight' or *sandhya* and *sandhyansa*, which are 200 divine years each.

Dwarfs   In Nordic mythology these are small men with large heads who are supposed to be born from the earth itself. They are a species of the SOUL BEINGS of the Earth element.

Dweller   A term used in Western occultism for certain astral residues of deceased humans which sometimes cause difficulties on the astral plane or even on the earth plane; in ordinary parlance these are 'ghosts', but in fact they are 'astral shells'. The term 'dweller' is not always used precisely, however, and may often refer to astral beings who have had no incarnate experience, unlike the DIAKKA. The word was appropriated (and seemingly misunderstood) by Bulwer-Lytton when he invented the term DWELLER ON THE THRESHOLD.

Dweller on the Threshold   A term derived from the occult romance of Bulwer-Lytton, *Zanoni*, but widely adopted in Theosophical and Anthroposophical circles. There is some confusion in popular occultism about what this being is (see, for example, DWELLER). In serious modern occultism the term is now restricted to the projection of the untransformed karmic consequences (of all previous incarnations) which each undeveloped human must eventually meet, either before initiation into the spiritual world or at the point of death. In this precise sense the Dweller on the Threshold is the unredeemed selfhood, the 'self-haunting'. The threshold is that region which marks off the ordinary world of experience (bathed as it is in etheric and astral powers) from the higher spiritual world. Sometimes the Dweller is called the 'double' or the 'shadow self'.

Dynamis The beings of the CELESTIAL HIERARCHIES linked with the planet Mars and the rulers of the fifth sphere, which is the sphere of Mars. They are sometimes called the Mights, although the Greek term is actually cognate with the modern 'dynamic'. Steiner calls them Spirits of Movement. In Christian symbolism these beings are often represented as subduing devils, a clear association with the powerful duality of the Aries–Scorpio rulership (see NEGATIVE MARS), which visualizes the higher nature of Mars as linked with the EAGLE, the lower nature with the Scorpion; for the higher to develop, the lower demonic element must be thrust down.

Dyzan Sometimes Dzyn or Dzen, a Tibetan corruption of the Sanskrit *Dhyan* meaning 'divine knowledge'. See BOOK OF DYZAN.

The fifth letter of the alphabet, linked by occultists with the Hebraic He. The modern form of the letter is usually said to be derived from a hieroglyph for a window, but in the Qabbalistic system it is linked with the womb, with a numerical value of 5, which of course is the number of both Virgo and Venus. This explains why in medieval images Virgo often holds a flower with five petals, and why Venus is linked with the PENTAGRAM and with the changeability of the number FIVE. Because of the aspiration of H, E is sometimes linked with it numerologically.

Eagle A term with several occult connotations. It is the English translation of the Roman Aquila constellation. There is an 'alchemical eagle' in the process of the manufacture of the spagyric *Lapis* in ALCHEMY. In astrology the image of the eagle is associated with the Evangelist St John, and hence with the zodiacal sign SCORPIO (see TETRA-MORPH). Some astrologers insist that the eagle was used in ancient times to stand in place of Scorpio itself, but there is no direct evidence of this in surviving records, even though the survival of esoteric ideas in the use of the eagle in astrological symbolism points to a lost tradition in art. The rationale seems to be that since Scorpio is the sign in which redemption takes place, then it alone of all the twelve signs of the zodiac may be symbolized by two images. The image of the earth-bound scorpion represents the unredeemed nature, while the image of the aspiring eagle symbolizes the redeemed nature. The eagle is also the attribute of the god Jupiter and is used as a symbol of the planet.

Earth Chain In the Theosophical cosmo-conception the Earth is regarded as a unit globe in a series of seven globes, each possessed of counterparts (see GLOBES), called the Earth Chain. This chain is classified according to a convention of alphabetical letters which refer to equivalents in similar septenary chains (see CHAIN). A and G are lower mental and invisible to ordinary sight. B and F are astral and invisible to ordinary sight. C is the physical planet Mars (and its invisible counterparts). D is the physical planet Earth (and its invisible counterparts). E is the physical planet Mercury (and its invisible counterparts).

Earth element The Earth element finds expression in the zodiac through the three signs Taurus, Virgo and Capricorn (see EARTH SIGNS). It is the element most deeply associated with the physical body and environment (in which connection see EARTH TRIPLICITY. Earth is primarily the nourishing element, the supporter of life (in that it invests spirit with visible form), which means that it is pre-eminently the esoteric incarnating principle, seeking to draw the immaterial into physical form. Any incarnating spirit inevitably feels the weight of such form, with the result that the element is also associated with inertia, with physical and mental passivity and so on, and is inclined to find pleasure in material wellbeing and physical comforts. See also MELANCHOLIC.

Earth scheme See EARTH CHAIN.

Earth signs The three zodiacal signs Taurus, Virgo and Capricorn are expressions of the EARTH ELEMENT, sometimes (wrongly) called the 'Earth asterisms' rather than the 'Earth signs'.

Taurus is Earth expressed through Fixity and seeks to remain in one place, seeking enjoyment in a conservative dependence on the environment and delight in the earth. Virgo is Earth expressed through Mutability and is therefore practical in a material sense, finding pleasure in rhythmic service to others. Capricorn is Earth expressed through Cardinality and is therefore driven by a sense of fulfilment which is linked with social climbing or ambitions.

Earth triplicity   The Earth triplicity consists of the three signs derived from the element of Earth – Taurus, Virgo and Capricorn (see EARTH SIGNS). Taurus is visualized as the broad and fertile region of earth, the scene of productive agriculture; Virgo is visualized as a deep valley, pervaded by a degree of gloom and sadness; Capricorn is visualized as a high peak, impressive in its sense of serene age. See also EARTH ELEMENT.

Eastern angle   In astrology an alternative name for the Ascendant of the HOROSCOPE or for the cusp of the first house. It represents the symbolic point of sunrise in every chart, the point where the Ego (or associated Mars, ruler of Aries) begins to assert itself.

Eblis   The demon AZAZEL, after being thrust from Heaven, is renamed Eblis and becomes the ruler of the devils. The word 'eblis' means 'despair'.

Echidna   The mother of CERBERUS and the prototype of many medieval images of the tempting serpent, derived ultimately from Egyptian mythology.

Ectenic force   In psychism a name given to an energy force or EMANATION of a medium under the control of a spirit, by means of which he or she is able to move objects in ways contrary to the ordinary laws of the material universe. The making of an APPORT is said to be done by means of an ectenic force. The word appears to have been originated by Thury to account for the phenomenon of TABLE TURNING.

Ectoplasm   A term derived by the French psychic researcher Richet from the Greek *ektos* ('outside') and *plasma* ('mould' or 'substance') and applied to the manifestation of a semi-matter

outside the physical structure of a person. It is believed that this substance is derived from within the inner being and energies of the medium. The ordinary manifestations of ectoplasm in mediumistic seances is of an ETHERIC nature and has been studied in detail by many scientists and occultists – notably by Schrenck-Notzing. Ectoplasm in its primary state is invisible etheric material, yet under certain circumstances it may be imbued with a solid nature and become quite visible. It has frequently been photographed in such a form, when it appears as a white, viscous substance with an ozone-like smell. Sometimes ectoplasm is produced without the conscious participation of the medium and almost always it extrudes from the natural orifices – especially from the mouth. Schrenck-Notzing writes of it as possessing 'some of the properties of a living substance – notably that of the power of change, movement and the assumption of definite forms'. In fact the varieties of ectoplasmic manifestation appear to be almost infinite and in its nature we may trace the 'matter' from which MATERIALIZATION takes place in seance rooms. See also ECTENIC FORCE and ETHERIC DOUBLE.

Edimmu   A hungry and restless ghost in Assyrian demonology. See GENIUS.

Egg-born   A term used in modern occultism, derived from the Theosophy of Blavatsky, and applied to humans who lived on earth before dual sexual generation had developed. See also SWEAT-BORN.

Egkosmioi   A Greek term used to denote the intercosmic gods. The supralunar gods (sometimes called the PLANETARY SPIRITS) were ruled by the supercelestial *Huper-Ouranioi*, with the lower hierarchy of *Egkosmioi*.

Ego   A term adopted by occultists from the Latin word meaning 'I' and applied to the eternal individuality, the part which is said to dwell in the CAUSAL BODY and which is also seen as a link between the lower levels and the higher TERNARY of the human being. It must not be confused with the term used in modern psychology. In occultist thought the ego is visualized as the reincarnating vehicle of consciousness, dwelling within the sheaths of physical, etheric and astral in order to gain the necessary experience of the material plane. The ordinary self is merely an experience of a faint shadow of the eternal, unchanging, wise self of the Ego. Sometimes this ordinary self is called the 'personality', and the Ego proper is called the 'individuality'.

Egregores Celestial beings who are said by some occultists to be shadows of the higher PLANETARY ANGELS. Probably a Hebraic term originally, sometimes written as 'Egregori'.

Egyptian Days A series of calendrical lists of fortunate or unfortunate days, said with good reason to have originated from Egyptian astrological practices but probably derived ultimately from Assyrian sources. The Egyptian days are sometimes called the 'Lucky and Unlucky Days'.

Egyptian demon See VUAL.

Egyptian descent of the soul In his commentary on a section from Virgil's *Aeneid* Servius refers to a tradition linked with the descent of the soul through the planetary spheres prior to rebirth which postulates a progress inimical to the good of the soul (see, however, ORPHIC DESCENT OF THE SOUL). His account of the descent pictures the 'sluggishness' of Saturn, the 'desire for domination' of Jupiter, the 'passionateness' of Mars, the 'lustfulness' of Venus and the 'cupidity' of Mercury. It is as though the pure soul is blinded by these influences and is afterwards unable to use its own powers. The imagery is partly Platonic in that it insists that ordinary life is that of a 'stunned' spirit, passed in a sort of shadow realm.

Egyptian Hermes See TRISMEGISTUS.

Egyptian spirit See VUAL.

Eidolon The Greek singular term meaning approximately 'image', but used in Western occultism to denote the shadow or image of a human which is left on the astral plane after the death of that human. It is the equivalent of the Astral image, sometimes popularly called a 'ghost' when seen on the earth plane. The *eidola* have only a short-term existence in the astral plane, for they disintegrate and are absorbed into that plane, in much the same way as the constituent elements of the physical body are absorbed into the realm of nature. See also SUBTLE BODY.

Eight The perfect balance of the two small circles of the numeral 8 point to the hermetic maxim that 8 is the number of Justice. In modern times it is, of course, the figure of eternity (which now means 'extension in time', but which in earlier days meant 'outside time'). The number 8 is said to be the figure of prosperity and happiness; it is linked with the letter H (which is again a balance, but this time an open one) and with the Hebraic letter Cheth. It is an intellectual number, with a magnetic power of its own, linked with hidden things (note the double enclosure of its form), versatile in interest and confident in its own powers. It is said by numerologists that the 8 must at times stand alone, 'to collect its considerable forces' – this is the rationale to be seen in the image of the monad (1) standing in front of the spiritual (7) in order to draw from this spiritual forces (1 + 7 = 8). See NUMBERS.

Eighth Hierarchy See ARCHANGELS.

Eighth house The eighth of the twelve astrological HOUSES, linked with the sign Scorpio and (in modern astrology) with the planet Pluto. While popularly said to be the house of death, it is actually the house governing regeneration, of which the postmortem experience is merely the extreme condition. It is called the 'occult house' because it has rule over hidden things – exoterically over legacies, but esoterically over KARMA, the final legacy. It is linked through SCORPIO with the sexual parts; more properly with the generative system.

Eighth sphere A much misunderstood occult term, the real meaning of which may be grasped only from its context. In popular occultism the term is sometimes used to denote PURGATORY or KAMALOKA, but serious occultists have argued that this is a wrong application. The use of the term has a long history: in the Ptolemaic system it was used of the sphere of the fixed stars (the STELLATUM), although this designation changed as the model was adapted. Eventually, by the later medieval period the Stellatum was the ninth sphere. In the early cosmoconceptive models the spheres were numbered from the centre outwards, although the actual numbers were merely designations, for the theory of the SPHERES was complex and required a large number of interacting spheres within the designate concentrics. There were, for example, a number

79

of elemental spheres encasing the geocentric earth; this alone means that even if we regard the spheres as numbered bands of interacting spheres, the eighth sphere Stellatum should really be numbered as the twelfth. However when Copernicus introduced his own model of the cosmos he retained the theory of spheres (somewhat modified in the beginning, but totally rejected eventually), numbered them inwards, towards the heliocentric centre. In the diagrammatic representation of this system the Stellatum is now often numbered as the first sphere.

This rather tiresome distinction must be made here in order to explain why the term 'eighth sphere' is used in astrology and occultism for both the sphere of Heaven (Stellatum) and the sphere associated with Hell. In popular occult literature the eighth sphere is indeed equated with the sphere of the Moon, which in esoteric tradition is linked with the postmortem purgatorial experiences. Allied to this, the eighth sphere has been called the planet of death (the planet being the Moon, of course), and it is said to mark the sphere where lost souls find their dwelling (which, of course, makes it a very different place from Purgatory). In fact, there is an extensive and highly potent literature dealing with the modern esoteric astrological conception of the eighth sphere, a literature spearheaded by Harrison.

El In the Qabbalistic system the name given to the God-aspect dwelling in the World of Origins (ATZILUTH) in the Sephirah of CHESED. The name, and its many derivatives such as Al, or even Bel and Baal, are usually translated as meaning 'God', although it should more specifically be translated as 'divine one'.

Election A term used to denote a chart cast according to the rules of ELECTIONAL ASTROLOGY.

Electional astrology A form of casting and interpreting charts to determine suitable times for commencing any specific activity, such as marriage, journeys, law suits and so on.

Elemental An occult term literally meaning 'relating to the elements' (see therefore, ELEMENTS). It is important to distinguish this term from ELEMENTARIES. The word 'elemental' is most frequently used to denote the soul beings who are linked with the four elements (see, therefore, ELEMENTALS). In Theosophical literature the word 'elemental' is also used to denote a THOUGHT FORM engendered by a strong feeling or wish, most usually a result of hatred or fear; such an entity may take on an autonomous existence and entirely leave the control of the person who originated it. There are records in the literature of spiritualism of such elemental forms possessing human beings (see POSSESSION). These, sometimes called 'artificial elementals', must not be confused with the ELEMENTARIES, or with the ELEMENTARS, or with the ELEMENTAL ESSENCE from which they are said to be engendered as forms.

Elemental aspects The original theory upon which the doctrine of ASPECTS was based related to the supposed harmonies and lack of harmonies (the 'sympathy') between the elemental natures of the signs. Thus planets in trine were said to be operating in a harmonic sympathy because they each fell into a sign of a particular element; for example, Mercury in Aries trine Jupiter in Leo were both working through FIRE SIGNS, and were thus in unison.

Elemental essence A name given in occult literature to the protean, semi-intelligent materiality of the ASTRAL PLANE. It possesses no definite form of its own but readily and rapidly adapts itself to every nuance and every vibration of mental and emotional action in its search for form. The forms taken by the elemental essence are myriad, but it is said that the nature of such forms is very much the reflection of the collective thoughts of humanity (see, therefore, THOUGHT FORMS.

Elemental soul beings See SOUL BEINGS.

Elementals A term properly applied to the class of nature beings, the so-called elementary spirits or Sugani of esoteric lore. It is important to distinguish the term from ELEMENTS and from ELEMENTARIES (a word properly applied to a class of disembodied spirits or to the astral shells of disembodied spirits). The four groups of elementals are often mentioned in astrological literature – especially in esoteric astrology – because they are the expression in the invisible etheric spheres (which support the manifestations of nature) of the four elements from which they take their generic name. The GNOMES are the Earth beings (Figure 32); the SYLPHS are the Air

Figure 32 *Elemental: a gnome, the soul being of the earth*

beings; the UNDINES are the Water beings; and the salamanders are the Fire beings (see Figure 68 under SALAMANDER). It is erroneous to call these beings 'spirits' (see SOUL BEINGS).

Elementaries Blavatsky correctly writes of the elementaries as souls which for one reason or another have separated from their divine spirits; they are usually a trouble to themselves and to humans. It is probably true to say that the majority of events which pass for hauntings in the popular mind are the effects of elementaries. In misuse the term is often applied to ghosts, phantoms or *eidola* (see EIDOLÓN) which are generally not depraved or harmful. The term is in fact frequently misused: properly denoting the soul residues of depraved humans or (even nonhumans – as for example in the case of DIAKKA, which are often called elementaries), it is applied to a wide range of different beings (distinguish, for example, ELEMENTALS) and psychic phenomena with which these elementaries have no connection. Elementaries, themselves a result of depraved behaviour or misuse of psychic energies, may be attracted to a particular location by depravity or

by the misuse of psychic energies and may haunt such localities, but it is wrong to call all ghosts elementaries, as is often done.

Elementars A word used to denote the astral shells of the deceased or even certain malevolent beings (whose proper dwelling is on the astral plane) who for one reason or another invade the material plane. The word has many different shades of meaning, according to the context, and has been thoroughly confused in popular literature with 'ELEMENTALS' and 'ELEMENTARIES'.

The poltergeist has often been called an elementar, which at least has the virtue of being more accurate than calling a sylph or an undine by this name. The spiritual beings (more properly astral entities) which populate seance rooms are more often than not elementars, but they are called by quite different names by the majority of spiritualists (see, however, DIAKKA). One of the roots of the confusions has been the instance of certain Theosophists in calling all disembodied souls of the depraved by the name 'elementaries', even though earlier writers in this field (even such as Eliphas Levi) distinguished between elementaries and elementars. What might have been clear to the early Theosophists (namely, that souls were spoken and written about) was later forgotten, and the name was then used of spirits as though there were no cosmic difference between the two.

Elements In occultism the elements are said to be five in number – the four elements of Earth, Air, Fire and Water, which are held together in pact or union by the fifth element, the QUINTESSENCE, which bears many different names in hermetic literature although it is often called the 'AETHER'. It is widely recognized that this Quintessence will in the future become visible to human beings, indeed, it is already visible to certain individuals. Blavatsky takes this projection further, however, and speaks of two other elements, which will long remain invisible, rounding off the present tetrad (or pentad) as a septenary. This septenary is said to be the conditional modification of the one and only element, which is 'not the Aether', to quote Blavatsky once more, 'not even Akasa but the Source of these' (see AKASHA). In astrology and alchemy the four elements play an important role both in regard to temperament (the so-called HUMOURS), and in regard to their influence through what are called

Table 13

Element	Humour	Cardinal	Fixed	Mutable
Fire	Choleric	Aries	Leo	Sagittarius
Earth	Melancholic	Capricorn	Taurus	Virgo
Air	Sanguine	Libra	Aquarius	Gemini
Water	Phlegmatic	Cancer	Scorpio	Pisces

the triplicities: each of the four elements manifests through a different QUALITY (the Cardinal, Fixed and Mutable) three times to make up the twelve divisions of the zodiac, as in Table 13. This table also gives the related humour for each of the elements. For a full survey of the elements of astrology see AIR ELEMENT, AIR TRIPLICITY, EARTH ELEMENT, EARTH SIGNS, FIRE ELEMENT, FIRE SIGNS, WATER ELEMENT and WATER SIGNS.

For an alchemical view of the elements, see GRADES OF FIRE. See also SEVEN COSMICAL ELEMENTS.

Eleventh house The eleventh of the twelve astrological HOUSES, linked with the sign Aquarius and the modern planet Uranus (traditionally with Saturn). It is associated with the native's ideals in relation to social life and evolution, as well as with the kind of acquaintances and friendships he or she will attract. The house is said to relate directly to the aspirations of the native, and for this reason it was called once the 'house of hopes and wishes', yet it does not have the same heartfelt drive of the FIFTH HOUSE in these matters, such impulses often arising more from ideals and intellectual attractions than from direct emotional involvement. The house indicates the areas which will open up the native to higher levels of consciousness – often involving connections with development groups or political-awareness groups – as the ruling Aquarius would suggest.

Eligor One of the seventy-two SPIRITS OF SOLOMON. He is said to appear in the form of a knight.

Elixir A term derived in its occult sense from ALCHEMY and used to denote the supposed liquid, a draught of which would give eternal life or some similar required extension or intensification of being. While in popular imagination the Elixir is regarded as being a liquid, the early alchemical manuscripts make it clear that it is a powder. The origin of the term is probably Arabic, for a word of similar sound denotes a powder used for healing wounds. The Elixir of the alchemists, powder or liquid, was used for healing the wound of Fallen Man. Sometimes it was believed that the Elixir was the so-called Philosopher's Stone, which could be used to turn ordinary dross metal into gold or silver – a concept which is actually a sort of occult blind. The sought-after Elixir was really connected with the achor which is supposed to have been the blood of the gods. Anyone who is able to make this Elixir within his physical frame becomes one of the gods and is no longer subject to mortal limitations. The esoteric alchemists speak of three different forms of Elixir, however, and it is only the 'Elixir of bodies' which is concerned with the achievement of this inner state.

Eloah va Daath In the Qabbalistic system this is the name given to the male–female God-aspect in the fourth world of Atziluth, in the solar Sephirah of TIPHERETH. 'Daath' means (approximately) 'knowledge' or 'total comprehension', and the whole name has been translated as 'omniscient one'. Eloah va Daath has been described as 'the stillness in the motion, the silence in the sound'; it is the place where past and future meet, the heart of the creative system. Within the human being it is the place where the light of the divine spark is kindled. See DAATH.

Elohim The Elohim (sometimes Alhim or Aleim) are the ancient sun gods. The word is a Hebraic term which is said in occult circles (if not in theological circles) to be the plural of the feminine *Eloah* formed from the masculine plural ending *im* (see, however, SEPHIROTHIC TREE). In the Qabbalistic numerological system the term is the equivalent of 86 and is said to represent a sevenfold power of godhead.

Elohim Gibor In the Qabbalistic tradition this is the name of the God-aspect who dwells in and controls the Atziluthic world of GEBURAH. Gray has given the nearest English equivalent as 'Almighty God', while pointing out that in terms of its position in the SEPHIROTHIC TREE, the name should be feminized as 'Giborah'. It is usual for Qabbalists to translate the name as meaning 'God of Battles' and All-Conquering Strength, yet he is not so much a destroyer as a rectifier and his action is cathartic.

Eloi   One of the names given to the planetary spirit of Jupiter.

Elongation   In a strictly psychic context the word is used to denote the elongation of the physical body of the medium (sometimes to meet the demands of the control). The famous medium Home was frequently seen to elongate almost as much as 10 inches during seances. Such disturbances on the material plane are said to arise from disturbances in the rhythm of the ETHERIC or in ECTENIC FORCES.

Emanations   In a psychic context a name used to denote the subtle (sometimes astral, at other times etheric) effluences of a magnetic nature which are supposed to proceed from all bodies. Those who attend seances (and mediums in particular) are said to open themselves up in sensitivity to such emanations. See also ECTENIC FORCE.

Empusa   A Greek term for an evil demon who manifests in a variety of frightful forms; a vampire.

Empyrean   One of the ancient names for the TENTH HEAVEN, although sometimes used (in post-medieval sources) to denote the extralunar spheres and even as a synonym for the heavens generally. See also MACROCOSM.

Enchiridion   One of the GRIMOIRES. More exactly it is a collection of charms and prayers, probably printed for the first time in 1523, although (spuriously) linked in legend with both Charlemagne and a Pope Leo (probably a misunderstanding for the Qabbalist Abravanel, Leo the Hebrew.

Endorism   A rarely used word meaning approximately 'witchcraft', but sometimes used to mean 'haunting'. It is derived from the biblical Witch of Endor (1 Samuel, 28), who was not a witch in any modern sense of the word, but a pythoness. See OBOTH.

Enochian   The name given by certain occultists to the language spoken in lost ATLANTIS. One of the SECRET SCRIPTS is also called Enochian (made famous in a slightly different form by the magician John Dee), but this has nothing to do with Atlantis and is merely late medieval in construction. This script is linked with the so-called 'Enochian Tables' and with the related 'Enochian Demons', lists of demonic values and spiritual correspondences. The names of the demons vary from list to list, but the sixty-one recorded in a modern text by McClean are derived from the SPIRITS OF SOLOMON and from the so-called OLYMPIC SPIRITS, as from other GRIMOIRES. The choice of the biblical Enoch may originally have been an occult blind for ENOICHIAN.

Enoichian   A Greek term meaning 'inner eye', the eye of developed imagination.

Ens   A term derived from the Greek and meaning approximately 'being'. It is adopted widely in alchemical literature to designate various occult principles. The most frequently used appear in *Ens astrale* (see ASTRAL) and ENS VENENI, although the third of these so-called Paracelsian *Ens* is the DEALE.

Ens astrale   See ASTRAL.

Ens veneni   A name given by Paracelsus to the invisible force in nature which is approximately the equivalent of the modern occult term ETHERIC (see VENENI).

Enoptromancy   See CATOPTROMANCY.

Ephemeris   In astrology a tabular listing of the positions of the planets and nodal points, usually in longitudes, latitudes and declinations, along with related astronomical data, often including relevant tables of houses.

Epoch   Originally a term used to designate a point of reference in the calculation of dates, but more recently used to designate the EPOCHAL CHART. The term is also used as a synonym for 'perodicities' or 'cycles' (see, for example, AGES). See also PLATONIC YEAR and PRECESSION.

Epochal chart In astrology a horoscope figure designed to present symbolically in chart form information allegedly relating to the cosmic configuration attending the moment of conception. This information is derived by extrapolation from the natal chart. It is sometimes called the conception chart or the pre-natal chart.

Esoteric The word 'esoteric' still retains its original Greek meaning, for *esotericos* meant 'inner', 'concealed' and 'secret'. See ESOTERICISM.

Esoteric Buddhism A term once applied to modern Theosophical teachings, even though the founder of Theosophy, Madam Blavatsky, points out that the book by Sinnett in which the term was first used was concerned neither with esotericism nor with Buddhism or Budhism.

Esoteric Moon In esoteric astrology the hypothetical planet LILITH has been called the 'Esoteric Moon', although in ordinary astrology Lilith is the 'Dark Moon'. In her system of Intuitional Astrology the esotericist Bailey pictures the Moon of our Earth as a sort of veil for the influence of planets which she variously identifies as Vulcan and Neptune.

Esoteric planets In astrology this term has several applications, depending upon context (see, therefore, ESOTERIC SUN, ESOTERIC URANUS and ESOTERIC VULCAN). Within the cosmoconception of Intuitional Astrology the term is used sometimes as synonymous with SACRED PLANETS and sometimes in a more exclusive sense. Within this system, which traces the arising and manifestations of the SEVEN RAYS, the sacred planets (called also the esoteric planets) are given the curious rulerships set out in Table 14.

Esoteric Sun Blavatsky puts into words an idea which is implicit in several esoteric strains of astrological thought and which is openly mentioned in the hermetic literature of the immediate post-Christian era – that the Sun was later called the 'esoteric Sun' in the Intuitional Astrology of Bailey. The Esoteric Sun is said to be the image of divine intelligence and wisdom. The Triple Sun of esotericism is linked with the Esoteric Sun, being a veil for the Trinity: the 'spiritual Sun' is God the Father; the 'heart of the Sun' is God the son; and the 'physical Sun' is God the Holy Spirit.

Table 14

Constellation	Orthodox planet	Esoteric planet
Aries	Mars	Mercury
Taurus	Venus	Vulcan
Gemini	Mercury	Venus
Cancer	Moon	Neptune
Leo	Sun	Sun
Virgo	Mercury	Moon
Libra	Venus	Uranus
Scorpio	Mars	Mars
Sagittarius	Jupiter	Earth
Capricorn	Saturn	Saturn
Aquarius	Uranus	Jupiter
Pisces	Jupiter	Pluto

Esoteric Uranus Both Blavatsky and Bailey write of an Esoteric Uranus. As the former says, 'Uranus is a modern name, but one thing is certain, the ancients had a mystery planet which they never named.' It is this Esoteric Uranus which figures in the Intuitional Astrology of Bailey, as one of the three synthesizing planets (the other two being Neptune and Saturn) through which Sirius influences our solar system.

Esoteric Vulcan Modern esotericism describes a Vulcan development which relates to the distant evolution of the present Earth. In her system of Intuitional Astrology the esotericist Bailey has proposed an important role for her planet Vulcan, sometimes called an esoteric planet, at other times one of the SACRED PLANETS.

Esotericism It has long been recognized by occultists that behind exoteric knowledge there lies an esoteric knowledge – sometimes called the 'secret doctrine', sometimes called the 'arcane knowledge' – which proclaimed a communal teleology between man and the angels. The image of man projected by this ancient esotericism is very different from that projected by modern scientists, and it is the tacit warfare between the ancient wisdom and the modern view of things which is the subject of Blavatsky's profound introduction to *The Secret Doctrine*, which had such a galvanizing effect on Western civilization during the last part of the nineteenth century, and which continues working through the fissiparous tendencies of modern Theosophy.

The esoteric doctrine proclaims more than a unity in all religions – more than what Huxley called the 'perennial philosophy' – for it expresses a precise relationship between the microcosm (which is man) and the macrocosm (which is a spiritually populated universe). In this esoteric doctrine man is visualized as being caught between the involuntary power of the demons and the evolutionary power of the gods, through which conflict he learns to develop the powers of love and freedom. Such lessons are learned through a series of many lifetimes or incarnations (see REINCARNATION) in which adjustments are made for failures and successes through the operation of what has in recent years been called KARMA in Western occultism. It is further taught that the true esoteric wisdom (for all its partial unveiling in recent years) is still in the hands of initiates who release such wisdom and knowledge as is required into the stream of human history, and solicitously guard and guide the individual lives of those who are dedicated to the evolution of mankind.

An important aspect of esoteric teaching is the abstruse idea of a cosmogenesis which is entirely foreign to the modern scientific view of things, in that it is inclined to see the physical universe, with its four kingdoms (man, animals, plants and minerals), as pointers to the story of the evolution of man. In this sense the animal kingdom is the development of powers which were once a part of the human nature but which had to be rejected (given an objective form) at a time when they began to impede human development. The three kingdoms of mineral, plant and animal each mark stages of such 'objectification' in human evolution, and each is linked with important cosmogenetic developments. It is apparent to all students of occultism that the stream of esoteric knowledge which sprang from the ancient Mysteries is still available – at least, to those who are prepared to make the considerable effort to reach into the spiritual realms from which it proceeds. The theory of spiritual historicism upon which this account is based contains concepts very different from those usually considered valid in academic circles, yet evidence for its truth is superabundant.

The Neo-Platonic astrology derived from Gnosticism was essentially born of an esoteric stream designed to counter certain of the destructive elements inherent in orthodox theology. Through the medium of Arabian astrology and philosophy, this esoteric antique seed flowered in medieval astrological forms, many aspects of which were encapsulated in the symbolism of cathedrals and basilicas. The 'new' esotericism of the Renaissance, which so completely informed the arts and literature of that period, appears to have been born of an esotericism nourished in Florence, rooted in the new image of man derived from Neo-Platonic sources, certain oriental ideas and a spiritual cosmoconception which is now little understood. The esoteric stream seems to have gone into partial occultation during the period of the intellectual Enlightenment, and survives mainly in prolix alchemical and religious texts linked with Rosicrucianism, but in the decades around the turn of the present century there was a proliferation of different esoteric systems, some of which were syncretic and orientalizing rather than truly esoteric.

The main difference between the esoteric astrology of modern times and the various exoteric forms is in the cosmogenetic and teleological aspect of the science: almost all esoteric astrological systems are founded on the premise that the cosmos is a living being, that the destiny of the solar system is intimately bound up with the destiny of humanity, and that human beings reincarnate periodically onto the earth.

See also SECRET DOCTRINE.

Essence   A term used in many different senses in occult contexts. In ALCHEMY it is used to denote the spirit embodied within matter, and it is probably something along these lines that Gurdjieff had in mind when he used the term 'essence' to refer to the indestructible and eternal part of man, thus distinguished from the persona or personality, which is the husk of essence. For a specialist use of the term, see ELEMENTAL ESSENCE. The QUINTESSENCE of alchemy suggests that the ELEMENTS themselves should be thought of as essences, although the Elixir is sometimes written of as being one of the *essentia*. Many of the alchemical terms which make use of this word (such as the 'Essence of the Greater Circulatum') are no longer understood. The term 'ENS' appears to have been approximately the equivalent of the modern 'essence', however, relating as it does to the inner principle.

Estrie   A demon said by some to be a witch, although according to Hebraic demonology it is possessed of vampire-like tendencies. The estrie is sometimes called a 'broxa'.

Ethelia   See AZOTH.

Ether   See AETHER.

Ether-goer   See KESHARA.

Ethereal planets   A term probably originated by the astrologer Harris and applied by him to a number of planets (invisible to all but advanced clairvoyants) said to be in orbit between Mercury and the Sun. This chain of planets he called the 'Sisterhood' and claimed they were AROMAL PLANETS. See HYPOTHETICAL PLANETS.

Etheric   In occultist literature a name given to the force which lends form to life within our cosmos. The etheric forces are the formative integrative forces which work on inert matter to produce the rich diversity of natural phenomena, the growth of plants, animals and human beings, the cycles of nature, and much of the planetary phenomena observed from the earth. All living forms are imbued with etheric forces, and indeed the phenomena of the kind and quality of life depends almost entirely upon the nature of the etheric forces at play within a given being. When the etheric forces are withdrawn, then the body becomes inert and quickly disintegrates into its constituent elements. It is the etheric force which restrains form from such disintegration, from what is popularly called 'death'. The etheric forces of the occultist have little to do with the 'ether' of science, however.

According to occult tradition, there are four distinct etheric forces at work in our solar system, and these have been linked in an ingenious way by Wachsmuth with the four ELEMENTS. There is a warmth ether which brings about the conditions of heat, corresponding to the ancient FIRE ELEMENT. There is a light ether, which brings about the gaseous conditions and which corresponds to the AIR ELEMENT. These two etheric forces are of a centrifugal nature, striving constantly to leave behind the material realm. There is the so-called chemical ether, which induces fluidic conditions; this corresponds to the WATER ELEMENT. There is the life ether, which supports the solid or earthly conditions and which corresponds to the EARTH ELEMENT. The action of these last two is of a centripetal nature. We may see that much of the phenomena of life is to be understood in terms of the tensions engendered by the pull between the warmth and life ethers against the chemical and life ethers.

Etheric Body   A term used to denote the sheath of ETHERIC forces which permeates the physical body. It is called by Steiner the 'Body of Formative Forces' and in some occult systems the ETHERIC DOUBLE. However, see also SUBTLE BODY.

Etheric death   See SECOND DEATH.

Etheric double   A name given in esotericism to a delicate body, invisible to ordinary vision, which sheaths the physical body and suspends it in a state of life (see, therefore, ETHERIC). Without the life-giving power of the etheric the physical body remains inert and rapidly disintegrates into its constituent atoms, which perhaps explains the alternative name 'life body' for the etheric. In almost every respect this human etheric double is virtually a copy of the physical body, although when described by occultists capable of clairvoyance it is said to be slightly larger than the physical, appearing as a pale, luminescent vibration extending about half an inch around the physical, and of a blue-grey to violet-grey colour. This should not be confused with the other luminescent sheaths around the body – the AURA (which actually arises from the etheric) – or with the ASTRAL BODY, which absorbs cosmic vitality from the sun. Under normal conditions the etheric double does not leave the body until death, but in certain individuals the link between the etheric and the physical is looser than normal, a condition which often gives rise to clairvoyant ability. Some occultists claim that it is the etheric double of man which gives out ECTOPLASM, which is of a semi-etheric, semi-material nature.

Etheric globule   See VITALITY GLOBULES.

Etheric race   See FIRST ROOT RACE.

Etheric vision   A name given to the vision developed in an advanced state of clairvoyance. A person with such vision may see the forces which are continually supporting and vitalizing the material forms on the earthly plane.

Eudaimon   Sometimes 'eudamon' or 'eudaemon', a Greek-derived term meaning approximately 'good spiritual influence'.

Evangelists   The Christian symbolism relating to the four Evangelists is derived from pre-

Christian astrological lore and Mystery wisdom. The bull of St Luke is from the image of Taurus; the lion of St Mark is from the image of Leo; the angel of St Matthew (carrying a book or scroll) is from the image of Aquarius (carrying an urn). The eagle of St John is the 'redeemed' image of Scorpio (see EAGLE). The cosmic imagery of the Evangelists is ultimately linked with the hierarchies of the CHERUBIM and the SERAPHIM. See also TETRAMORPH.

Evestrum A Paracelsian term used to denote several aspects of the eternal substance of Heaven. It is the ethereal and invisible substance (or rather agency) of the heavens, and the Sidereal Body, the Starry Body or Astral Body of man, which is itself built from that substance or agency. The term is sometimes used in later-medieval texts for the ETHERIC DOUBLE or for the SUBTLE BODY of man.

Evil eye An important idea underlying the practice of witchcraft and black magic is that certain individuals have the power to cast evil spells or to project evil THOUGHT FORMS merely by looking at another person. Indeed, Elworthy, in his authoritative work on the subject, takes the evil eye 'to be the basis and origin of the Magical arts'. The idea of this evil power in man is just about universal, and there exists in virtually every language an equivalent term – the *boser Blick* in German, *malocchio* in Italian, *mauvais oeil* in French; and from the Latin *fascinum*, which was originally connected with the idea of binding, we derive the English 'fascinate', which was originally connected with such ideas as binding by means of diabolical powers or PACT. The modern English 'to overlook' is also connected with the evil eye. Maclagan, who records numerous examples of the evil eye in Scotland, quotes a woman from Mull who says that the evil eye is 'just an eye

Figure 33 *The* Mano pantea, *a famous Roman amulet against the evil eye, incorporating several traditional motifs (after Elworthy)*

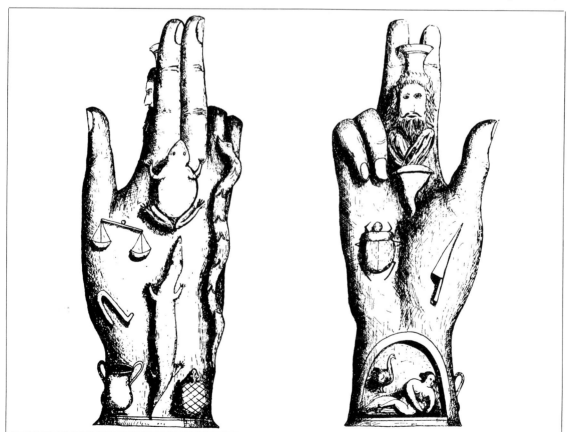

with great greed and envy', and the remark by an old man that 'it used to be said by old people that the greedy eye could split asunder the very rocks.' On a more exalted level the great medieval schoolman, Thomas Aquinas, lends his considerable authority to the belief that one mind may indeed influence another through forces which proceed from the eyes. We find a survival of the evil eye principle in our word 'cast' in reference to a slight squint, which was itself associated with the evil eye. The Latin *jacere* means 'to cast or throw away', and to this day a *jettatura* in Italy is one who possesses the evil eye.

The fact of the evil eye has given rise to numerous protective devices against it. These include a wide range of magical SIGILS, AMULETS, reflective surfaces (to 'throw back' the *jettatura*), and in particular a number of obscene or phallic figures and amulets which are intended to deflect the evil. Images of eyes are also used to avert evil, on the grounds of SYMPATHETIC MAGIC, and many of the more ancient gems and sigils are designed with this in mind (Figure 33). A highly efficient protection was found in the horn, often explained as phallic in origin, but in fact linked with the lunar crescent; thus the Moon reflecting back the light of the Sun is astrologically linked with the eyes. The horned lunar crescent is also linked with the curious hand gesture used in modern times in Italy against the evil eye (see Figure 3 under AMULET), and it is probably the basis for the survival of the horsehoe as an amuletic device. See also CHARM and MAGIC NAILS.

Exorcism The expulsion of evil spirits by adjuration; the casting out, by one means or another, of evil spirits. The magical arts of exorcism involved CEREMONIAL MAGIC, and the official demonifuge rites of the modern churches are themselves not so far removed from such ceremonials. See THARANA.

Exsusiai The name given to the spiritual beings of the sphere of the sun. See CELESTIAL HIERARCHIES.

Extispicy Divination by means of entrails. The *extispices* of the Roman religious colleges were the *aruspices* or augurs. See HARUSPEX.

Extra A term used in SPIRIT PHOTOGRAPHY to denote any phenomenon, recorded on a negative or film, which was not present (at least, to ordinary vision) at the time when the picture was taken. Thus, in a sense, all images of spirits or ghosts are really 'extras'.

Eye See EVIL EYE.

Eye of Dangma Sometimes Dangma's Opened Eye or Eye of Siva, a term derived from Theosophical literature and used to denote the opened inner spiritual eye of the seer, intimately connected with the opened THIRD EYE. The Dangma is sometimes said to be the purified soul.

The sixth letter of the alphabet, given in occultism the number 6 (see SIX). Occultists link the F with the double F⏋, which some say gave rise to the diagamma. In the occult sound system it is an excarnating sound, an idea which may be expressed by the fact that the equivalent of F, the Feoh of the RUNES, means 'belongings' – that is to say, things on the outside of the person.

Face   In astrology a face is a 5-degree division of a zodiacal sign, there being six equal divisions in each sign. In connection with Qabbalistic thought, see PARTZUPHEEM.

Fairy   Name given to a SOUL BEING of the Air element, whose natural dwelling is on the astral plane (see ELEMENTALS). The body of a fairy is described as being of a pulsating iridescence, but it is said that when they materialize on the physical plane they adopt the traditional THOUGHT FORM created by humans as their vehicle. This is why they so frequently appear as small, delicate creatures with wings and wearing flimsy clothing. Gardner, who has studied fairies through his developed clairvoyance, says that they have an intelligence comparable to that of a pet dog, being alert and observant but not rational. See also UNDINES, with which fairies are sometimes confused. In modern times the fairies are often confused with the DEVAS.

Fama   See ROSICRUCIAN.

Familiar   A name given to spirits attendant upon witches or magicians. Usually familiars are visible to ordinary sight, as, for example, in the form of dogs or cats, but in some cases it is claimed that such people as witches are followed by a swarm of invisible familiars. The word is from the Latin *familiares*, but alternative Roman names were *magistelli* and *martinelli*, while the Greeks called them *paredrii*. It is claimed in the witchcraft literature that the familiar is given to

the witch by the Devil to aid in the work of black magic. See also AGATHION.

Familiarities   The 'familiarities' of planets were the ASPECTS between them.

Farvarshi   A Zoroastrian term used to denote the shadow side of a god, the adversary of that god. AHRIMAN is the *farvarshi* of ORMUZD, for example.

Fascinate   A term from the Latin *fascinare* ('to enchant') and used as a general term for the act of casting spells or (in particular) of throwing the EVIL EYE upon another. In late-medieval literature a person 'fascinated' was usually under the spell of a magician or witch. See also *fascinum* under EVIL EYE.

Fatae   The Greek and Roman mythologies included three spiritual beings called in Greek the *Moirai*, in Latin *Parcae* or *Fatae*, who were supposed to control the individual life of man (see, however, FATE). They were named (probably after Hesiod) Clotho, who held a distaff on which was the material of life; Lachesis, who spun the thread from this material; and Atropos, who made that final cut of the thread which ended life. Sometimes the three are called the Harsh Spinners, even though they do not all spin. Their 'spinning' was said to take place at birth, and in some periods also at marriage, when a new life or fate was made. The general word *moirai* means

89

'share' or 'apportioned lot'. *Lachesis* means approximately 'obtaining by lot' and *atropos* 'irresistible'. The three witches in *Macbeth* have been linked with these three spinners, from the old English term *weird*, which means approximately 'destiny'; the three 'weird sisters' were the Fates who control destiny.

Fate   The word 'fate' is derived directly from the Latin *fatum*, which really means something like 'that which has been spoken'. Fate, as a life pattern, is therefore (etymologically at least) determined by the gods, as a sort of verbal fiat. In that sense Fate is more an equivalent of predetermined DESTINY rather than KARMA, with which it is sometimes linked. The modern derivatives, such as 'fatalistic' and 'fatal', confirm this important distinction. The determinative of Fate, even though it might have been involved with lot or chance, was certainly seen as a fiat from the spiritual realm of the gods. It is indeed from the Roman *Fatae*, the sisters who determined Fate, that we ultimately have our word 'fairies'. See, however, FATAE.

Father-Ether   See ARCHAEUS.

Feng-shui   These two Chinese words, meaning literally 'wind' and 'water', are used to denote the ancient occult study of the hidden currents and forces that cover the surface of the earth. The direction and spiritual qualities of these forces are of paramount importance in determining the suitability of locations for living, burial and religious centres. Those who practise the discipline of *Feng-shui* have an intimate knowledge of the workings of the magnetic *Kung-lei* (dragon paths) which trace out the powerful earth currents and which appear to be the equivalent of the ley lines of certain writers (see GEOMANCY). The Chinese name for the force conducted along the *Kung* lines is *Sha*. *Feng-shui* is usually mistranslated by sinologists, and even by historians of the occult, as 'geomancy', but the Chinese system is not predictive, nor is it concerned with the manipulation of earth materials for predictive purposes (see, therefore, GEOMANCY). Under the curious term *Fong-chur*, Spence made nonsense of the ancient Chinese art, and his term still persists in popular circles.

Fiducial   The fiducial or fiduciary is a point (in astrology very often a fixed star) determined as a fixed position for a basis of comparative measurement. The term is derived ultimately from the Latin *fides* ('faith') and refers to something in which one may place trust.

Fifteen stars   Many of the medieval star lists pay special attention to fifteen fixed stars, of comparable visual magnitude, each of which was accorded a SIGIL and a special place in relation to the lore of magical gems and talismans used for amuletic and therapeutic magic. Their modern names and their ancient sigils are listed in Table 15.

Table 15

1 Aldebaran	6 Procyon	11 Polaris
2 Pleiades	7 Regulus	12 Alphecca
3 Algol	8 Algorab	13 Antares
4 Capella	9 Spica	14 Wega
5 Sirius	10 Arcturus	15 Deneb Algedi

Fifth element   This is the QUINTESSENCE, the secret etheric force which unites the four elements of Earth, Air, Fire and Water.

Fifth heaven   A term used synonymously with 'fifth sphere', which in the occult cosmoconception was the sphere of Mars, ruled by the DYNAMIS.

Fifth Hierarchy   See CELESTIAL HIERARCHIES.

Fifth house   The fifth of the twelve astrological HOUSES, the house of creativity and children, linked with the nature of Leo and with the Sun, representative of the creative power, organizational abilities, approach to pleasures and the general talents of the native. While the old title 'house of children' may be taken quite literally, it must be seen as relating to a more general idea of 'offspring', such as works of art, creative concepts and so on.

Fifth Race   A term derived from modern Theosophical literature for the Aryan race, the progenitors of whom were the last subrace of the ATLANTEANS. This Fifth Root Race was established on the plains of what is now northern India. The five subraces of the Fifth Race which have already established themselves on the earth are the Indo-Aryan, the Aryo-Semitic, the

Five

Iranian, the Celtic and the Teutonic. See SEVEN RACES.

Fire baptism Originally a baptism of fire was exoterically martyrdom by fire – that is, real death. Napoleon III used the term of those who went into military action for the first time but did not necessarily die. The term was esoterically used of baptism by the Holy Spirit and denoted a process of initiation into higher wisdom, perhaps on the basis that it was believed that there was a ring of fire around the earth which had to be passed by those who sought knowledge of higher things. The secrets of many spiritual fires were taught in the Mystery wisdom.

Fire element The fire of the occultists and the alchemists is something altogether greater than the incandescent gases of familiar experience (these being merely the manifestation on the material plane of the Fire element itself). Fire is regarded as the highest of the spiritual etheric forces, the most spiritualized of the ELEMENTS, linked as it is in occultism with the highest TERNARY of man, sometimes with the EGO; it is the warmth ether of modern occultism (see ETHERIC). In late medieval occultism it was called the principle and spiritual of the four elements, the efficient cause of things. The alchemist makes use in his spagyric art of different GRADES OF FIRE, themselves linked with the fourth element, which relate to the different levels of spiritual experience and growth in the path towards illumination and INITIATION. The 'Fire of the Philosophers' is, according to Paracelsus, 'a close, aerial, circular, bright fire, which the philosophers call their Sun'. It is this psychological truth which is the reason for the esoteric name of the alchemists as 'FIRE PHILOSOPHERS', which is really an occult blind to hide the true nature of the 'Great Work'.

In astrology the fire element is expressed through the signs of the zodiac Aries, Leo and Sagittarius. On the microcosmic level the element works through the temperament of the CHOLERIC.

Fire Mist See LORDS OF FLAME.

Fire of the Philosophers See FIRE ELEMENT.

Fire philosophers A term used of alchemists, hermeticists and Rosicrucians in the late-medieval period. They were also called 'philosophers'. See also VULCAN.

Fire signs The three signs of the zodiac linked with the element of Fire are Aries, Leo and Sagittarius. The Fire nature is linked specifically with the impress of selfhood, so that each Fire sign is in one way or another involved with itself, most wholesomely when supported by a creative cast of mind or a creative aptitude. The Fire nature drives towards independence and love of material luxury and splendour; the world is seen as a quarry for decorative material to adorn spirit and self. The Fire signs tend to be exhibitionist, but they are often full of altruistic idealism and warmth of being, tinged with an impulsive and original way of expressing themselves.

Fire Spirits A name given in modern esotericism to the ARCHANGELS.

First house In astrology the first house is the first in the sequence of twelve HOUSES, linked with the idea of selfhood and all that appertains to the incarnated Ego. Since this is the subject of the entire horoscope, it is helpful to visualize the first house as a sort of lens through which all the other activities in the remaining eleven houses are projected, or even distorted. This house participates in the nature of the associate sign ARIES and is linked with the CARDINAL nature, as with the FIRE ELEMENT.

First point In astrology almost always a reference to the first point (degree) of Aries in the tropical ZODIAC.

First Race Sometimes the 'First Root Race', a term derived from modern Theosophical literature to denote the first race of man, the Adamic Race – human souls who were still preparing for the descent into a body of matter. They were said to possess only the faculty of hearing and to dwell in protean ASTRAL BODIES. See SEVEN RACES.

Five The number 5 is said to be a dangerous and changeable number, and its form in European symbolism expresses this idea in the opposing directions of the two open forms – the top of our modern 5 pointing to the right (which in occult systems is the future) and the bottom pointing to the left (which in occult systems is the past). It is essentially lacking in purpose, for it seeks to find a direction by revolving upon itself, caught between past and future. This condition arises from the conflict between the materiality of the preceding number and the tendency towards isolation of the monad (4 + 1 = 5). This must lead either down even deeper into matter or upwards into a higher realm. Therefore the 5, rather like the 3, is involved in choice. The movement downwards becomes a preoccupation with time, the movement upwards leads into the spiritual realm of the ETHERIC. It is the element of the 'now', the feeling of being balanced between past and present, a deep concern with what some occultists have called the 'specious present' that makes the number 5 a dangerous number. Its strength lies in the fact that it points to a higher realm, where (and only where) the tensions inherent in its form may be resolved. This becomes evident in the QUINTESSENCE, the fifth essence or fifth element, which is the invisible supporter of the material realm of the four elements that appears to underlie the phenomenal world (see FOUR). This again points to the redemption implicit in the 5. From this one may see why 5 is called the 'number of life'; however, the phrase has a deeper meaning, for it is associated with the pentagram, which is in turn linked with the etheric forces, the formative forces of the universe. Figure 55 under MORNING STAR illustrates the relationship which the number 5 has to the pentagram and Venus, for this planet is said to have rule over the physical body, and occultists often draw the body inscribed within a five-pointed star. The Hebraic equivalent letter is He. See NUMBERS.

Fixed signs In astrology the four fixed signs are Taurus, Leo, Scorpio and Aquarius. See also TETRAMORPH.

Fixity In astrology the word 'fixity' is used to denote a state of being which impedes motion or the free flow of energies. There are four signs of the zodiac which operate through Fixity or induce Fixity into the microcosmic plane: Taurus, Leo, Scorpio and Aquarius. These fixed signs are linked with the image of the TETRAMORPH.

Flaga A name used by Paracelsus to denote a GUARDIAN ANGEL.

Flame In some esoteric systems initiates are called 'Sons of the Flame' or 'Sons of the Holy Flame' (see HOLY FLAME and LORDS OF FLAME). For the Qabbalistic flames, see YESOD.

Flauros One of the seventy-two SPIRITS OF SOLOMON. He is said to appear in the form of a leopard.

Fleurety A demon supposed to have the power to perform any labour on behalf of a conjuring magician during a single night. He has the power to cause hailstorms.

Flying salve See AZOTH.

Fluvii transitus Literally, 'crossing the river', a name given to one of the more popular of the many SECRET SCRIPTS.

Focalor One of the seventy-two SPIRITS OF SOLOMON. He is said to appear in the form of a man with wings. Like the spirit VEPAR, he has power over the sea and may be conjured to cause shipwrecks and death by drowning.

Fohat A Tibetan term which is sometimes explained in Theosophical literature as meaning 'kosmic electricity' – a conscious principle of cosmic will. Blavatsky's oft-quoted words suggest something of the nature of this curious principle: 'Fohat is the steed and thought is the rider'; it is clearly more than merely the 'vital force of the universe'. It is really primordial light, the active male potency of the feminine reproductive power in nature.

Fong-chur See FENG-SHUI.

Foras One of the seventy-two SPIRITS OF SOLOMON. He is said to appear in the shape of a man and will confirm invisibility on those who successfully conjure him.

Forfax One of the names for MORAX.

Formative forces A term used by Steiner to denote the ETHERIC forces – the body of formative forces is the Etheric Body.

Formators See YETZIRAH.

Forneus One of the seventy-two SPIRITS OF SOLOMON. He is said to appear in the shape of a sea monster.

Fortuna A name given to two of the sixteen figures of GEOMANCY – the Fortuna Major and the Fortuna Minor. In astrology these terms are sometimes used of Jupiter and Venus respectively. Also in astrology the term is also frequently used as a short form for the PARS FORTUNA.

Fortuna Major　The Greater Fortune, one of the sixteen figures of GEOMANCY; but see also FORTUNA.

Fortuna Minor　The Lesser Fortune, one of the sixteen figures of GEOMANCY; but see also FORTUNA.

Fortunes　A collective term for Jupiter and Venus; the former is the Greater Fortune, the latter the Lesser Fortune.

Fortune-telling　A popular term for personalized prediction or DIVINATION.

Foundation chart　A term used for a horoscope cast in relation to the founding time or date of a building or an important reconstruction.

Four　The 4 is the number of the material world, as expressed in the idea of the FOUR ELEMENTS and so on. It is said to be the builder of the forms envisaged by the 1, to be loved by the 3 (1 + 3 = 4), and is perhaps the most active of all numbers. Indeed, it is the line of 4 which supports all the other numbers in the esoteric TETRACTYS. Its links with the four elements, the four fixed signs, the TETRAMORPH and all the tetrads indicate its importance in occult lore as a supporter of material forms. However, it is the FIVE which really holds together the 4, and it is therefore more fitting to see the 5 in its role as the underlying QUINTESSENCE, as the thing which lends structure to the created forms of the world. The 4 is practical and worldly wise, and so it does not give without expecting return. This concept of a sense of payment and restraint is expressed in the vastness of the D with which it is associated – this is a containing form, which is almost a vestigial drawing of a belly. The related delta Δ of the Greek alphabet is really a container of power; it is the space contained within the triangle which induces occultists to link the D with 4. Sometimes, because of the exoteric symbolism of the triangle, D is linked directly with the number 3. The sound of D is said to be an incarnating sound which moves down into the depths of

matter. The Hebraic equivalent letter is Daleth. Four is the number of material life (see THREE). See also NUMBERS.

Four ages　In *Metamorphoses* Ovid mentions four previous ages prior to his contemporary age: he called them the ages of Gold, Silver, Bronze and Iron, these being separated from his present fifth age by a great flood. These four ages may be linked with the esoteric theory of cosmogenesis (see, for example, SUN PERIOD, which corresponds to the Golden Age); there is also a correspondence with the Hindu theory of cycles (see YUGA). In early times an important analogy was established between the four world ages and the ages of man, the seasons, the elements and so on. The GOLDEN AGE was Fire, the youth of man; the SILVER AGE was Air and adolescence; the BRONZE AGE was Water and maturity; the IRON AGE was Earth and old age.

Four animals　The occult four animals are actually three animals united by a (fourth) human figure – the lion, the bull and the eagle linked by the winged human. These are derived from the images of the four FIXED SIGNS of the zodiac. In the esoteric astrological melothesia (see MELOTHESIC MAN) the lion represents the feeling element in man (the heart); the bull represents the will-life or physical element; the EAGLE represents the capacity for higher thinking; while the winged human represents the union of these three capacities in the human form. See TETRAMORPH and FOUR ZOAS.

Four elements　The so-called four elements are actually five in number. The exoteric four are Earth, Air, Fire and Water, but these are united by the fifth, which is the QUINTESSENCE (see, however, ELEMENTS). The esoteric natures of the elements are very different from the materialities by which they are symbolized in modern times. The medieval occultists were aware of this and often chose to symbolize their elements by less exoteric means. In the personifications of the four elements in Figure 34, for example, while tongues of flame emerge behind the leading figure (which is Fire), the other symbols are more potent – the drawn sword links to the CHOLERIC nature of the sign, with its incipient violence, while the lion links it with the creative force of the fire of zodiacal LEO.

Figure 34 *A fifteenth-century woodcut of the four elements with their symbols. From left to right: Fire (Choleric), Air (Sanguine), Water (Phlegmatic) and Earth (Melancholic)*

Four principles See PRINCIPLES and FOUR QUALITIES.

Four qualities Sometimes called the 'four principles' to distinguish them from the qualities, these are the four states of being associated with the planets and zodiacal signs in early astrology: Hot, Cold, Humid and Dry. See QUALITY.

Four zoas A term originated by the poet Blake, probably under the influence of the esotericist Boehme, from the Greek plural *zoa*, and derived from occult astrological lore. Blake follows the esoteric tradition in identifying the four beings with the fourfold nature of man – Tharmas is the body (probably a word derived from the Greek *thumos,* the equivalent of the etheric – see AETHER); Urizen is reason (thinking – probably a play on the Germanic *Ur* and the English 'horizon'); Luvah is the emotional life (probably a play on the word 'love'); while Urthona is imagination (probably again the use of the Germanic *Ur* and the English 'earth-owner'). These four zoas correspond to the four fixed signs of the zodiac (with which the word *zoa* is cognate) – Taurus, Scorpio, Leo and Aquarius, respectively – and the four beasts which figure in the tetramorph (see FOUR ANIMALS).

Fourteen Stars The list of star names set out under the medieval FIFTEEN STARS contains one asterism (the Pleiades); the list is therefore sometimes more correctly referred to as the 'Fourteen Stars'.

Fourth heaven Sometimes this term is used as synonymous with the 'fourth sphere', which in the cosmoconception built around the Ptolemaic system was the sphere of the Sun, ruled by the EXSUSIAI. In the Qabbalistic system this heaven is sometimes called Machonon and, in common with all Western esoteric systems, was assigned rulership of the Archangel Michael.

Fourth house The fourth of the twelve astrological HOUSES, linked with the nature of Cancer and with the planet Moon. It represents the domestic life of the native and is linked with the early environment, especially with the mother (indeed, it was formerly called the 'house of the mother'), although esoterically it deals with the whole experience preceding birth (see GATE OF BIRTH). This house is a useful index of the imaginative faculties and moods, and relates to 'hidden things' on account of which it has unfortunately been called 'the Grave'. It is essentially associated with the ribcage, the protective guard around the heart, which is reflected in the protective attitude of the Cancerian to kith and kin.

Fourth race Sometimes the Fourth Root Race, a name given in Theosophical literature to the fourth of the SEVEN RACES' stream of evolution. This race is sometimes called the Atlantean, and was said to occupy mainly the lost continent of ATLANTIS (also called Kusha), located approximately over the present Atlantic Ocean.

Fourth sphere The sphere of the Sun in the occult cosmoconception, ruled by the celestial hierarchies of the EXSUSIAI.

Frontal chakra See AJNA.

Furcas One of the seventy-two SPIRITS OF SOLOMON. He is said to appear in the form of an old man, riding a horse and carrying a spear.

Furfur One of the seventy-two SPIRITS OF SOLOMON. He is said to appear as a deer with wings and a fiery tail.

The seventh letter of the alphabet. The modern form is said to be derived from the Latin C, itself from the Greek gamma. Blavatsky makes much of the fact that the word 'god' begins with this letter, for this, along with related derivatives in many languages, is said to refer as a three-letter word to the Trinity. She also points out that the origin of the G and the C, which are said to be derived from a vestigial drawing of a camel or a camel's neck, is actually from a vestigial drawing of an erect serpent. However, the Hebraic Gimel, with which the G is associated, means 'camel'. The association between the G and the numeral 4 insists upon a link with the sacred TETRACTYS; see therefore FOUR.

Gaap One of the seventy-two SPIRITS OF SOLOMON. He is said to appear in human shape, attended by four kings.

Gabriel The Archangel accorded rule over the sphere of the Moon and over elemental Water. Gabriel is the Angel of the Annunciation, an association which derives from the esoteric cosmology, which gives him rule over the lunar sphere. This is the last of the planetary spheres through which the descending spirit passes on the way to incarnation (see, for example, DESCENT OF THE SOUL and GATE OF BIRTH). Gabriel is one of the SECUNDADEIAN BEINGS. See also YESOD.

Gamalei Certain natural stones or gems, which, because of some powerful astrological influence, were said by medieval occultists to be magically efficacious. Artificial gamalei are those engraved with astrological, Hermetic or magical sigils, towards talismanic ends. They are sometimes called 'gemetrei' and 'gamathei', but Paracelsus calls them 'gamahei' and says that they are 'stones graven according to the face of heaven'. See Figure 35; see also BIRTH STONES and SEALS.

Figure 35 *A man taking from a frog a stone which is supposed to be located in its forehead. Such stones were said to have magical properties and were supposed to be used for making gamalei and amulets*

Gamaliel The name of an Adversary of the ARCHANGELS OF THE SEPHIROTH.

Gamchicoth The name of an Adversary of the ARCHANGELS OF THE SEPHIROTH.

Gamygyn Sometimes Gamigyn, one of the seventy-two SPIRITS OF SOLOMON. He is said to appear in the shape of a horse or donkey. He is the necromantic demon, consulted by those who wish to raise the dead for their own personal reasons.

Gate of birth In occultism it is said that the incarnating soul enters the physical realm through the sphere of the Moon, which is, of course, associated with rule over CANCER and also accounts for the term 'gate of birth'. The esoteric basis for the term is most clearly set out in Macrobius in his description of the descent of the soul through the seven zones of the planetary spheres.

Gate of death Name applied to the sign CAPRICORN, sometimes to the sphere of Saturn. In esoteric astrology it is said that the soul in its postmortem experience aspires to travel to the sphere of Saturn, which marks the boundaries of time, and it is almost certainly this association which gives rise to the term.

Gati A Sanskrit term meaning approximately 'moving out' in the sense of passing from one mode of existence into another, and applied specifically to the passage between the grades of sentient existence. The esoteric list is different from the exoteric. The esoteric range downward through the *dhyanic* (*anupadakic* – see ANUPADAKA), the Devas, men, elementals (or nature spirits), animals, lower elementals, to organic germs. The exoteric range downward through the Devas, men, Asuras, beings in Hell, the Pretas, to animals.

Geburah The fifth Sephirah of the Qabbalistic SEPHIROTHIC TREE. Its name means 'strength', 'justice', 'severity' and 'fear', and is concerned spiritually with the clearing of dross and the re-establishing of balance in the universe, and this role it plays in union with the fourth Sephirah CHESED. Geburah, for all its Martian associations in the popular mind with violence and pain, may be understood correctly only when it is seen not as a cause of violence, but as a necessary cure for imbalance; this often requires as a last resort such operations as give rise to violence and pain. In the lowest World of Expression (ASSIAH) Geburah is connected with Mars, and with the stringent forces which turn in upon themselves. In the World of Formation (YETZIRAH), it is ruled by the angelic order of the Seraphim (the so-called Fiery Serpents) who work through heat; it is through heat that the Seraphim destroy in order to regenerate and preserve the balance of the world. In the World of Creation (BRIAH) we find at Geburah the Archangel Khamael, whose name means 'burner of God' and who is also linked with the destroying angel SAMAEL. Khamael has been described as the built-in resistance that modifies the divine powers so as to make them useful lower down in the Tree, especially on the plane of Assiah. In the world of Origins (ATZILUTH) the ruler is Elohim Gibor, whose name means 'all-conquering strength', although as with so many of the Hebraic names the precise meaning is richer, and there is much argument as to how the word should be translated. This being controls the forces which eliminate things seeking perfection; this is why he is sometimes pictured as a warrior or devouring god.

Gedulah A name for the Sephira CHESED.

Gematria A method popularized from Qabbalistic praxes, based on the fact that the letters of the Hebrew alphabet have been accorded numerical equivalents, in which the numerical value of letters in words are added together to give specific values. Words of similar numerical values are regarded as having correspondences or analogies and are often subjected to ingenious interpretation as a result. Trachtenberg lists seven different ways of abstracting such analogic correspondences by means of numerical reductions. In popular occultism gematria may be defined as a method of extracting hidden meaning from letters, words and sentences by numerical analogy. See also NOTARICON and TEMURA, with which gematria is sometimes confused.

Gemini The third sign of the zodiac, and one of the constellations. It is linked with the TAROT arcanum of 'The Sun' and with the Hebraic letter Koph. The constellation is said to represent the twin sons of Jupiter and Leda, Castor and Pollux, the former being mortal, the latter immortal. They each figure as stars in the asterism, the alpha and beta respectively. The modern sigil for

Gemini ♊ is said by some to be a drawing of the twins holding hands, but some occultists see the significance of the sigil as deriving from the space within the rectilinear structure, for the rule of Gemini over the human lungs points to the permanent rhythmic relationship which the human being holds to the outer world. By breathing man is constantly taking in air and oxygen, so that the inner becomes the outer, the outer the inner (Gemini, in fact, has rule over all dualities). Gemini is of the AIR ELEMENT and of the Mutable quality, the influence being mental, intellectual and versatile. The Geminian exhibits a strong need to relate to others and is at worst histrionic. This airy nature of the sign is expressed in the many key words attached to it by modern astrologers: versatile, idealistic, communicative, imitative, inventive, alert, inquisitive – in a word, all those qualities which may be associated with an Air nature expressing itself with a view to establishing communication with the world. In excess the Geminian nature may be described in terms which express the tendency to superficiality of all Air types, the key words being restless, impatient, unstable, superficial, lacking in concentration, inconsistent and diffused. The type tends to remain (at worst) childish and immature and (at best) retains its youthful mentality and physical appearance. Gemini is ruled by the planet Mercury.

Gems   See BIRTH STONES.

Genethliacal astrology   A term derived from the Greek and applied in general to natal astrology, which deals with the casting and interpretation of personal charts for the moment of birth.

Genii   In the Gnostic hierarchies the genii are the ranks of Angels. In Arabic lore the genii are the *jinn*. See GENIUS.

Geniture   A term used both to denote a personal horoscope and (incorrectly) the interpretation of the same.

Genius   In Assyro-Babylonian demonology the genii or *jinn* were demons, sometimes called the *utukku*, who participated closely in the everyday life of humans, although they themselves were invisible and superhuman. Good *jinn* were called *shedu* or *lamassu* and would act as guardians (although they required propitiatory rites). Evil

jinn, called *edimmu*, were said to be the souls of the dead who had not been properly buried. See AGATHODAEMON, which may be translated 'good spirit' or 'good genius'.

Geomancy   The name given to any system of constructing a predictive figure according to the rules of earth magic. In practice geomancy nowadays is a matter of making such predictions by means of stones, or indeed any inorganic material, such as twigs, in order to select from a possible sixteen figures (see Table 16) a certain configuration, which is then subject to interpretation by a series of fixed rules. Of late, due to an ignorance of historical terminologies, the word 'geomancy' has been misused, and applied to the study of telluric forces, the so-called ley lines (invisible earth currents) which have nothing to do with the predictive art of geomancy (see FENG-SHUI). Geomancy proper was originally unrelated to astrology and was limited to consideration of the sixteen basic figures in a simple formal pattern. Eventually, however, the simple geomatic method was rendered complex by permitting an influx of astrological ideas, such as

Figure 36   *The medieval image of the Moon shows the two lunar geomantic figures – 'Via' and 'Populus' – on either side of the goddess's head (drawing after an astrological manuscript by Michael Scot in the Bodleian Library)*

Table 16

Geomantic figure and name	Element	Planet	Zodiacal sign
Via – Way	Water	Moon	Leo
Populus – People	Water	Moon	Capricorn
Coniunctio – Joining	Air	Mercury	Virgo
Carcer – Prison	Earth	Saturn	Pisces
Fortuna major – Greater good	Earth	Sun	Aquarius
Fortuna minor – Less good	Fire	Sun	Taurus
Acquisitio – Gain	Air	Jupiter	Aries
Amissio – Loss	Fire	Venus	Libra
Loetitia – Joy	Air	Jupiter	Taurus
Tristitia – Sadness	Earth	Saturn	Scorpio
Puella – Girl	Water	Venus	Libra
Puer – Boy	Fire	Mars	Aries
Albus – White	Water	Mercury	Cancer
Rubeus – Red	Fire	Mars	Gemini
Caput – Head	Earth	Caput	Virgo
Cauda – Tail	Fire	Cauda	Sagittarius

the doctrines of elements, aspects, planetary rulerships, houses and signs, into a divinatory system to which they did not properly belong. As a predictive method geomancy is therefore only peripherally connected with astrology, and then only because the early practitioners of the art in medieval Europe chose to introduce a system of recording the results of divination within a chart which resembled the horoscope figure and which brought to the system a series of associations derived from astrological lore. The personification of the Moon in Figure 36 illustrates the double rule which this planet is supposed to have over the geomantic figures 'Via' and 'Populus', symbolized on either side of the woman's face. Table 16 sets out the traditional nomenclature and astrological associations. See also GEOMANTIC CHARACTERS.

Geomantic characters   A term used to denote a series of SIGILS each derived from a graphic play with one of the basic figures of GEOMANCY, as set out in the tabular form of Figure 37.

Germ-thread   See PRANA.

Ghost   A term probably from the Middle English *gaest* (perhaps meaning something like 'anger') and applied to a variety of different ideas. A ghost is an incorporeal being, but sometimes it is also an evil spirit, so that the word 'ghost' may sometimes refer to a DEMON. The term is also used to denote the incorporeal appearance of a dead person, or a spectre or apparition. The modern term 'ghostology' is really concerned only with the word in its last sense and was probably designed to distinguish it from the study of evil spirits (properly 'demonology').

Figure 37   *Geomantic characters: on either side are the geomantic characters with their associated planets on the right. In the centre are the geomantic characters which are derived from the individual figures (nineteenth century, after Barrett)*

99

Ghoul A word said to come from the Arabian *ghul* (to seize) and used to denote an evil spirit, reputed to haunt graveyards and to gain sustenance from human remains.

Gibborim The name given to the giants who are said to have lived on earth during the epoch of ATLANTIS. See also RAKSHASAS.

Glastonbury Scripts A general name given to a series of manuscripts produced through AUTO-MATIC WRITING between 1907 and 1912, under the guidance of F. B. Bond, with specific regard to the restoration of Glastonbury Abbey. Bond was the medium, although not the amanuensis, during the seances, and the discarnate agencies claiming to be former monks of the thirteenth to the fifteenth centuries were the spirits producing the scripts. Many details concerning the dissolution of the monastery, seemingly known only to the spirit world, were revealed to Bond and later verified by him. In the last series of scripts appeared accurate prophecies relating to the coming and ending of the Great War.

Glastonbury zodiac The name given to a supposed earth zodiac, contained within a circle of about 9 miles in diameter, with Butleigh (Somerset) at the centre and Glastonbury Tor to north-northwest of the circle. The figures were originally traced out by Maltwood (after whom the zodiac is sometimes named) in the 1920s. In the sixteenth century the scholar John Dee had mentioned the existence of a zodiac in or around Glastonbury, but his descriptions are vague and there is no evidence that this so-called Dee Zodiac corresponds to the Glastonbury zodiac. The images (which do not in every case correspond to either zodiacal or constellational images) are supposed to be traced out in landscape contours, roads, earthworks, rivers, pools and other 'natural' formations. Sometimes called the Somerset Giants, their antiquity is (unconvincingly) claimed to have been derived from initiate knowledge brought to Britain by Sumer–Chaldean priests. The supposed zodiac, whatever it is, is certainly not Chaldean, and the images portrayed by Maltwood are not zodiacal, but constellational.

Glasyalabolas One of the seventy-two SPIRITS OF SOLOMON. He is said to appear as a winged dog and, in addition to teaching all sciences, will cause murder.

Glauneck The name of one of the demons of the GRIMOIRES.

Globe period In the Theosophical cosmo-conception the period of time during which any of the GLOBES in a CHAIN is fully active (which is to say, supportive of the main stream of life) is called a 'globe period'. The passage of such life support through all the seven globes of a particular chain is called a 'round', a septenary of rounds make up one chain period, and seven chain periods (that is, 343 globe periods or forty-nine rounds) make up what is called a single SCHEME OF EVOLUTION. In any specific globe round seven ROOT RACES are said to be born, attain fulfilment and pass away.

Globe round See GLOBE PERIOD.

Globes In the Theosophical cosmoconception the Earth and the planets are called globes. However, each individual globe is said to possess a counterpart, often described in terms of graduations of finer substance than ordinary matter. A physical globe, such as our own Earth, for example, is regarded as the dense centre of seven interpenetrating worlds, each occupying the same space, yet all of different qualities of materiality. Such counterparts are approximately analogous to the invisible subtle sheaths which are said in occult circles to surround and interpenetrate the body of man (the so-called ASTRAL BODY, LOWER MENTAL, HIGHER MENTAL, BUDDHIC and so on). Not all the globes are regarded as being physically rooted, however. For example, the globes of our EARTH CHAIN consist of three physical globes, along with two astral and two mental globes.

Glyph A term often wrongly used as being synonymous with 'SIGIL', and one of the most misused of all occult terms – even the careful Blavatsky misuses it. The word 'glyph' has a proper application to relief symbols in sculptural and architectural forms, but not to written forms. Some glyphs have undoubtedly become sigils; for example, some of the bas-relief symbols on Egyptian tombs (properly glyphs) have become sigils by virtue of being translated to the written form on papyrus or paper. The modern sigil for the Sun ⊙ was once precisely such a glyph as the Egyptian determinate for 'god' and for 'time'; it became properly the sigil for the Sun in the fifteenth century AD, when it was adopted by Italian astrologers.

Gnomes The class of ELEMENTALS linked with the earth. They have many different names in popular lore, but two types of gnomes mentioned in esoteric lore are the Diemeae (the kind which live in large stones) and the Durdales (tree spirits). In certain of the astrological CALENDARIA MAGICA they are often called Pigmei.

Gnosis A Greek term meaning 'knowledge', but in occultism usually limited to the meaning 'knowledge obtained by initiation'. See GNOSTICISM.

Gnosticism A term derived from the Greek GNOSIS and applied to a large and varied syncretic literature and sect, which had roots in oriental, Zoroastrian and Platonic teachings and which were to some extent Christianized. The basic difference between doctrinal Christianity and Gnosticism lies in the concept of the nature of the material world. The Gnostics saw this world as being separate from God (even the creation of a demiurge) rather than as a manifestation of, and instrument of, his divine will. It was the surviving literature of the Gnostics that contributed most forcefully to the development of non-Judaic occultism in the West.

God-aspects A term used in Qabbalism in respect of the divine rulership over the SEPHIROTHIC TREE in the world of ATZILUTH.

Goetic Pertaining to that magic involving the evocation and binding of evil spirits to service on behalf of humans. See WITCHCRAFT.

Golden Age See FOUR AGES and KRITA YUGA.

Golden Number In astrology the term is applied to a method for determining the calendrical fall of the METONIC CYCLE by referring to a table of such cycles. In a non-astrological context the same term is also used of a ratio, the 'divine proportion' of the ancients, which results from the division of a line in such a way that the smaller part is in the same proportion to the greater part as that greater part is to the whole.

Golleb An adversary of the ARCHANGELS OF THE SEPHIROTH.

Gomory The only demon among the seventy-two SPIRITS OF SOLOMON to appear in the shape of a beautiful woman.

Grades of fire A term used by the alchemists for four different forms of fire, each related to the four elements – the Aerial of Air, the *Cineris* of Earth, the *Igne aperto* of Fire, and the *Balneum mariae* of Water. For the esoteric aspect of these grades, see FIRE ELEMENT.

Grand Grimoire The name given to a confused and fantastic collection of invocations, spells and elementary magic, supposedly from the pen of King Solomon, but almost certainly no older than the sixteenth century. The text varies from edition to edition, but (with indifferent spellings) the chief infernal spirits are given as Lucifer, Beelzebumb, Astaroth, Lucifuge, Satanachia, Agaliarept, Fleurety, Sargatanas and Nebiros. As Waite points out, it is in the first part of this work that the name LUCIFER, the 'light bearer', becomes Lucifuge, 'fleeing from light' – a name for a spiritual agency which has been adopted by almost all popular occultists since that time. The rather inconsequential, even polite, Satanism within the text has little foundation in real black magic and yet it has been accorded much importance by such magicians as Levi.

Grand Work A term used in ALCHEMY to denote the purpose of the art itself – the manufacture of the spagyric *Lapis*.

Great Breath The esoteric term for the 'eternal ceaseless motion'. Blavatsky, who defines Deity in terms of the motion from which the OCCULT TRINITY proceeds, derives the Greek *theos* from the verb 'to move'. See also OCCULT CATECHISM. The Great Breath is the fount of all individual consciousness and the source of pre-cosmic thought formation.

Great Dragon A term with a variety of applications in occult, esoteric and astrological contexts. In astrology the term is sometimes used in reference to the path of the Moon (or indeed to the sphere of the Moon) which, in its intersection of the ecliptic, gives the nodes, themselves named after the image of an encircling dragon (see DRA-GON'S HEAD) and often depicted as a scaled dragon. The term is also sometimes used in astro-logical contexts of the constellation Draco. In alchemy the reference is often to Time, as the great destroyer, frequently imaged as the OUROBOROS dragon, an image often found in esoteric astrological contexts. In occult thought, which touches upon modern esoteric astrology, the name is sometimes given to the dark Adver-sary Ahriman, who is often depicted as a scaled dragon under the feet of Michael. In spiritualist circles it is a term (first used by Davis) for a mysterious portion of the heavenly Summerland, inhabited by the morally deficient beings called DIAKKA. While apparently relating to very dif-ferent ideas within these several contexts, there is actually a unifying principle in this term, for the sphere of the Moon is traditionally linked with the diabolic postmortem existence (but see EIGHTH SPHERE). See also ASTRAL LIGHT.

Greater Benefic   See BENEFICS.

Greater Guardian   See GUARDIAN OF THE THRESHOLD.

Great Ilech   The hidden virtue in medicine, derived from the planets and stars.

Great Serpent   See ASTRAL LIGHT.

Great Year   Said by some authorities to be the period taken for all the planets to return to a given fiducial point. In medieval astrology and alchemy there is much argument as to how long this period is: Petarius, quoting classical sources, gives 350,635, but the theologian Conches gives 49,000. The former is probably nearer the mark. Some authorities confuse the Great Year with the platonic year of 25,920 years. See CYCLES.

Green lion   A term used in ALCHEMY for a stage in the spagyric operations, often symbolized in the image of a (green) lion swallowing the (golden) sun – as in Figure 38 – which is one of the root secrets in the manufacture of the PHILO-SOPHER'S STONE.

Grey Brothers   See BROTHERS OF THE SHADOW.

Grimaud pack   See TAROT.

Figure 38   *Green lion: the lion devouring the Sun, a standard alchemical image of a process in the manufacture of the Philosopher's Stone (sixteenth century)*

Grimoires   A general name given to a variety of texts setting out the names of demons, along with instructions for raising them to do the bidding of the magician or 'operator'. The *Grimorium Verum* lists seventeen of the names and characters of such spirits, each with its own particular field of inter-est: for example, Glauneck, who has power over riches and hidden treasures, Bechard, who has power over winds and tempests, and so on. This grimoire insists that the spirits are in truth invis-ible, but that they may borrow or manufacture a semi-tangible body to manifest themselves. It is up to the magician to ensure that they appear in forms which are not too hideous for human sight (see SPIRITS OF SOLOMON). The *Lesser Key of Solomon* (also called the *Lemegeton*) gives the names and sigils (characters) for seventy-two spirits. For example, Agares is a duke who rides a crocodile and carries a goshawk on his wrist; his main function is to stop runaways, teach languages, destroy spiritual and temporal digni-ties, and to cause earthquakes. Behemoth is a demon concerned with the pleasures of the belly with (according to de Plancy at least) the head of an elephant (Figure 39). Sytry is a great prince with a leopard's head; his function is to procure sex or love for the magician. Bune is a powerful duke with the heads of dog, griffin and man; his function is to change the place of burials and to answer all questions put to him by the magician. Astaroth is a powerful duke, appearing in the guise of an angel or a dragon, with a viper in his right hand. The magician must not permit him to approach because of the stench of his breath, and must protect himself with a special magical ring. Astaroth will answer truthfully about all manner of past, present and future questions. Similar grimoires are the GRAND GRIMOIRE, the HEPTAMERON, the *Enchiridion*, the *Grimorium Verum*, the *Grimoire of Honorius* and the *Key of Solomon*.

Grimorium Verum   See GRIMOIRES.

Group soul   According to occult doctrine, minerals, plants, bees, insects and animals are not ensouled by individual souls, stemming from a single MONAD (as are human beings), but receive their life force from what are called 'group souls'. The principle is that, from a large and undifferentiated matrix on the astral plane, a single ray is projected into a lower level of existence, as, for

Figure 39   Behemoth, demon of gluttony, as visualized in the grimoires (nineteenth century, after de Plancy)

example, into the body of an animal on the physical plane. This ray then proceeds to experience vibrations corresponding to that plane. At the death of that creature, instead of its soul retaining any individualized capability as an independent being, it is absorbed back into the collective undifferentiated matrix from which it arose. There are vast numbers of different group souls, each forming different types of minerals, plants and animals, and seemingly capable of splitting to encourage diversification on the earth plane. Thus, wolves, foxes, jackals and dogs are what are now differentiated group souls of what was originally one single group soul. As fission and experience of materialization develops, the specialization which results leads to a single group soul informing only one animal body, and what occultists call 'individualization' is established. In this way animal incarnations may result in the creation of 'spirits' which in a distant future age may be prepared for human existence. At the present time only a few animals are capable of such individualization – the cat, the dog, the monkey, the elephant and the horse. Premature individualization is not necessarily a good thing, however, for the keynote of evolution is natural growth. It is really only the human being who is capable of speeding up his or her own evolution by means of disciplines and meditative practices.

Grylli   See AMULET.

Guardian angel   The name given in popular theology to the personal angel who is the tutelary spirit of each human being. In esotericism it is recognized that this rank of celestial hierarchies act as guardians to humans through incarnation to incarnation (normally remaining with the same individual throughout the entire period of the earth evolution) – see ANGELS. In occult lore the guardian angel is sometimes called the 'flaga'.

Guardian of the Threshold   A name given by occultists to the demonic entity which stands on the threshold of the spiritual world and prevents the incarnate human from entering that world, without the human meets specific demands. This guardian is a sort of embodiment of the karmic debt which the human has to repay, a composite record of all the failures and errors of preceding incarnations. There is a sense therefore, in which each human being is himself the Guardian of the Threshold, with his failures externalized or objectivized into this awesome figure of demonic nature. It is a tenet of all forms of occultism that man cannot fully enter into the spiritual world with objective consciousness until he has passed the Guardian of the Threshold, which might normally be done only by means of trials and spiritual disciplines. Some occultists distinguish between the Lesser Guardian, which is this objectified karmic debt, encountered at a certain state of enlightenment or spiritual development, and the Greater Guardian, which is the ideal form of man's own being, the divine prototype of his higher self, freed of such debt. The Lesser Guardian must not be confused with the GUARDIAN ANGEL.

Guardian wall   A term used to denote the protective and invisible power built around the earth by the conscious activity of initiates and adepts, to protect humanity. It is not to be confused with the GUARDIAN OF THE THRESHOLD.

Gunas   Sometimes the TRIGUNAS, Sanskrit terms relating to the triune division of the qualities of matter. They are *rajas, sattva* and *tamas.*

Guru   A Sanskrit term meaning 'teacher'. See MAHATMA.

Gurudeva   A Sanskrit term meaning 'divine master'.

Gusayn   One of the variant names for GUSION.

Gusion   Sometimes Gusayn, one of the seventy-two SPIRITS OF SOLOMON. He is said to have the power to foretell the future and to make those inimical towards the conjurer friendly.

Gyromancy   Said to be a method of divination in which the diviner walks around a circle of letters until he is too giddy to continue; the letters against which he stumbles are supposed to spell out a prophetic message.

The eighth letter of the alphabet. The associated Semitic letter Heth, like the Runic Haegl, has two crossbars and is reasonably claimed to be a vestigial drawing of a fence. Blavatsky says that it is linked with Venus, and with 'opening or womb'; its occult number is therefore the Venusian FIVE. This connection may be derived from the fact that the H is often linked with E in aspiration (see E), and in the occult theory of numbers sound is more important than orthography.

Haborym   One of the variant names for AINI.

Hades   Name given to one of the HYPOTHETICAL PLANETS. Hades (or Aides) was the Greek equivalent of Purgatory (not of HELL, as is popularly believed).

Hagenti   One of the seventy-two SPIRITS OF SOLOMON. He is said to appear in the form of a bull with wings, reminding one of the Babylonian gate guardian. His demonic speciality is the alchemical transmutation of matter.

Hagiel   Name given by Agrippa (quoting ancient Qabbalistic sources) to the Intelligency of Venus.

Hall   A term adopted by Blavatsky as a metaphor for states of being. The Hall of Ignorance is the state on the physical plane, the Hall of Learning is the state on the ASTRAL plane, while the Hall of Wisdom is that on the causal plane, where experiences from various incarnations are gathered and eternally stored.

Hallucination   Popularly defined as a 'false perception' of more or less sensory intensity, seemingly arising without a corresponding stimulus of sense impression. In fact the majority of hallucinations are not in any sense 'false', and in the majority of cases there is an actual stimulus – it is a question of the stimulus arising from realms with which the recipient is not familiar. If a clairvoyant penetrates into the etheric or astral worlds, he or she will be more or less familiar with the strange entities that may be seen on that plane. If, however, an ordinary, untrained person penetrates into those realms, he will experience things well beyond the confines of his ordinary perceptive range. Such a person may be said to be suffering from hallucination, especially so if he attempts to describe to someone unfamiliar with the higher planes the entities he can see, or if he acts as though these entities have a validity independent of these planes. Such images (hallucinations) are 'real' in every sense of the word, although the normal human organism is protected from seeing them by virtue of the peculiar construction of the higher spiritual bodies which inform the physical body. Drugs, alcohol and will-forces may temporarily or permanently disturb this natural balance or protection and permit entities of an extremely low evolutionary level to make themselves known to the individual. This in turn increases the disposition to take drugs. The ordinary 'sick' or psychologically disturbed individual (victim) has no control over which of the astral entities may manifest to him. In contrast, an adept, using ancient methods of control, may work on the same astral plane with a power which makes it possible for him to choose which 'hallucinations' he may investigate or use; he is free to pick and choose among the vast store of images within the seemingly boundless astral plane. It is this distinction between a victim and an adept which distinguishes between results attained by drug-taking and results attained by conscious meditative praxes and moral disciplines. The realms explored are much the same (although usually the levels explored are different), but the methods differ.

Halomancy   See ALOMANCY.

Halpas   One of the seventy-two SPIRITS OF SOLOMON. He is said to appear as a dove.

Hansa   Sometimes Hamsa or Ansa, a swan or goose of oriental mysticism which is associated by most modern occultists with the pelican of the Rosicrucians. It is a symbol of the highest spiritual being (sometimes called the *Parabrahman*, the Sanskrit equivalent of the unnamed AIN SOPH) which, unsullied by contact with the material plane, will descend in part into incarnation, returning from the experience unsullied. The Sanskrit term *kalahansa* is said to mean 'the bird out of space and time'. Blavatsky says that the word 'Aum' (see OM) is linked with the *kalahansa*, the A being the right wing of the bird, the U its left wing, and the M its tail. The half meter of the sound is said to represent its head. See also KALAVINGKA.

Harmonics   In astrology a term applied to an entirely new form of astrological research and interpretation, based on statistical methods originally (at least) connected with numerological theory. The theory to which the now extensive literature of harmonics relates is largely derived from the researches of the astrologer Addey, stemming from a seemingly indefatigable application of statistically derived astrological data.

Harmony of the Spheres   See MUSIC OF THE SPHERES.

Haruspex   The Latin name for a diviner, originally derived from the Etruscan method of divination which involved the foretelling of future events from an examination of the entrails of slaughtered animals. The word may have been derived from the Sanskrit root *hira* ('entrails'). A synonymous term is 'extispicy'.

Hasmodai   A name given by Agrippa (quoting ancient Qabbalistic sources) to the 'daimon' of the Moon.

Hatha-Yoga   The system of oriental meditations and praxes concerned with manipulating the body in order to achieve specific inner states.

Healing   See CHIROTHESY.

Heart chakra   See ANAHATA.

Heart doctrine   The esoteric school of Buddha's doctrine was called the 'Heart'. The exoteric school was called the 'Eye'.

Heaven   A word of disputed etymology (Old english *heben* or *hefen*) referring to the habitation of God and the CELESTIAL HIERARCHIES, called in modern occultism DEVACHAN. See also EMPYREAN.

Heavenly man   See ADAM KADMON.

Heliacal rising   The first rising of a star after its period of invisibility due to conjunction with the Sun.

Heliacal setting   The last setting of a star prior to its period of invisibility due to conjunction with the Sun.

Heliocentric astrology   Heliocentric astrology is founded on the calculation and interpretation of charts cast from an imaginary viewpoint of an observer in the centre of the Sun. Since the ZODIAC proper is based upon a point calculated in geocentric terms, heliocentric astrology tends to postulate and rely upon a constellational zodiac in which there appears to be no precise consensus as to the limits of the twelve asterisms. The heliocentric chart differs considerably from the geocentric equivalent, as the Sun itself is absent and there is no system of houses, no Ascendant, and no Moon (as this is incorporated in the orb of the Earth). Thus the three fundamental influences of the normal horoscope figure – Sun, Moon and Ascendant – are missing. Heliocentric astrologers place great emphasis on planetary nodes and the axes arising from these, as well as upon heliocentric ASPECTS.

Helioedes   See SUBTLE BODY.

Heliophobe   Name given to a type of DEMON.

Helios   The Greek astrological term for the Sun, but see APOLLO.

Hell A term cognate with 'hole' and 'hollow', formed from the Anglo-Saxon *helan* (to hide), implying a dark or hidden place and in a general sense now applied to some sort of final place of torment after death. In most theological interpretations Hell is given as a translation of the Greek Hades, the Hebraic Sheol and Hinnom (or Gehenna), although changes in the concept of Hell require that the word should be used as an equivalent only of the last term. Hades and Sheol were shadow lands, in which the shades of the human dead wandered. The Babylonians designated this place of the dead as 'the country whence none return', locating it within the planetary spheres. This location corresponds roughly to the occult view, for Hell is located in the lowest of the seven planetary spheres (see EIGHTH SPHERE). This Hell of occultism really corresponds to the PURGATORY of theology, however, for the soul is not condemned to remain within its domain for ever, but only until its sins have been purged. A system of beliefs such as that which the occultists accept as valid involves the idea of reincarnation, which in itself must reject the idea of a permanent Hell. In fact, the very idea of an eternal Hell, as an everlasting Hell, is based on a misunderstanding of the meaning of the word 'eternal' in ancient texts; 'eternal' merely meant 'outside time' and had nothing to do with prolongation of time or even with temporal sequence. Occultists actually take issue with all the attached concepts of the theologial Hell, as a place of eternal punishment, as a limbo for infants, and as a pre-Christian limbo. Within the occult framework there is no place of eternal damnation, and Blavatsky quite rightly dismisses the idea of a hot Hell as 'an afterthought, the distortion of an astronomical allegory'. Within the occult terminology Purgatory is a result of the internal fire of guilt produced contemporaneously with any sin – the sin is indulged in this present life, but its purgatorial equivalent is not experienced until after death. The Purgatory of modern occultism is called KAMALOKA, itself linked with the sphere of the Moon. For an account of demons, see INFERNAL HIERARCHIES.

Heptameron The title of a book dealing with the invocation of spirits in the style of the GRIMOIRES, with a second part touching upon elementary magical praxes, such as the secrets of hidden things, love procuration and the conveyance of evil thoughts. The first part of the text is supposed to be by the Italian magician-astrologer Peter of Abano, although it was certainly not written before the fourteenth century.

Hercules The name given by the astrologer Wemyss to one of the HYPOTHETICAL PLANETS. Also the name of one of the CONSTELLATIONS.

Hermann Prophecies A series of prophecies, first printed about 1722, as allegedly the work of a monk called Hermann. These consisted of a hundred sentences of a predictive nature and gained much popularity in France (especially in the First World War) as they prophesied the eventual downfall of Germany and the Hohenzollern, and the redistribution of German lands.

Hermes One of the names given to Mercury in Graeco-Roman astrology. Hermes was the son of Zeus and Maia, and messenger of the gods, his winged feet being a symbol of this function, his staff (see CADUCEUS) an emblem of his ability to interpenetrate the realm of man. Hermes is also the name given to one of the HYPOTHETICAL PLANETS in the system proposed by the Dutch astrologer Ram, accorded rule over zodiacal Gemini. The same name was also used of a hypothetical planet by Thierens. See also TRISMEGISTUS, who is sometimes called Hermes.

Hermetic This term was probably derived from the name Hermes Trismegistus, the Egyptian Thoth, who gave us the so-called HERMETIC CANON of secret texts. The word has long been used to denote the occult sciences in general, especially the alchemical branch, as well as esoteric lore. The fact that the ancient esoteric mysteries were protected by a vow of silence probably gave rise to the modern use of the word 'hermetic' to mean 'sealed off' or 'airtight'.

Hermetic canon Sometimes Hermetica, Hermaica and Trismegistian literature, a body of work supposedly written by the legendary TRISMEGISTUS. Cyril of Alexandria writes of fifteen books within this canon, but, while the initiate–author was supposed to have lived prior to Moses, the style of the surviving work points only to the post-Christian Alexandrian school of esotericism. The most influential book from the canon is the POEMANDRES.

Hermetic Mercury The mercurial forces linked with planetary Mercury in hermetic lore is something different from that associated with ordinary Mercury – that is, with the Mercury of the non-esoteric astrological forms. It is termed 'Permanent Water' and 'Vitalizing Spirit', and is linked with the quintessential forces of the world. Often the magical symbol for the SEAL OF SOLOMON is drawn with the sigil for Mercury in the central space, to link it with the Quintessence, and so placed it is no longer the ordinary exoteric Mercury. For Qabbalistic connections, see HOD, but see also MERCURIUS and THREE PRINCIPLES. Many of the esoteric names for this planet suggest the idea of liquid, a symbolic form for the quintessence of etheric forces – the Blessed Water, Virtuous Water, Philosopher's Vinegar, Dew of Heaven, Virgin's Milk and so on. Esoterically, the power of this hermetic Mercury is a unifier in the human being, bringing into harmony the polarity of thinking (imaged as Salt) and the will-life (imaged as Sulphur). Sometimes the thinking element in man is symbolized by POSITIVE MARS and the will-life by NEGATIVE MARS (the former ruling Aries, which in turn rules the head of the human being; the latter ruling Scorpio, which in turn rules the sexual parts of the human being). Without the unifying control of hermetic Mercury, these two polarities would run riot in the life of man.

Hermetic rule Sometimes called the Trutine of Hermes, a general law sometimes used in astrology, derived from the supposition that the Moon of a given natal chart is on the degree of either the Ascendant or the Descendant of the conception chart, while the Ascendant of the conception chart marks the same degree as the Moon of the natal chart.

Herschel See URANUS.

Hesperus One of the names given to the planet Venus, as the Evening Star. See also LUCIFER.

Hexagram In the Chinese divinatory system of the I CHING, a name given to a six-line figure made from two TRIGRAMS. Within this figure the Chinese diviner will trace a second pair of trigrams, called the NUCLEAR TRIGRAMS. The hexagram, its basic and nuclear trigrams, and the associations drawn between these three elements are combined by the diviner to give responses to questions. Sometimes a consultation of the classical text of the *I Ching* is also resorted to. The sixty-four hexagrams of the Chinese canon are given in Figure 40.

Hierarchies See CELESTIAL HIERARCHIES.

Hieroglyphic In a specialist occult sense a name given to spiritual symbols appearing in seances, which the American clairvoyant Davis interpreted as 'friendly messages' from the spirit realm. See, however, GLYPH.

Hieroglyphic Monad See MONAS HIEROGLYPHICA.

Hierophant A term from the Greek meaning literally 'one who explains sacred things', and applied to the highest adepts responsible for teaching the Mysteries.

Higher Manas See MANAS.

Higher self A name used in modern esotericism for the ATMA, sometimes for the MANAS. See TERNARY.

Higher ternary See TERNARY.

Higher triad A term sometimes used in popular occultism to denote the higher nature of the human constitution, consisting of ATMA, BUDHI and MANAS. In popular occultism the three are sometimes grouped together under the term 'EGO', but in esoteric centres the Ego is the link between the higher triad (the TERNARY) and the lower ternary of ASTRAL, ETHERIC and physical.

Hindu zodiac From very ancient times the Hindu astrologers have distinguished between the tropical and sidereal zodiacs, wisely providing different names for the two systems. The Sanskrit terms for the two have been given in different ways, but Table 17 sets out the correspondences given in the Theosophical literature. These names have become important to European occultism because of the profound influence of Theosophy on modern esoteric thought. The Theosophical

Figure 40 (opposite): *The sixty-four hexagrams, from* Khien *to* Wei Chi *(after Legge)*

8	7	6	5	4	3	2	1
pî	sze	sung	hsü	măng	*k*un	khwăn	*kh*ien

16	15	14	13	12	11	10	9
yü	*kh*ien	tâ yû	thung zăn	phî	thâi	lî	hsiâo *kh*û

24	23	22	21	20	19	18	17
fû	po	pî	shih ho	kwân	lin	kû	sui

32	31	30	29	28	27	26	25
hăng	hsien	lî	khan	tâ kwo	î	tâ *kh*û	wû wang

40	39	38	37	36	35	34	33
*k*ieh	*k*ien	khwei	*k*iâ zăn	ming î	ǯin	tâ *k*wang	thun

48	47	46	45	44	43	42	41
ǯing	khwăn	shăng	ǯhui	kâu	kwâi	yî	sun

56	55	54	53	52	51	50	49
lü	făng	kwei mei	*k*ien	kăn	*k*ăn	ting	ko

64	63	62	61	60	59	58	57
wei ǯî	*k*î ǯî	hsiâo kwo	*k*ung fû	*k*ieh	hwân	tui	sun

concepts were often couched in Sanskrit and oriental terminologies.

Table 17

Western name	Hindu tropical	Hindu sidereal
Aries	Mesham, Maish	Acvini
Taurus	Rishabham, Vrishab	Krttika, Krittika
Gemini	Mithunam, Mithun	Mrgacirsha, Mrigasitas
Cancer	Karkatakam, Karka	Punarvasu
Leo	Simham, Simha	Magha
Virgo	Kanya	Phalguni
Libra	Tula, Tulam	Citra
Scorpio, Scorpius	Vrishikam, Vrishchik	Vicakha
Sagittarius	Dhanus, Dhanu	Mula
Capricorn(us)	Makaram, Makar	Ashada, Ashadha
Aquarius	Kumbham, Kumbh	Dhanishta, Cravishta
Pisces	Meenam, Meena, Minam	Bhadzapada, Bhadrapada

Hippomancy   A method of predicting the future from the movements of horses.

Hismael   Name given by Agrippa (quoting ancient Qabbalistic sources) to the daimon of Jupiter, for whom he gives the magical number 136. See IOPHIEL.

Hochmah   Another version of CHOKMAH.

Hod   The name given to the eighth Sephirah of the SEPHIROTHIC TREE, the word usually translated as meaning 'splendour' or 'renown'. In the World of Expression (ASSIAH) it is ruled by Mercury, who is tutelary of the art of living in the material realm – the true spagyric art of the hermetic science. In the World of formations (YETZIRAH) the Angels of Hod are the Beni-Elohim, the Sons of God, who encourage a unity of mind and soul – Yetzirah tending to give more attention to the former than the latter. In the realm of BRIAH, which is the World of Creation, the Sephirah is protected by RAPHAEL, the Mercurial Archangel, a healer of injuries (specifically injuries of the soul, since Briah deals with the soul element in man). In the highest World of Origins, the realm of ATZILUTH, Hod is linked with the God-aspect Elohim Sabaoth, the feminine divine in every created individual, in which the androgyne nature of Mercury (the esoteric planet of Hod) finds its real completion.

Holy Flame   An oriental name for the ANIMA MUNDI. Initiates are sometimes called Sons of the Holy Flame.

Homer's Golden Chain   A name given to a series of ten sigils, usually depicted as connected in a chain (the *Aurea catena Homeri*), linked with an alchemical notion of progression from the receptivity of Chaos to the perfect consummation of the universal QUINTESSENCE.

Honorius   The name of a GRIMOIRE which has been described by Waite as the 'most frankly diabolical of all the Rituals concerned with Black Magic'. The oldest exant copy is Italian, dated 1670. One of the rituals requires the slaughter of a black cock, the tearing out of its eyes, tongue and heart.

Horary astrology   The astrological art of interpreting specific questions in terms of a chart erected for the moment when the question is formulated.

Horoscope   In modern astrology the word 'horoscope' is used to denote the symbolic figure of the heavens, the chart, sometimes indeed called

Figure 41   *The birth horoscope for the German poet Goethe, who was born on 28 August 1749. The outer concentric circle contains the signs marking the angles and the intermediate houses, while the inner concentric contains the planetary placings*

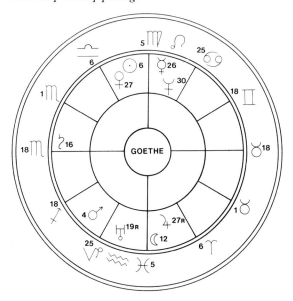

the horoscope figure or the horoscope chart, of which Figure 41 is an example. Until the eighteenth century the word 'horoscope' was frequently used to denote also the ASCENDANT degree, the *horoscopos* of the Roman and medieval astrologers.

Horoscopos See HOROSCOPE.

Horus Name given to one of the HYPOTHETICAL PLANETS by Thierens.

Hot See FOUR QUALITIES and PRINCIPLES.

House of Death Traditional astrology uses this unfortunate term for the eighth house of the horoscope figure, because of its link with the NEGATIVE MARS of Scorpio. The matter dealt with in the eighth house is related more to the regeneration principle than to death (which is merely the ultimate experience of regeneration).

Houses In astrology the traditional horoscope figure is divided into twelve arcs, which are symbolically presented as being equal either in a spatial system or in a time system. This division is superimposed upon the projected celestial sphere, with the symbolic horizon line (usually) marking the cusps of the first and seventh houses (the east point and west point, respectively). The tenth house cusp marks the symbolic zenith, called the *Medium coeli*, while the fourth house cusp marks the symbolic nadir, called the *Imum coeli*.

Human artificial An astral entity formed from the ELEMENTAL ESSENCE by the conscious thought of a human – usually a black magician – and invested with a life of its own, with some specific purpose in view. Leadbeater claims that many of the materializations of the nineteenth century were human artificials.

Human ascent See DEVIC ASCENT.

Humours A conception of a tetrad of bodily fluids which were recognized as influencing the disposition (later itself the 'humour') of a person, through excess or deficiency. The four humours were Phlegma, Black Bile, Yellow Bile and Blood. These humours were dominated by a theory which held that certain excesses or deficiencies produced illness (physical or psychological). A man could be said to be 'out of humour'

through lack of a bodily fluid. This theory – called the perisomata theory – eventually led to the development of the conception of the TEMPERAMENTS which were associated with each of the four humours, the modern names being derivations from the Greek. The four humours are linked with the FOUR ELEMENTS, as set out in Table 18.

Table 18

Humour	Temperament	Element
Yellow Bile	Choleric	Fire
Blood	Sanguine	Air
Phlegma	Phlegmatic	Water
Black Bile	Melancholic	Earth

Huna A Polynesian word meaning 'secret'. See KAHUNA.

Hunting the Moon A phrase used by astrologers to denote an ASPECT of 90 degrees (square) between Saturn and the Moon, which is said by some to be the most baneful aspect cast by the planets.

Hutriel 'Rod of God', the name of one of the seven Angels of Punishment.

Hydromancy A name given to a large number of different methods of predicting the future by means of water. Such were popular techniques in ancient times, and Psellus writes of one practised with a basin full of water which, at the behest of the diviner, is activated by spirits in order to vibrate to a point where it appears to boil and give off meaningful sounds. It has been suggested that Nostradamus used such a technique in the production of his famous CENTURIES of predictive verse. Another technique, recorded by Augustine, says that the diviner could see reflected in the water the forms of spirits; he mentions that when blood is used instead of water it is possible to conjure the shades of the dead from the Underworld – the true SCIOMANCY. However, Augustine wrongly records that this latter technique is called necromancy. Methods of disturbing water (by means of suspended rings or by means of pebbles being dropped into the bowl) are also described as legitimate hydromantic techniques, and some diviners are supposed to read from the reflections on the surface or from the colour of water, as well as from the movement of water in fountains.

Hyleg In astrology a term derived from the Arabian astrological system and used of a planet which (by virtue of its position in a special mundane arc) is regarded as the giver or sustainer of life, the APHETA.

Hyperborean In occultism the term 'Hyperborean' is used to denote a now lost continent (located in the present wastes around the North Pole and the northern parts of Asia) which in the distant past knew no winter. It was the ancient land of the gods, the name being given to the second continent (and associated race of humans) preceding that of LEMURIA. In classical mythology the Hyperboreans were the ancestors of the gigantic Titans, but in the esoteric lore these mighty beings did not incarnate into physical bodies in the way of modern man. The one-eyed Cyclop giants may be seen as racial memories of these beings, who had a developed inner vision now associated with the central Third Eye of clairvoyance.

Hypnosis The name given to a technique for inducing a state of dislocated consciousness, somewhat resembling sleep, but accompanied by a heightened state of sensitivity to suggestion and ordinary stimuli. Properly speaking, hypnosis is not a phenomenon which is occult in any sense of the word. Most modern occultists would recognize the techniques of hypnosis – designed as they are to permit the will of one person to override the will of another – as belonging to the LEFT-HAND PATH, and as a promulgator of undisciplined HALLUCINATION. However, popular misconceptions have undoubtedly linked hypnosis with occultism, and the subject must be touched upon in this present context.

Hypnosis is regarded by esotericists and occultists as distinctly harmful, as a sort of spiritual murder, in that it displaces or dislocates the normal relationship between the upper TERNARY and the LOWER QUATERNARY of anyone who is subject to being hypnotized. It is for this reason that Blavatsky speaks of it as 'the most dangerous of practices, morally and physically'. The seemingly beneficial effects that may be gained through hypnosis are counterbalanced by the less obvious effects on the spiritual plane. The psychic worker Myers was quite wrong (uninformed as he was about esoteric matters) to write of hypnotism as 'an empirical development of sleep'. Sleep is a natural union with the spiritual realms, whereas hypnotism is not. Occultists distinguish between hypnosis, or the state of ideoplasty as it is sometimes called in occult circles, and the seeming hypnosis of the mediumistic TRANCE.

Hypnotism was at one time called 'braidism' or 'mesmerism' after early practitioners. Mesmerism, which involved the use of what was then called ANIMAL MAGNETISM, was developed by Mesmer from about 1770 onwards, but the techniques of ideoplastic hypnosis were not officially recognized by the British Medical Association as 'genuine and theurgic' until over a hundred years later, even though Esdale had shown at the beginning of the nineteenth century that operations might be painlessly and successfully performed on subjects by means of mesmerism. Hypnotism, animal magnetism and mesmerism are often confused by the layman but, as Boirac says, 'they too much resemble each other's path not to betray a secret relationship'.

Hypothetical moon See LILITH.

Hypothetical planets Some astrologers have claimed the existence of a number of planets in our own solar system which are neither visible nor recognized by science, but which have been located (largely) by such psychic means as clairvoyance. Some astrologers have postulated the existence of over a thousand such planets, while Blavatsky claims that there are six ETHEREAL PLANETS. At least twenty-five of the more widely used hypotheticals have been described and listed in modern times.

I

The ninth letter of the alphabet, associated with the Hebraic Yod. Blavatsky points out quite rightly that in occultism the I is to be regarded as the equivalent of both 1 and 10, and as phallic. However, the significance of the 1 and 10 depends upon the upright being regarded as separative consciousness and the zero as the external world. What is important in the figure 10, therefore, is the space between the two units, and the contrast in their forms. The separation or alienation experienced by upright consciousness in the face of the entire world is really only expressed in TEN.

I Ching The name of a Chinese divinatory system, and the title of the sacred book used in this system. The title is usually translated as meaning *Book of Changes*, but the word *I* (sometimes *Y*, as in *Y King*) has connotations which are difficult to translate into European contexts. As a method of divination the *I Ching* involves the manipulation of fifty yarrow stalks according to a sequence of prescribed numerological and symbolic procedures. The result of such a manipulation is a hexagram, a six-lined figure composed of YIN AND YANG lines, the sequence of which is given in Figure 40 under HEXAGRAM. This hexagram is viewed in the first instance as a union of two three-lined figures each called a TRIGRAM, and in the second instance as a union of two interlinked trigrams call NUCLEAR TRIGRAMS. In classical Chinese consultation it is possible for the diviner to read the answers to specific questions from consideration of such a figure, and its transformation into other figures (according to prescribed laws), but it is also possible for the diviner to refer to a sequence of texts relating to each of the hexagrams within the corpus of the *Book of Changes* itself.

In the West the system of the *I Ching* has been partly misunderstood, and instead of relying on direct interpretation of the figures (which requires considerable knowledge of both Chinese and Chinese symbolism) there is an undue reliance upon the text of the *Book of Changes* itself.

However, the evidence is that the text used for interpretation (unlike the important commentaries within the book as a whole) were really case histories, or records of responses to specific questions which are not really applicable to other questions which have given rise to a similar figure. Another tendency in the West, due largely to the popularization of the method by Wilhelm (whose translation leaves a great deal to be desired), is that operators use three coins instead of manipulating sticks in response to questions. Some Chinese specialists warn against the use of coins, however, as being both disrespectful to the spirits who control this divinatory method and ultimately destructive of the divining faculty itself.

Iatric Strictly speaking, 'itatric' means 'medical', from an equivalent Greek word, but the term is often used in various combinations to link occult subjects with medical concepts and virtues of healing. For example, 'iatromatical' is often used to denote the practice of astrology in conjunction with healing praxes, and in former times 'iatrochemical' was used of certain alchemical praxes.

Iatromathematics A term used for that division of astrology concerned with medicine.

Ichthyomancy Divination from the movements of fish or, according to some accounts, from the inspection of the entrails of fish.

Iddhi   A Pali word sometimes used in Theosophy to denote the supranormal psychic faculties in man. It is said to be the equivalent of the Sanskrit SIDDHIS.

Ideoplast   There is some confusion in occultist circles over this word. Strictly speaking, anything 'ideoplastic' is moulded or modified by mental activity, and in ordinary usage the term may be applied to the human ability to shape mental images. A more specific use was suggested by Durand in 1855, to denote the unconscious reception of verbal suggestions in HYPNOSIS. Another use of the term is to denote the externalized manifestation of an etheric force (see ELEMENTAL ESSENCE) which may be sufficiently developed to resemble an independent living human being or animal. In this use it is related to ECTOPLASM.

Ideos   Paracelsus gives this word as the equivalent of the MYSTERIUM MAGNUM, in its sense of being primordial matter.

Idolomancy   Divination of the future from idols. In Roman times it was believed that certain idols would make movements to indicate oracular advice.

Igne aperto   See GRADES OF FIRE.

Ilech   A term from the Paracelsian thesaurus. The Great Ilech is the star of medicine, that is, the hidden principle or VIRTUE behind the medicinal element. It is the healing power (derived from the planets and stars) which we assimilate when we take medicine. The Supernatural Ilech is defined by Waite as 'the supercelestial conjunction and union of the stars of the firmament with the stars of things below'. It is, in other words, the name given to that subtle connection which the ancients insisted links all sublunary things with the celestial realm. Crude Ilech is said to be a composition of the three alchemical principles of Salt, Sulphur and Mercury, which represent (in the microcosm of man) the thinking, willing and feeling life respectively. The Paracelsian term is linked with the ILIASTER.

Iliaster   A term from medieval esoteric astrological lore (linked with alchemy), apparently originated by Paracelsus from the Greek word *hyle* ('matter') and *astrum* ('star' or the 'power of heavenly thing', in classical Latin). It is applied to that spiritual force in matter which strives towards perfection and towards the building of forms. It works against the CAGASTER.

Image   Many of the AMULETS derived from occult symbolism were even in medieval times called *imagines*, and as a result these are even now sometimes called 'images'. Paracelsus defines the 'science' of the image as that of representing the properties of heaven and 'impressing them' into the material realm. In the occult tradition the man-made (or, more appositely, magic-made) image is far more powerful than a natural SIGNATURE, for a 'like virtue is not found in any herbs'. See GAMALEI.

In astrology the word 'image' is properly applied to the pictorial symbols associated with the zodiacal constellations and signs. They must be distinguished from the SIGILS for the twelve signs. In Figure 42 there is a circular zodiac with each of the twelve signs as images; below the date of 1484 in the centre of the zodiac are the images for Pisces, Aries, Taurus and Gemini. In the outer part of the square in Figure 43, which is one of the forms used in medieval times for a horoscope chart, are the twelve sigils for the signs of the zodiac. At the top are the sigils for Taurus, Aries and Pisces. Figure 44 shows one of the images of Gemini, while the sigil for Gemini is ♊ .

Imagination   The occult view of imagination is far removed from the popular concept of 'fancy'. Blavatsky well defines it as 'one of the plastic powers of the Higher Soul . . . the memory of the preceding incarnations' (it is probably such a thing that Plato had in mind when he wrote of knowledge in terms of remembering). As a power it seems to be linked with the reading of the Akashic Chronicles (see AKASHA), which explains why the training of the imagination, through meditative disciplines, is one of the most important phases in the development of man in most occult systems. The occultist Steiner uses the word in a specialist sense, and says that 'imaginative cognition' is to be understood as the faculty of cognition that results from the soul having attained to a supersensible state of consciousness in a realm to which the ordinary senses have no access. This represents a preliminary stage of higher cognition.

Impersonation   In a specialist sense a term used to denote the state of a medium who is so controlled by the (supposed) spirit of a dead person

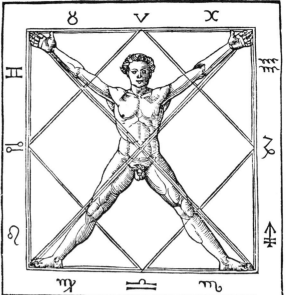

Figure 42 (left): *The zodiacal circle above the man contains the images of the twelve signs of the zodiac. These are not to be confused with the sigils for the signs, or with the constellations (after Albrecht Dürer)*

Figure 43 (above): *The sigils of the twelve signs are shown on the outer frame of the picture of cosmic man (after Agrippa's* Occulta Philosophia, *1531)*

Figure 44 (below): *The image of Gemini, the Twins (from a fifteenth-century translation of Albumasar)*

that he or she takes on a faithful imitation (impersonation) of gestures, voices, even an element of physical appearance, of the deceased. One of the (rare) results of impersonation is the strange phenomenon of ELONGATION.

Imum coeli In astrology a Latin term ('the lowest part of the heavens'), used to denote the point opposite the MEDIUM COELI. It is often wrongly applied to the cusp of the FOURTH HOUSE, which in many chart systems falls on the northern angle of the horoscope figure.

Incubus In popular lore a demon in male form which seeks intercourse with women, usually while they are sleeping. In romantic occultism it is an ELEMENTARY of the male sex, called into a shadowy existence on the earth by human lust and said to copulate with living women (usually at their behest). The incubus is sometimes called the 'spirit husband'. In non-occult circles the incubus is merely a name for a nightmare. The female equivalent is the SUCCUBUS.

Individuality The name given to the higher EGO, in contradistinction to the personality. See ESSENCE.

Individualization A term used to denote a more or less natural process by which humans, through their treatment of animals on the earth plane, induce in them a state of 'individuality' which is not proper to beings without an EGO. The soul element of an animal which has to some extent been individualized, by training or love, does not return completely to the GROUP SOUL to which the animal properly belongs, but takes on another existence which is in some respects advanced upon the group soul condition from which it is fragmented. Certain of the ELEMENTALS are said to be created in this way, by the action of human love on group souls. It is claimed by some occultists that only a few animals are presently capable of individualization – the dog, the cat, the horse, the elephant and the monkey.

Indwellers According to Blavatsky, a name given to the seven inner enemies of man, the seven capital sins – lust, hatred, avarice, ignorance, pride, envy and sloth.

Inferior planets In early astrology this term was applied to the planets below (inferior to) the Sun, in the concentrics of the SPHERES of the geocentric Ptolemaic system. Hence, the 'inferiors' were Venus and Mercury.

Infernal hierarchies There does not appear to be an official equivalent of the celestial or Dionysian hierarchies for the DEMONS, although several attempts have been made in both antiquity and relatively modern times to provide such a classification (see, for example, DEMONS). The orderly sequence of Purgatory and Hell presented in the vision of Dante suggests that a hierarchy of functions and specific rules does exist, yet Dante does not provide names for the various hierarchies. Most of the attempts to classify the diabolic hierarchies, or even to give names to individual demons, have been based on the communications with these entities themselves, who are notoriously dishonest and usually reluctant to give their names. Many names which have survived have been derived from conflicting reports in witch trials and from exorcisms, in which it was common for those suspected, as for those under intense forms of torture, to name demons involved in work against humanity and Church. In recent times the various garbled reports of pseudo-occultists and low-grade mediums who have obtained their material from spiritualistic seances (seemingly ignorant of what Davis himself wrote about DIAKKA) have added to the farrago of nonsense and the proliferation of demonic names.

The classical attempt to discuss demons and their operations is that of Psellus, although much of what he had to say about the infernal hierarchies through his *Dialogue* has been basically misunderstood by later commentators. Psellus describes a sexted of demons, but he by no means suggests that this is a complete classification. He lists the Lelirium (or Igneus), the Aerial, the Earthly and the Subterranean (or Terrestrial), the Aqueous and the Lucifugi (or Heliophobes), thus attempting a classification in terms of the localities and elemental natures of the demons. Yet even Psellus admits that there are many demons 'of every possible variety of figure and conformation, so that the air is full of them . . . the seas are full of them, and the lowest subterranean depths.' Classification and nomenclature for such vast hordes is obviously out of the question, and we find that Psellus is not the only demonologist to point to this. While all demons are 'haters of God' and the enemies of mankind, the Aqueous and

Subterranean are especially malignant, the Lucifugi worse, seeking not only to impair man's intellect by fantasy and illusions, but even to destroy his mind completely. The Aqueous will suffocate humans in water, while the Subterraneans and Lucifugi attempt to insinuate themselves in to the lungs of those they meet, in order to choke them or to render them epileptic and insane. The Aerial and Earthly work on many by attempting to instil material lusts and by deceiving the mind.

Contemporary European demonology has had various names and nomenclatures grafted upon it, but most of these are of dubious value and authenticity. The demons described by the Louviers nuns, *circa* 1630, are fairly typical of the kind: Putifar, Dagon, Leviathan, Ancitif, Arfaxat, Consangue, Crogade, Phaeton, Asmodeus and Calconix are of mixed heritage, some being ultimately Zoroastrian, others Greek, and the rest the product of derangement of a French-speaking individual. Robbins correctly points out that the list given by the nun Jeanne Fery, who named eight demons who tortured her after her seduction by the Devil (Traitre, Sanguinair and Homicide), reads almost like a clinical diagnosis of hysteria – unimaginative hysteria to boot.

Since it is the inclination of the demons to lie, and since the name is a power source in itself, all information about names and ranks given by the demons, or recorded by those who have had close encounters with demons, must be suspect. In spite of this the names provided by Sebastien Michaelis have passed into the bloodstream of demonology. This list includes the traditional demons, such as BEELZEBUB as Lord of the Flies (Figure 27 under DEMONS), down to fairly obvious and unimaginative inventions – but the point is that the information was supposedly derived from a demon who offered his own name as Balberith, who claimed to be merely one of a vast number of incredibly powerful demons inhabiting the body of poor Sister Madelaine.

More recently a degree of confusion has been added by such writers as Barrett and Collin de Plancy, who have shown themselves sufficiently influenced by demons to issue confused descriptions of an 'orderly' hierarchy of devils when it is certain that such an order would for very good reasons be hidden from man. Thus Barrett lists nine orders of demons, but is confused and unconvincing in his arguments, and when this demonic hierarchy is related to the numerous portraits of demons in the GRIMOIRES, we sense a disappointment both in the demons and Barrett alike.

Almost all the demons which might be termed 'classical' in terms of name or specific function are derived from one of the four pre-Christian cultures or religions – Zoroastrian, Buddhist, Egyptian and Hebraic. The prototypes of the most famous of all medieval demons, the male INCUBUS and the female SUCCUBUS, are found in pre-Christian demonologies, as are many of the different praxes involved with the EXORCISM of demons. Alphonsus de Spina named ten varieties of demons, partly Christian and partly pagan: the FATAE, poltergeists (such as Duende de Casa), incubi (and succubi in the same class), marching hosts, familiar demons (not to be confused with FAMILIARS), nightmare demons, a class which may only be called semen demons, deceptive demons, clean demons and a curious group called Bruxae or Xorguinae. Binsfeld associates seven of the more powerful demons with specific powers over the seven deadly sins (see, therefore, DEMONIC SINS).

The most comprehensive list of demonic names and functions – that given by Michaelis in 1612 – is an inverted hierarchy, a diabolic mirror image of the nine CELESTIAL HIERARCHIES, which are confronted by Christian saints rather than by the equivalent celestial hierarchies, as in the Qabbalistic demonologies (hinted at under SEPHIROTHIC TREE). The Michaelis list is set out in Table 19 (p. 118).

Before glancing briefly at the demonic pantheons which preceded the Christian and formed its tenuous hierarchies, it might be as well to observe that they all hold in common three different types of demons, of which only the higher two are really demons in the full meaning of the term. The first is the malignant type under the control of a supreme and evil 'prince', such as Beelzebub in the European tradition or Kingu in the Babylonian and Ahriman in the Zoroastrian. The second are those without personal names, operating under general class names, such as the *jinn* of the lower-quality elementars. The third are said to be born of human parentage, usually through immorality – either as a result of depraved emotions, malignant or uncontrolled thought formations or through insufficient attention to death rites. An example of this would be the PRETA, which is really a ghost, although often called a demon.

Table 19

Hierarchy of Fallen Angels		Name of demon	Saintly Adversary
First	Seraphim	Beelzebub	Francis
	Seraphim	Lucifer	John the Baptist
	Seraphim	Leviathan	Peter the Apostle
	Seraphim	Asmodeus	John the Baptist
	Cherubim	Balberith	Barnabas
	Thrones	Astaroth	Bartholomew
	Thrones	Verrine	Dominic
	Thrones	Cressil	Bernard
	Thrones	Sonneillon	Stephen
Second	Powers	Carreau	Vincent
	Powers	Carnivean	John the Evengelist
	Dominions	Oeillet	Martin
	Dominions	Rosier	Basil
	Principalities	Verrier	Bernard
Third	Virtues	Belias	Francis de Paul
	Archangels	Olivier	Lawrence
	Angels	Iuvart	(not listed)

In the ancient Buddhist cosmologies, stemming from which we find a vast demonology, there is a confused but extensive range of demons. Waddell classes the various groups of Indian Buddhist demons as the *nagas* and the *mahoragas*, these being snakelike beings, sometimes in the shapes of clouds, living in the sky or under water; the *yaksas*, who devour men and yet appear sometimes to be capable of being friendly to man; the *asuras*, giant demons under the control of Rahu; and such varied demons as the *raksasas*, the *diatyas*, *kumbhandas* and *pisachas*.

The demons of Assyrian demonology are perhaps as vast as those of the Buddhist. Those identified and listed by Thompson include the sexless demons *gallu*, the female *labartu*, the lurking *rabisu*, the *sedu* and *lamassu*, the last two of which may be taken into the service of mankind. Thompson also discusses the so-called Seven Spirits of the demonic kind, which interfere with man and the earthly environment. A cuneiform tablet describes them as creeping on their bellies like snakes, making the chamber stink of mice and giving tongue like a pack of hounds. They eat flesh and drink blood and are the cause of eclipses.

The Egyptian demons are formidable both in ability and number. The Book of the Dead claims that there are 4,601,200 demons, although few of these are listed in what survives of Egyptian demonology. Most of the low-grade demons, while invisible to ordinary sight, resemble wild beasts, lizards, serpents, crocodiles, monkeys and the like. They inhabit swamps, deserts, burial grounds and so on, and their power is greatest at night-time. A complex system of talismans and magical praxes was developed to keep these astral beings at bay. The generic term for demon – *khuu* – also means 'spirit of the dead', so that the distinction between demon and spirit is not so clear as in Western demonology, although the *biu* appear to be more beneficient than the *khuu*. According to Foucart, the Egyptian demons were anonymous groups, so that a demon might be identified by an individual name properly belonging to a god. Thus Sorku is a crocodile god (demon), Ririt a hippopotamus god (demon) and so on. The majority of such named gods and demons appear to have astrological or cosmological functions, for they represent such things as time, natural phenomena, the mansions of the Moon, planets, stars, decanates and so on. The panoply of demons might be seen as dominated by Set, the Egyptian equivalent of Beelzebub. There is certain linguistic and literary evidence to suggest that Set might have become confused in the later Coptic with SATAN.

The demonology of Hebraic tradition is complex and many of the individual demons are derived from composite sources. Within the Talmudic tradition it is taught that God created the demons as part of his divine plan, on the first Sabbath eve, towards twilight. He had merely constructed their souls when the Sabbath overtook him and he was obliged to cease his labours. This is why the demons have no physical bodies and exist only on the etheric or astral planes. This

Figure 45 *Infernal hierarchies: demonic monsters (after* The Nightmare, *by Simonet)*

popular account vies with rabbinic legend which holds that, after the expulsion from Eden, Adam was parted from Eve and during this time took to wife LILITH, from which liaison were born the demons. In reference to the invisibility of demons, the Talmud quite sensibly points out that we should regard this as good fortune for, should we see the myriad demons swarming around us, we would collapse from sheer terror (Figure 45). The Hebraic demons are described under the general names of *mazzikin*, the *lilin*, demons which have human forms although with wings, the *shedim*, with forms resembling humans, and the *ruhin*, which are formless.

Influence   In a general sense the term means 'to have an effect on something', but the etymology of the word, which is from the Latin *influere* ('to flow into'), indicates that in origin 'influence' was once directly linked with occult and astrological concepts, for it was held that the macrocosm flowed into the microcosm. There is actually no more satisfactory theory of influences than that expressed in the tradition of SYMPATHY which underlies the doctrine of the CHAIN OF BEING, although admittedly this is descriptive rather than explanatory. A related term from Paracelsian astrology is ILECH. See also SYNCHRONICITY.

Infortune Major   A term used for the planet Saturn, and employed in this sense to denote one of the figures of GEOMANCY.

Infortune Minor   A term used for the planet Mars, and employed in this sense to denote one of the figures of GEOMANCY.

Infortunes   In astrology the two planets Mars and Saturn are traditionally the Infortunes, the Infortune Minor and the Infortune Major respectively. To this traditional classification some astrologers add Uranus. See also MALEFICS.

Ingress   In astrology a term used to denote the entry of a planet or nodal point into a sign.

Initiate   A term from the Latin *initiatus* and applied to any person to whom the Mysteries have been revealed. In modern times it is often applied to those who have so developed themselves as to have as clear consciousness in the spiritual realm as in the material. In a more popular sense, however, an initiate is one who has

been allowed entry into a secret organization, sometimes involving the acceptance of a personal prayer, mantra or inner discipline. However, such an initiate does not have entry to higher vision by virtue of such admittance to the society. For nomenclature, see INITIATION.

Initiation   The various stages of the making of an INITIATE are sometimes called 'degrees' or 'levels'. In some initiation systems there were seven such levels, linked with the planetary sequence (as, for example, in the Mithraic Mysteries), in other systems four, linked with the elements. In this latter series Fire was linked with deity, Water with spirit, Air with *pneuma* or the breath of God, and Earth with matter, as well as with a symbolic death and resurrection which was really a symbolic birth into the spiritual realms not accessible to the uninitiated. This symbolic birth, or death, was important to virtually all the ancient Mystery centres where initiation was practised. The Greek word *teleutao* signifies in the active voice 'I die', and in the middle voice 'I am initiated'; *teleutan* is 'to die', while *teleisthai* is 'to be initiated'. *Pastos* or *taphos* are the names for the sarcophagus in which the would-be initiate is placed prior to the symbolic death, and the word *pastos* is linked with our modern term 'Paschal' in reference to Easter. Such observations might suggest a significance in the etymology of the word 'sarcophagus', which means 'flesh-eater'. Initiates have always been known by secret names, but the generic terms used for a true initiate include 'serpents', 'dragons', 'dragon-men', 'fish-men' (see ANNEDOTUS), 'sons of the dragon', 'sons of the serpent god' and so on.

Inner sight   A term used for clairvoyant vision, or for that vision which comes from the development of the THIRD EYE.

Insufflation   A term derived in recent times to denote the method of transmitting forces by means of breathing upon people or things. The word appears to have originated mainly to designate a healing technique, by which the warm breath of the operator was used to heal, in the manner of CHIROTHESY, but the same term may be applied to the destructive use of breathing. It is not the breath itself which is said to heal, but the vital essence contained within the breath.

Intellectual Soul   A name given by Steiner (with the alternative 'Mind Soul') to designate that part of the soul which develops the faculty of the EGO for receiving impressions and making such impressions its own, free of the external world.

Intelligency   A term used to denote a class of spirits, originally the Intelligencies, who regulated the movement and life of the celestial SPHERES. Some medieval images show angels winding the mechanism which drives the series of geocentric spheres – these are the *Motori* or the Intelligencies. However, the function appears to have been forgotten by about the seventeenth century, so that the term was (quite wrongly) equated with intelligence. Agrippa, still aware of the actual function of these beings as spherical regulators, gives the names listed in Table 20, along with a series of sigils and MAGIC SQUARES for the Intelligencies of the planets (by which he meant 'planetary spheres') and the corresponding *daemonia* (see DAIMON).

Table 20

Planetary sphere	Intelligency	Daemonium
Moon	Malcha	Hasmodai
Mercury	Tiriel	Taphthartharach
Venus	Hagiel	Kedemel
Sun	Nachiel	Sorath
Mars	Graphiel	Barbazel
Jupiter	Iophiel	Hismael
Saturn	Agiel	Zazel

Intuitional Astrology   The name given to an esoteric system of astrology proposed by Alice Bailey, which is partly an extension of esoteric principles formulated by Blavatsky, and involves many unconventional astrological conceptions, among which is the important teaching concerning the SEVEN RAYS.

Invocation   A word used in a specialist sense for the calling up of DEMONS by ritual magical techniques. The invocation of supposed spirits in seances is usually termed 'calling'. See, however, CONJURATION.

Ioel   In the Qabbalistic system of the SEPHIROTHIC TREE a name given to METATRON. See KETHER.

Iophiel   Name given by Agrippa (quoting ancient Qabbalistic sources) to the Intelligency of Jupiter. He gives the magical number of Iophiel as 136, which is four times the linear sum of the MAGIC SQUARE of Jupiter (34). See ZAPHKIEL.

Ipos   Sometimes Aypeus, Ayporos or Ipes, one of the seventy-two SPIRITS OF SOLOMON. He is said to appear in the form of an angel or lion, or in the combined forms of the two.

Iron Age   As a specialist occult term, derived from the Hindu chronology and from modern esotericism, see KALI YUGA and FOUR AGES.

Ishtar   One of the ancient Babylonian names for a goddess regarded as the equivalent of Venus. But see also VIRGO.

Isis   The name Isis has several applications in occultism. First, it is linked with the constellations: the Egyptian goddess of this name was the pre-Christian prototype of the Virgin Mary, and inevitably esoteric astrology has linked the Egyptian name with both the constellation and zodiacal sign VIRGO. It is also a name given to three different HYPOTHETICAL PLANETS. The first was that identified by the astrologer Sutcliffe, who claims for it a periodicity of 360 years. The second Isis was that proposed by Thierens as the future ruler of Taurus. The third is that listed by the astrologer Jayne.

Israfel   One of the names of the angel who will blow the final trumpet which announces the Resurrection.

Ithuriel   In earlier traditions, the name Ithuriel was used of one of the Cherubim (as, for example, by Milton in *Paradise Lost*), while in the popular demonological tradition it was the name of a spirit linked with the sphere of Mars. In modern occultism, however, it is the name given to the Archangel who acts as ambassador from the planet Uranus.

Iuvart   Name of a demon. See Table 19 under INFERNAL HIERARCHIES.

Izards   The second series of creations of ORMUZD, the Zoroastrian Being of Light. They are twenty-eight in number and are said to watch over the virtue of the world, acting as interpreters of human prayer. The Izards are often linked with the lunar cycle of twenty-eight days and with the twenty-eight LUNAR MANSIONS.

J

The tenth letter of the alphabet and (through association with the Hebraic Jod or Yod) ascribed the numerical significance of TEN. Since in medieval times (when the Hebraic occult numerology was introduced to Europe) the J and I were interchangeable, it is also linked to with the number ONE. See also I, and NUMBERS.

Jael In some forms of CEREMONIAL MAGIC the governor of zodiacal Libra.

Janus The oldest of the Roman gods, his name (from *ianua*, door) and function involved with the spirit of opening, from which we derived the name of our month January. He is usually symbolized as a god with two faces, one young and the other old, one looking into the future, the other into the past. In astrology a name given to HYPOTHETICAL PLANET by Wemyss, who accorded it rule over zodiacal Sagittarius.

Jesod See YESOD.

Jettatura Popular (Italian) word for the EVIL EYE, as something thrown.

Jetzirah See YETZIRAH.

Jhana Sometimes *jnana*, the Sanskrit term for knowledge, especially for occult knowledge.

Jinn See DJIN and GENIUS.

Jivatma Sanskrit for the divine spirit in man.

Jnanachaksha See THIRD EYE.

Jupiter The planet in orbit between Mars and Saturn, ruler of the zodiacal Sagittarius, and in traditional astrology the ruler of zodiacal Pisces. Modern astrologers generally give the throne of Pisces to Neptune, however. In the Boehmean occult cosmoconception Jupiter is linked with the sixth of his SEVEN PROPERTIES and is visualized as a higher development of Venus, an expression of a fuller self-perception and understanding of the material world – the inner source of wisdom, which has to descend into the concrete realm in the seventh phase (linked with the Moon). In numerology Jupiter is linked with the mystic number 9 (but see NUMBERS). The sigil for Jupiter ♃ is said to represent the semicircle of spiritual potential lifting the heavy cross of materiality, which certainly symbolizes the uplifting nature of the planet, although this sigil is actually not earlier than the fourteenth century in origin. Jupiter represents the profound side of the mental life: it stands for the speculative thought of the native and for the spiritually expansive side of his nature. In particular Jupiter offers an index of the moral nature of the native and of the degree to which he will respond enthusiastically to life and its responsibilities. When Jupiter is beneficially emphasized in the chart it gives a generous, optimistic, loyal, popular and generally successful nature. Traditionally Jupiter has rule over the thighs and liver (see MELOTHESIC MAN).

Jupiter Chain See JUPITER SCHEME.

Jupiter Period The name given in esoteric astrology to a future condition of the earth, when humanity (having learned the lessons relating to objective consciousness in the present cycles) will attain to self-directed 'picture consciousness'. Distinguish from JUPITER SCHEME.

Jupiter Scheme The Jupiter Scheme and the Jupiter Chain are terms derived specifically from the Theosophical cosmoconception linked with the SCHEME OF EVOLUTION and are not to be confused with the JUPITER PERIOD. It is claimed that, while Jupiter is not yet inhabited, its moons are, and the future evolutionary development of this chain will reach a very high level, particularly in regard to what is called 'picture consciousness', which is the faculty of ideation at present working in the ASTRAL BODY of man.

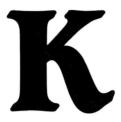

The eleventh letter of the alphabet. It is said that the Egyptian hieroglyphic equivalent for K (the Greek kappa, and the Hebraic Kaph) was a bowl, a spiritual container. As a sound value the K is regarded in occult circles as being the equivalent of the cutting or severing C. The ancient Greek punishment for false accusers involved the branding of the letter K on the forehead of those found guilty of *kalumnia*; it is likely that the sound value was the most important element here, rather than the fact that it was the first letter of the word. The numerological equivalent of the letter is usually given as 20, but some link it with THREE or EIGHT, as equivalents of the hard G and the soft C respectively.

Kabbala See QABBALA.

Kabbalistic Faces According to Blavatsky, this is the generic term for body (*nephesh*), soul (*ruach*) and mind (*neschamah*) in Qabbalism.

Kabiri Sometimes Cabiri, a name probably derived from a Phoenician term for what Blavatsky calls 'mystery gods', whom the uninitiated were not permitted to name or discuss.

Kadmon Usually ADAM KADMON, the Hebraic term for the archetypal man.

Kahuna A name, meaning 'keepers of the secret', given to the native magicians of the Polynesian islands and to their modern followers. Their 'secret' is that of Huna, a system of magic which was studied in depth by Long. As a result of Long's researches, several useful terms derived from this system have been introduced into European occultism – for example, AKA, UNIHIPILI (an entitive force of the subconscious) and the UHANE (an entitive force of the conscious mind). See also DEATH PRAYER.

Kakodaemon See CACODAEMON.

Kalagni A Sanskrit term usually translated as meaning 'flame of time' and used of a monster with a thousand heads created by the Hindu goddess Siva.

Kalahansa See HANSA.

Kalavingka Sometimes *kuravinkaya* or *karanda*, a Sanskrit term said to indicate the 'sweet-voiced bird of immortality', which some occultists say is the higher Ego (see HANSA). The sound of the sweet-voiced bird is said to be heard at certain advanced stages of meditation.

Kali Yuga A Sanskrit term which has been Europeanized mainly through the influence of Theosophy, and translated as meaning 'Iron Age', 'Black Age' or 'Dark Age'. The term often crops up in modern esotericism because it is widely acknowledged that we now live in this age, which the Hindus claim began in 3102 BC with the death of Krishna. It is said by some occultists to be a period of 360,000 years, by others 432,000 years, yet others insist that the age has already terminated (*circa* 1880). Blavatsky says that this is the last of the ages into which the evolutionary period of man is divided; she further claims that the first cycle of 5000 years, which began in 3102 BC, ended between 1897 and 1898. See YUGA, which sets out the additional periods of 'twilights' for the Kali Yuga.

Kalpa In the Hindu chronology a *kalpa* is a 'day of Brahma', a period of 4320 million years. The 'night of Brahma' is of the same length. One 'year of Brahma' (a solar *kalpa* in modern parlance) is made up of 360 such pairs, while a century of such years makes up an entire cycle, the *mahakalpa* of 311,040 trillion years. Unfortunately, it is apparent that the word *kalpa* is used fairly indiscriminately in reference to ages. For example, Purucker records that a *kalpa* is also a *mahamatava*, a period equivalent to a whole lifetime of the globes in a PLANETARY CHAIN.

Kama A Sanskrit term for 'lust' or 'evil desire', which involves the clinging to material-bound existence. Distinguish from KARMA.

Kama-rupa See ANIMAL SOUL.

Kamadhatu Name given in the Buddhist cosmology to the lowest of the three regions, comprising the six realms of the DEVAS and the Earth itself.

Kamaloka A Sanskrit name for the equivalent of the Christian Purgatory, certain levels of the Egyptian Amenti and the Greek Hades, where the purgatorial experiences of recently deceased souls must be undergone. See, however, HELL.

Kamea A Hebraic term for an AMULET.

Kanya The Sanskrit term for zodiacal VIRGO.

Karana sarira The Sanskrit term for the CAUSAL BODY.

Karanda See KALAVINGKA.

Karcist An obscure term used in the set of instructions for evoking infernal demons in the GRAND GRIMOIRE, and applied to the operator or magician who seeks to bind the spirits to his service. The word may be derived from the Latin *carcer* ('prison') in reference to the attempts to imprison demons by pact. Theoretically anyone who practises CEREMONIAL MAGIC is a karcist, however. Distinguish KARDECIST.

Kardecist Name given to any follower of the spiritualism propounded by the nineteenth-century French spiritualist Rivail (an adherent of reincarnation theories), who adopted the pseudonym 'Allen Kardec'.

Karma Term derived from the Sanskrit root *kri* ('to do' or 'to make') and applied to one of the fundamental concepts underlying occult teaching – namely, that every single thought, feeling and action on the physical plane has a consequence proportional to its original intention and intensity. Karma may therefore loosely be described as the law of consequences. In a popular sense, karma is sometimes regarded as the oriental equivalent of the Western DESTINY or FATE, but this is an erroneous view. Karma is properly regarded as the fruits of action in a previous lifetime which determines the conditions of a life in a subsequent incarnation. This is quite different from the Western concept of Destiny or Fate, which is not necessarily connected with deeds of a previous existence and which may arise from a random fiat of the gods. Attempts to translate the laws of karma into modern European terms such as Fate or Destiny may lead only to a misunderstanding of the original Eastern concept.

The Hindu view of karma as 'inescapable retribution' is in effect highly complex and even pedantic, yet it may be distilled to the simple idea that 'everything is karma', which tends to displace somewhat the function of the human power of will in determining personal and social change. In a sense the Hindu tradition holds that nothing survives each individual life other than karma, the fruits of thought and feeling, and it is this which alone is reborn to become the 'cause' of the next life. In this view of karma we find the 'Knower' displaced. Western occultism insists that the eternal EGO is informed of the consequences of karma in which it is projected during a lifetime. Blavatsky rightly calls karma 'ethical causation', and one senses that it is through the efforts of the Theosophists (who perhaps introduced the word in its popular sense to Europe) that a softer and less mechanistic view has become available to the Western mind, which grasps the idea of 'survival' in terms of the survival of an Ego and which does not seek to displace the 'Knower'.

The simple operation of karma through a sequence of lifetimes has been set out in a reasonably simple form by Annie Besant: the desire to do a thing in one life usually precipitates itself as a compulsion and capacity to act out that desire in a subsequent life. Repeated thoughts in one life precipitate as a distinct tendency in a later life, while the will to perform certain acts will become transformed into the actual ability to perform them in a later lifetime. In such a process, experience is translated into wisdom, and painful experience into conscience. A more complex account of the laws underlying karma has been set down by Guenther Wachsmuth, who links it with cosmic periodicities. Steiner, who has written most convincingly about karma in relation to Christianity, sees karma as a creative formative force in the development of the human Ego. The doctrine of karma is found in almost all Far Eastern religions and, since the importation of such religions to the West, has become intimately bound up with all occultist theories and praxes in which the tenets of REINCARNATION are upheld.

Reincarnation is (for the ordinary soul at least) the consequence of karma, built up from previous incarnations – rebirth is seen as the opportunity given to the soul to purify itself from the previous effects of 'bad' karma, which have arisen from immoralities or weaknesses in earlier lives. It is widely recognized by occultists that one of the functions of personal struggle against karma (the gradual liberation of the self) is the enriching of the eternal element within the human psyche. Thus, when it is understood correctly, karma is concerned neither with punishment nor reward, even though it is sometimes referred to by occultists as the 'law of retribution'; it is rather a system of justice, by which the simple demand is made that the human being learn to accept full responsibility for thought, feeling and action.

For an astrological connection, see EIGHTH HOUSE.

Kemedel The name given by Agrippa (quoting ancient Qabbalistic sources) to the daimon of Venus.

Kephalonomancy A method of divination practised in connection with baking or boiling the head of an ass; the crackling of the skull is supposed to give response to questions.

Kephziel One of the several variant names for the ruler of Saturn.

Keshara Sometimes in modern occultism *khechara*, a Sanskrit term sometimes translated as 'sky-walker' or 'ether-goer', and used to denote a high state of development attained by means of religious disciplines or Yoga. The state permits conscious astral travel, an understanding of the devic languages and the ability to read into the minds of all created beings.

Kether Name given by Qabbalists to the topmost Sephirah of the SEPHIROTHIC TREE, usually translated as meaning 'crown' or 'summit', which marks the summit of the human progress through the Tree. At Kether we reach the highest point of the Tree, and stand at the furthest remove from the 'incarnating fall' which the lowest point of MALKUTH symbolizes. In the World of Expression this Sephirah is linked with the *Primum mobile* and with the nebulae on the very edge of our visible world. Some modern esotericists have attempted (quite wrongly) to establish a connection with the planet Uranus, but the workings of this Sephirah are well beyond the level of the merely planetary, for it is the staging post for man's leap into that inner space which is the unknown realm beyond the stars; it is the 'impossible' leap inside and outside in one movement. In the World of formation (YETZIRAH) Kether is under the tutelage of the angelic order called in Qabbalist literature the Chioh ha Qodesh, the holy living creatures, which are linked with the living beings of the zodiac, the source of all life below the sphere of the *Primum mobile*. In BRIAH, that World of Creation, the Sephirah is in the hands of the mighty METATRON, the Archangel of the Presence, who, so to speak, presents man to God (his Qabbalistic alternative name Ioel means something like 'I am God'). In the highest level of ATZILUTH the Sephirah is linked with the untranslatable Ahih, the 'first and the last', the eternal Amen, the in-breathing and out-breathing of the godhead.

Ketu The Sanskrit term for the DRAGON'S TAIL, which is accorded much importance in Hindu astrology. The Hindu *Caput* is RAHU.

Key of Solomon A name given to a late-medieval text of the GRIMOIRE type. But see SPIRITS OF SOLOMON.

Khamael Sometimes Camael, a name given in the Qabbalistic tradition to the Archangel who operates within the Sephirah of GEBURAH. His name means 'burner of God', as a result of which his function has been radically misunderstood in popular lore. Khamael works as a creative force in BRIAH, with the ability to make divine heat useful (albeit hurtful) for the lower spheres. He is linked with the Destroying Angel SAMAEL.

Klippoth A widely used Hebraic term originally intended to denote astral shells, but now also confused with demons and even elementaries. The word is also sometimes used to denote the whole realm of demons, the dwelling of SAMAEL.

Kobold A demon originally from Hebraic lore. He is described as a small creature, rather like a human in form, who delights in confusing men by mimicry and the use of echoes.

Koilon A term derived from the ancient Greek *koilos* ('hollow') and used by esotericists to denote the basic root matter from which the material world is made. The word is sometimes used of the unit of such matter, the occult equivalent of the atom. Koilon is invisible to all but the most highly developed of clairvoyants.

Kore Greek term, sometimes Romanized as Koure, of Attic origin, meaning 'maiden', and in occult contexts sometimes used to denote zodiacal and constellational VIRGO. She was especially called Staxeodos Koure ('wheat-bearing maiden'). See SPICA.

Kosmic electricity A theosophical term (or analogy) for FOHAT.

Kosmos In occult literature 'kosmos' (as opposed to 'cosmos') means the entire spiritual and material universe. See MACROCOSM.

Krasis See MUSIC OF THE SPHERES and TEMPERAMENTS.

Krita Yuga The Hindu Golden Age, a periodicity of 1,728,000 years, sometimes called the Satya Yuga. This period includes the 'twilights' – *sandhya* and *sandhyansa* – of 400 divine years each. See also YUGA.

Krittika The name for the constellation TAURUS in the Hindu astrology. See also RISHABHAM.

Kronos Sometimes Chronos, a name given by the Greeks to the planet Saturn, but not originally the Greek god equivalent of Saturn. Kronos was in Greek mythology the youngest of the giant Titans, the son of Uranus and Gea, and was later identified with Saturnus by the Romans – presumably through his ancient association with agriculture (Gea being the Earth Goddess). The same name (Kronos) is given to one of the several HYPOTHETICAL PLANETS used in a specialist modern system of astrology, and is said to have a meaning linked with 'authority'.

Kumara The Sanskrit term means 'virgin boy', but in esotericism the word is linked with the solar angels.

Kundalini A term derived from the Sanskrit meaning approximately 'spiral energy' and used by occultists in reference to one of the three fundamental solar forces in our planetary system. In its human context Kundalini is the serpent fire or the serpent power which wreaks havoc on any individual who attempts to tamper with its workings without a sufficient occult knowledge of moral discipline. It is an energy sometimes used by black magicians who seek to further their involutionary aims through other individuals. Clairvoyant vision sees the activated Kundalini as a kind of liquid fire rushing in a sort of spiral through the CHAKRAS of the body, although in normal man the Kundalini energy lies dormant near the root chakra, the MULADHARA. The awakening of this serpent fire, by meditation or by yogic practices, is arduous and filled with danger. However, its legitimate awakening is necessary for all modern would-be INITIATES in order to bring into physical consciousness the experiences of the ASTRAL BODY, which is, for the ordinary man, quite unconscious at the present stage of evolution.

Kundalini Sakti A Sanskrit term usually translated as meaning 'power of life', but in fact used properly only in reference to powers developed by difficult acts of meditation and disciplines. See KUNDALINI.

Kung-lei See FENG-SHUI.

Kushiel The name of one of the seven Angels of Punishment, meaning 'the rigid one of God'.

Kyriotetes See DOMINIONS and CELESTIAL HIERARCHIES.

L

The twelfth letter of the alphabet, with the numerical equivalent of 30. It is usually claimed that the associated Lamed of the Hebrews was an ox-goad, linked with the equivalent of Mars. However, in the Egyptian hieroglyphics it was represented as a lioness and is therefore a solar letter. The sound value of the letter L is an expression of change, especially of changing form.

Lachesis See FATAE.

Lahgash A Qabbalistic term usually translated (inadequately) as 'secret speech' or 'esoteric incantation'.

Lamassu See GENIUS.

Lamb A term sometimes used of zodiacal or constellational Aries, derived from the talismanic magic of the medieval period.

Lamia See LILITH.

Language of the Birds A phrase used to denote the language used by initiates when talking among themselves. See also SPIRITS OF SOLOMON.

Lapis The *Lapis* of Alchemy is the PHILOSO-PHER'S STONE, the *Lapis philosophorum*, which actually goes under very many names. The *Lapis exilis* is a name used of the mysterious Grail in the Eschenbach legends. The *Lapis judaicus* is said to be a talismanic stone, sometimes called the Theolithos, which is supposed to have fallen from the crown of Lucifer as he fell from heaven. It is often confused with the Phoenix Stone which renews the youth of its owner. See also MAGIC STONES and MAGNESIA.

Lares A Latin term for a spirit – in Roman times they were tutelary or guardian spirits – especially so the *lares familiares*, the household *lares*. They

appear originally to have been elementals, but in later Roman times they were visualized as being the shades (or *manes*) of humans who had died, and were identified with the LEMURES and the LARVAE.

Larvae A Latin name for the shades of deceased humans – ghosts. In modern esotericism the same name is used to denote animal-like low-grade spirits which will attach themselves to humans to suck their spiritual forces.

Laya A Sanskrit term derived from the root *li* ('to dissolve') and applied to a point through which some form of differentiation or new manifestation may take place. The 'laya centre' of modern occultism appears to be something equivalent to the point of chaos within a seed from which a new cosmos may be developed. There is a specialist form of Laya Yoga concerned with developing the latent power of inner hearing, through which inner development is made possible.

Law of Retribution See KARMA.

Lecanomancy A term derived from the Greek *lekane* ('dish') and *manteia* ('divination') and applied to a form of predicting the future from the inspection of water, or glittering objects covered by water, in a dish.

Left-Hand Path One of the names given to the pathway directed towards the attainment of personal aims at the expense of the evolutionary scheme of the cosmos. This is the pathway pursued consciously by dark magicians, the Brothers of the Left-Hand Path, and unconsciously by criminals and immoral humans. Stripped of its symbolism and ritualistic trimmings, this is the destructive path of BLACK MAGIC, which (consciously or unconsciously) calls to the aid of the practitioner evil spirits and demons. See also RIGHT-HAND PATH.

Lelirium The Igneous class of the sexted of DEMONS described by Psellus. They are said to inhabit the air and to be a genus which has been expelled from the regions adjacent to the Moon.

Lemegeton The name given to a seventeenth-century text of the GRIMOIRE type, sometimes called the *Lesser Key of Solomon*. Its four main parts are 'Goetia', 'Theurgia Goetia', 'Pauline Art' (which deals with the planetary hours in relation to the invocation of spirits, and with the zodiacal rulerships of spirits) and 'Almadel', which lists the choirs of evil spirits.

Lemures A Latin term for ghosts or SHELLS. See LEMURIA.

Lemuria A term taken by modern occultists from natural science and applied to an ancient continent which was the main centre of activity for the THIRD RACE in the early history of humanity. Roughly speaking, the Lemurian Age was contemporaneous with the Mesozoic or Reptilian Age, and as an epoch preceded that of ATLANTIS, the culture which supported the Fourth Root Race. It was located in the southern hemisphere, as a huge equitorial continental strip, so vast as almost to surround the globe. After its destruction by volcanic action only fragments were left, such as modern Madagascar, the Seychelles, Easter Island and Australia. Occultists claim that it was on Lemuria that man learned for the first time how to incarnate into earth-made bodies, although the forms of such bodies were different from those of today. It was in Lemurian times that mankind gradually separated into two distinct sexes and developed womb birth. In its occult sense the term is not to be confused with the Roman festival held in mid-May to appease ghosts (the Latin *lemures*, meaning approximately 'shades of the departed').

Leo The fifth sign of the zodiac and one of the constellations. It is associated in occultism with the Hebraic letter Kaph and the TAROT arcanum

Figure 46 *Leo: the Tarot arcanum 'Strength' which is associated with the constellation Leo. This arcanum image is derived from the medieval image of the Cardinal virtue 'Strength' (from the Grimaud pack)*

'Strength' (or 'Force'), itself derived from an image of one of the Cardinal virtues (called '*La Force*' in French, but often 'Strength' in English) who subdued the lower demonic lion (Figure 46). The asterism is said to be the lunar Nemean lion which Hercules killed, but it was a lion in Babylon long before Grecian mythology was heard of. The modern sigil for Leo ♌ is said by some to be a corruption of the initial of the Greek term for the asterism; however, the present form of the sigil appears to derive from a late-medieval form, itself derived from the Byzantine Greek, neither of which is like the lamda, and the significance remains hidden. Leo is of the FIRE ELEMENT, and of the Fixed quality, the influence being creative, self-reliant, enthusiastic, warm-hearted and positive. As with all Fire types, there is a strong element of selfishness, but the Leonine is rarely insensitive to the needs of others. The warm and creative outlook of Leo is expressed in many key words attached to the sign by modern astrologers: self-expressive, dignified, inspirational, exuberant, magnanimous, flamboyant (sometimes theatrical), hospitable and altruistic – in a word, all those qualities which may be associated with a Fire nature expressing itself without fear and with a wish to be creative. In excess the Leonine nature may be described in terms which express its underlying selfishness, the key words being vain, demanding, predatory, imperious, dogmatic, self-satisfied, ostentatious and militant. Leo is ruled by the Sun, and the sign marks the detriment of Saturn, while some astrologers say that it marks the fall of Mercury.

Lerajie One of the seventy-two SPIRITS OF SOLOMON. He is said to appear as an archer, clothed in green. His demonic speciality is that of delaying the healing of wounds.

Lesser Benefic See BENEFICS.

Lesser guardian See GUARDIAN OF THE THRESHOLD.

Leviathan The word 'Leviathan' in Hebrew means approximately 'that which gathers itself into folds' or 'that which is drawn out'. There is much confusion about the translation of the word in its biblical context, however, and theologians agree to differ about its meaning, though the general idea is that it refers to some huge animal, almost certainly linked with water. In Job, 41, 1, the word might well refer to a crocodile. Some translators have seen the Leviathan as a whale, and the more literal-minded theologians have insisted that it is an Egyptian crocodile, pointing to the crocodile as an emblem of Egypt and its adoption as one of the images of Typhon, 'as the evil demon . . . popularly worshipped under the form of a crocodile'. The words in Psalm 104, 25–6, have been taken by some to refer to a large ship, though

some read the Hebrew as ponting to a Leviathan who is a ruler of dragons. The Leviathan of the poet Blake was a coiled sea serpent, in Blake's vision a 'crooked serpent' (closer to the Hebraic meaning than any mere crocodile was a symbol of the warring evil in man (but see BEHEMOTH). Blavatsky (*Theosophical Glossary*, 1892) sees 'Leviathan' as a term formerly used in initiation – 'the Mystery of the Serpent of the Great Sea' – insisting that esoterically Leviathan represents 'Deity in its double manifestation of good and evil'. See also DEMONIC SINS.

Levitation In spiritualist circles and in SEANCES the word is used to denote the rising into the air of objects or human bodies without visible agency. The phenomenon is far from being merely spiritualistic, however, for there are numerous records of holy men of both East and West levitating, especially when deeply involved in prayer.

Ley lines See GEOMANCY.

Libanomancy A term derived from the Greek *libanos* ('incense') and *manteia* ('divination') and applied to a form of divination from the movement of the smoke from burning incense. The term is sometimes mispelled as 'livanomancy', due to a mistake in Gaule's *Mysmantia* of 1652.

Libra The seventh sign of the zodiac, which corresponds neither in location nor extent with the constellation of the same name. In occultism the asterism is linked with the Hebraic letter Heth and the TAROT arcanum 'Justice'. While in Greek astrology the asterism was at first part of SCORPIUS and called the Chelae or Claws (and was sometimes pictured in an image of a scorpion grasping the balance in its claws, even as late as medieval times), it was formed as a separate image to represent the balance upon which Astraea would weigh the good and evil deeds of men immediately after death. It is therefore symbolically linked with the outcome of the life forces inherent in the opposite sign and constellation Aries, and is naturally followed by the death element of the adjacent Scorpio, which some astrologers have linked with the realm of KARMA. The sigil for Libra ♎ is said by some astrologers to be a vestigial drawing of a pair of scales, with which the sign and constellation have been associated from the very earliest times, the Babylonian name for the asterism being Zibanitu ('scales'). However, one of the more frequently used of the Egyptian hieroglyphics for the sign shows that the sigil is derived from a picture of the sun setting over the earth, an appropriate image for a sign which is now associated with the Descendant, that symbolic place of sunset. Libra is of the Air element, and of the Cardinal quality, its influence being harmonious, elegant, orderly, comparative, peaceful, changeable and helpful. The nature of Libra is manifest in human beings in terms of the many key words used by modern astrologers: gentle, artistic, sensitive, helpful, peaceful, spiritualized, delicate, perceptive, affectionate – in a word, all the qualities which may be associated with an Air type expressing itself with a delicate awareness of others. In excess the Libran nature may be described in terms which express an impractical nature, as well as a lazy streak: untidy, easily persuaded, 'lost in the clouds', unable to cope and so on. Libra is ruled by the planet Venus, marks the exaltation of Saturn and the fall of Pluto.

Life body A name sometimes used as an equivalent for the ETHERIC BODY.

Life essence One of the European names for PRANA.

Life ether See ETHERIC.

Life-spirit The name given by Steiner (in German, *Lebensgeist*) to BUDDHI.

Life waves A term derived from Theosophy; they are (approximately) the will, wisdom and activity, seen as the evolutionary activity of the Trinity in cosmogenetic manifestation.

Light ether See ETHERIC.

Lights In astrology and alchemy the Sun and Moon are the 'lights' (also the 'luminaries'): the Sun is the Greater Light, the Moon the Lesser Light.

Lilin Properly *lil-in*, a name given to the children of LILITH – demons. The *lilin* are said to attack newborn children and to seduce men in their sleep in order to promote nocturnal emissions. See SUCCUBUS.

Lilith The word 'Lilith' appears to have been derived from the Assyrian *lilitu*, a semihuman SUCCUBUS whose name was introduced into rabbinic literature as the first wife of Adam. From this ancient liaison were born devils, spirits and the LILIN. Some occultists call Lilith the second wife of Adam, however. In medieval occultism she is figured as the female demon Lamia. In popular tradition Lilith is said to have spawned the succubi or to be their demon princess (see INFERNAL HIERARCHIES). The same name is also given to a planet generally described as one of the HYPOTHETICAL PLANETS, although it is really a hypothetical moon of the Earth, invisible to ordinary sight save (it is said) when its body passes between the Earth and the Sun. This lunar Lilith is called the Dark Moon.

Limbus In ALCHEMY a term used to identify CHAOS – the conflicting elements unbound by the Quintessence into a cosmos.

Linga sarira The Sanskrit name given to the ASTRAL BODY in oriental occultism. See also SARIRA.

Lipika A term derived from the Sanskrit root *lip* ('to write') and applied to the celestial beings who record (or 'write down') all the thoughts, feelings and deeds of human beings while they dwell on earth. These writings of the recording angels (as they are called in the Christian tradition) are inscribed in what modern occultists call the Akashic Chronicles (see AKASHA).

Lithomancy A term derived from the Greek *lithis* and *manteia*, meaning 'divination from stones', and applied to a method of predicting future events from signs given by stones, such as the random patterns of thrown stones and so on. Some diviners had special MAGIC STONES which they used for SCRYING. The word is now little more than an alternative term for GEOMANCY, which originally was itself only a form of lithomancy. However, in ancient times it was believed that certain stones (or statues carved from stone) could predict the future by making special noises, or by moving in a mysterious way.

Livanomancy See LIBANOMANCY.

Living dead In modern esotericism those who are ignorant of the truth enshrined in the esoteric wisdom are called 'the living dead'. Some esoteric schools more kindly (and indeed more accurately) call such people 'sleepers'. The living dead or sleepers are passing through their present existence unaware of the spiritual realities. It is likely (indeed, eventually certain in the majority of cases) that in a future incarnation their sleeping parts will be sufficiently awakened for them to begin the process of speeding up spiritual development, which is the real concern of the esoteric and occult schools.

Living fire   See OCCULT TRINITY.

Loetitia   'Joy', a name for one of the sixteen figures of GEOMANCY.

Logarithmancy   A term used to denote divination from logarithms, as reported by John Gaule.

Lohitanga   The Sanskrit term for the planet Mars.

Loka   A Sanskrit term for 'region' or 'place'; see, for example, KAMALOKA.

Lord of Karma   A term used by the esotericist Bailey of Saturn, the planet which imposes retribution and which demands payment of all debts.

Lord of the Land   See MALKUTH.

Lords of Flame   In Theosophy the name Lords of Flame or Lords of the Flame (sometimes Children of the Fire Mist) is used to denote adepts from the sphere of Venus who came to help earthly evolution. However, see SATURN PERIOD.

Lords of Form   The name given to one of the TWELVE CREATIVE HIERARCHIES, associated with zodiacal Scorpio, who according to the esoteric cosmogenesis are especially concerned with the evolution of man as a spiritual being during the present Earth Period. They are in the present stage of evolution linked with the EXSUSIAI, and therefore with the sphere of the Sun. See SPIRITUAL HIERARCHIES.

Lords of Harmony   See CHERUBIM.

Lords of Individuality   The name given to one of the TWELVE CREATIVE HIERARCHIES, asso-ciated with zodiacal Libra, who according to the esoteric cosmogenesis prepared the Desire Body of man during the MOON PERIOD. See also SPIRITUAL HIERARCHIES, in which they are called 'Spirits of Wisdom'.

Lords of Light   See DHYAN-CHOHANS.

Lords of Love   See SERAPHIM.

Lords of Mind   The name given to one of the TWELVE CREATIVE HIERARCHIES, associated with zodiacal Sagittarius, who according to the esoteric cosmogenesis formed the equivalent of humanity during the SATURN PERIOD. They are in the present stage of evolution linked with the ARCHAI.

Lords of Will   Esoteric name for the THRONES.

Lords of Wisdom   The name given to one of the TWELVE CREATIVE HIERARCHIES, associ-ated with zodiacal Virgo, who according to the esoteric cosmogenesis prepared the vital body (the etheric body) of men during the SUN PERIOD. They are called the KYRIOTETES in some systems (see SPIRITUAL HIERARCHIES).

Lost soul   See SOUL.

Lotus flowers   See CHAKRA.

Lowell–Pluto   A name suggested for the planet Pluto, shortly after it had been discovered by Lowell.

Lower face   A Qabbalistic term for the MICRO-PROSOPUS, the so-called Long Face. Distinguish FACE.

Lower Manas   See MANAS.

Lower quaternary   A Theosophical term used to denote the perishable fourfold nature of man which is used by the Ego (see TERNARY) for the aims of incarnation. This lower quaternary con-sists of the four bodies: Ego, Astral, Etheric and Physical (in some systems the Ego is wrongly called the MANAS). In the pre-orientalizing terminology the lower quaternary was denoted by the names of the four elements: the Ego body was that of Fire, the Astral Body was that of Air, the Etheric Body was that of Water, and the physical was that of Earth.

Lower self In European occultism a term for the lower MANAS. Sometimes the term is used also to denote a part of man very different from the manas, namely the DOUBLE.

Lower ternary See TERNARY.

Lucifer In demonology Lucifer is the celestial being wrongly equated with Satan (probably due to a misreading of Isaiah, 14, 12). The general view, adopted in the literary tradition, is that Satan was called Lucifer before the Fall from Heaven. At all events, the name has been adopted in esoteric circles to represent the modern equivalent of the being of the Sun (originally named ORMUZD in the Zoroastrian dualism) opposed by the darkness, the Prince of Lies, who was called Angra Mainyu, in modern occultism AHRIMAN. This dualism has been carried into several of the esoteric astrological systems of modern times. In astrology the name is sometimes given to the planet Venus when it appears before the Sun, when it is also called the Morning Star. Another astrological use is linked with the asteroids, for Butler has suggested that these (which he rightly calls 'planetoids') mark the remains of a lost planet, which he calls Lucifer or Morning Star.

Lucifuge Rofocale The name given to an infernal spirit who is said to have power over all the wealth and treasures of the physical world.

Lucifugi The name applied to the lowest class of the sexted of DEMONS described by Psellus. They are of such a lower order of being that they may scarcely be considered sentient beings. The Lucifugi inhabit the interior of the earth and correspond to the lowest type of Ahrimanic being. See INFERNAL HIERARCHIES.

Lucky and Unlucky Days See EGYPTIAN DAYS.

Luminaries The Sun and Moon are often called the 'luminaries'.

Luminous arc A term evolved by Theosophists to denote the passage of life-bearing waves or streams carrying the evolving monads; it is essentially an image of the evolutionary process in a spiritual (rather than a Darwinian) sense. An alternative name is the 'ascending arc', which is curiously contrasted with the 'descending arc' of incarnation, which might imply that the pathway into incarnation is not linked with spiritual evolution, when in fact incarnation is one of the most intense periods of spiritual development.

Luminous waters A name said by some authorities to have been used in medieval alchemy and occultism to denote the Akashic Chronicles. See AKASHA.

Lunar gods The term is usually a Theosophical equivalent for the Pitris, the ancestors of previous human races, according to occultism. In Western terminology, however, the lunar gods are really the ANGELS.

Lunar intelligency The governing spirit of the sphere of the Moon. In modern occultism this is said to be GABRIEL. Following ancient Qabbalistic sources, Agrippa records the Hebraic *Schedbarschemoth Schartathan* as relating to both the 'daemon of the lunar demons' and the 'intelligency of the lunar intelligencies'.

Lunar mansions An ancient method of dividing the ecliptic belt into arcs of 12 degrees 51 minutes, corresponding approximately to the daily mean motion of the Moon through the ecliptic. By such divisions, twenty-eight segments, the lunar mansions, are obtained (the word 'mansions' appears to be derived from the Arbian *manzils*). Each of these mansions is named and has been subject to astrological interpretation along the lines of a lunar zodiac.

Lunar Race See PITRIS.

Luvah see FOUR ZOAS.

The thirteenth letter of the alphabet. It is generally argued that the M form (certainly from the Phoenician equivalent) represents the waves of water. The associated Hebraic Mem means water, and the Sanskrit *ma* (an important root which gives MAYA) is the equivalent of the Venusian 5, and also linked with water through many derived words (for example, the *mare* of Latin, the *mer* of French). It is also connected with the ancient constellation or sign Makara, which was originally a water creature (like the Babylonion Capricornus), sometimes wrongly described as a crocodile (in this connection, see also MARA). Blavatsky says that among the esotericists the M is a symbol of the higher Ego, the MANAS; in his esoteric poem *Commedia* Dante makes use of this notion, deriving from the letter M the face of man. Perhaps there is some connection with the fact that the Egyptian equivalent hieroglyphic is an owl. See also HANSA. The numerical equivalent of M is usually given as 40, which reduces to 4 – the incarnating number.

Macrocosm A Greek term meaning 'great arrangement' and applied to the ordered system of the celestial bodies and spheres of the celestial fabric, as much as to the vast range of different consciousness within this system. The macrocosm is sometimes called the 'kosmos' by occultists, who are anxious to distinguish it from the 'cosmos' and to emphasize the fact that this system is the larger model of what man (the MICROCOSM) is on a smaller scale, both in terms of consciousness (potential) and spiritual bodies. Within the esoteric tradition it is maintained that man is a microcosm only while living in a physical body. Before birth and after death he is integrated into the macrocosm. Occultists divine the macrocosm into three parts. There is the Empyrean, which corresponds in the microcosm to the intellectual part of man (usually termed *ratio*, reason), located in the head; the Aethereum (a name linked with the modern ETHERIC), which corresponds to the vital faculties, located in the heart; and the elementorum (a name linked with ELEMENTS) or the natural faculties, located in the human stomach. These correspond in the alchemical system with Salt, Mercury and Sulphur, respectively (see THREE PRINCIPLES). In ASTROLOGY, which is rooted in a study of the relationship held between the macrocosm and the microcosm, these correspond sequentially to the realm of the fixed stars, the planetary SPHERES and the sphere of Earth.

Macroprosopus A Greek word adopted into Qabbalism to denote the Great Countenance (see PARTZUPHEE). It is the entire universe, within which the microprosopus is an image, the ADAM KADMON.

Magi A term sometimes used as meaning 'astrologers' (but see MAGIAN). The *magi* of Chaldea are said to be the descendants of the ancient priests of the Sun (in Sanskrit *maga*). The word is, of course, the root of the English 'magician'.

Magian A name given to certain ancient priests connected with the worship of a fire god, in Assyrian, Babylonian and Persian cults, probably from the Old Persian *magu*, applied to a subrace of Medians reputed to have tremendous theurgic and occult powers. Blavatsky links them with the Sanskrit term *maga*, which is used of priests of the Sun, mentioned in the *Vishnu Purana*. The same Sanskrit root has given us such words as 'magic', 'magician', 'image', 'imagination' and so on. Since the Wise Men who sought out Jesus by means of the so-called Star of Bethlehem have been called Magians (the Greek being *magos*), it is clear that they were more than astrologers (see MAGI). They were INITIATES.

Magic A name used to denote various techniques of breaking through the barriers imposed by the material plane into the spiritual realms which lie behind that plane. For possible etymology, see MAGIAN. In its widest application magic may be defined as the act of influencing the course of events through the persuasion or coercion of spiritual agencies. Such a definition includes both WHITE MAGIC or theurgy (which makes use of the beneficient spirits) and BLACK MAGIC or goety (which makes use of evil spirits). Theoretically there is a third kind of magic, sometimes called 'natural magic' by the early occultists, which does not have recourse to the agency of spirits. The fact is, however, that occultism maintains that everything on the earth plane is spiritual, and therefore it is impossible to have praxes or art forms which are not involved with the manipulation of 'spiritual forces', which are in occultism always seen as 'spiritual entities'. 'Magic', says Blavatsky, 'is the science of communicating with and directing supernal, supramundane Potencies, as well as of commanding those of the lower spheres; a practical knowledge of the hidden mysteries of nature known to only the few, because they are so difficult to acquire, without falling into sins against nature.'

In modern times there is a distinction (sometimes tacit) made between white magic and black magic, the former being called 'divine magic' in occultism, the latter 'sorcery' or the 'magic of the Left-Hand Path'. The so-called transcendental magic of modern magicians really has no link with the transcendental purposes underlying religious and mystic praxes, by which the spark of divinity in man seeks for reunion with the divine. In reality this term should be 'practical magic', for its aim is in effect that of overcoming the ordinary limitations of the physical realm, with a view to breaking through into direct and

manipulative communication with spirits – either good or bad.

As in so many other occult derivations, the etymology of the word 'magic' has given rise to unfortunate associations. It is said to come from the Greek *mageia*, itself pointing to the dualist Magian sect, or at least to Zoroastrian dualism. The Church, which took over the word, saw in all dualism a threat, and in fact consciously or unconsciously strove to define its spiritual sense by opposing itself to dualism. Thus magic, since in name and practice it savoured of dualism, was from the beginning of our era linked with heresy, with skills verging on devil worship or with practices against the law. It is therefore not surprising that all examples of magic recorded by the pagan Apuleius in *The Golden Ass*, or by the Christian Saint Augustine, are actually records of goetia; the miracles were not acts of magic but acts of faith. There was from the beginning a marked reluctance to contrast the pagan goetia with the Christian theurgy, even though the Christian praxes were in effect all based on early rituals of a theurgic kind.

This attitude to the pronounced 'magical' nature of Christian ritual and worship, rooted as it is in a profound belief in the miraculous, has never been adequately reconciled to the pagan forms of magic. It has never been sufficiently noted how the invocations of the black magicians are really debased forms of prayers used by priests and white magicians (see, for example, SABBAT). The complex, wearisome and usually ineffective conjurations of the black magicians as recorded in the GRIMOIRES found a parallel in the complex operations underlying real alchemy, which was a search for inner principles rather than for outer domination. The study and use of talismans, rituals and diabolic hierarchies, along with all the other flotsam and jetsam of black lore, found a parallel in the deep concentration and effort demanded of anyone who wished to understand the microcosmic structure through that most complex of all philosophical machines, astrology. Agrippa quite rightly insists that someone who wishes to practise magic must be skilled in natural philosophy, by which he or she will understand the qualities of beings, in mathematics, by which he or she will understand the natures of the stars and virtues, and in theology, by which he or she will understand the nature of immaterial substances, 'for there is no work that is magical that does not comprehend these three faculties'. We see therefore that the urge to point to the theurgic basis of religion came not from official theology but from the realm of the magicians themselves. See also SYMPATHETIC MAGIC.

Magic circle The magical operators or karcists who sought to bind spirits to their service by pact would protect themselves initially from such dangerous things as elementars, diakka and so on by standing in a specially prepared magical circle. In some cases the circle was drawn on the ground or on skins in special inks, blood or as invisible tracings by magical stones. Such a circle is usually of a complex design; only rarely is it a simple circle. Most frequently it is one of the triangles or

Figure 47 *Black magicians sacrificing a goat and raising spirits in a magic circle*

pentagrams or rings associated with the name of Solomon and often using the name of Jesus or Christ and religious symbols. Within the circle the name or character of the spirit being called for binding was usually drawn or set out in sigillic form, and in many cases the horoscopic characters or sigils for the relevant time were also put into the circle, certain times (not only days, but even hours within such days) being regarded as especially efficacious for such evocations. The somewhat dramatized image (Figure 47) of the magicians disembowelling a goat in preparation for a goetic practice is perhaps not too far from being an accurate picture. The magician in the magic circle to the right of the picture is holding symbols of the two extremes of the cosmos – a model of the heavens and a skull, a symbol of inert matter and death.

Magic nails   The driving of a nail into a substance has for many centuries been regarded as a symbolic act, or as an actual means of transmitting magical power. The idea is that the magician carries in his soul a strong wish as he drives in a

Figure 48   *The four sides of an inscribed magic nail from the Collegio Romano (nineteenth-century print, after Elworthy)*

nail with a hammer, and that the act of hammering gives power to that wish. By exerting force in this way, the magician is operating a SYMPATHETIC MAGIC, driving his own wish deeply into the world. Sometimes the nail will have been prepared according to occult praxes, with magical invocations or with special virtue-bearing symbols, sigils or inscriptions scratched upon its head or slender body. Such 'prepared' nails have survived from several ancient sources, one of the most interesting being a large nail from the Collegio Romano which has on one face a magical formula and on the three remaining faces many of the devices and sigils commonly found on magic AMULETS, such as a snake, frog, scorpion and hare (Figure 48). There are many traditions concerning the efficacy of such magical nails, from the ancient Roman belief (recorded by Livy) that the plague in a city might be stopped by the Dictator driving in a nail, to the talismanic use of the holy-relic nails from crucifixes, and the relatively recent belief that the nail from a shipwreck may be used as a specific against epilepsy.

The idea of such sympathetic nail magic underlies many occult procedures and may be linked with the occult virtue of iron, which is the metal of Mars, and hence linked with the Devil. The esotericist Elworthy tells us that the mere utterance of the word *defigere* (originally 'to fix down') implies that a nail has been driven in and that thereby the EVIL EYE has been counteracted. There are records of magicians impressing Martian aggression (or the 'death wish') into objects representing living creatures, such as WAX IMAGES or animal remains, to bring about illness or even death.

Magic numbers   See the entries for each of the letters of the alphabet, MAGIC SQUARE, SOUL NUMBERS and TETRACTYS. For numerology, see NUMBERS.

Magic square   The name given to an amuletic device used in the medieval magical tradition and linked with the series of numbers ascribed to the planets or to the spiritual rulers of the planets. The origination of magic squares ranges from very simple to highly complex manipulations of groups of numbers. The act of manipulation and the resulting numerological sequences have been shown to have given rise to graphic sigils, seals and characters used to represent planetary

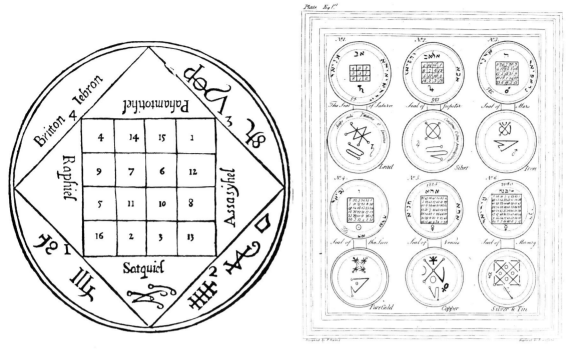

Figure 49   *The magic square of Jupiter*

Figure 51   *The planetary magic squares, along with the planetary seals derived from them (after Barrett)*

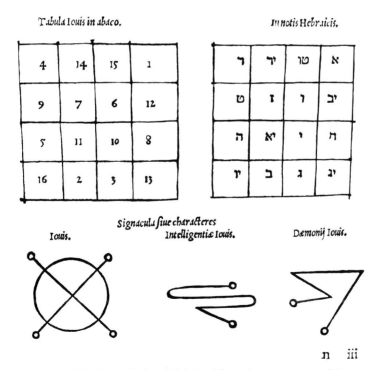

Figure 50   *The magic square of Jupiter with the sigil derived from the construction of this square from an ordinary numerical sequence. To the right is the Hebraic magic square (the letters representing numerical equivalents)*

137

daimons. To see how these are derived we may examine more closely the magic square for Jupiter, which is at the centre of the magic seal in Figure 49. This sequence of numbers is derived in the following way. From the simple numerical sequence:

```
 4   3   2   1
 8   7   6   5
12  11  10   9
16  15  14  13
```

the inner pairs of peripheral numbers – (3 2) (8 12) (15 14) and (5 9) – are transposed diametrically. This then gives the sequence in the magic square, thus:

```
      14  15
 9           12
 5            8
       2   3
```

The corresponding sigil or secret symbol for Jupiter (beneath the Latin 'Iovis' in Figure 50) is nothing more than a graphic analysis of this process of manipulation. The four small circles on the cross and the cross itself point to those numbers which were fixed in relation to the original sequence, while the large circle marks out those numbers which were turned around. Each of the planets has a similar manipulated magic square, and similar series of sigils, derived in a related manner. The magic square to the right in Figure 50 is the Hebraic form of the square to the left, the letters of the alphabet being the equivalent of numbers. Figure 51 gives the traditional magical squares of Saturn, Jupiter, Mars, the Sun, Venus and Mercury. In the Saturn square each line of figures adds up to 15, which is the number of Saturn. The seal beneath this magic square is derived by linking together all the numbers in the square with a series of straight lines.

Magic stones Certain stones (precious, semi-precious or otherwise) were regarded by occultists as having specific properties which enabled them to be used as TALISMANS or as prophylactic sources of power. Occult literature is replete with mention of such stones and their imagined VIRTUE. For example, the stone called Amandinus enables the wearer to solve any questions relating to dreams or enigmas; the black stone Antiphates was a specific against witchcraft or the evil eye; the Androdamus from the Red Sea sands was credited with the power over anger and lunacy; the Anacithidus was a necromantic stone,

with the power to evoke demons, and so on. The names given to stones were often blinds to cover principles and cosmic properties of value in alchemy – see, for excample, MAGNES, which is so often translated in exoteric sources as meaning 'lodestone', whereas it actually denoted the Akasha. Some of the magical stones, and even ordinary stones such as gems and diamonds used only for decoration, were manufactured into certain forms by means of the incision of magical sigils, symbols or words, and the observation of certain rites at relevant astrological hours. Such 'manufactured stones' were often called artificial GAMALEI. See also BETYLES.

Magnes A term used in ALCHEMY, exoterically of the lodestone but esoterically of the AKASHA. The derived word 'magnetic' was used in healing MESMERISM and hypnotherapy for a long time, originating in the belief that the healing powers so derived were from the Akasha (see also IATRIC). Animal magnetism was itself derived from the Akasha (sometimes described as a 'fluid', but really an emanation as palpable as a fluid – see ECTENIC FORCE), although the term was seemingly derived to distinguish this from the spiritual or cosmic magnetism, which was the Magnes itself.

Magnesia An esoteric term used in ALCHEMY. Although it is certainly linked with the idea behind the MAGNES, there is much dispute about the esoteric significance of this word. According to Waite it is the 'matter of the stone.' 'Outwardly', Waite says cryptically, 'she is a stone, and yet she is no stone'. The word 'Magnesia' is certainly linked with the secret of the LAPIS, which the alchemists sometimes called Red Magnesia, sometimes White Magnesia. On the other hand, it is also said to be the name of Mercury or quicksilver, although here again it is not the liquid quicksilver which the alchemists have in mind, for it is a Magnesia 'of such a celestial and transcendental brightness, that nothing on earth can be compared to it.' The 'catholic Magnesia' is the 'sperm of the world', out of which all created things are generated. Magnesia is also called the 'Water of Life'. Altogether there are some fifty or so different names for the Magnesia, and the majority of these (along with the few esoteric definitions) point to the name being an alternative for AKASHA.

Magnetic See ANIMAL MAGNETISM and MAGNES.

Magnum opus Latin for 'great work' or 'great labour'. In occultism it is almost always used in an alchemical sense – sometimes for the alchemical art as a whole, and sometimes for the final stage of that art, the actual manufacture of the PHILOSOPHER'S STONE or the ELIXIR. See ALCHEMY.

Magos See MAGIAN.

Magus A term sometimes used as meaning 'astrologer', at other times 'magician'. But see MAGIAN.

Mahaguru The Sanskrit term meaning 'great teacher'.

Mahamara See MARA.

Mahamaya The Sanskrit term meaning 'great illusion' – the entire universe. But see also MAYA.

Mahat A Sanskrit term meaning 'great one' and applied to the first principle of universal consciousness.

Mahatma A Sanskrit term (see MAHAT) used in reference to the perfected human being. These are the true gurus, the masters, teachers of humanity, who have gained mastery over the lower quaternary of their nature, have perfected to the utmost of possible development the higher ternary, and are thus fitted as esotericists to lead humanity by education towards its evolutionary purpose.

Mahavidya The Sanskrit term meaning 'great esoteric knowledge'.

Major Arcana See TAROT.

Makatiel The name of one of the seven Angels of Punishment, the 'plague of God'.

Malachim The Hebraic term for the ANGELS. There is a secret script, recorded by Trithemius, called Malachim writing; it is sometimes also called Enochian. See SECRET SCRIPTS.

Malachy prophecies Title given to a series of prophecies dealing with the sequence of the papal succession up to the end of the world, supposedly written about 1139 by the Archbishop of Armagh as a result of a vision he experienced while attending Innocent II during the Second Lateran Council. He was said to have given the sequence of prophecies to the Pope in order to console him during the difficult period arising from the contemporary schism. The manuscript was said to have been placed by the Pontiff in the archives of the Vatican, where it was discovered in 1590 (certainly it was published shortly after this date).

While it has been reasonably claimed that this story is apochryphal, there may be no doubt that the prophecies are of a remarkably apposite kind. Each of the prophecies (save for the last one) consists of two or three Latin words. Together they list 112 future popes, from Coelestinus II up to the end of the world, which, according to the prophecies, is due in the present century. The terse epithets of the prophecies often summarize an important aspect of the life or work of an individual pontiff, or seize upon some unique quality by which he might be identified, such as a reference to a coat of arms, place of birth, dignity held and so on. Examples culled from the list are often pertinent: Pius VII (1800–1832) was held captive by Napoleon, who annexed the Papal States to France in 1809. In the prophecies Pius was designated by the phrase *Aquila rapax* ('rapacious eagle'), with obvious reference to Napoleon, whose symbol was the eagle. Leo XIII (1878–1903) was called *Lumen in coelo* ('light in Heaven') and he had on his crest a comet. When, in 1789, O'Brien was surveying the prophecies attached to the popes then still to come, he was disturbed by the coming threat of *Religio depopulata* ('religion laid waste') which proved to apply to the papacy of Benedict XV (1914–22), the years of the reign alone providing reason for the stark prophecy. The present Pope, the first to come from behind the Iron Curtain, is called *Lux Orientalis* ('light from the East').

The last Pope, sometimes called *Petrus Romanus*, from the long Latin sentence designated to him, is supposed to witness the end of the world. The translation runs: 'In the final persecution of the Holy Roman Church there will preside Peter the Roman, who will feed his flock amid many tribulations. When these things are done, then the seven-hilled city will be destroyed, and the dreadful Judge will judge the people.'

Malaphar One of the variant names for VALEFOR.

139

Maleficia A word carried over into medieval literature from the Latin for 'evil doings' and applied to misfortunes and calamities of all kinds for which no immediate causal explanation might be given. Maleficia became inextricably woven into the idea of witchcraft, and with the work of the Devil, to a point where the word became a synonym for 'witch'.

Malefics In astrology the term is used to denote both harmful planets, such as Mars and Saturn, as well as harmful ASPECTS, such as the square aspect.

Malifiecus Sometimes 'malefiecus', an old term for a sorcerer or one who interprets dreams, incantations and magical characters. See MALLEUS MALIFICARUM.

Malkuth In the Qabbalistic SEPHIROTHIC TREE Malkuth is the first world of the sequence, sometimes called the Kingdom, and linked with the earth and with man (more properly, with the microcosm, which is a little more than man). In the realm of ASSIAH Malkuth is the World of Man and Elements, where they find their full expression in incarnate states. In the World of Formations (YETZIRAH) Malkuth is governed by Angels. This last Qabbalistic truth has been misunderstood by some writers, who know that the sphere of the Angels is that of the Moon, and they have accordingly confused Malkuth with the Moon. However, the realm of activity for the Angels is within the spiritual destiny of man, which is why each human being is linked with a particular Angel, through incarnation to incarnation – it is this concern which is the esoteric connection between the Angels and Malkuth. In the World of Creation, which is that of BRIAH, Malkuth is ruled by the Archangelic being Sandalphon (some say by Metatron, and yet others insist that these are identical – see, however, KETHER). In the World of Origins Malkuth is directly linked with the God-aspect called Adonai Malakh and sometimes Adonai ha Aretz (Lord of the Land – but see in this connection YAWE), who is the 'Maker of Matter' in Gray's happy phrase. It is the name 'Kingdom' which is contained within the much repeated and little understood adage that 'the Kingdom of God is within you'. This is the Malkuth of Adonai Malakh, in which the foot of the Tree and the highest beings of the spiritual realm meet.

Malleus Maleficarum The title (in Latin, meaning 'hammer of witches') of the most important of the late-medieval theological texts against witchcraft, first printed in 1486, which in its definitions and legal codification became the instrument of most later witch-hunts in Europe (see, therefore, WITCH). Its authors were the Dominicans Jakob Sprenger and Heinrich Kramer. See also AMULET.

Malpas One of the seventy-two SPIRITS OF SOLOMON. He is said to appear in the form of a black bird and to have been the demon who helped King Solomon as a builder.

Mammon Mammon was not originally a demon or even a pagan idol, but simply the Syrian term for 'money' or 'riches'. He entered the lists of demons as what has been taken as a personification in the words of Christ (Matthew, 6, 24). By biblical exegesis and popular misunderstanding he developed a variety of corrupt names (for example, AMAIMON or MAYMON) which flourished in a number of demonologies, and eventually he emerged in popular consciousness as the demon of money or (more precisely) the demon love of money. From a Syrian term for value he aspired to become under the pen of Milton 'the least erected Spirit that fell'. The symbolism of this is more profound than is generally observed, for it was the plunder of the earth which gave rise to the dwelling of the demons, which men later called PANDAEMONIUM. In Book II of Milton's poem Mammon argues that, rather than warring on God or on his representative (man), the Fallen Angels should remain in Hell to exploit its wealth. He is already becoming the demon of the Romantics, as representative of the soulless materialism. In Blake's vision Mammon appears to be one of the few demons which the poet used unadulterated in significance, as a sort of deification of misuse of money.

Mana A Polynesian–Melanesian term for a mystery efficacy, much like an energy, which may reside in anything, and which may be used for protecting or destroying (at the will of the operator) things, animals and people. Each object and person is said to have its own *mana*, but this may be increased or decreased by magical rites. Objects highly charged with *mana* are regarded as having powerful magical potency. Spirits, whether evil or beneficient, have *mana* of their own, and it is this which may be used for the ruination or for the benefit of man. See also SYMPATHETIC MAGIC.

Manas   A word derived from the Sanskrit root meaning 'to think' and applied to a wide range of mental activities. In present times the centre of Ego consciousness is said to lie in Manas, as the permanent indestructible and knowing 'I'. The Theosophists distinguish a dual Manas, the higher and the lower. The higher spiritual entity of Manas may not descend directly into matter, but towards this end it will project downwards a ray, which is usually called the 'lower Manas'. It is this lower Manas which manifests through the brain, and which in ordinary man becomes involved with the emotional life. In terms of this definition what we call the mind or intellect is merely a shadow of the true Manas, which is possessed by all men but manifests purely only in the very rare cases of initiates or men of genius (see TERNARY). In esotericism the development of the Manas is said to be a result of conscious work on the Astral Body.

Manasa rupa   See TAIJASI.

Manes   A Latin term for the shades of the dead or SHELLS. See LEMURES.

Manipura   A Sanskrit name for the Navel CHAKRA, which has ten lotus petals and is said to be predominantly of a red colour, with a quantity of green within its moving form.

Mantic frenzy   A term used in Greek times to denote a state of possession in which diviners permit spirits to occupy their bodies or to make use of their speech organs, with a view to making predictions about the future (see, therefore, POSSESSION). The Greek word *manteis* means 'prophets', and the practice of frenzy is sometimes called 'manticism'. Some forms of mediumship verge on mantic frenzy. See PYTHIA.

Manticism   See MANTIC FRENZY.

Manushis   A name given to the sages of the THIRD RACE.

Manzils   The Arabian term for the twenty-eight LUNAR MANSIONS, from which the European word 'mansions' appears to have been derived.

Mara   In the exoteric oriental religions Mara is a demon, one of the demoted ASURAS. In esotericism Mara is, as Blavatsky puts it, 'personified temptation through men's vices'. The Sanskrit term means 'that which kills', referring to that which, through such successful temptations, kills the soul. The king of the Maras (Mahamara) carries a jewel on his staff (sometimes in his crown) with which he blinds men. The symbol is probably intended to show how Mara works through the illusion of MAYA, which is external nature.

Marbas   One of the seventy-two SPIRITS OF SOLOMON, a great president of Hell.

Marchosias   One of the seventy-two SPIRITS OF SOLOMON. He is said to appear in the form of a winged wolf, breathing fire.

Margaritomancy   Divination by means of pearls. Sometimes the pearls are used as instruments for SCRYING, but other methods of divination are recorded involving the animation of pearls by spiritual agencies intent on giving responses to questions.

Mark   See PRICKING.

Mars   The planet in orbit between the Sun and Jupiter. It more clearly resembles the Earth in regard to physical factors than any of the other planets, although it has a diameter just over half that of the Earth. In the esoteric structure of Boehme's SEVEN PROPERTIES Mars is the third form which is likened to a turning wheel representing a fusion between the centripetal direction of Saturn and the centrifugal power of Mercury, and which is called the 'turning wheel of desire'. The result of the meeting between the flight of Mercury and the restraint and fixity of Saturn is a fusion of the centripetal and centrifugal, which means that both the destructive and the creative powers are locked within its nature. In occultism Mars is always the representative of that desire which will bind itself to the material realm, to flesh, either by domination or by carnal desire. This explains why Mars is at once the planet of war (domination) and the planetary god who seeks to be the lover of Venus (carnal desire). In modern astrology Mars is the ruler of zodiacal Aries, but in traditional astrology the duality of Mars was more adequately expressed in its second rulership over Scorpio (now displaced by Pluto). Some astrologers say that it is exalted in Capricorn, with its corresponding fall in Cancer. In exoteric astrology Mars represents the physical side of the native's life and is an index of his energy, endurance, his ability to carry projects through and the active side of his temperament. Mars is directly linked with the sex drive, in which it cooperates with the planet Venus, the former being active, the latter passive. When Mars is well emphasized in a chart, the native is courageous, enterprising, confident, active and proud. In particular the planet bestows great energy, with an ability to construct or destroy. A badly placed Mars tends towards disruption and explosions: the native is rough, reckless, destructive and self-centred. Traditionally Mars has dominion over the sexual parts in the human being. The planet is a useful index of how quickly the physical energies may be called into play as a result of disturbances on the physical or astral plane. The Martian type usually finds expression on the physical plane through activities demanding the exertion of physical energy, and especially in connection with activities which give rapid results. All work involving the use of iron and steel, sharp tools and weapons of war are connected with Mars, so that military establishments, slaughterhouses, waste-disposal units, mortuaries and so on are its dominion. See MATTER.

Marseilles pack See TAROT.

Marthim See BATHIN.

Martinelli See FAMILIAR.

Mary's bath Se BALNEUM MARIAE.

Masak Mavdil A Qabbalistic term for the ABYSS, meaning 'place of rejected failures'.

Mash-mak A term explained in occult and Theosophical literature as having survived from the time of ATLANTIS, originally used as the name of a cosmic force which was said to be powerful enough to reduce whole cities to dust and to disintegrate the material world. See VRIL.

Maslem One of the Qabbalistic names for the ruler of the zodiac. See ARCHANGELS OF THE ZODIAC.

Master See MAHATMA.

Mastiphal One of the several names given to the Prince of Demons. See LUCIFER.

Materialization The appearance, particularly in seances, of organic-seeming entities, which seem to have an existence contiguous with the material plane. Spirits which under normal conditions are invisible to ordinary eyes may under certain circumstances materialize by means of the ELEMENTAL ESSENCE or by means of ECTOPLASM. Such materializations are generally of a temporary nature, and the energy for such events appears to be derived from the medium conducting the seance or from a willing or unwilling participant within the seance. Very many cases of materializations of spirits have been studied and recorded by scientists interested in such things. A large number of materializations have been photographed in varying stages of composition and decomposition, or 'dematerialization'. While a whole human figure may take up to twenty minutes to materialize completely, it may dematerialize in a few seconds. There are several cases of animal materialization. The more or less instant materialization of inorganic objects is usually linked with APPORTS, although flowers, jewels and such like sometimes materialize slowly and dematerialize in the full sight of those present in a seance. See also PROTOPLASTUS.

Mathematicians Sometimes 'mathematicals', a term used as synonymous with 'astrologers' in early treatises.

Mathesis A word from the Greek root of a word meaning 'to learn'. In medieval occult lore the two Latinized Greek words for 'mathesis' were distinguished by an accent over the a, which is now rarely used. The first was taken to denote knowledge gained from mental study, the second was taken to denote knowledge gained by means of divinatory practices, usually involving forbidden conference with demons. The name *Mathesis* is used also to denote the longest ancient text on astrology, written by Firmicus Maternus. See also PANSOPHIA.

Matter In the secret doctrine the materiality of the world is at once an illusory veil over spiritual entities and forces and at the same time the most highly evolved expression of the Logos. Matter is said to be compounded light and may be examined only when bathed in the forces from which it was created. It is an important part of the esoteric doctrine that one of the main purposes of human life is the redemption of matter, the returning of dark materiality to its original light-formed nature. Matter is generally associated with the dark principle of nature, which is of a receptive feminine kind, which explains the almost universal use of the root *Ma* (in 'matter', 'maya', 'Mary' and so on) to denote concepts of this kind. MARS is symbol of imprisoned matter awaiting the redemptive future.

Maya A Sanskrit term meaning 'illusion', almost the equivalent of our modern 'phenomena', but used mainly of the realm of nature, which is visualized as being an illusory surface behind which there is a spiritual reality. It is often claimed that the word was originally used as the equivalent of 'puppet show', suggesting that the material realm is an ephemeral play of the gods. See MATTER.

Maymon A name given to the Demon King, conjured as a monstrous bird-headed humanoid, along with a dragon-like steed (Figure 52). The word is perhaps a corruption of 'MAMMON'.

Figure 52 *The Demon King Maymon (from a fifteenth-century manuscript book of conjurations, private collection)*

Mazzikin See INFERNAL HIERARCHIES.

Medium In popular use this term is applied to those who have the ability, conscious or unconscious, to communicate with one or other of the realms of spirit. Ignorance of the true nature of these realms has led many individuals (even serious investigators) to believe that the spiritual entities raised or contacted are actually the spiritual relics of those who have passed from the material plane into death. There is very little evidence for the truth of this, however. Even Andrew Jackson Davis, an influential American spiritualist, warned that the spiritual beings who were prepared to invade seances or to participate in such gatherings, were not always what they seemed (see, for example, DIAKKA). Occultists usually distinguish between the mediumship which is a result of atavistic clairvoyant abilities, and that mediumship (really 'spiritual vision') which is a result of conscious development (by means of moral and spiritual efforts) of the higher bodies. The true occultist never seeks to practise mediumship as such, but is none the less conversant with the post-mortem conditions of diseased humans through direct spiritual vision. It is generally regarded as harmful to the dead to seek to bring them down into the darker realms of the material plane.

Medium coeli In astrology a term derived from the Latin meaning 'middle of the skies' and used to denote the Midheaven of the horoscope figure, that point directly above the place for which the figure is cast. This should not be confused with the tenth house cusp. The opposite point on the chart is the IMUM COELI. *Medium coeli* is sometimes abbreviated to M C.

Melancholic One of the four TEMPERAMENTS, derived from an excess of Earth element in the make-up of the personality. The melancholic type is withdrawn, conservative, practical and reliable. In astrology the melancholic nature is associated with the three Earth signs, Taurus, Virgo and Capricorn, though it is the last which is most deeply of this elemental nature. Under extreme conditions the melancholic is narrow, miserly, unadventurous and egotistical, most of the faults arising from lack of fluidity.

Melothesic man Popularly termed the 'zodiacal man', the melothesic man is that symbolic image of man which is linked with the twelve zodiacal signs – an image which was introduced to Europe with Arabian astrology in the twelfth century. The simple exoteric diagrams show the human head ruled by Aries, the throat by Taurus, the arms by Gemini, the ribcage by Cancer, the heart by Leo, the stomach by Virgo, the pelvis by Libra, the private parts by Scorpio, the thighs by Sagittarius, the knee and skeletal frame as a whole by Capricorn, the lower leg by Aquarius, and the feet by Pisces. This exoteric rulership is merely the occult blind front for a more complex esoteric series of rulerships, however.

Menstruum universale Se ALCHEMY.

Mercurial Waters See AKASHA.

Mercurius One of the medieval names for MERCURY, and in esotericism one of the names for TRISMEGISTUS. In astrology it is also a name given by Thierens to a future development of his own Hermes as Mercury–Vulcan (see, however, VULCAN PERIOD), which is said to be a principle of transmission. The name is also used in ALCHEMY to denote the unifying agency of Mercury (see, for example, THREE PRINCIPLES).

Mercury A name given in ALCHEMY to the spagyric secret of the LAPIS and to quicksilver (see MAGNESIA and CADUCEUS, which is the emblem of Mercury and the alchemical MERCURIUS). It is also the name given to the planet in orbit nearest to the Sun, although in traditional astrology, founded on pre-Copernican models, it was thought to be in orbit between the Moon and Venus. In esoteric lore Mercury is seen as the unifying element in the THREE PRINCIPLES, and in the cosmology of Boehme it is the second form of the SEVEN PROPERTIES which strives in freedom against the restraint imposed upon it by Saturn; it is therefore centrifugal and outgoing as a cosmic power, 'in eternal flight from fixity', as Freher puts it. For the Qabbalistic tradition relating to Mercury, see HOD. The sigil for Mercury ☿ has been interpreted in many different ways, but most astrologers see in it a union of the three forms of crescent, circle and cross, as representative of the ability of Mercury to bring things together and to unify. This is the exoteric level of looking at the esoteric tradition connected with the planet in astro-alchemical circles (see ALCHEMICAL

MERCURY, and for some mention of the occult background see NUNTIUS). Mercury has rule over Gemini and Virgo, with corresponding detriments in Sagittarius and Pisces. Some astrologers say that it is exalted in Aquarius, with its fall in Leo. Mercury represents the ability of the native to communicate with others: in traditional astrology it ruled human speech and such activities as letter writing. It is also an index of mentality, although it is concerned with the details, with short-term reactions, with memory and with day-to-day problems, rather than with profound metaphysical thinking, which is really the domain of Jupiter. A badly placed Mercury, or one badly aspected, tends towards exaggeration of speech – in lying, sarcasm or excessive volubility. Traditionally Mercury ruled the hands and arms of the human body, as well as the lungs.

Mercury of the Philosophers In ALCHEMY one of the names given to the spagyric LAPIS, the development of which is the aim of the Great Work (see, however, MERCURY). The 'philosophers' are the alchemists.

Meru See ABIEGNUS MONS.

Mesham The Sanskrit name for zodiacal Aries, but see also ACVINI.

Mesmerism See ANIMAL MAGNETISM.

Mesukeil A name given to the spiritual guardian of the ABYSS.

Metagraphology A term applied by certain psychic research workers to PSYCHOMETRY by means of manuscripts.

Metatron Sometimes Metraton, in the Qabbalistic system Metatron is the first of the ten Archangels of the world of BRIAH, and is called the King of Angels, the Liberating Angel and the Heavenly Scribe (not to be confused with the LIPIKA, however); see KETHER. When invoked on the physical plane he is said to appear as a pillar of fire, with a face more dazzling that the sun. According to the *Zohar* he is of the size equal to the breadth of the whole world (a fine esoteric symbolism). The same name is also used for the higher of the two inseparable companions of man on the earth plane; he is virtually the equivalent of the GUARDIAN ANGEL of Christian esotericism. See also SAMAEL, by whom he is opposed.

Metempsychosis A Greek term meaning the 'passage of the soul (or spirit) of a human being or animal after death into a new body'. This body might in theory be that of a human being or an animal, but esotericism teaches that under normal circumstances a human may metempsychose only into a human state; the metampsychosis of animals is of a different order altogether (see GROUP SOULS). In popular thought metempsychosis is equated with transmigration of souls. Occultists suggest that the term 'metempsychosis' has been misunderstood and misused for centuries, and should apply only to animals. Human beings are properly subject to the laws of personal REINCARNATION.

Metensomatosis A Greek term meaning approximately 'changing of body after body' and applied in a more general sense than the word REINCARNATION. The idea behind metensomatosis is that the human spirit does not always descend into corporeal flesh, that the body in distant times was of an altogether different constitution from that of today, and in the far distant future human bodies will no longer be formed from flesh but from an etheric material. In a more specific sense, therefore, the word may be defined as meaning 'the periodic changing of the human vehicle in accordance with human evolutionary aims'.

Methetherial A term coined by Myers to indicate the world in which spirits exist – literally 'beyond the ether'. Since occultists maintain that spirits exist in every world, the term is meaningless from a strictly occultist point of view.

Metonic cycle A cycle of nineteen years, named after the Athenian astronomer Meton who first formulated its true nature. The cycle marks the return of a cycle of solar eclipses to a specific degree of the zodiac. Distinguish from the SAROS CYCLE. See also GOLDEN NUMBER.

Metraton Sometimes Metratton. See META-TRON.

Michael The Archangel linked with the rule of the sphere of the Sun, and said by some to be the leader of the Archangels; Trithemius makes him the leader of the SECUNDADEIAN BEINGS. The name Michael is properly pronounced 'Mikhaiel'. In the esoteric Christian tradition Michael is the guardian of the newly dead soul, on whose behalf he will fight the demonic hordes. He is linked in the astrological lore with rule over the element of Fire, and is often depicted with the attributes of a golden sword and a pair of scales, derived from Egyptian symbolism, for the weighing of souls. See also FOURTH HEAVEN.

Microcosm A term from the Greek meaning 'little world' or 'small arrangement' and usually applied in astrological contexts to man, who is the small arrangement of the cosmos (see MACRO-COSM). Technically, any complete entity which contains within it a summary of all the working of the laws within the macrocosm is a microcosm. In terms of the occult theory of cosmogenesis, man is defined as the vehicle which spans the gulf between the highest and lowest manifestations of a particular world system. By such definition each man is a model of the entire universe and contains within him (either in developed form or in potential) each and every manifestation to which the universe may be subject. For example, in the triadic world of the present age the solar force represents the creative energies of the highest order, and these find a link with the brain and heart of man. The lunar and earthly forces, representing the lowest energies working from beneath man (sometimes indeed termed the demonic), find a centre in the sexual sphere. Thus man is 'inhabited' by the (solar) angels and by the (telluric) demons, and is the unifier of these two different beings, through which he learns to exercise consciousness and love. The unifying force is the emotional part of man, called in alchemy the 'Mercurial' (see THREE PRINCIPLES). This triad is preserved in a vast number of ancient images depicting universal or microcosmic man, from the theological image of the crucified Christ between the Sun and Moon, to the occult images popularized by Fludd. The solar image always represents the angelic nature and the lunar image the demonic nature.

A glance at the microcosmic man described by Fludd will indicate something of the triadic nature of the micro-macrocosm. Man is pictured within the ambient of the macrocosm, as a threefold being inhabiting a physical body (Figure 53). The lowest part, the *Regio elementaris*, is quite mortal, a shade which returns after physical death to the realm of darkness – it is of the matter of Earth, of the four elements. This is the realm charged with the faculty of perceiving colours, dimensions and materiality – the word 'matter' and the Sanskrit

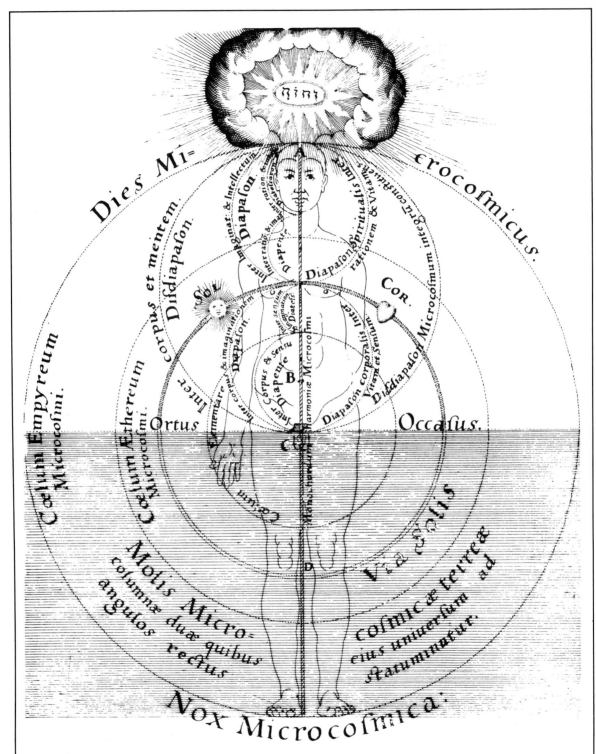

Figure 53   *Man the microcosm standing in the three worlds (seventeenth century, after Fludd)*

maya ('illusion') are cognate. The highest spirit, the *Regio inellectus*, is linked with the stars and presents the clarity of selfhood. It governs the intellectual life of man, being objective in its view, capable of developed wisdom and justice. Connecting these two is the 'spirit of life', the *Orbis solis seu cordis* (the Orb of the Sun or of the Heart). The function of this third part is to remain within the true divine light within man and to resist error. It is linked with the emotional life, detects spiritual similitudes and likenesses, and echoes the realm of the planets.

No great difficulty would be required to link this triadic model with the triadic astro-alchemical model of the Paracelsian Crude Ilech (which is really another name for the microcosm – see ILECH). The Crude Ilech consists of Salt (the thinking part, which is linked in the alchemical model with the lunar forces), Sulphur (the will part of man, linked in the alchemical model with the Mars forces and with sexuality), and the mediator, Mercury (the emotional part, in the seat of the heart). This triadic relationship between the microcosm and the ambient macrocosm is sometimes dispensed with in occult and astrological literature, and a septenary relationship (directed to the planetary forms) is etablished as an alternative model of man. It is maintained in occult circles that any valid spiritual model of the microcosm (and hence of the macrocosm) must be at once a triad and a septenary. The theory of the nature of the microcosm in its specific relationship to the macrocosm actually constitutes the bulk of modern occult studies, as, for example, developed by such esotericists as Blavatsky, Steiner and Bailey. The five-pointed star is sometimes called the 'microcosm' (see Figure 55, under MORNING STAR).

Microprosopus   See MACROPROSOPUS.

Midas   Name given to one of the HYPOTHETICAL PLANETS, said to be in trans-Plutonian orbit.

Midheaven   In astrology the 'Midheaven' is a term properly applied to the culminating degree of the ecliptic.

Mights   See DYNAMIS.

Minam   Sometimes Minas or Meenam, the Sanskrit terms for zodiacal Pisces, as used in Hindu astrology.

Mind Soul   A term used by Steiner (in the German *Gemutseele*) to denote the INTELLECTUAL SOUL, the activity of which is linked with the operation of the EGO. By taking cognizance of external objects the Mind Soul increasingly liberates itself from the external world of perception to work within its own spiritual realm.

Minor Arcana   See TAROT.

Minos   Name given to one of the HYPOTHETICAL PLANETS.

Mithunam   The Sanskrit name for zodiacal Gemini, but see MRGACIRSHA.

Mixtum   Sometimes the QUINTESSENCE is called *mixtum* in medieval occult and alchemical texts, presumably on the grounds that it is the fifth element which permits the four mutually antagonistic elements to work in harmony as a mixture.

Modern planets   The so-called modern planets are those which have been discovered since the development of advanced optical instruments, and added to the planetary schema of seven planets used by the ancients. These planets are URANUS, NEPTUNE and PLUTO, although some astrologers also include the ASTEROIDS.

Modern Rosicrucianism   See ROSICRUCIANISM.

Modern zodiac   The modern zodiac, sometimes called the 'modern astronomical zodiac', was defined during the 1928 conference of the International Astronomical Union (hence, it is sometimes also called the 'IAU zodiac'). Strictly

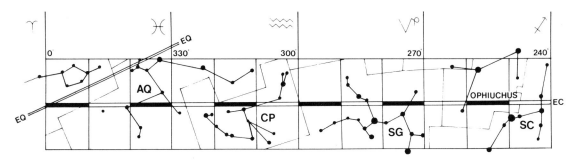

Figure 54   *A section of the modern zodiac of Delporte, along the ecliptic from the constellation Scorpius (SC) to Aquarius (AQ). Note how the constellation Ophiuchus is part of this 'zodiacal' sequence. Observe also the position of the tropical zodiac (marked with the sigils of the zodiacal signs) for these asterisms. The line marked EQ is the equator*

speaking it is not a zodiac but a constellational grid definition. It was published by Delporte in 1930. The sequence of asterisms, with their curious grids defined by complex geometric means, are set out in Figure 54.

Moirai   See FATAE.

Molybdomancy   A term derived from the Greek *molibdos* ('lead') and *manteia* ('divination') and applied to a method of divination from studying the shapes made by cooled lead, rather like that of CEROMANCY.

Monad   In its original Greek etymology the term 'monad' was applied to the basic indivisible unit of a cosmos or numerical system; thus the word might apply equally to the vast solar system, which was viewed as a cosmos, or to the tiniest atom. The word was adopted into astrological and occult terminology with a similar meaning, although with a special application to the realm of spirit rather than matter (see, for excample, DEALE). Thus in Theosophical literature it is often taken as representing the unity of the spiritual ternary Atma–Buddhi–Manas, 'that immortal part of man which reincarnates in the lower kingdoms', as Blavatsky puts it. In this sense the human monad is in modern occultism that indestructible element within each individual human that continues through the cycles of reincarnation. In popular occultism the monad is equated with the EGO, however, and not with the developed TERNARY. For another meaning of the term, see MONAS HIEROGLYPHICA.

Monas hieroglyphica   A name given by Dee to a sigil sometimes called the 'monad' or 'monas', which he used as the basis for an erudite treatise on graphic symbolism. The sigil ☿ consists of the standard form for Mercury inserted into the open sigil for Aries. The importance of the sigil lies not so much in its form as in the esoteric argument used by Dee to explain the magical nature of its structure, in his *Monas Hieroglyphica* of 1558.

Monomoiria   A term derived from Hellenistic astrology, although probably related to earlier astrological forms, and linked with the tradition that each degree of the ecliptic is associated with a planetary influence.

Moon   The satellite of the Earth, called in astrology a 'planet'. In esotericism the Moon is usually linked with the development of the ASTRAL nature of man, with his animal nature. For the Qabbalistic tradition, see YESOD. The Moon is the seventh form in Boehme's influential SEVEN PROPERTIES and is involved with the 'final concrete realizations' which must follow on the sequence of planetary interactions, leading inevitably from its own natural fluidity of form into the fixity and death grip of Saturn, and thus starting the sequence anew. In astrology the Moon has rule over zodiacal Cancer and is exalted in Taurus, with its corresponding fall in Scorpio. In a horoscope chart the Moon represents the imaginative, reflective side of the native and is justifiably linked with the subconscious element in the modern image of man. It is an index of the receptive, withdrawn, secluded part of the person. When the Moon is emphasized in a chart it is usually an indication of a highly sensitive, impressionable and changeable nature, often linked with a personality in some way associated with the past or with childhood. A badly placed Moon, or one badly aspected, tends to give rise to a personality which is hypersensitive, untidy, withdrawn, morbidly concerned with self and strangely subject to misfortune. Traditionally the Moon is given rule over the breasts in the human body and, through its rule over Cancer, with the ribcage. However, in some systems both the womb and the lymph glands are associated with this planet.

Moon Chain   A term applied in the Theosophical cosmoconception to the third CHAIN of the evolution of the Earth. This was the equivalent of the Moon in the present EARTH CHAIN, and the present physical body of the Moon is visualized as a disintegrating crust, much diminished in size and on its way to destruction. This Theosophical teaching is much opposed by several other esoteric doctrines (see, for example, EIGHT SPHERES). The most highly developed beings to emerge from the Moon Chain are called the Sons of Twilight and sometimes the Barhishads. These are the modern angels.

Moon forces   See SUN FORCES.

Moon Period   The Moon Period is said to represent the third of the planetary evolutionary states, following on the SATURN PERIOD and the SUN PERIOD. Initially it was a condition of moisture, which was said to densify, although it did carry spiritual elements from previous stages of cosmogenesis, so that while the ancient Moon body is said in occult circles to be of its Water element, the equivalent of its atmosphere is Firefog. This Moon Period, which is only tenuously linked with the present Moon of our system, is sometimes called the Old Moon. The period of the evolutionary state was said to have been overseen by the hierarchy of Seraphim.

Moon Revolution   A term derived from modern esoteric astrology, and relating to cosmogenesis. It is said that the path of the evolution of our solar system, with its periods of activity and sleep, must recapitulate the entire sequence of evolution. Since the third stage of the cosmogenesis of our present system took place in the MOON PERIOD, the term 'Moon Revolution' pertains to the third of these recapitulations.

Morax   One of the seventy-two SPIRITS OF SOLOMON. He is said to appear as a sort of Minotaur, with the body of a man, merged with the head of a bull.

Morning Star   In esoteric lore one of the names given to the PENTAGRAM, and in exoteric lore to the planet Venus (see, for example, LUCIFER). This form is linked esoterically with what art historians call the *orans* or 'praying' gesture. This gesture is imitated in the five points of the pentagram (which echoes the two feet, the two outstretched arms and the head); see Figure 55. Strictly speaking, it is not an *orans* gesture so much as an image of the departed soul, symbolized in the ETHERIC, at the beginning (or morning) of his postmortem existence; hence (perhaps) the esoteric link with the Morning Star, Venus. This five-pointed star is sometimes called the MICROCOSM.

Motori   See INTELLIGENCY.

Moving Fire   See OCCULT TRINITY.

Mrgacirsha   The Sanskrit name for the constellation Gemini, but see MITHUNAM.

Mudra   A Sanskrit term used to denote certain positions of the fingers in devotional or meditative praxes.

Mukti   When, as a result of spiritual development, the trammels of illusory MAYA are lifted

Figure 55   *Morning Star: the power of Venus (ruler of the physical body) in the five-pointed star (sixteenth century, after Agrippa)*

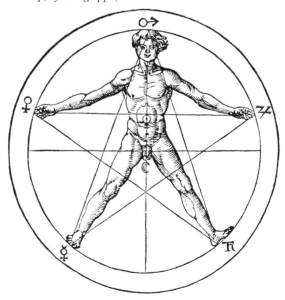

from the eyes of an initiate, he is said to have reached Nirvana or Mukti.

Mula The Sanskrit name for the constellation Sagittarius, but see also DHANUS. The same term (meaning 'root') is also used of the seventeenth of the Hindu NAKSHATRAS.

Muladhara The Sanskrit name for the Root CHAKRA, which radiates in four lotus petals. It is often symbolized as a flaming cross, to indicate the fiery nature of the KUNDALINI force which lies dormant within it.

Mulaprakriti A Sanskrit word usually translated as meaning 'primordial substance'. It is said to form the basic matter for every phenomenon on the material, mental and psychic plane.

Mumia Originated as an occult term by Paracelsus to indicate the life force which permeates all nature, it is the force which (in modern images) changes ordinary molecular structure into cellular life and which (when withdrawn) allows matter to sink back to its molecular components (see ANIMAL MAGNETISM). It is therefore something equivalent to the ETHERIC and is perhaps linked with the alchemical MAGNESIA, being the therapeutic element derived from this. Paracelsus emphasizes its healing power – indeed, according to him the function of the doctor should be merely to aid the Mumia to heal the body in his charge. 'Mummy', an unfortunate English equivalent used in certain translations, has given rise to misunderstandings about the occult virtue of Mumia. See also SYMPATHETIC MAGIC.

Mummy See MUMIA.

Mundane astrology Astrology limited to casting and interpreting specialist charts directed towards the exmination of national trends – a subdivision of what has been called 'historical astrology'.

Murmur One of the seventy-two SPIRITS OF SOLOMON. He is said to appear in the form of a duke, riding a griffin. He is one of the necromantic demons, second only in power or popularity (with the magicians) to GAMGYN.

Music of the Spheres It is one of the most insistent ideas of occultism that the macrocosm

resounds with the beauty of celestial music. The nine MUSES of Hesiod have been associated by occultists with this music; these were the daughters of Zeus and Mnemosyne (whose name means 'remembrance'), and so we are inclined to find in classical literature a link with occult teaching which would have our souls 'remembering' the celestial world, in the Platonic sense of the word. The idea of a planetary music has been attributed wrongly to Pythagoras. He did, however, lay the basis for the idea of planetary ratios when he showed that intervals of the scale could be expressed in simple ratios: the intervals known to the ancients were the 4th, 5th and octave. Pythagoras applied these ratios to the supposed distances of the planets. He maintained that since the ratios of the scales extend into the heavens, then the whole of the substellar realm should echo to a heavenly music. When the concept of the planetary spheres was developed, the original Pythagorean idea was extended and popularly called 'Music of the Spheres'. It was thus passed into the Neo-Platonic tradition which elaborated on the basic ideas. The architect Alberti, and such musicologists as Gafurus, drew a detailed picture of the planetary relationships and corresponding tones and intervals which profoundly influenced humanistic art and literature in respect to the notion of planetary harmonies, and which in fact still reverberate in many of our modern conceptions of ratios and planetary natures.

Several explanations have since been given as to why we in the sublunar sphere do not hear this music. Pythagoras was of the opinion that we did not hear it because our souls were out of *krasis* (out of 'harmony') with the stellar music. Some say that we are deafened by its perpetual sound, while others maintain that we hear it in our sleep, when our spirits are not so tightly bound to the body. The Rosicrucian school, which has so deeply influenced the development of esoteric astrology, maintains that humans are not permitted to hear the music itself, but may hear copies through ordinary mortal music, and thus not lose the longing for the celestial world beyond the material realm. The Rosicrucian Fludd, who believed that the music is produced from the impinging of the moving Sun upon the paths of the planets, says, 'music is a faint tradition of the angelic state'. Modern esotericism insists that the music may be heard only by INITIATES on the earth plane, but that it becomes part of the later postmortem experience for every other human.

In modern times the esotericist Collin has introduced a sophisticated concept of the harmonic relationships between planets, based no longer on supposed distances (as is the Pythagorean model) but on revolutions and revolution periodicities, which he links to the tonic scale. He shows that in theory thirty-six octaves separate human time from what he calls 'solar time', and the same interval separates the vibrations of human music from the vibrations of the planetary motions.

Mutability   In astrology the term applied to one of the three qualities (see CARDINALITY and FIXITY) which acts as a unifier of the impulsiveness of Cardinality with the rigidity of Fixity, and may even be said to carry a quality common to both. Indeed, the Mutable signs (Gemini, Virgo, Sagittarius and Pisces) are sometimes called the 'common signs'. The Mutable nature is that of changeability and adaptability, but under pressure it will give rise to instability.

Myalba   An esoteric Tibetan name for the Earth, sometimes used in modern Theosophical literature. It is said to be regarded as one of the stages of Hell (although properly of Purgatory). See AVITCHI.

Myomancy   Divination from the movement of mice and rats, or from the sounds such creatures make; a form of THERIOMANCY.

Mystagogy   A word derived from the Greek *mystis* and *agogos* ('to lead') and used to denote any system of interpreting the Mysteries or the instructions given prior to initiation into the Mysteries.

Mysteries   The word is derived in its European context from the Greek *muein* ('to close the mouth'), relating both to the esoteric content of the Mysteries themselves and to the strict silence to which those who had been initiated were foresworn (see INITIATES and INITIATION). The esoteric lore of the ancient world was preserved by the ancient Mystery centres such as Delphi, Eleusis and Delos, and in the esoteric forms of many of the ancient cults such as the Mithraic, the Sybellian or the Dionysian. Much of this wisdom and attendant symbolism passed into the early Church, which even in name kept certain of the *mysteria* from the profane.

Mysterium magnum   The Latin for 'great mystery', a term used in alchemy, usually in reference to the secrets of the art itself – the making of the ELIXIR or the LAPIS.

Mystic number   See NUMBERS.

Mystic tetrad   See TETRACTYS.

Mystical planets   See SACRED PLANETS.

N

The fourteenth letter of the alphabet. In esotericism the N is seen as the symbol of the female principle and birth (or the womb); the Egyptian hieroglyphic of the equivalent sound represents a line of water. The significance of the associated Hebraic Nun has been linked with the Christ, for it means 'fish', and the final Nun in the Hebraic script, and hence in some occult numerological systems, is sometimes given the numerical value of 700, which of course reduces to SEVEN, the sacred number. The N at the beginning of a word, or in any other place than the final position, is linked with 50, which reduces to 5. See, however, NUMBERS and ZERO.

Naberius One of the seventy-two SPIRITS OF SOLOMON. He is said to appear in the shape of a cock or black crow – though some grimoires insist that he appears with three heads, and a bird-like body.

Nabia A Hebraic term for 'seership', associated with clairvoyance and oracles, whose insights arise from heavenly grace. The related *nebirah* looks into futurity, while the *nebi-poel* is the magician.

Nachiel A name given by Agrippa (quoting Qabbalistic sources) to the Intelligency of the Sun, to whom he ascribes the magical number 111, the linear sum of the MAGIC SQUARE of the Sun.

Nada A Sanskrit term often translated as 'soundless voice', though as Blavatsky points out, it is really 'the voice in the Spiritual Sound'. It was the word she had in mind in her title *The Voice of the Silence*, derived from the ancient mystical text known as *The Book of the Golden Precept*.

Nadigranthams General name given in Hindu astrology to collections of palm-leaf manuscripts used in consultative astrology. The origin of these nadigranthams is unknown. It is often said that the palm-leaf manuscripts contain horoscopes, but specialists in Sanskrit claim that the astrological material is not horoscopic in any recognizable form.

Naga A Sanskrit term meaning 'serpent', which is given an extraordinary etymology by Blavatsky. She says that in the Indian Pantheon the *nagas* were the serpent or dragon spirits of Patala (Hell) – but the word *patala* means 'antipodes' and was the name originally given to America by those ancients 'who knew and visited the continent before Europe had ever heard of it.' The term is probably akin to the Mexican *nagals*, now sorcerers and medicine men. Since 'dragon' and 'serpent' were terms often used to denote INITIATES, the *nagas* were often wise men or even tutelary spirits.

Nagals See NAGA.

Nakshatras The Hindu equivalent of the LUNAR MANSIONS. While there are the usual twenty-eight mansions or *nakshatras* in the Hindu system, only twenty-seven of these are used in ordinary astrology.

Naraka A Sanskrit term popularly translated as meaning 'Hell' or 'prison beneath the earth', but more properly purgatorial spheres. In the Buddhist lore Naraka is presided over by the Lord of Death, Yama, who is himself finite and periodically tortured.

Naros cycle A name given to a periodicity or cycle, sometimes called the Naronic cycle or the Neros cycle, claimed in esoteric circles to be one of the Mystery secrets, but exoterically said to be a period of 600 years. Blavatsky claims that there were three kinds of Naros cycle – the greater, the middle and the lesser, and that only the last corresponds to the cycle of 600 years. See PHOENIX.

Natal astrology That branch of astrology which is concerned with the casting and interpreting of birth charts, from the Latin *natus* meaning 'birth'. See ASTROLOGY.

Native The subject for whom a horoscope (the NATIVITY) is cast.

Nativity In a specialist sense the term used for the chart cast for a particular birth (from the Latin *natus*, 'birth'). In modern terminology the equivalent is HOROSCOPE.

Natural magic In the medieval period a concept of natural magic was developed which was supposed to work wonders (that is change the course of nature by means of spiritual influences) through the use of occult forces inherent in nature. The natural magician made use of the virtues or powers within such natural forms as the stars, stones, plants and even words and numbers. This kind of magic was distinguished from ordinary magic (never called 'unnatural', however) which was concerned with the invocation of spirits and demons, the kind of magic which the thirteenth-century magician Michael Scot himself dubbed the 'mistress of all iniquity and evil'. The point was that the ordinary magic was condemned by the Church, whereas natural magic was at least tolerated.

Naturale A name given (probably first by Paracelsus) to one of the *entia* or body forces. This is the earthly body in man, which, occultists maintain, represents the meeting of past and future, on the grounds that only in the physical body is the expression and experience of continuity in time possible. The eternal body lives out of time, and is often contrasted with the natural body, or the natural man. The spirit participates in the life of the *naturale* through the mediation of the soul or the ENS VENENI.

Nature souls See NATURE SPIRITS.

Nature spirits Sometimes the ELEMENTALS are called 'nature spirits', although properly speaking they are not spirits but souls and should be called 'nature souls' or 'soul-beings'. In certain modern schools of occultism the controlling spirits who guide the elementals are called DEVAS.

Navel chakra See MANIPURA.

Nebo A Chaldean god, sometimes equated with the planet Mercury.

Necromancy The popular term for divination by means of dead bodies, which involves the calling back into temporary 'life' a corpse, in order to persuade it to give information about the future (and, indeed, sometimes about the past). The term is often popularly misused for SCIOMANCY, the art of conjuring the shades of the dead, rather than the physical bodies of the dead, in order to gain knowledge of futurity. The famous necromanteions of the Greeks were places where the true sciomantic art was practised, as a careful reading of Homer will show. In the great majority of cases the spiritualism of the modern seance rooms is involved with sciomancy, and not with necromancy.

The whole operation of genuine necromancy is of dubious value: besides the logistic difficulties of obtaining reasonably 'fresh' dead bodies, there is the problem of the quality of spirit which is being invoked. Occultists recognize that a spirit called back to galvanize a dead physical body is unlikely to be that which had inhabited it prior to death; since only low-grade ELEMENTARS or DEMONS would deign to operate in this way, the value of the predictions gained might be more than dubious. The operation of necromancy itself originally involved a system of occult conjurations, as well as blood sacrifices, and was an off-shoot of black magic. Inevitably it was condemned from the very earliest times, Iamblichus and Porphyry being among the earliest to argue in literature against its morality and utility. Modern attitudes to both necromancy and sciomancy are perhaps most clearly reflected in SPIRIT PHOTOGRAPHY.

Necromantic demon This is GAMYGYN. See SPIRITS OF SOLOMON.

Negative Mars In the traditional system of planetary rulerships over the signs Mars was assigned to Scorpio. In accordance with this schema the Scorpionic Mars was said to be feminine, nocturnal and negative, in contrast to the masculine, diurnal of POSITIVE MARS which ruled Aries.

Nehaschim A Qabbalistic term meaning 'serpent's works', applied to the ASTRAL LIGHT during certain magical praxes. It is so called because magicians work surrounded by the light of the primordial serpent which they perceive in heaven as a luminous zone, composed of myriads of small stars.

Nenuphars See SYLPHS.

Neophyte A Greek term for a candidate entrant to the Mystery wisdom.

Nephesh In Qabbalism, the name given to the source of the physical appetitive life – the ETHERIC BODY. See SOUL.

Nervengeist See PSYCHIC BODY.

Neptune A planet in orbit between Uranus and Pluto, discovered in 1846, although it had been observed (but mistaken for a star) as early as 1795. Since its discovery Neptune has displaced Jupiter from its traditional rulership over Pisces. Astrologers see it as a dissolving influence: it bestows nebulousness and confusion, even deceptiveness when working under pressure. When working through its beneficient side, however, it induces an imaginative, inspirational, idealistic and artistic nature. Neptune is linked with the Roman equivalent of Poseidon, the god of the seas, and astrologers use this connection to indicate the ease of contact which the planet facilitates with the 'sea' of the unconscious. The sigil for Neptune ♆ is popularly explained as being derived from the trident of Neptune.

Neptune Scheme The Neptune Scheme and the Neptune Chain are terms derived specifically from the Theosophical cosmoconception linked with the SCHEME OF EVOLUTION. It is claimed that the three planets in this chain include Neptune and two others beyond its orbit, perhaps even Pluto, which was unrecognized when the schema was originated. Blavatsky claimed that Neptune is not in our own solar system, so that the formulation of this scheme is derived from her followers (probably influenced by the teachings of Besant and Leadbeater).

Nergal A Chaldean name, probably for a personification of Mars as the giant king of war. The same name is used in Hebraic astrology for Mars, although seemingly of the darker side of his nature.

Neros See NAROS CYCLE.

Netzach The seventh Sephirah of the Qabbalistic SEPHIROTHIC TREE, the name meaning 'victory'. It is connected with the emotions, with the underlying beauty of life, as well as with the growth of understanding through emotional experiences; it balances the eighth Sephirah HOD. In the lowest World of Expression (ASSIAH) it is connected with Venus, and with all the soft receptivity of that planet, as well as with the emotions of love, such as tenderness, joy, sexuality and sympathy. In the World of Formation (YETZIRAH) it is ruled by the angelic order of the ELOHIM, the Divine Ones. In the World of Creation (BRIAH) we find at Netzach the Light of God (Auriel), who, through the faculty of the human soul and aided by the Elohim, enables man to become aware of the higher spiritual world. In the World of Origins (ATZILUTH) we find at Netzach the male divinity Yawe Sabaoth, who (in the words of Gray) 'must not be considered as the Male Divine Aspect of human life, but of all life as regenerative phenomenon.' In Netzach we find humanity seeking for divinity through the operations of the emotional life.

New planets This is the curious term often applied to the three planets of the solar system which have been added to the traditional seven of the ancient astrological model – in order of discovery, URANUS, NEPTUNE and PLUTO.

Nidana The Sanskrit term for the twelve causes of existence.

Night of Brahma See KALPA.

Nigromancy Some give this term as alternative for NECROMANCY. However, it is derived from the Latin *niger* ('black') and should really be applied to methods of prediction through occult means, including the dark demons.

Nine The 9 is the mystic number of great power – it is 3 + 3 + 3, which is the sacred triad multiplied by itself (3 × 3 = 9). It is called by the mystics the 'number of love', by which they mean both universal love and personalized love; it is strong, unswerving, protective and creative, and is harmoniously related to the spiritual world. This harmony is reflected in its form, for the enclosure in the upper half is linked with Heaven and the open form in the lower half is linked with

Earth. The number may therefore accumulate spiritual forces and give them freely to the material world. This is why it is called the number of the 'writer, teacher and lecturer'. The 9 also stands for journeys and philosophy (witness the NINTH HOUSE of astrology), although usually there is a rugged individualism expressed in both these realms. It is linked with the letter T, and with the Hebraic Teth, which is an incarnating sound once again (less deep in incarnation than the D). This idea of incarnating from the upper spiritual to the lower material (in the circle and curve below) is expressed in the adage of the numerologists that '9 is the alpha and omega of human possibilities, the beginning and the end'. In the beginning is the creative force of love, and in the end is death, that end which is also the beginning of another cycle, marking the completion of the cycle which began with 1 and ends in 0, the great zero, which is the question mark of existence. See NUMBERS.

Nine Orders   See CELESTIAL HIERARCHIES.

Ninib   A name derived from Chaldean sources and generally equated with the planet Saturn, although originally it was the name of a god.

Ninth heaven   At one time the name given to the PRIMUM MOVENS, the *Primum mobile* of the geocentric cosmoconception of the ancients – that sphere above the eight spheres which gave the diurnal revolution to all the others. Sometimes it was called the 'crystalline Heaven', the 'diaphanous' or 'transparent' heaven (even though all the other spheres were themselves said to be both diaphanous and transparent (see, however, TENTH HEAVEN). The ninth heaven was also called the 'ninth sphere', but unfortunately this same term was also later applied to the Earth itself, as some cosmoconceptions reckoned the concentrics in descending order from the periphery, with the *Primum movens* (the old ninth heaven) as the first.

Ninth Hierarchy   See ANGELS.

Nirmanakaya   A Sanskrit term (meaning approximately 'transformed body') for a state of being – an adept who has attained to the Nirvanic state yet chooses to live within the samsaric wheel (that is, rejects his own bliss for ordinary life conditions) to be of service to others and the evolution of the world. See BUDDHIC BODIES.

Nirvana   A Sanskrit term for a state of consciousness in which the human Ego has reached the highest degree of perfection and bliss. It is said that the word is derived from the Sanskrit compound for *nir* ('out') and *vana* ('to blow'), in reference to the idea that the lower principles in man have been 'blown out' or annihilated, leaving the perfect Ego of man in a state of absolute consciousness, untrammelled by the demands and limitations of the lower quaternary. The word is widely misunderstood in popular occult writings: it should not be translated as meaning 'heaven'.

Niyama   See YOGA.

Nodes   The nodes are the two points in the orbit of a planet where they intersect with the ecliptic. In astrology they usually refer to the DRAGON'S HEAD and DRAGON'S TAIL, which are the nodes of the Moon. In heliocentric astrology the nodes of all the planets are considered as being influential in a chart.

Notaricon   A name given to a Hebraic method of cryptographic wordplay involving the interpretation of each letter of a word as though it were an abbreviation of another word. Originally it appears to have been a method of abbreviation in which the initial or final letters of several words were made to form single words for purpopses of what Trachtenberg calls 'anagogic homilectics'. From this method arose some of the most important names in the mystic catalogue. For example, the magical word 'Agla' is really a notaricon of a Hebraic phrase meaning 'Thou art mighty for ever, O Lord'. Another example may be seen under ARARITHA. Notaricon is sometimes confused with GEMATRIA or TEMURAH.

Nous   A Greek word which in its occult application appears to be the equivalent of the higher mind of the MANAS or perhaps of the EGO. Blavatsky says that the Greek word was itself derived from the Egyptian *nout*, which meant 'one-only-one'. See AGNOIA.

Nuclear trigram   In the Chinese system of I CHING a term used to denote a pair of TRIGRAMS within the hexagram, revealed when the line at the beginning and the topmost line are discounted. The arrangement below shows how the two nuclears are derived from a basic hexagram. In the Chinese reading of such figures the nuclears are said to play a most influential role, especially in regard to the future outcome of the conditions implicit within the radical HEXAGRAM.

Numbers Almost all occult systems have proposed a series of correspondences between numbers and esoteric ideas. The supposition is that every number corresponds to a spiritual vibration, or sound, which is in turn reflected in the material realm. Within this (Pythagorean) view of things, all sublunar forms of nature have a corresponding number, and a complex occult system has been built around the relationship between numbers, letters, words and ideas. For specific number symbolism, therefore, see ONE, TWO, THREE etc., through to ZERO. In Qabbalistic thought the numerological correspondences have been taken to incredible depths of extrapolation and refinement, especially so in the techniques of GEMATRIA, which has to some extent influenced the European occult view of numbers. The standard correspondences between the Qabbalistic systems and the letters of the Hebraic and European alphabet are set out under the individual letters (for example, see A for Aleph, B for Beth, and so on). Several magical sequences are also set out under individual headings, such as NUPTIAL NUMBER, SOUL NUMBERS, TETRACTYS and OCCULT NUMBERS.

More specifically in relation to Western occult systems, however, it must be observed that there are many different systems of numerology and that the following merely gives a digest of the most satisfactory rationales. As the basis of numerology is reduction – the reducing of any number to its basic constituents and adding these to give a single number – only the first nine numbers are considered in any depth, along wth the final zero, which carries the individual number into the cosmos, prior to the reduction which brings that number back to itself. As an example of reduction we might consider the number 372, which is first reduced (3 + 7 + 2 = 12), and then (1 + 2 = 3). In these terms, then, the number 372 contains the symbolic equivalent of 3. The numerical equivalents given in occult texts for the Hebraic and European is as follows:

Aleph	A	1
Beth	B	2
Gimel	G	3 and 4
Daleth	D	4
He	H and E	5
Waw	W	6
Zayin	Z	7
Cheth	C	8
Teth	T	9
Yod	Y	10
Kaph	K	20
Lamed	L	30
Mem	M	40
Nun	N	50 and 700
Samech	S	60
Ayin		70
Pe	P	80
Sadhe		90
Koph	Q	100 and 90
Resch	R	200
Sin	Sh	300
Tau	T	400

F is linked with 6. U and V, being numerologically interchangeable, are linked with 21 and its reduction 3 – see, however, U. X is linked with 10. Y is linked (through association with I) with the number 1, as well as 10. See also ZERO, which is linked with the letter O, and with the number 11.

Numerology See NUMBERS.

Nunctator See NUNTIUS.

Nuntis A Latin term for the plant Mercury. See NUNTIUS.

Nuntius One of the medieval esoteric names for MERCURY, which pictures the planet in its anthropomorphized role as messenger. It is sometimes called Nunctator, although in both forms it is found most often in the astrological terminology linked with alchemy. Blavatsky writes of astrological Mercury as 'still more occult and mysterious than Venus', and likens the word 'Nuntis' (a term seemingly derived from the Mystery wisdom) with 'Sun-Wolf' – no doubt a reference to the Hermetic Anubis (see Figure 16 under CADUCEUS). She is, of course, touching upon the esoteric tradition which links Mercury with the Sun – the Saint Christopher Mercury who carries the Sun Child on his shoulders was originally a dog-headed Latinized Anubis.

Nuptial number In effect, the number 60, derived from the properties of the Pythagorean triangle, a right-angled triangle, the shorter sides of which were ascribed the values 3 and 4, and the hypotenuse 5. The multiples of these three figures (3 × 4 × 5) equals 60. This mystical number was linked with the so-called SAROS CYCLE, as well as with the harmonics of the spheres.

O

The fifteenth letter of the alphabet, associated by occultists with the number 11; as 11 reduces numerologically to 2, see TWO. In Semitic languages the equivalent of the O was called 'the eye'. It is usual in occult texts for the O to be regarded as equivalent to the ZERO, with all the attendant anagogic implications. In occult symbolism the enclosed circle was the basis for a highly significant system of symbolic language, ranging from the theta-derived ⊖, which means Death, to the Egyptian-derived ⊙, which means God, or Sun, and Life.

Oannes A man-fish, sometimes called Dag or DAGON (although these latter terms appear to refer to the Annedoti as a whole), an occult teacher of the Chaldeans, linked by the Kircher with the zodiacal sign Pisces (Figure 56). Blavatsky points out that the Greek *amphibios* means 'life on two planes', and was often applied in antiquity to those men who, although still wearing a human form, had made themselves almost divine through knowledge and parti-

Figure 56 *The image of Oannes, under his name Ichthon, is contained in the segment relating to Pisces in this seventeenth-century syncretic zodiac devised by Kircher*

cipated in full consciousness on two planes – the spiritual and the physical. See, therefore, INITIATES.

Ob A Hebraic term relating to the evil use of the ASTRAL LIGHT. True diviners were said to be possessed by the Spirit of Ob. See OBOTH and OD.

Oboth A Hebraic word for a special kind of diviner, and wrongly used of a necromancer (see, therefore, NECROMANCY). One with OB has the power to make contact with the souls of the dead. The so-called Witch of Endor (1 Samuel, 28, 7) was in fact a mistress of Ob, and is properly a pythoness, not a witch. See ENDORISM.

Obsession The term is derived from the Latin *obsidere* ('to besiege') and is used in occult circles to denote the overshadowing of a human being by an evil spiritual entity. See, for example, AGATANA YENE.

Occult blind A term used to denote a technique (usually literary) employed by certain occultists to hide or disguise a truth behind a façade or pretence (sometimes an outright distortion). This façade, or blind, is presented in such a way as to be immediately evident to an initiate, yet confusing or misleading to all others. For an example of a possible occult blind, see ENOCHIAN.

Occult catechism In the 'Proem' to *The Secret Doctrine* Blavatsky sets out the so-called occult catechism at length in relation to the symbols of the BOOK OF DYZAN. ' "What is it that ever is?" "Space, the eternal Anupadaka." "What is it that ever was?" "The Germ in the Root." "What is it that is ever coming and going?" "The Great Breath." "Then there are three Eternals?" "No, the three are one. That which ever is is one, that which ever was is one, that which is ever being and becoming is also one: and this is Space." ' '

Occult numbers   As the individual entries for the letters of our alphabet indicate, each letter is linked with an occult number, ultimately derived from Hebraic Qabbalism. Certain numbers also have an occultist sanctity attached to them in connection with their symbolical or cyclical import. For example, the number 7 is the greatest of numbers in the divine Mysteries, even superior to the number 3. In the secret doctrine the figure 3 is masculine and the 4 is feminine – these work together to produce the 7, and all the phenomena of the world have been seen in terms of the resultant septenaries. In this numerological connection, however, see NUMBERS. Again the number 666 is called in occultism the 'number of the Great Heart' and is linked with the NAROS CYCLE. See also the 1460 cycle of the SOTHIS PERIOD. For other number symbolism, see PRECESSION and MAGIC SQUARES.

Occult script   A name sometimes used in modern occultism for the Akashic Chronicles (see AKASHA; see also SECRET SCRIPTS). Steiner says that the knowledge acquired through higher inspiration comes from 'reading of the Hidden Script'.

Occult trinity   The so-called occult trinity are Light, Heat and Moisture, 'the eternal witness to the unseen presence of the Deity', the 'cause of every phenomenon in Nature', according to Blavatsky. The occult trinity proceed from occult Fire (sometimes called 'Living Fire', at other times 'Moving Fire'). But see also GREAT BREATH and OCCULT CATECHISM.

Occultism   The term occult appears to be derived from the Latin *occulta* ('hidden things') and refers to the study of the invisible, esoteric or secret things in life. The original application of the word was to the study of things which were hidden from men who were of an ordinary level of development; things were not hidden by some

act of God or by fiat of the celestial hierarchies, but merely by the ignorance of men. Enlightenment would mean that what was previously hidden, or occult, would be revealed. The disciplines and praxes of occultism in its various guises were all designed either to open up the spiritual eyes of individuals, so that what was hitherto hidden should be revealed, or to prepare such individuals for this initiation. In this sense, therefore, occultism was originally linked with INITIATION and with the stream of ESOTERICISM which flowed from the ancient Mystery centres. Unfortunately the use of the term has in recent years become more than slipshod, and it is now widely applied to virtually any study of unusual phenomena, from psychic experiences in seances to BLACK MAGIC, both areas of human interest which the true occultists would have rejected as being involved with the degredation of humanity or, more simply, as being immoral.

Och   Name of a daemon listed in the GRIMOIRES as one of the seven supreme angels of the Qabbalists and said to possess all the attributes of the Sun. He is supposed to have a complete knowledge of medicine and healing, and to be able to change base matter into gold. He is said to be capable of prolonging human life to 600 years, which is a scarcely veiled reference to the ancient NAROS CYCLE, itself linked with the cycles of reincarnation.

Od   A term derived from the Greek *odos* ('passageway') and used in modern occultism to relate to the force developed by ('passing from') such agencies as magnets, gems, chemicals and so on. It was called by Reichenbach the Odyle, the Odic force or the Odylic Force, and was regarded by him as an entitive force, which radiates from every thing in the universe. The word was popularized in spiritualism, and some psychic workers regarded the manifestations in seances as nothing other than the product of odylic vapours arising from the medium and connected with a thought atmosphere. Blavatsky, more interested in the occult side of the Od, linked it with the life-giving aspect of the Chaldean *Aour*, or 'astro-etheric' light, the shadow of which was the 'death-giving' OB.

Odic Force   See OD.

Odylic Force   See OD.

Ogham The name of a so-called Mystery language used by the Celts and believed by some to be the secret writing of the Druids. There may in fact be nothing secret about the Ogham script, although its significance has been largely lost.

Ogygia A name given to one of the islands which for a time survived the sinking of its parent land ATLANTIS. It is said to be the Calypso of the ancients.

Old Moon See MOON PERIOD.

Old Saturn See SATURN PERIOD.

Old Sun See SUN PERIOD.

Olympic spirits These are the seven planetary spirits, distinguished from the planetary SENATORS and named under PLANETARY ANGELS.

Om A Sanskrit syllable of high potency, used as an invocation, as well as a sound technique, to bring beneficial vibrations to an already pure body. The word is often spelled 'Aum' or 'Avm', and Blavatsky tells us that in popular belief these letters stand for Agni, Varuna and Maruts, who are the Fire, Water and Air gods respectively. Esoteric lore maintains that it is wrong to pronounce the word in any place which is unholy.

Omens See OMINA.

Omina The art of divination by means of *omina* or 'celestial omens' is not, strictly speaking, a part of genuine astrology, although the early forms (widely practised in Babylonian and Egyptian societies) were incorporated into later forms of astrology.

Omphalomancy A term derived from the Greek *omphalos* ('navel') and *manteia* ('divination') and applied to a method of predicting the number of children a woman will have from the number of knots in the umbilical cord of the first-born. Sometimes the method is called umbilicomancy.

One The numerical equivalent of Aleph is linked with Taurus, yet it is changing and unstable in its influence. It is masculine and logical, constant and upright – the European 1 stands upright like the human I, (EGO). Being single and Taurean, 1 is fixed, although intense in feeling,

opinionated, argumentative. It is called the 'symbol of the Creator' or the 'Architect' and it is the MONAD, the archetypal designer. Numerologically, 1 seeks to stand alone and defines itself against the vast space of the universe (the space within the 0) in the magical number 10, which is always reduced in the numerological method back to 1 (1 + 0 = 1). In this way does the 1 challenge the circumference and represent the cosmic situation of 'aloneness' which every conscious being experiences in life. The figure 1 is the number of loneliness. See NUMBERS.

Onimancy Sometimes 'onymancy', divination by means of the nails of the human hand. One of the subdivisions of palmistry, in which futurity, or even the past, is sought in the natural signs or blemishes on the nails, and from their shape, length and conditions. There is a related ONYCHOMANCY.

Onomancy A term derived from the Greek *onomas* ('to name') and *manteia* ('divination') and applied to a wide variety of different methods of divining the future from letters, the numerical equivalents of letters, and given words or groups of words. The word is sometimes 'onomomancy' or more properly 'onomatomancy'.

Onomatomancy See ONOMANCY.

Onomomancy See ONOMANCY.

Onychomancy A term derived from the Greek *onech* ('nail') and *manteia* ('divination') and applied to a method of divination from the nails of the human hand, involving the study of the forms revealed by the reflections of the sun on the surface. It is sometimes also called ONIMANCY, which is really a different form of divination.

Onymancy See ONIMANCY.

Ooscopy Sometimes 'oomantia', a method of divination by means of eggs.

Ophanim Sometimes Auphanim, the Hebraic plural for the spiritual 'wheels' of the biblical Ezekiel, which Blavatsky rightly links with the world spheres. The word is Hebraic for 'Angels of the Stellatum'. Blavatsky identifies these with the spiritual beings now called CHERUBIM (perhaps the Assyrian *karoubs*, sphinxes) figured in the zodiac as the four fixed signs, Taurus, Leo, Scorpio and Aquarius. See TETRAMORPH.

Ophiel Name (sometimes Oriphiel) given to the fifth of the supreme angels of the Qabbalists. He was said to possess the attributes of Venus and to have the curious unalchemical ability to transmute solar forces (gold) into the Venusian forces (copper).

Ophiomancy A term derived from the Greek *ophi* ('serpent') and *manteia* ('divination') and applied to a method of divination from the movement and behaviour of snakes.

Oracle A term often used of a site where the gods or spiritual beings manifest to man in some way and appear to be prepared to give answers to questions. Sometimes the term is applied to a god or a spiritual being who gives such answers, and sometimes even to the priest who officiates as a medium for the god. The oracle at Delphi, where the oracle god was Apollo, was served by a woman known as the pythoness (sometimes also called the 'oracle'). A similar oracle linked with the god Jupiter was at Dodona, and a dark oracle, in which futurity was sought in an underground chamber by means of the sciomantic art, has recently been restored at Ephirus. There were well over fifty major oracle centres in the ancient Mediterranean world.

Orai One of the Gnostic names for a ruler of Venus.

Orb In astrology that area of influence (expressed in degrees of arc) within which planets in ASPECT may be said to exert an influence while still forming or separating. Also in astrology one of the now archaic terms for the planetary spheres and later for the planetary body itself.

Orenda See SYMPATHETIC MAGIC.

Orias One of the seventy-two SPIRITS OF SOLOMON. He is said to appear as a lion with a serpentine tail, riding a great horse. His demonic powers include a boon to would-be astrologers, for he is prepared to teach the complex art of astrology in an instant, demanding no effort on the part of the student.

Oriphiel See OPHIEL.

Ormuzd Sometimes called Ahura Mazda (Great Being of Light), Ormuzd or Ormazd is the creative power of Zoroastrianism who worked against the darkness and lies of AHRIMAN, the Prince of Lies and Darkness (more exactly, against Angra Mainyu, who was later called Ahriman in Western occultism). While the latter is often identified with the lunar forces, Ormuzd is linked with the solar forces, and Blavatsky records the esoteric teaching that he is the synthesis of the Elohim, the creative Logoi, which are in turn associated with the realm or sphere of the EXSUSIA. The equivalent of Ormuzd in the dualism of modern occultism is LUCIFER. See IZARDS.

Ornithomancy Divination from the movement or flight of birds (see, for example, ALECTROMANCY).

Orphic A term derived from the associations built around the legendary magician Orpheus, who is said to have founded the Greek cult of Orphism, which remained connected with several ancient Mystery centres. When the term is used in (non-scholarly) astrological contexts it is generally as a synonym for 'esoteric' or as pertaining to the secret doctrines which pervade astrological lore.

Orphic Ages According to an account of the Orphic theogony recorded by Servius, there are four ages of the world. The first is that of Saturn, the second of Jupiter, the third of Neptune, and the fourth that of Pluto. The gods must (for once) be distinguished from the planetary beings, since it is clear from the context that they are intended to personify the four elements: Saturn is Fire, Jupiter is Air, Neptune is Water and Pluto is Earth.

Orphic Descent of the Soul In his commentary on an esoteric section of Plato's *Republic* Macrobius quotes what he describes as Orphic initiation knowledge relating to what the descending soul learns in its passage through the planetary spheres prior to rebirth. This description has entered the stream of occultism under the title the 'Orphic Descent of the Soul'. A summary of this descent reflects much of the ancient teaching of the influences of the planets themselves.

The soul, wrapped in a luminous body, descends into the sphere of Saturn where it develops the power of reasoning and theorizing (contemplative reason). In the sphere of Jupiter it develops the power of putting into practice (*vis agendi*). In the sphere of Mars it takes on the power of ardent vehemence (although the word translated is actually *thumikon*, which in esoteric lore is linked with magical powers). In the Sun sphere the soul learns sensing and imagining – in a word, PHANTASY, the power of pictorial visualization or representation. In the sphere of Venus the soul takes on the power of desire, which is linked with love. In the next sphere (Mercury) the soul is given the power of giving expression and of interpreting feelings (those feelings engendered in the previous sphere). In the final sphere, that of the Moon, the soul begins to learn about physical bodies – actually about how to make physical bodies move and grow, which is esoterically connected with the ETHERIC forces. In the lower realm, the spheres of the Earth, where it takes on through incarnation the 'terrene' physical body, the soul is imprisoned in a dark shroud of the physical. As the historian Mead remarks, the 'planetary energies thus imbibed are in no way regarded as being either beneficient or maleficient', and there is no question of good or bad emanation in the spheres; see, therefore, the contrasting EGYPTIAN DESCENT OF THE SOUL.

Ose One of the seventy-two SPIRITS OF SOLOMON. He is said to appear in the form of a large and graceful leopard.

Osiris In astrology a name given to one of the HYPOTHETICAL PLANETS.

Ouija The ouija board was originally a wooden tripod, usually on rollers, directed by the hands of a medium in such a way as to slide over a flat surface marked out with letters of the alphabet, with a view to spelling out messages supposed to come from the world of spirits. The word, which is said to be from the French and German words for 'yes', suggests that at one time the sliding device was used to indicate only alternative responses to questions. Such a device is mentioned in classical literature. In modern seances the ouija is more often than not a spinning pivot, centred on a circle of alphabet letters. See also AUTOMATIC WRITING.

Ouranos Sometimes Uranus, the ancient Greek name for the expanse of the heavens, the Waters of Space. The god Uranus was the husband of Gaia (Earth), through whom the Titans were fathered. Esoterically, Ouranos and Gaia are the original parents of man, who belongs partly to the realm of spirit (*ouranos*) and partly to the realm of elemental forces (*gaia*). See URANUS.

Ouroboros Name given to the snake or dragon which is usually depicted and described as devouring its own tail, often explained as a symbol of reincarnation, of time cycles and recurrence.

Outa Sometimes Uta, the name for the symbol called in modern occultism the 'Eye of Horus'.

Over-Soul See SECRET DOCTRINE.

P

The sixteenth letter of the alphabet. In the Hebraic tradition the Pe, equivalent of the modern P, is said to correspond to the mouth. This may well explain the readiness with which the early Christians adopted the Chi-Ro symbol for the Christ, as in at least one language the central symbol would be linked with the idea of the descending Word. It is also associated with 80 (see, therefore, EIGHT).

Pact The term is used in demonology and witchcraft in connection with the idea of making a compact or pact with the demons. Accounts as to how a pact is made vary from age to age. Some authorities insist that a person need only request the aid of a demon (even with an innocent-seeming oath) and this will be immediately granted, at the usual price of soul. However, the MALLEUS MALEFICARUM lent its tremendous authority to belief in a ritual pact, basing its descriptions on actual confessions wrung from the lips of tortured witches:

Now the method of profession is twofold. One is a solemn ceremony, like a solemn vow. The other is private, and can be made to the devil at any hour alone. The first method is when witches meet together in conclave on a set day, and the devil appears to them in the assumed body of a man, and urges them to keep faith with him, promising them worldly prosperity and length of life: and the witches recommend a novice to his acceptance. The devil then asks whether she will abjure the Faith and forsake the holy Christian religion, and the worship of the Anomalous Woman (for so they call the most Blessed Virgin Mary), and never venerate the Sacraments. And if he finds the novice willing, then the devil stretches out his hands, and so does the novice, and she swears with upraised hand to keep that covenant. And when all this is done, the devil at once insists that this is not enough, and when the disciple asks what more is needed, the devil demands the following oath of homage to himself, that she gives her body and soul to him for ever, and to do her utmost to bring others of both sexes to his power. He adds finally

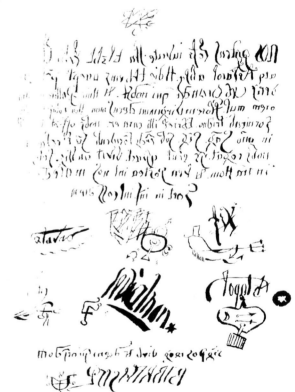

Figure 57 *The last page of the pact made between devils (the sigils and signatures of such high-ranking demons as Satanas, Beelzebub and Lucifer may be seen) and Urbain Grandier, c. 1643. The pact is in Latin and in mirror writing, said to be typical of the demons' wish to reverse civilized Christian procedures*

that she is to prepare certain unguents from the bones and limbs of children, especially those who have been baptised.

Later accounts garnish the details of such pact with lewd sexual encounters as part of the deal.

In spite of the thoroughness with which such a pact is described, and the exactness of the forms which require the potential witch to abjure the faith, we are surprised to find the authors of the *Malleus Maleficarum* claiming that they had learned 'from the confessions of those we have caused to be burned that they have not been willing agents of witchcraft', but have been beaten into submission by the Devil. The idea of a written pact – popularized by the Faust legends – is very common, and several signed and sealed documents have survived. One of the oldest records of a pact is that signed in his own blood by St Theophilus of Cilicia (sixth century), and perhaps the most famous is that of 1634, signed by Urbain Grandier, who was burned alive in 1634 at Loudun (Figure 57). A written pact mentioned by Summers is that of Stevenote de Audebert, who was burned in 1619. This document was shown to the judge at her trial and was described as 'a foul piece of parchment, all crocked and grim, scrawled with blood and feculent matter, enough to turn a man's stomach to see.'

See also INVOCATION.

Paimon One of the seventy-two SPIRITS OF SOLOMON. He is said to appear in the form of a king (he is supposed to be very obedient to Lucifer, and some demonologists place him directly under the supreme devil). He has the ability to teach instantly, and without effort from the student, all arts, sciences and arcane knowledge.

Palingenesis A word derived directly from the Greek, meaning 'new birth' or 'transformation', and generally taken as being the equivalent of 'REINCARNATION'. However, the word is not necessarily always applied to the idea of rebirth into matter or reincarnation. See also PALINGENESY.

Palingenesy A word originated in the seventeenth century by alchemists to denote the resurrection of dead plants by alchemical means. This 'rebirth' was of an ASTRAL nature, however – a sort of 'vegetable ghost', which resembled the dead plant in every way save in actual materiality. Methods derived from the vegetable palingenesy

were eventually applied to the bodies of men, as Ferrier records.

Palmistry The study of the human hand as a guide to character interpretation and as the basis for the prediction of the future. The main tradition of nomenclature attached to the fingers, the lines and the so-called finger mounts, is linked with planetary names, as may be seen from the comprehensive illustration from a classical text by Belot (Figure 58). The fingers, from right to left, are ruled by Mercury, Sun, Saturn, Jupiter and Mars (for the thumb, which in Figure 58 Belot unaccountably links with Venus, which really has rule over the lower part of the thumb). The lower part of the hand (right in Figure 58), the so-called hypothenar eminence, is ruled by the Moon, and the centre of the palm is ruled by Mercury. Belot also ascribes the phalanges of the fingers to the signs of the zodiac, though not all palmists would

Figure 58 *A seventeenth-century chiromantic diagram designed to show the allocation of the lines, mounts and parts of the hand to the planets and zodiac. The upper thumb is here allocated to Venus, while in most systems of chirognomy it is given to Mars, while Venus rules the ball of the thumb (after Belot)*

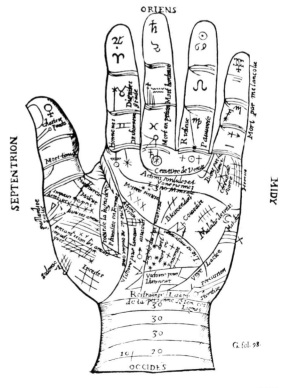

agree with this ascription. The lines themselves have special associations, as indicated on the separate analysis in Figure 58.

While there are very many different systems of palmistry, one may generalize and say that there are basically two methods of hand-reading: one method, whch has been called the 'deductive method', is involved with a detailed analysis of the lines of the hand, in relation to the form of the hand, from which rules of interpretation are applied in order to build up a composite picture of the personality. The other method, which has been called 'intuitive palmistry', is involved with using the hand as an autoscope for a mediumistic examination. In the latter practice a *soi-disant* palmist may need to know nothing of the theory of the art, being prepared to work entirely from intuition. In the majority of cases it is this latter kind of palmistry which is used. However, this should not disguise the fact that very many serious attempts have been made to establish systems of palmistry by which a person entirely without mediumistic ability may learn to read hands and palms.

Due almost entirely to historical factors, two lines of thought concerning the interpretation of hands have developed side by side and have in many respects not yet been integrated into one single practice. These are involved with the study of the lines of the hand, properly called CHIRO-MANCY, and the study of the form of the hand, properly called CHIROGNOMY. The tendency in the medieval practice of the art was to concentrate almost entirely upon the study of the lines of the hand. The characteristic of such palmistry was the reliance upon methods of interpreting lines and symbols on the hand as though they were capable of fixed interpretation, regardless of the quality and meanings inherent in the remaining lines and formations, and independent of the hand as a whole. However, the pioneer work of such nineteenth-century specialists as Carus (who devised a fourfold system) and D'Arpentigny (who devised a sevenfold system) contributed to a formulation of the laws of chirognomy which now play a great part in the study and interpretation of hands. In recent years some effort has been made to establish a relationship between personal

Figure 59   *Two plates from books on palmistry. Left: from Barthemy Cocles,* Ciromantia, *c. 1530; right: Joannes Indagine's* Introductiones Apotelesmaticae . . . , *1582*

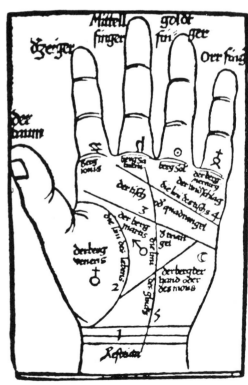

horoscopes and the chirogno-chiromantic laws. See also Figure 59.

Palmoscopy   A term derived from the Greek *palmos* ('pulsation') and *skopia* ('examination') and applied to a method of divination from the surface palpitation of the nude human body. In some cases the body was stimulated into palpitation by the applications of juices or by massage.

Pan   Name given to one of the HYPOTHETICAL PLANETS.

Pansophia   A term used specifically by the historian Haase as denoting an attitude of mind rising from the hermetic tradition, which (he says) strives towards presenting a unified harmonic picture of the world, often using fantastical and seemingly obscure materials in the picture-building. It is a holistic and hermetic attitude, which Haase contrasts with the fissiparous attitude of the *Mathesis universalis* (see MATHESIS).

Pantacle   Another name for the five-pointed star, the PENTACLE.

Parabrahman   A Sanskrit term meaning literally 'beyond even Brahma'. See HANSA.

Parcae   See FATAE.

Paredrii   See FAMILIAR.

Pars   Sometimes 'part' or 'point', a term used in astrology to denote a variety of different methods of determining significant degrees within a horoscope figure, by establishing certain numerical and angular relationships between such planets as the Sun, the Ascendant ·and other planets. The most frequently used of Pars in modern astrology is the PARS FORTUNA.

Pars Fortuna   The Part of Fortune, a term used to denote a significant degree within a horoscope, determined by revolving the Sun until it is exactly on the Ascendant of the figure; the Moon is then projected to a new place in that figure, so that it bears the same angular relationship to the Ascendant Sun as it did to the original Sun placing (Figure 60). This Pars is sometimes regarded as an indicator of personal destiny.

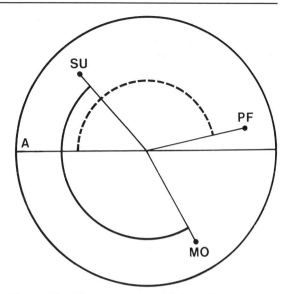

Figure 60   *The construction of the* Pars Fortuna *(PF), which, in terms of arc, bears the same relationship to the Ascendant (A) as the Moon (MO) does to the Sun (SU)*

Partile aspect   An exact ASPECT between two or more bodies.

Partzupheem   A Qabbalistic word given in a variety of spellings, usually translated as meaning 'faces'. It is said that when matter was differentiated all future forms were contained in the three heads or faces of the Trinity. Specialist terms, now translated as 'Long Face', 'Short Face' and 'White Face', were given to these storehouses of the future.

Pass-Not   An abbreviation for RING-PASS-NOT.

Passiel   Name given to two quite distinct spirits with separate functions. In certain methods of ceremonial magic the name is one of several attached to the governer of zodiacal Pisces. In the Qabbalistic tradition it is the name given to one of the angels who has rule over Abaddon.

Passing bell   The name given to the bell which is rung in the church when a person is near to death; it is said to have the effect of frightening away the evil spirits which are ready to take the soul as it passes from the body. In the medieval period bells were sometimes rung to destroy witches, as it was supposed that the sound of bells

165

threw them off their night flight and rendered their diabolic magic ineffective.

Passing the River See SECRET SCRIPTS.

Pastos See INITIATION.

Patala Patala is said by occultists to be the ancient name for the Americas. By a different etymology, it is also the name applied to Hell. See NAGA.

Path of Shadows See BROTHERS OF THE SHADOW.

'Pauline Art' See LEMEGETON.

Pentacle Specifically, a geometric figure linked with the number 5, such as the five-sided pentagon or the PENTAGRAM or the PENTALPHA. However, the term is often used in a general sense for any simple geometric figure constructed for magical or amuletic purposes. Thus the six-pointed SEAL OF SOLOMON or the septenary order of the planets in diagrammatic form, the Chaldean Order, is sometimes called a pentacle. See also the so-called PYTHAGOREAN PENTACLE.

Pentagram The pentagram, sometimes called the 'pentalpha', is the five-pointed star regarded as a symbol of many esoteric qualities. It is indeed the symbol of the microcosm, as well as of the etheric (see MORNING STAR). See also NUMBERS. From very early times the pentagram has been linked esoterically with the planet Venus. In this latter connection, as the work of Schultz demonstrates, when the patterns of conjunctions between Venus and Sun are plotted over synodic periods, a pentagram is traced in the skies around the Earth.

Pentalpha One of the names for the five-pointed PENTAGRAM, so called because it reproduced in its sigillic form the letter A (the Greek alpha) five times. See Figure 55, under MORNING STAR.

Perfect body See SUBTLE BODY.

Perisomata See HUMOURS.

Permanent atom A term and concept derived from modern Theosophy. It is a name applied to an invisible (and indeed hypothetical) atom which is said to be a residue of experience and knowledge gained on each of the mortal planes by the human being from incarnation to incarnation. The concept has given rise to much difficulty and disagreement within modern occult circles and not all occultists subscribe to the theory which the term evinces. Perhaps the major difficulty arises from the unavoidable link with materialism which the word 'atom' conjures in the modern mind. The experience and knowledge which is carried from lifetime to lifetime is stored within the human TERNARY.

Permanent Water See ALCHEMICAL MERCURY.

Persephone Name given to one of the HYPOTHETICAL PLANETS.

Personality In occultist circles it is usual to distinguish carefully between the words 'personality' and 'individuality' (see EGO). 'Personality' is usually applied to the characteristics, memories and karmic strengths or deficiencies of one life, while 'individuality' is applied to the reincarnating Ego, to the higher TERNARY. Personality is, therefore, the more or less impermanent clothing of one lifetime, capable of refinement and adjustment during that lifetime, which (while it certainly leaves seed traces and consequences for future incarnations) may be said to be perishable.

Phainon The Greek name (meaning 'shiny one') for the planet Saturn.

Phaleg The third of the seven supreme angels of the Qabbalists, described as the War Lord, and possessing the attributes of Mars.

Phalguni The Sanskrit name for the constellation Virgo, but see KANYA.

Phantasy A term used to denote the image-making faculty of the ASTRAL BODY. But see SPECULATION.

Phantom In general use a ghost or spectre, but see ASTRAL BODY.

Philosopher A term used in occult contexts to denote an alchemist.

Philosopher's Egg There was a medieval specific against poison and plague, called the 'Philosopher's Egg', which should not be confused with its alchemical namesake, which was the secret of 'incubation' – that is, the whole secret of the alchemical art – by which the inner life was germinated. The Egg is sometimes said to be the 'product' of alchemy – that is, the PHILOSOPHER'S STONE – rather than the equivalent of the alchemical search itself.

Philosopher's Stone The name given in ALCHEMY to a stone, powder or substance which will transmute base metals into gold; the 'philosopher' is the alchemist. It has very many names – it is the Powder of Projection, the LAPIS, the universal Quintessence. Naturally, as with all alchemical ideas, it has a spiritual or allegorical significance.

Philosopher's Tree Sometimes called 'Diana's Tree' (Diana being a lunar goddess), a name given in ALCHEMY to an amalgam of cystallized silver obtained from Mercury. Sometimes the tree of the PHOENIX is also called the Philosopher's Tree.

Philosopher's Vinegar See ALCHEMICAL MERCURY.

Phlegethon One of the rivers of Hell. It is said to be a river of liquid fire.

Phlegmatic One of the four TEMPERAMENTS, arising from an excess of the WATER ELEMENT in the psychological make-up of the personality. The phlegmatic temperament is withdrawn, sensitive and unstable, and within the astrological tradition is associated with such key words as receptive, confused, emotional, fluctuating, lacking in direction, self-protective and slow. The type is usually very methodical and, when the forces of the temperament are rightly canalized, has a strong power of soul, yet its exterior is often deceptive, unrevealing of the depths within. Faults in the temperament arise from oversensitivity to physical phenomena, which often produces fear or an inability to cope.

Phoenix Sometimes the 'Arabian bird', or even the 'Egyptian bird', a name given to the Arabian equivalent of the Egyptian benu bird, which was said to live for a specific number of years, and to terminate its life in a characteristic manner by building a nest of spices, sitting in this nest, flappings its wings to start a fire, and burning itself to ashes. From the ashes of bird and nest it arises in a new phoenix body. The bird is often used in esotericism as a symbol for reincarnation, but it was also used as a symbol of alchemy (being involved with the idea of transmutation of ashes to living being). There was also in esoteric literature a phoenix tree (*Phoenix dactylifera*), a date palm which was supposed to have the power to rejuvenate itself if it was in any way destroyed. The periods of rejuvenation for both bird and tree vary from culture to culture, but cycles of 500 and 1500 years are sometimes given, whilst esotericists favour the 1456-year period of the Sothic cycle.

The same name, Phoenix, is also used for one of the seventy-two SPIRITS OF SOLOMON. He is said to appear in the form a bird with a beautiful voice, and is therefore nothing other than a demonized form of the Arabian bird.

Phrenology A term from the Greek meaning literally 'the study of the mental faculties', but in an occult sense used to denote a specialist theory, first announced by Gall and Spurzheim, that the mental faculties, and certain aptitudes of soul, were located on the surface of the brain, and that a study of the surface of the cranium would therefore reveal the peculiar nature and qualities of these faculties and aptitudes in individual cases.

Phreno-mesmerism Sometimes called PHRENOLOGY, this is the art of using the principles of mesmerism in the reading of the human head. As a 'science' it was developed by such men as Braid when it had been discovered that a somnabule in a mesmeric state would respond with appropriate emotions to the touch of a hand on various parts of the head, in accord with the then fashionable theory of phrenology.

Phul The seventh of the seven supreme angels of the Qabbalists, said to possess all the attributes of the Moon.

Phylactery An AMULET, probably from the Greek *philakterion* (a 'watchman's post' or a 'safeguard'), in the form of a series of holy texts enclosed in a small leather box or bag.

Phyllorhodomancy Divination from rose leaves or, more precisely, from the sound made by rose leaves when they were crushed in the hands.

Pilgrim An occult term used to denote the MONAD or the incarnating spirit in man. Blavatsky says that in the *Vedanta* it is called the 'thread soul' (the SUTRATMAN).

Pirsoyn One of the variant names for GUISON.

Pisachas A Sanskrit term for demons. In some oriental cultures and modern Western occultist circles also a name applied to LARVAE and astral SHELLS.

Pisces The last of the twelve signs of the zodiac and one of the constellations. It corresponds as a zodiacal sign neither in location nor extent with the asterism of the same name, which is linked by the Qabbalists with the Hebraic letter Pe (see P) and with the TAROT arcanum 'The Star'. The modern sigil for Pisces ♓ is said by some to be a drawing of the two fishes united by the so-called SILVER CORD which joins together their mouths in the constellation image (Figure 61). In this image the two fish usually face in opposite directions to symbolize the altercation between spirit and soul in the human being. Pisces is of the WATER ELEMENT and of the Mutable quality, the influence being pre-eminently emotional, intuitive and insecure. There is a strong tendency to withdrawal or towards artistic expression, and the Piscean type tends to be hypersensitive to the emotional needs of others. The sensitive nature of

Figure 61 *An image of the constellation Pisces (from a late-fifteenth-century astrological text)*

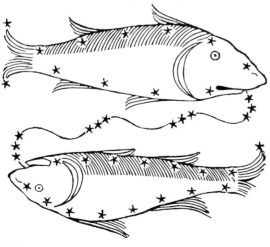

Pisces is expressed in the many key words attached to the sign by modern astrologers: sympathetic, imaginative, poetic, suggestible, emotionally malleable, poetic, self-pitying, easy-going, self-indulgent, sentimental, kindly and inconstant. In excess or under pressure the Piscean nature expresses itself in terms relating to its underlying insecurity and lack of drive, the key words being dreamy, impractical, lazy, restless, unstable, chaotic, hypochondriac, fickle, lacking in self-reliance. Pisces is ruled by the nebulous and sensitive modern planet NEPTUNE in most modern astrological systems, although in traditional astrology it was ruled by the beneficient and expansive Jupiter. The sign marks the exaltation of Venus and the detriment of Mercury.

Pitris A Sanskrit term used to denote the ancestors of mankind, those beings which preceded the ADAMIC race. Sometimes they are called 'Lunar Ancestors', 'Lunar Race', or 'Lunar Pitris'. In the Theosophical literature they are said to consist of seven classes, three of which are incorporeal.

Pituita A late medieval term for the PHLEGMATIC humour.

Plaksha See SECOND RACE.

Planchette Name given to an instrument designed for use in SEANCE rooms. It is a sort of mounted pencil on castors, which permits the hand to rest, yet move freely to the supposed direction of the spirit control as in the direct method of automatic writing (see SLATE WRITING). It is said to have been invented by a spiritualist named Planchette in 1853. See also OUIJA.

Planetary angels As with the ZODIACAL ANGELS and the ZODIACAL SPIRITS, there is much confusion of nomenclature and role of the planetary angels, or planetary spirits as they are sometimes called. The true planetary angels of medieval astrology are the governors of the spheres, which are listed under their esoteric name of SECUNDADEIAN BEINGS. However, the names of planetary angels most widely used in modern occultism are: Moon – Gabriel; Mercury – Raphael; Venus – Haniel; Sun – Michael; Mars – Hamael; Jupiter – Zadkiel; Saturn – Zaphkiel.

Planetary Chain A term introduced into esoteric astrology through the Theosophy of

Blavatsky. It is claimed that each of the physical GLOBES of the cosmic bodies is accompanied by (and indeed nourished by) seven superior globes which remain invisible to ordinary sight. These septenaries are termed a CHAIN.

Planetary Chain Logos In the Theosophical cosmoconception the Planetary Chain Logos is the title given to the individual spiritual entity deputized to take charge of a whole series of seven chains or an entire SCHEME OF EVOLUTION.

Planetary rulerships Each sign of the zodiac is assigned a planetary ruler. For example, the sign Aries is said to be ruled by the planet Mars. The order of rulerships is best set out in tabular form to demonstrate that the system of planetary ruler-ships is nowadays twofold. The first list in Table 21 sets out the sequence according to traditional astrology. The second list establishes the sequence according to modern astrology, which incorpor-ates into its system the so-called modern planets. The traditional system apportions two signs to each planet (save for the luminaries), one being a positive expression of the planet, the other a negative expression. The positive was sometimes called the 'day house', the negative the 'night house'. This explains why there is such a desig-nation as 'positive Mars' (which means Mars as ruler of Aries), and 'negative Mars' (which means Mars as ruler of Scorpio). The modern rulerships

Table 21

Traditional astrology

Positive sign ('day house')	Planet	Negative sign ('night house')
Cancer	Leo / Sun	Moon
Gemini	Mercury	Virgo
Taurus	Venus	Libra
Aries	Mars	Scorpio
Pisces	Jupiter	Sagittarius
Aquarius	Saturn	Capricorn

Modern astrology

Sign	Planet		
Cancer	Moon	Capricorn	Saturn
Leo	Sun	Aries	Mars
Virgo	Mercury	Taurus	Venus
Libra	Venus	Pisces	Neptune
Scorpio	Pluto	Aquarius	Uranus
Sagittarius	Jupiter		

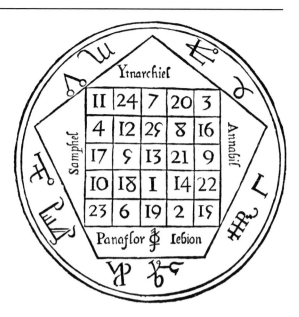

Figure 62 *The planetary seal for Mars, containing the magic square for this planet along with a number of Martian sigils and the names of the demonic rulers (from Kircher's* Oedipus Aegyptiacus, *1652)*

have continued a number of these traditional associations, but in most modern systems of astrology the three moderns – Uranus, Neptune and Pluto – have replaced three of the traditionals.

Planetary seals Graphic symbols or sigils denoting planets and supposed in themselves to exert a corresponding planetary influence (see, however, SEAL). The example seal in Figure 62 is part of a larger complex seal (or magic pattern) designed to evoke a spirit of Mars. Until this present century planetary seals were accorded little serious attention and were regarded largely as (little understood) survivals from late-medieval astrology. However, in our present century Steiner designed a number of remarkable seals, one for each planet, the forms arising from deep meditative consciousness.

Planetary spheres See SPHERES.

Planetary spirits The esotericist Bailey defines the term much in accord with tradition as 'another term for the Logos of a planet'. See also PLANE-TARY ANGELS and SEPHIROTHIC TREE.

Planetoid See ASTEROID.

169

Planets In modern astronomy the name 'planet' is applied to all celestial bodies (with the exception of comets and meteors) which revolve around the Sun of our system and have no light of their own. The ancients, however, believed that the planets did have a light of their own, and called the SUN and MOON planets in addition to the five 'visible' bodies MERCURY, VENUS, MARS, JUPITER and SATURN. This traditional seven of the early astrology was in relatively modern times augmented by the so-called modern planets, URANUS, NEPTUNE and PLUTO, while some astrologers include the ASTEROIDS and even the so-called HYPOTHETICAL PLANETS.

Plastic soul Sometimes the 'protean soul', a term used in Theosophy as the equivalent of the ASTRAL BODY, which properly speaking is not a soul body at all. The term is derived from the faculty of this body for receiving into itself the impress of images from the astral light or other powerful spiritual sources.

Platonic age See PLATONIC CYCLE.

Platonic cycle This term is sometimes wrongly identified in popular thinking with the so-called platonic year, which is a period of PRECESSION, about which Plato probably knew nothing. The platonic cycle is actually the *Magnus annus*, the GREAT YEAR, in which it is visualized that the movement of the eight spheres causes them to arrive together in a great union at the same points (the same fiducials) from which they began their period or cycle. In terms of the ancient cosmoconception, once a platonic cycle was completed, a retrograde motion of the spheres set in and a backward unfolding began, to continue for another vast periodicity until the planetary spheres were once more aligned to their common fiducials. The motion forward was linked in antique times with the AGE OF SATURN, under the direction of an inner harmony. In the retrograde motion time is visualized as being reversed, so that men and other creatures grow young with the progression (or rather retrogression) of time.

Platonic month A misnomer (in that it has nothing to do with a month or even with the Moon) derived from analogy with the twelve lunar months related to the PLATONIC YEAR. It is used to denote the PRECESSION of the Vernal Point through one sign of the zodiac, which takes 2160 years.

Platonic year The Vernal Point retrogrades through the constellations in a period which is approximately 52,920 years (but see PRECESSION). This is the so-called platonic year, the *Annus platonicus* of traditional astrology, although it is misnamed by being linked with the Greek philospher (see PLATONIC CYCLE). This period is divided into twelve equal lengths (the so-called PLATONIC MONTHS), corresponding to the arcs of the zodiac, and the periods during which the Vernal Point retrogrades through the arcs are named after the relevant signs.

Pleroma A term derived from Gnostic speculation, meaning approximately 'fullness', and often taken to refer to the universal soul. In popular occultism the term is sometimes used as though it denotes the abode of the gods, the Devachan of oriental lore, the fullness of divine emanations.

Pluto A planet discovered in 1930 by the Lowell Observatory. When first announced by astronomers it was named Pluto–Lowell or Lowell–Pluto, but it had been mentioned before this time under a variety of different names by astrologers; these names included 'Pluto'. Astrologers see it as an eruptive and disturbing influence, involved with the processes of elimination and regeneration. When involutionary, it is connected with the underworld, with crime and all that is dark and unregenerate in our society; when evolutionary, it is connected with esoteric movements, with all that seeks to redeem. Since the modern Pluto was discovered, it has displaced the traditional NEGATIVE MARS from its rule over the zodiacal Scorpio.

Poemandres A Greek title, sometimes given as *Pymander*, meaning approximately 'shepherd-man', given to one of the most influential of the HERMETIC CANON, presenting (partly in the manner of Platonic dialogue) knowledge of spiritual and esoteric matters, mingled with early Christian concepts.

Pollux Se GEMINI.

Poltergeist A term, compounded from the German, meaning 'noisy or troublesome spirit' and applied to a variety of invisible entities which manifest in an unruly and disturbing manner, often involving unexplained noises, the moving or throwing of objects, the breaking of material things, as well as such curious phenomena as APPORTS. While some occultists claim that the majority of poltergeist activities arise from SHELLS, DIAKKAS or ELEMENTARS, certain modern psychic workers tend to think that the disturbances are derived from the energies of living humans, who project them unconsciously. Such phenomena often appear to be linked with the energies of children. The term PSYCHO-HARAGGIC DIATHESIS has been proposed to denote such phenomena. It is sometimes claimed that while a ghost will haunt a house, a poltergeist will haunt a person. This, however, is a simplification, for there are cases of extensive poltergeist activity in empty houses. Poltergeists certainly appear to take pleasure in frightening human beings, although only rarely do they hurt humans seriously – a possible exception is the BELL WITCH, although some researchers dispute that this curious manifestation was really connected with poltergeist activity at all. The most dangerous manifestation produced by poltergeist activity is that of fire, which may seemingly be generated from nowhere. Such poltergeist fires have been the cause of substantial destruction of property. Poltergeists appear to be fond of throwing stones and other objects, such as cups and saucers, or of causing such things to be thrown, dislodged and so on. The odd thing is that the objects observed in such flight appear to move more slowly in their trajectory than they would if thrown by an ordinary agency. Such thrown objects have been found to be warm, even hot, after transits. Poltergeist activity has been reported in all ages and in all countries, and is in fact a remarkably common occurrence even outside professionally conducted seances. The Italian psychic researcher Bozzano investigated 532 cases of hauntings and found that 158 of them were directly connected with poltergeist activity. However, a great many poltergeist activities go unrecorded, while many others are 'treated' by clairvoyants, psychic workers and religious orders, in order to have their influences removed. See also EXORCISM and TRARAMES.

Polygraphy In an occult context a term used to denote both the art of writing in secret alphabetic languages and of deciphering these. See SECRET SCRIPTS and STEGANOGRAPHY.

Poppet A term derived from the French *poupée* (doll) and used to denote a figure, usually in human form, made in clay or wax for magical purposes. See SYMPATHETIC MAGIC and WAX IMAGE.

Populus 'People', a name given to one of the sixteen figures of GEOMANCY.

Poseidon Name given to one of the HYPOTHETICAL PLANETS. Since Poseidon was in Roman times called Neptune, the term is sometimes used as a synonym for the modern planet NEPTUNE.

Poseidonis The name given to the last remaining land area of ATLANTIS after the main continent had sunk beneath the ocean. See also RUTA and DAITYA.

Positive Mars A term which is a survival from the ancient Ptolemaic astrological system, relating to the classification of planetary rulerships over the zodiacal signs. Each of the planets (save for the luminaries) were accorded rule over two signs of the zodiac (see PLANETARY RULERSHIPS), and such pairs were deemed positive or negative, solar or lunar and so on. Mars was accorded a negative rule over Scorpio and a positive rule over Aries. Thus the term 'Positive Mars' really means 'Mars as ruler of Aries'. See NEGATIVE MARS.

Possession Technically, possession is the name applied to a condition in which a person is so completely under the control of a demonic power that the demon is able to 'sit within' his or her body. The word is from the Latin *possidere* ('to take possession of'), and is distinguished by demonologists from the related word 'obsession' by virtue of the fact that a demon in control of a human 'obsesses' from outside (the Latin *ob* meaning 'towards' and implying bearing on the outside). The concept of possession was well established in pre-classical times, but few wrote so personally about its effects than the Desert Fathers, those fourth- and fifth-century hermits who did so much to contribute to the theories of demonology and witchcraft which would wrack Europe almost a thousand years later. A more frequently used term for possession in the demonological literature was *energumenus*, a word derived from the Greek, and meaning 'possessed by the devil'. The demonologist witch-hunter

171

Guazzo uses this word when describing the manner in which a priest may determine if a person is truly possessed or merely pretending possession. The underlying idea was that the spirit of the person possessed in such a manner was made subservient to the will of the demon, so that sometimes the voice of that person changed, sometimes even his or her appearance. The body might be thrown into convulsions, and strange objects and even creatures were said to be passed from the orifices, mainly the mouth and anus.

For all the strange behaviour associated with possession, it was sometimes not possible to determine whether someone was really possessed or merely eccentric, although the professional witchfinders and those who set themselves up as advisers in these matters rarely put too fine a point on the distinction. The ecclesiastical attitude was rooted in the belief that it is largely the reaction to sacred images, words or symbols which reveals possession, and it is the part of the body which reveals the affliction most acutely which is taken to be the locality favoured by the possessing demon: vomiting is a sign that the demon is in the stomach, a sense of strangling accompanies possession in the throat, and so on. Having determined the fact and place of possession, a priest might try to exorcise the demon.

Powers   A term used of one of the ranks of CELESTIAL HIERARCHIES, sometimes called the Potestates or DYNAMIS.

Practical magic   See MAGIC.

Praestigiosus   A medieval term for a witch who deludes men by fantastic illusions or transformations.

Pralaya   A Sanskrit term used to denote a period of rest or dreamless sleep between cosmic ages, sometimes called 'twilights'. See YUGA.

Prana   A Sanskrit term usually translated as meaning 'life principle' or 'breath of life'; it is sometimes called 'life essence'. The word appears in many combinations, from highly spiritual and symbolic concepts of breathing (the idea being that living organisms breath in prana from the ambient) to relatively materialistic concepts. For example, *pranatman* is one of the names given to the eternal *sutratma*, the 'gem thread' of beads which symbolize the sequence of incarnations; while *pranayama* is the regulation of the breath in

certain yogic exercises. See also VITALITY GLOBULES.

Prana globule   See VITALITY GLOBULES.

Pranamayakosha   The Hindu name for the ETHERIC DOUBLE.

Pranatman   See PRANA.

Pranayama   See YOGA.

Pratyahara   See YOGA.

Pre-existence   See REINCARNATION.

Precession   The 'precession of the equinoxes' is the term used to denote the retrograde movement of the Vernal Point through the constellations, a phenomenon which is perhaps connected with the nutation of the Earth upon its poles, although the fact is that there is no really convincing explanation of precession. In simple terms one has to visualize the two so-called zodiacs, the tropical and the constellational, one of which 'moves' and one of which is 'fixed'. Because of precession the fixed stars appear to advance (in longitude) one arc of just over 50 seconds each year, which means that the First Point of tropical Aries (which marks the spring equinox) seems to retrograde through the constellations. In 1 year the rate is 50,25 seconds; in 72 years the rate is 1 degree 0,3 minutes; in 2160 years the rate is 30 degrees, and in 25,920 years (72 × 30 × 12) the rate is 360 degrees. The 2160 span is called a 'precessional year' and wrongly a 'GREAT YEAR'. As the Vernal Point retrogrades through one 30-degree arc in 2160 years, it is maintained that the relevant zodiacal sign leaves its own distinctive impress on the history of that era, and that civilizations of particular characters, with particular natures and purposes, succeed each other in epochal series of 2160 years. It is widely believed that we are at present living in the age of Pisces (which is to say that the Vernal Point is progressing through the sign Pisces), and that this age is intimately connected with the destiny of Christianity and with Christ (symbolized as a fish and the centre of much Piscean imagery). See also PLATONIC YEAR.

Precessional age   A period sometimes supposed to be 2160 years in duration, but see PRECESSION.

Precessional year   A period of 25,920 years. See PRECESSION.

Precipitation   A term used by psychic workers and occultists for a little-understood phenomenon in which matter appears to 'condense' from a non-material state and/or to pass through matter, as when an APPORT is carried by psychic means into a locked room. The term itself is derived from the idea that the solid apport 'precipitates' into its basic atoms, and then reprecipitates after passing through the solid objects. The word was widely used by the early Theosophists in regard to letters and written instructions which were said to be received directly from the Mahatmas by such psychic means.

Premonition   A warning, arising from within the soul, of an impending event.

Prenatal chart   See PRENATAL EPOCH.

Prenatal epoch   Sometimes simply the 'epoch', the prenatal epoch was originally defined as a time. It was claimed to be that moment (said to occur approximately at the beginning of the gestative period) when the degree ascending on the eastern horizon and the longitude of the Moon at that moment were interchangeable with the longitude of the Ascendant degree and the longitude of the Moon (or their respective opposite points) at birth. Some astrologers would cast a chart for such a time, and regarded this chart as a conception chart, relating it to the destiny of the native as they would an ordinary birth chart. The term is sometimes used to denote a chart cast for the putative moment of conception.

Prenestine lots   A variation on an ancient system of divination, the *Sortes prenestinae*, in which the letters of the alphabet were placed in a jar, shaken according to prescribed rites and then emptied upon the floor. The words formed by chance were taken as relating to futurity.

Preta   A Sanskrit term meaning 'hungry demon', but used to denote the astral shell of a morally deficient man after death. Pretas are sometimes wrongly said to be elementaries.

Prevision   The faculty of foreseeing or having insight into the future. In popular occultism this is also linked with the edea of SPIRITUAL BILOCA-TION and with PROPHECY.

Pricking   During the witchcraft craze of the sixteenth and seventeenth centuries self-appointed WITCHFINDERS would search out suspects and prick malformations on their bodies such as warts, birthmarks and the like with needles or bodkins. It was widely believed that witches did not feel pain when such a malformation was pricked, and it was for this reason that pricking

Figure 63   *The bodkins to the left are trick knives, used by witchfinders who, for personal gain, were intent on showing innocent people to be witches. As the illustration indicates, the blades of these knives will slide into the handles, giving the impression that they are sinking into the flesh of the suspect without causing pain. The bodkin to the right is one proposed by those who were more fairminded: it is obvious that this blade cannot slide back into the handle*

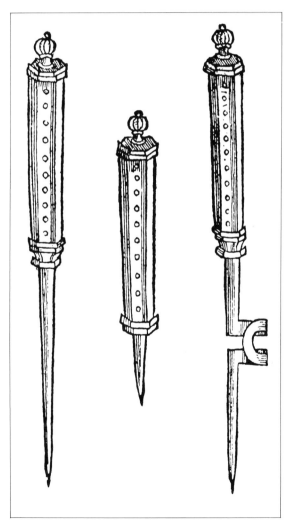

was regarded as a reliable indication of their true nature. However, it was recognized even in the heyday of the witch-hunts that many of the witchfinders were dishonest, and the writer Scot reproduced pictures of a special trick pricking knife or bodkin used by some of the witchfinders (Figure 63), the blade of which would slide into the handle (left and centre in Figure 63). With the aid of the trick bodkin the witchfinder could appear to stick the knife into the flesh of the subject and when he or she showed no sign of pain, pronounce him or her to be a witch. The bodkin on the right is a proposal for a design which would make such trickery impossible.

Primary system In astrology one of the forms of prediction from the radical chart rests on the idea that each Earth day is the equivalent to the advance of the Sun by approximately 1 degree. By analogy this degree is taken to be equal to the passage of one year in the life of the native.

Prime essences One of the names given by Paracelsus to the traditional THREE PRINCIPLES of astrology and alchemy.

Primordial Seven An esoteric name for the DHYAN-CHOHANS.

Prince of Darkness See AHRIMAN.

Principalities See ARCHAI and POWERS.

Principles In Theosophy the word 'principles' is used to denote the seven individual and fundamental aspects of the one universal reality in the kosmos and man. Each of these seven is sometimes called a 'principle'; thus, for example, there is the 'Divine principle', the 'Astral principle' and so on. In descending order these principles in man are Atman, Buddhi, Manas, Ego, Astral, Etheric and physical, although, of course, there are many alternative names for these, depending upon the occult system used. Alchemists used the same term in their own occult THREE PRINCIPLES. The early Greek astrologers employed the Aristotelian Four Principles which ruled matter – terms translated as 'Hot', 'Moist', 'Dry' and 'Cold'. These were the pairs of interacting opposites said to underlie all phenomena: Hot and Moist united forms and brought increase; Dry and Cold separated forms and brought destruction. The polarities or principles

(sometimes popularly called the Aristotelian principles and often confusingly called the 'qualities' – see QUALITY) played a most important part in early astrological doctrines.

Procel Sometimes Pucel, one of the seventy-two SPIRITS OF SOLOMON. He is said to appear in the form of an angel.

Progressed horoscope Sometimes called the 'progressed figure' or 'progressed chart', it is an astrological term used to denote a horoscope figure calculated for a specific time after the natal chart and schematically derived from the same.

Progressions In astrology this term is generally regarded as being an equivalent of DIRECTIONS, a method of calculating futurity from a consideration of a natal horoscope chart.

Projection A term with two different meanings in occultism, one used in connection with alchemy and the other with astral travel. In ALCHEMY projection is the last of the twelve stages of transmutation by which the alchemist penetrates ordinary metals and stones with the prepared powder of the finished work ('the Powder of Projection') to invest this power on the unprepared matter. In astral travel the term is used in the sense that the consciousness of the operator has been so developed for him or her consciously to project the astral body (that is, cause it to travel) while leaving the sleeping physical in an inert position. Unconscious astral travel is not called projection, which is properly involved with the idea of conscious participation in the astral realm.

Prophecy The foretelling of the future. There are a vast number of different occult and quasi-occult systems designed to peer into futurity. All the important methods are listed under the specific names within this present text (see DIVINATION), but it is usually admitted that the basis of such mantic prophecy is the use (conscious or unconscious) of demons or spirits. Certain systems which appear not to make use of spiritism are none the less explained by occultists in spiritist terms. For example, the basis of the TAROT predictive method is linked with a higher quality of spiritual agency, while the Chinese occultists insist that the beings who regulate the working of the I CHING are of a special evolutionary level. The use of direct mantic frenzy, as, for example, in ORACLES, involving the priest or pythoness as a sort of mouthpiece of the gods or gods, is clearly involved with what is now called spiritualism. In relation to astrology, which would appear to be involved with intellectual processes rather than with making contact with spirits, the art of foretelling the future is properly one of the specialist fields connected with the art of PROGRESSIONS and DIRECTIONS, by which the promise of a radical chart is unfolded and revealed in terms of cycles and dates relating to the life of the native. Unfortunately, astrology has been linked with other forms of prophecy – perhaps more accurately termed 'astromancy' – which really play no part in the philosophical background of the science. For example, a surprising number of people use the horoscope as an autoscope, and make predictions according to clairvoyant principles which have nothing to do with genuine astrology. For examples of famous prophecies, see HERMANN PROPHECIES and MALACHY PROPHECIES.

Protoplastus   A word probably originated by the occultist Paràcelsus and intended to denote the living human being, with the driving force of what he called ILIASTER within him. The Iliaster was a sort of cosmic life force, a power from the stars, which had the power perpetually to regenerate matter, probably the equivalent of the modern AKASHA. In a slightly different sense the word survives in the modern 'protoplasm', the basic living material of animal and plant cellular life. Sometimes occultists apply the term as meaning 'that which is first formed', with the result that the protoplastus is sometimes called the ADAMIC, as the first representative form of the human being; more often this is the 'protoplastic man'.

Psyche   A Greek term adapted into the occultism of Theosophy to mean the lower MANAS or the animal, terrestrial soul. For the ancient Greeks, however, it was something different. See SOUL.

Psychic   A name sometimes applied to a human who is particularly sensitive to the invisible agencies which constitute in the popular mind the spirit world. In reality all humans are psychic, so that the word points to a degree or quality, rather than to an attribute.

Psychic body   A term seemingly derived from spiritualistic circles in the nineteenth century to describe an ill-defined soul body of rarefied matter which radiates a spiritual energy or force. It is said that this psychic body becomes visible as materializations in seances by some (again ill-defined) method of attracting to itself a more dense materiality. The term appears to be approximately the same as ETHERIC BODY as described by people who have little or no awareness of what this spiritual body really is. The psychic body has also been called the *Nervengeist*.

Psychic cold   A name given to a phenomenon sometimes observed in seance rooms or haunted houses when there is a sudden drop in temperature or the feeling of a cold breeze. A related phenomenon is the experience of a chill or frisson down the spine. It has been shown by psychic researchers that the experience is not entirely subjective, for not only is there a marked drop in temperature in certain seances, but there is also at times a sufficient movement of air to move the hairs on the heads of sitters or to bend the heads of flowers in vases. A table of temperature has been constructed to show that there were falls of from 1 degree to 11 degrees during the course of one- or two-hour sittings, while in one case (where psychical phenomena had been recorded) there was a drop of 20.5 degrees!

Psychic photography   Another term for SPIRIT PHOTOGRAPHY.

Psychic writing   See PSYCHOGRAPHY.

Psychograph   A term with two different meanings in psychic research. It was first used to denote a mechanical OUIJA board, which had a rotating disc moved by the fingers of the medium to facilitate the spelling-out of messages from the spirit world. It was also used to denote a photograph of a manuscript or document produced by a discarnate agency. See SPIRIT PHOTOGRAPHY.

Psychography   A word used to denote spiritist writing in which the writer follows the dictation of his own soul power. Sometimes the word is used to denote psychic writing, which is not always to the dictate of a soul power but to the dictates of disincarnate or non-incarnate entities. Unfortunately the same term has been used in connection with SPIRIT PHOTOGRAPHY (see, therefore, PSYCHOGRAPH).

Psychomancy A term derived from the Greek *psychomantia* (the proper equivalent of sciomancy) and applied to a method of divining the future from men's souls. John Gaule defined it as 'divining by men's souls, affections, will, religious or moral dispositions', from which description it appears to be the kind of clairvoyance commonly used in spiritualistic circles nowadays. The word is sometimes used to denote occult intercommunication between souls and spirits, and should therefore be used for the kind of commerce with the supercelestial world described by such occultists as Swedenborg, Davis and Blake. It is sometimes wrongly used as an equivalent of NECROMANCY.

Psychometry A Greek-derived term meaning 'soul measurement', but applied to the method of sensing or 'reading' from physical objects the history of each object (and indeed the history of things and people associated with these objects) which is hidden to ordinary sensibility. Psychometry is perhaps the oldest of all the divinatory faculties, but the modern name was not used to distinguish it until the last century, by Buchanan, who was of the opinion that all objects contain within them the history of the world as a result of the connection between them and the Akashic Chronicles; see therefore AKASHA.

Psychoharragic diathesis A name coined by the psychic worker Myers to denote a hypothetical unconscious projection of spirits. In terms of this theory (which is largely dismissed by occultists) spirits are themselves merely projections from the unconscious mind of a disturbed person – which is to say that under certain circumstances ghosts and related psychic phenomena (particularly that of POLTERGEISTS) are a result of the splitting-off of psychic energies, which are, by some unexplained means, given a tangible reality in order to release tensions within the psyche of the disturbed personality.

Puck Sometimes Puckril, a name derived from the Old English *puca*, meaning 'mischievous demon', and applied to an evil, malicious or otherwise harmful spirit.

Puckril A name given to a witch's FAMILIAR, probably a dimunitive of PUCK.

Puella 'Girl', a name given to one of the sixteen figures of GEOMANCY.

Puer 'Boy', a name given to one of the sixteen figures of GEOMANCY.

Purgatory The name given to a stage of being (often identified with a place in popular thought) experienced after death, in which more or less painful adjustments are made for sins and errors committed during the preceding lifetime. Purgatory has a limit in time, for it is experienced only until the stains of sin have been washed or wiped away. Purgatory is sometimes confused in popular occultism with Hell, although most occultists deny the reality of Hell as an eternal state of damnation. The corresponding purgatorial experience in oriental occultism is KAMALOKA. The occultist insists that while the direct painful consequences of sin are not experienced until after death, they are even so carried within the spiritual bodies of the sinner during the preceding lifetime from the moment of the sin, and to some extent work their influences from those bodies into the present lifetime. In that sense, but only in that sense, may Purgatory be said to be here on earth; in every other sense it is properly related to the postmortem state, in the astral plane.

Puruel The name given to the angel who probes the human soul, and who is termed the 'fiery and pitiless angel'. He has been identified with the Archangel URIEL and confused with PUSIEL.

Purson One of the seventy-two SPIRITS OF SOLOMON. He is said to appear in human form, with the head of a lion, riding a bear, and with a snake in his hand.

Purusha A Sanskrit term usually translated as meaning 'the spiritual self' of man – the archetypal man.

Pusiel One of the seven Angels of Punishment, his name meaning 'fire of God'.

Pymander See POEMANDRES.

Pyroeis One of the Greek names for Mars, meaning 'fire'. It is variously spelt in medieval astrological and alchemical texts.

Pyromancy The prediction of the future by means of fire. This was one of the most popular of predictive techniques with the ancients, who would predict from large fires, from the nature and sizes of flames, as well as from oil and candle flames. Many related techniques have evolved around the burning or boiling of things and from studying the nature of charred remains; however, such techniques should not be called 'pyromantic', even though they are often so described in popular lore. Thousands of years ago the Chinese evolved a method of prediction through burning tortoise shells (the nature of the cracks being the signs of futurity), and it is thought that from this basic technique the highly spiritualized predictive method of the I CHING was evolved. While it is generally believed that Nostradamus used astrology to arrive at his remarkable *centuries* of quatrains relating to the future of Europe, he in fact admits in a letter to his son that he used a special kind of pyromancy, although it is very likely that this was actually a method of HYDRO-MANCY. From certain of the quatrains we may reconstruct the method used by Nostradamus, which appears to owe its form to the technique of the Grecian PYTHIA. The magician pictures himself sitting alone in his secret study, leaning on a brazen tipod and watching a little flame within the bowl. His feet and the hem of his robe are bathed in water. Although Nostradamus does not say as much, the flame may be floating on the surface of a bowl of water or may have arisen from a vaporous oil upon the water, since such predictive methods had been used in earlier times. Indeed, it is possible to argue from ancient texts, notably from Iamblichus, that the 'little flame' is not external at all, but rather an internal ray of illumination, which is often pictured as a flame of fire.

Pythagorean harmonies See MUSIC OF THE SPHERES.

Pythagorean letter The name given to the letter of the alphabet Y (which see, along with NUMBERS).

Pythagorean pentacle The name given to a six-pointed star, with an eagle figured at the highest point, and below a bull, a lion and the face of man (the image of the four fixed signs of the zodiac – see, for example, TETRAMORPH). The imagery of the Pythagorean pentacle (which has nothing to do with Pythagoras, even though the numbers 4 and 6 (4 + 2) were derived in this context from the Pythagorean SOUL NUMBERS) was widely adopted in proto-Renaissance ecclesiastical sculpture and appears in many medieval astrological, alchemical and occult texts.

Pythagorean triangle See NUPTIAL NUMBER.

Pythia According to the ancient Greek and Roman sources the pythia was a priestess chosen to reside in the temple or *temenos* and to give oracular responses to questions. The pythia of Delphi, who was probably the most famous in the ancient world, was said to sit on a tripod when delivering such oracles. But see ORACLE.

Pytho A Grecian word sometimes wrongly associated with PYTHIA and said to denote the same evil influence as that of the OB.

Pythoness A name given to the PYTHIA.

The seventeenth letter of the alphabet, associated with the Hebraic Koph and in some occult systems ascribed the number 100, in others it is said to represent 90, which reduces to NINE.

Qabbala The word 'Qabbala' (sometimes 'Cabbala', 'Qabbalah', 'Kabala', 'Kabbala', etc.) relates to a complex philosophy and cosmo-conception which has an oral tradition, transcribed for over a thousand years, rooted in a mystical and esoteric interpretation of the Scriptures. Some indeed argue that Qabbalism is the root of modern occultism. It is usual to distinguish 'Qabbalism' as the Hebraic hermetic tradition from 'Cabbalism' as the European system of secret ciphers, acrostics, arcane terms and symbolism, but there are many variant spellings of the name. The influence of occultism on Qabbalistic thought – or, more accurately, on Christian Qabbalism – has been profound. Equally, the influence of Christian and Jewish Qabbalism on esotericism has been extensive; indeed, so extensive are these fruitful influences, which may be traced through Agrippa, Boehme, Dee, Fludd, Paracelus and Welling (to mention only those authorities whose terms are touched upon in the present work), that it is entirely beyond the scope of a short article to deal with them. By far the best method of setting out the relevant terminologies and classifications which have influenced occultism is by means of tables. See SEPHIROTHIC TREE for some indication of the main entries in the present work.

Qadmon A Qabbalistic term for ADAM KADMON.

Q'lippoth See KLIPPOTH.

Quadruplicities Each of the twelve signs of the zodiac have been grouped into fours in such a way as to reflect the communality of QUALITY: Car-dinality, Fixity and Mutability. These three groups are called quadruplicities:

Cardinal – Aries, Cancer, Libra and Capricorn
Fixed – Taurus, Leo, Scorpio and Aquarius
Mutable – Gemini, Virgo, Sagittarius

Qualities See QUADRIPLICITIES and QUALITY.

Quality This term has (confusingly) two important technical applications in astrology. The first meaning is related to the idea of four qualities linked with the innate natures of the elements: Fire is said to be of the Hot and Dry qualities; Earth is one of the Cold and Dry qualities; Water is of the Cold and Moist qualities; Air is of the Hot and Moist qualities. In this sense the four qualities, apparently originated by the early Greeks, were a development of the Empedoclean theory of ELE-MENTS, in which Fire was hot, Air cold, Water moist and Earth dry. In relation to human beings illness was a sign that a person was 'out of quality' or suffering from some imbalance (see TEMPER-AMENTS).

A second meaning of the term is related to the astrological idea of the three qualities, by means of which each of the four elements finds expression in the twelve signs of the zodiac (see QUADRUPLICITIES).

Quartessence The term 'quartessence' is found mainly in the curious astrological terminology of alchemical texts. Philalethes denies the existence of the QUINTESSENCE but describes a 'quartes-sence', a 'fourth essence', which binds the THREE PRINCIPLES and is called by the curious designation 'moist and silent fire'.

Quaternary   See LOWER QUATERNARY and TERNARY.

Quicksilver   In ALCHEMY the name given to the spagyric Mercury, which is not the liquid metal of modern science, but a spiritual quality. See ALCHEMICAL MERCURY and MAGNESIA.

Quinanes   A name given by certain occultists to the race of giants who lived on the continent of ATLANTIS.

Quincunx   An ASPECT of 150 degrees, the two aspecting points being separated by five signs of the zodiac.

Quindecile   An ASPECT of 24 degrees, derived from dividing the zodiac into fifteenths.

Quintessence   In general occultism the term means 'fifth element' and is a reference to the invisible power or essence which binds in a unity the otherwise separate FOUR ELEMENTS (see CHAOS). In ALCHEMY the term is synonymous with 'elixir'. The term has had very many synonyms, of which the most frequently used are 'AETHER', 'Mercury of the Philosophers' and the modern 'etheric', which has been studied in some depth by Wachsmuth. See also SEVEN COSMICAL ELEMENTS.

Quintile   An ASPECT of 72 degrees, arising from a division of the zodiac into fifths.

R

The eighteenth letter of the alphabet, associated with the Hebraic Resch and the magical number 200. It is claimed that the curious cross on the ℞ in the short form for 'recipe' or 'prescription' is derived from the sigil ♃ for Jupiter, the god of medicines. However, the ♃ symbol was used even in the period before this was the standard sigil for Jupiter, the common medieval symbol for the planet being ♃. In any case, both the Sun and Mercury are just as associated with healing as Jupiter. Some have traced the R to a short form for *Responsum Raphaelis*, under the impression that it is the Archangel Raphael who is responsible for healing. Raphael is, of course, associated with Mercury. Blavatsky linked the form R with the esoteric notion of the 'walking man'.

Rabisu An evil spirit of Assyrian demonology. It is said that as he passes a human being he sets the body hair of that human on end – a phenomenon common to many unpleasant forms of psychic invasion (but see PSYCHIC COLD).

Radiant body A term coined by Mead in connection with his study of the various misunderstandings of the occult nature of the AUGOEIDES in the writings of Bulwer-Lytton and the Theosophists of his time. See SUBTLE BODY.

Radical In astrology the original position of a planet or nodal point in a given chart, as opposed to positions attained by techniques of PROGRESSION or by transit. The original chart is sometimes called the 'radix figure'.

Radiograph A photograph of psychic phenomena produced without a camera – sometimes called a 'skotograph'. See SPIRIT PHOTOGRAPHY.

Rahu The Sanskrit name for the DRAGON'S HEAD (the north node), which is accorded great importance in Hindu astrology. The same name is also used of a variety of different cosmologically linked demonisms, however. Rahu was the name of a demon who robbed the gods of a powerful elixir (*amrita*); he was punished with exile to the heavens, where he became the constellation Draco. This celestial position is sometimes confused with the lunar myth (see, for example, ATALIA) of the dragon swallowing the luminaries. See also KETU, the Sanskrit equivalent of the DRAGON'S TAIL.

Rajas See TRIGUNAS.

Raka A Sanskrit term for the day of the full moon, generally regarded as suitable for occult practices. A *raksha* is an amulet prepared during this time.

Raksha See RAKA.

Rakshasas A Sanskrit term meaning 'raw eaters' and in exoteric thought regarded as demonic beings. In esoteric lore they are said to be the giants of the period of ATLANTIS, the Gibborim or Quinanes. The related term 'Rakshasi-Bhasha', meaning literally the 'language of the Rakshasas', is the Sanskrit name applied to the speech of the Atlanteans.

Rapadhatu In the oriental cosmoconception, the region of form, freed from sensuality.

Raphael The Archangel linked with the sphere of Mercury and one of the SECUNDADEIAN BEINGS. In Qabbalistic tradition Raphael is the healer and is connected with the idea of knowledge gained through experience (see also HOD). Raphael is linked in Western occultism with rule over the AIR ELEMENT.

Rapping A term used in a specialist sense to denote the characteristic noises in seances which are apparently derived from non-human and discarnate sources. See TYPTOLOGY.

Rasi The Hindu term for a birth chart, usually cast for a constellational zodiac.

Ratziel See CHOKMAH.

Raum Sometimes Raym, one of the seventy-two SPIRITS OF SOLOMON. He is said to appear in the form of a blackbird.

Ray The term, now almost archaic in its original astrological sense, was once used in traditional astrological texts as being synonymous with 'INFLUENCE'. However, in modern times the term has been widely used in such systems as the Intuitional Astrology of Bailey, in a specialist sense – see, therefore, SEVEN RAYS and SEVEN RAY-TYPES.

Rebirth See REINCARNATION.

Reception In astrology a planet placed in a sign over which it does not have rulership is said to be 'received' by the planet which rules that sign.

Rechaka A Sanskrit term for one of the breathing exercises of Hatha-Yoga.

Recording Angels See LIPIKA.

Rectification A specialist astrological term used to denote the process of adjusting a birth chart (itself believed to be inaccurate) by reference to known events which are dated independently of the horoscope, and hence permit correction by adjustment.

Rectors The seven rectors are the seven planetary OLYMPIC SPIRITS.

Red lion A name given in ALCHEMY to a stage in the development of the spagyric LAPIS. See Figure 38 under GREEN LION.

Red Magnesia See MAGNESIA.

Reduction See NUMBERS.

Reincarnation A term derived from the Latin and meaning literally 'repeated embodiment in flesh'. It is used by occultists to denote the repeated descent of the human MONAD or EGO into a physical constitution (which is not entirely of the flesh). In its simplest form the theory of reincarnation holds that there is in man a permanent and eternal principle, which gains experience through a long series of rebirths. In its more complex aspects, however, the teachings surrounding the theme of reincarnation offer a wide and satisfying account of the nature of the soul, the evolution of the spirit, the reasons underlying individual human existence, as well as a completely integrated theory of cosmogenesis. The theme of reincarnation is incorporated into virtually all the ancient esoteric streams, permeates occult doctrines, and teaches unequivocally that the purpose of the repeated descent of a spiritual entity into the flesh is to inform and expand the permanent spiritual qualities of that self; in other words, it teaches that the aim of life is understanding and growth, and the experiencing of conditions which arise only on the earth plane.

In occultism the laws of reincarnation are intimately bound up with the laws of KARMA, and in modern times these have been well documented by Wachsmuth, whose main tenets are synopsized here. As a general statement it may be taken that the laws of reincarnation require that those factors which were internalized in one life will be externalized in the following life. Thus, for example, the moral propensities (inner qualities) of one life determine the appearance, physical condition and even actions (the outer qualities) of a following lifetime. The occult tradition insists that the time spent in earthly embodiment is of a short duration relative to the time spent in the noncorporeal worlds of KAMALOKA and DEVACHAN between death and rebirth; it would appear that an individual monad will incarnate only twice or three times during one zodiacal era (see PRECESSION). However, the length of the period between incarnations depends upon many factors, such as the spiritual level of evolution, the

181

length of the previous lifetime in the body, and indeed upon the cosmic aims of the incarnating element. Thus, an INITIATE is free to incarnate almost immediately after death, for his moral purity ensures that he has no need to experience the realm of Kamaloka, while an ordinary human may have as much as 700–800 years between incarnations. Although it is difficult to give precise rules without reference to individual cases recorded from examination of the Akashic Chronicles, it is a general rule that a monad will alternate between male and female incarnations in sequence.

Superficial notions of reincarnation often give rise to misunderstandings of the rich level of material available in the esoteric teachings within the doctrine. Although the term 'reincarnation' is properly applied to human beings or, more exactly, to their monads, it is possible to use the word in connection with all forms of consciousness. However, this has actually given rise to a number of different terminologies (as well as much confusion), especially so in connection with METEMPSYCHOSIS or transmigration, in terms of which theories it is often held that the human spirit may dwell within the bodies of animals, birds or even minerals. It is a peculiarity of the European occult tradition of reincarnation that it insists that the human spirit may dwell only in human bodies; there is no question of a human monad descending into animal existence or into lower levels of being. The reasons for this are ultimately involved with the nature of karma, but are too complex for adequate examination in this context. It is perhaps sufficient to set down the prevalent belief and its occult counter-claim. What is being claimed is that the whole concept of the transmigration of souls, through the mineral and animal kingdoms, is a fanciful idea, based in fact on a misunderstanding of certain writings that deal not with individual reincarnations but with the cosmogenesis of the world and the evolution of the human race, which at one time passed through equivalent stages of the mineral, the animal and so on (see METEMSOMATOSIS). While much of the literature connected with revealing the interconnections of various historical personages through reincarnations is of a romantic kind, and therefore academically suspect, Steiner has presented a serious study of such interrelationships in connection with landmarks of philosophy and culture in the Western world.

Relationship chart   In astrology a chart which presents in a single figure material derived from two horoscopes. The figure is cast for the midpoint in time and space between the two relevant birth dates.

Ressurrectional Body   See SUBTLE BODY.

Retrograde   A specialist astrological term derived from the Latin compound meaning 'to step backwards' and applied to the apparent motion of a planet or a nodal point (such as the vernal equinox – see PRECESSION) backwards along the zodiacal belt. In traditional astrology a planet which was retrograde carried a somewhat sinister connotation.

Rhabdomancy   A term derived from the Greek *rhabdos* ('rod') and *manteia* ('divination') and applied to a method of divination by means of rods or wands. The term is often used for a method of dowsing, or locating lost objects, minerals, streams and so on with the aid of rods, pendulums or twigs.

Rhapsodomancy   Divination by means of poetry. The method involves opening a book of poetry at random and taking the first line or stanza of a poem as being oracular.

Right-Hand Path   The name given (originally in esotericism) to the path towards the attainment of the evolutionary demands of the cosmos, as pursued by the disciplines and praxes of esotericists and white magicians. The Sanskrit term for the Right-Hand Path is *Dakshina-marga*. The Right-Hand Path is contrasted with the LEFT-HAND PATH of the black magicians.

Ring-Pass-Not   A phase or term used mainly in modern Theosophical contexts in reference to a serious and complete limitation to spiritual awareness and development. The student, occultist or chela is seen as being limited by (ringed in by) a delusion within his own consciousness, which prevents his expansion outwards into further spiritual and mental understanding. The Ring-Pass-Not has been likened by Purucker to a spiritual *laya* centre (see LAYA), a point of transmission between planes, which is blocked. A general misunderstanding of the term has resulted in the idea of there being an objective ring (presumably around the earth) which blocks certain undeveloped individualities from spiritual progress.

182

Rings See AMULET.

Rishabham The Sanskrit name for zodiacal Taurus (but see also KRITTIKA).

Rising sign A term frequently misused in popular astrology. Properly speaking it should apply only to the sign which marks the Ascendant degree on a particular horoscope.

Rogziel The name of one of the Angels of Punishment, meaning 'wrath of God'.

Rolamandri See SALAMANDER.

Roneve One of the names of RONOBE.

Ronobe One of the seventy-two SPIRITS OF SOLOMON. He is specialist in teaching the magician languages.

Root Chakra See MULADHARA.

Root Races Modern occultists have described a history of the world in which distinct types of humanity have lived at different periods. Occultists claim that during the evolution of the earth there have been so far five different Root Races (stages in the development of humanity); they insist that there will be a further two races in the future of the earth. Each of the five Root Races has been given a special name. Humans of the present period belong to the FIFTH RACE (called by occultists the 'Aryan'): the Fourth Race was that of the ATLANTEAN, the Third was that of the LEMURIA, the Second HYPERBOREAN, while the First was called the ADAMIC. The Root Races are sometimes called the Seven Races.

Rosicrucian A term which was first used in the fiteenth century, applied to the disciples of an INITIATE called Christian Rosenkreuz, who appears to have established a series of esoteric teaching centres during that time. The publication of a text called *Fama Fraternitatis* (1614) was the first literary sign of the existence of this esoteric group, although it had been in active existence for some considerable time prior to this date. The expressed purpose of the *Fama* was the regeneration of society by means of the spiritualization of individuals, according to Christianized esoteric and occult principles. While in the following century the original Rosicrucians appear to have gone underground, leaving behind a vast hermetic and alchemical tradition (which flowered later in the works of such men as Fludd

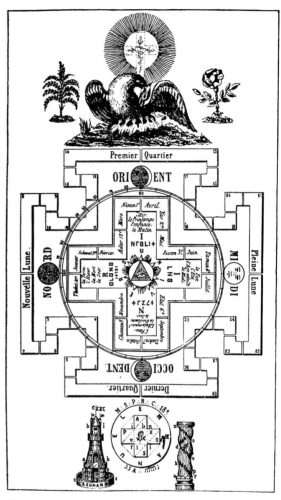

Figure 64 *Solomon's Temple, surrounded by Rosicrucian symbols (after a nineteenth-century engraving)*

and Boehme), several other groups appropriated for themselves the original name. In general the term is used loosely as an equivalent of Christian hermeticism, or even for Neo-Platonic occultism, but the hints of the original doctrines which have survived indicate that the movement was essentially Christian, although charged with an influx of occult and hermetic knowledge presented in the guise of alchemical, astrological and symbolical forms. The Rosicrucian school founded by Grasshoff in America appears to have derived much of its esotericsm from Steiner and Theosophy in general. It owes little to the original school of Rosicrucianism; it is a general practice to distinguish this school by the term 'Modern Rosicrucianism'.

In the occult image of Figure 64, which is said to be a plan for the famous Temple of Solomon, we may see several interesting Rosicrucian symbols. Note, for example, the cross, with the rose within it (the 'rosy-cross'), in the centre of the halo at the top of the picture. Below this is what appears to be a conventional image of the pelican piercing its side in order to feed its own blood to its chicks below. This pelican is regarded as being a symbol of Christ, who gave his blood for mankind. However, the pelican looks more like an eagle (the bird of the sun), and the shapes of the chicks are so drawn as to suggest the idea of flames. When seen from this point of view, one realizes that besides being the Christian pelican symbol, it is also the pagan phoenix, one of the ancient symbols for reincarnation.

Ru See ANKH.

Ruach In Qabbalism, the name given to the seat of the passions, the approximate equivalent to the ASTRAL BODY, sometimes the spirit. See SOUL.

Rubeus 'Red', a name given to one of the sixteen figures of GEOMANCY.

Rule This astrological term is used of planets and signs in a wide and often unsatisfactory manner to indicate particular relationships and congenialities. For example, a planet may be said to have rule over a particular zodiacal sign. The image of Venus in Figure 65 illustrates one of the traditional rulerships which is still used in modern astrology, for this planet has rule over Taurus (the bull, to the left of her feet) and Libra (the balance, to the right).

Figure 65 *A personification of the planet Venus as ruler over the signs Taurus and Libra (woodcut from an early-sixteenth-century German astrological text)*

Runes A name probably derived from the Gothic *runa* (secret) and applied to a group of Nordic alphabets which might have been developed initially for magical purposes. There are several different systems of runes, as Jensen shows, but Table 22 sets out the most frequently encountered sigillic forms, along with their names and (where known for sure) their meanings. See also SECRET SCRIPTS.

Rustu The gate of entry (from incarnation) of the Egyptian AMENTI.

Ruta The name given to one of the two islands which survived for a considerable time after the sinking of the main continent of ATLANTIS.

Table 22

Rune	Name	Meaning	Rune	Name	Meaning	Rune	Name	Meaning
ᚠ	Feoh	Property, wealth	ᚢ	Ur	Drizzle	ᚦ	Dorn	Thorn
ᛜ	Os	God	R	Rad	Wagon, ride	ᚻ	Cen	?
X	Gyfu	Gift	ᚹ	Wynn	Pleasure	ᚺ	Haegl	Hail
+	Nyd	Distress	I	Is	Ice	ᚤ	Yer	Year
ᛋ	Eoh	?	ᚻ	Peord	Horse (?)	ᚣ	Eolx	Elk
ᛟ	Sigel	Sun	↑	Tir	Tree	B	Beorc	Birch
M	Eoh	?	ᛝ	Ing	?	ᛗ	Man	Man
ᚱ	Lagu	Water	ᛞ	Daeg	Day	ᛟ	E(th)el	Property
ᚾ	Ac	?	ᚴ	Aesk	?	ᛠ	Ear	?
✳	Ior	?	ᚧ	Weord	Bait	ᛣ	Calc	?
ᛞ	Stan	?	ᚸ	Gar	?			

S

The nineteenth letter of the alphabet, linked with the Hebraic Samech and ascribed the number 60. Blavatsky records that Samech is regarded as being especially holy on the grounds that it is the sacred name of God. She says that in occult geometry it is represented by the encircled cross ⊕ which is the symbol of the incarnate god. In some occult texts the S is the graphic sigil for Saturn, probably chosen because of the serpentine structure of the letter, which evokes the notion of the OUROBOROS associated with the god and planet.

Sabao The Gnostic name for the ruler of the sphere of Mars.

Sabathziel One of several variant names for the spiritual ruler of Saturn.

Sabbat The idea of the Sabbat as a weekly convention of witches and demons does not appear to be much older than the late fourteenth century and seems to have emerged from the minds of the persecutors of witches rather than from the supposed witches themselves. The word itslf is not much older than the fifteenth century (perhaps being a play on the word 'Sabbath'), and its absence from the otherwise thorough MALLEUS MALEFICARUM would suggest that it is a relatively late development, perhaps from the idea of heretics meeting together to perpetrate their supposed indignities and blasphemies. The fact that the supposed practices in the witches 'Sabbat were said to be inversions of the Christian rituals and liturgies is further indication of a 'theological' origin at the hands of the inquisitors who pursued witches and heretics in those dreadful years. Some of the 'inversions' relate to Church rituals which were instituted only in the medieval period.

In these Sabbats the worship of LUCIFER, or of unnamed demon kings, was a sort of prelude to what eventually became the Black Mass of the GRIMOIRES, the anti-sacramental mockery of Christian ritual, involving sacrificial slaughter of animals and birds. In the minds of those who constructed the Sabbat all attention was paid to unlicensed bawdiness and sensuality – sexual practices with the Devil or with his demons was part and parcel of the general riot of the Sabbat, while the taking of the holy sacrament was reduced to drinking the blood of sacrificial victims, savouring the later CONJURATION rites of black magicians.

The Sabbat itself seems to have been a clandestine gathering of witches and warlocks in a part of the country remote from villages or towns. As the myth of the Sabbat grew the gathering became more and more spectacular, so that eventually the witches would transvect there, followed by a stream of invisible and visible familiars and demons (Figure 66). Sometimes the witches prepared themselves for such night flight by means of special unguents and flying salves. Having arrived in style, the proceeding involved making lewd homage to the demons and the worship of the Devil, who is supposed to have appeared in the guise of a huge goat – an image which persisted well into modern popular belief. The blasphemy of a Black Mass and the kissing of the Devil's anus soon became a standard requirement of the Sabbat legend and imagery (Figure 67), as did the grand finale of a huge banquet, followed by indiscriminate sexual indulgence between demons and witches, witches and warlocks, and warlocks and demons.

A vast and macabre literature has been constructed around these Sabbats, even though the

Figure 66 (left): *An imagined view of the witches' progress to a Sabbat*

Figure 67 (right): *Kissing the rear of the Devil in homage (sixteenth century)*

evidence suggests that they existed mainly in the minds of the theologians and monks sent to exterminate the supposed heresies and signs of witchcraft, possibly carried over from the almost eradicated 'heretical' movements which the Church had found it necessary to combat in the preceding centuries.

Sabeans The ancient Chaldean tribe of Sabeans, or Sabians, is sometimes regarded as being so deeply connected with early forms of astrology that the name is often used as synonymous with 'astrologers'. It is possible that in common with many pre-Christian tribes they were astrolators, but unlikely that they were astrologers. Sabean-ism is often regarded as being the religion of the ancient Chaldeans.

Sabnack One of the seventy-two SPIRITS OF SOLOMON. He is said to appear in the form of a

warrior, with the head of a lion, and usually riding a horse.

Sacred animals A term carried into English from the Hebraic *Sepher Jesirah* by Blavatsky in reference to the ZODIAC.

Sacred planets The esotericist Bailey dis-tinguishes seven sacred planets (as distinct from her five non-sacred planets, which are linked with the SEVEN RAYS of her Intuitional Astrology. They are Vulcan, Jupiter, Saturn, Mercury, Venus, Neptune and Uranus.

Sadhyas A Sanskrit name for the twelve great gods, the 'divine sacrificers'.

Sagittarius The ninth sign of the zodiac, which corresponds neither in location nor meaning with the constellation of the same name, which is

187

linked by Qabbalists with the Hebraic letter Vau and with the TAROT arcanum of 'The Lovers'. The sigil for Sagittarius ♐ is said by some to represent the arrow of desire being shot from a vestigial bow, but many occultists maintain that it actually consists of a fourfold cross, with an arrow lifting this symbol of materiality into the upper spiritual realms – an excellent symbol for the spiritualizing and expansive nature of the sign. Sagittarius is of the FIRE ELEMENT and of the Mutable quality, the influence being enterprising, open, honest, dignified, optimistic, independent, enthusiastic, philosophic, idealistic, generous, open-minded, loyal, magnanimous, frank and restless – in a word, all the qualities which may be associated with Fire working inspirationally. In excess the Sagittarian tends to be prodigal, sporty, indolent, self-indulgent, conceited, dogmatic and subject to 'pointless' wanderings. Sagittarius is ruled by the planet Jupiter.

Sahasrara   The Sanskrit name for the Crown CHAKRA, located on top of the head and said to be the Chakra of a thousand lotus petals, although modern occultists point out that it has only 960 such spokes or petals.

Sakti   The Sanskrit name for the feminine (active) energy of the gods. In occultism it is the name given to the crown of the ASTRAL LIGHT.

Figure 68   *The salamander living in the flames of a fire (from a seventeenth-century alchemical text,* Museum Hermeticum)

Salamander The class of soul beings of the Fire element (see ELEMENTALS) who correspond to the Trifertes of esoteric lore. They are sometimes called Aetnaei or Aethnici, and the list of correspondences in the CALENDARIA MAGICA names them as Silvani. In magical images the salamander is usually depicted as a lizard, living in flames (Figure 68). Paracelsus appears to call them Rolamandri, defined by Waite, however, as 'igneous men, otherwise essences of the race of the Salamander'. See also AMIANTHUS.

Saleos One of the seventy-two SPIRITS OF SOLOMON. He is specialist in causing love between the sexes.

Salt In alchemy a name used to veil the thought processes in man. See THREE PRINCIPLES.

Samadhi A Sanskrit compound from *sam* ('together with'), *a* ('towards') and the root *dha* ('to place'), meaning approximately 'to direct towards', although sometimes taken to mean 'self-possession through directed attention'. A man in the state of *samadhi* is said to have complete control over all his faculties. See YOGA.

Samael A name, meaning approximately 'venom of God' (*sam* meaning 'poison'), derived from the Hebraic tradition and applied to the Archangel acting as ruler of the sphere of Mars (see, therefore, GEBURAH). Samael is one of the SECUNDADEIAN BEINGS. In popular occultism the name is used to denote the Angel of Death. Westcott claims that it is from this last usage that the term SATAN was evolved, and in many traditions the name Samael is interchangeable with Satan, although there are many conflicting traditions concerning the role of Samael. The name Samael is also used within the Qabbalistic system to denote the lower of the two inseparable companions of man on the earth plane: he is virtually the personal Devil (some might say the DOUBLE) of Christian and European esotericism. The fact that Samael is opposed by the spirit of the Sun, METRATON, means that he is a personification equivalent in nature to AHRIMAN of the earlier dualism. Samael and Metraton are together sometimes called the Dual Ego, although this term must not be confused with the Ego of occultism.

S'ambhala A variant spelling for SHAMBALLA.

Sambhogakaya See BUDDHIC BODIES.

Samil A variant for SAMAEL.

Samma sambuddha A Pali term used to denote the Buddhist technique or faculty for recollecting all of one's previous incarnations.

Samsaric wheel In Western occultism, this is a word derived from the SAMSKARA of Sanskrit terminology to denote what is often called 'the wheel of rebirth', the round of existence.

Samskara The Sanskrit term, from the roots *sam* and *kri*, meaning 'to refine' or 'to improve', is used to denote the impressions left on the spirit of a human, as seeds which are capable of improvement in future times. The *samskara* are, therefore, germs capable of development, carried over from one birth to another.

Sandalphon See MALKUTH.

Sanguine One of the four TEMPERAMENTS, derived from an excess of the Air element in the psychological make-up of the personality. The Sanguine temperament strives to understand the material world through the intellect, and is freedom-loving and idealistic. The Air temperament is associated with the following key words: communicative, inquisitive, original, intellectual, quick-witted, companionable, discriminative and refined. Faults in the temperament arise from the fact that the intellect tends to divorce the subject from external compulsions, thus leading to daydreams, complex ideologies and to an inability to relate emotionally to others; under such circumstances the type may become emotionally arid, diffused and even dishonest in speech. See also HUMOURS.

Sariel A name given to one of the Grigori, who (according to Hebraic legend) taught men the nature of the course of the Moon and its influences, as well as (probably) the nature of the twenty-eight LUNAR MANSIONS.

Sarira Sometimes *sharira*, a Sanskrit term used in Theosophy to denote a body or vehicle, its meaning being approximately 'something easily worn out'. The *linga sarira* is the ASTRAL BODY, the *sthula sarira* is the coarse body, the physical body.

Saros cycle   A cycle of eclipses. The two nodes of the Moon regress along the celestial sphere, and the rate of movement is such that it takes 223 lunar months (18 years, 11 days, and 8 hours – a figure which must be adjusted for extra or deficient leap years) for the regressing points to return to their original positions. This periodicity is the Saros cycle. See also METONIC CYCLE. The name Saros cycle is also applied by some occultists to a cycle of 60 days or 60 years ('days' and 'years' and 'ages' being interchangeable in some ancient systems – see, for example, the 'days' of biblical creation, which are actually 'ages') or even multiples, such as 60 x 60, or 3600 days or years.

Sat   A Sanskrit term for the divine essence or Absolute. See ASAT.

Satan   One of the chief names given to the Prince of Evil, the enemy of God. We have it on authority of Revelation, 12, 9, that the Devil, Satan, dragon and the serpent are one and the same, and that he was thrown to earth from Heaven. In almost every way, however, Satan is clearly marked as a king of demons, as the Adversary. The Hebraic term 'Satan' means 'adversary', and it is clear that certain passages in which the word is taken in translation to refer to Satan actually refer to a general concept of 'someone who opposes'. There is indeed much confusion in translation and in later biblical exegesis between Satan, LUCIFER and the Devil (Diabolos). The terms 'Satan' and 'Diabolos' might well be regarded as referring to the same being. However, the word 'Lucifer', which in popular lore is regarded as the equivalent of 'Satan', is not interchangeable with either 'Satan' or 'Diabolos', although it is often used as though it were.

Satan is the Christian equivalent of the Zoroastrian Angrimainyu (see ARIMAN and DAIMONIARCHION).

Satanachia   An infernal spirit said to have power over women, who must at all times bend to his will and to the will of those who have successfully conjured and bound him.

Sathariel   The name of an Adversary of the ARCHANGELS OF THE SEPHIROTH.

Saturn   The name given to the outermost of the seven traditional planets, the planetary orb within the sphere ruled by the celestial THRONES. In medieval occultism time was said to end at the sphere of Saturn, which probably explains the late-medieval origin of the sigil for the planet ♄ which is said to be a vestigial drawing of a scythe. One of the Greek names for Saturn was Kronos, linked with time. In the esoteric cosmology of Boehme Saturn is the first form of his SEVEN PROPERTIES, representative of the harsh, hardening and centripetal force, which 'indraws and compacts about its chosen centre' in the manner of an embrace of death. In Qabbalism Saturn is linked with BINAH. The influence of Saturn in the microcosm represents the restrictive side of a person's nature, and stands for the manner in which the human being is prepared (or is able) to pay for things received and to demand payment from others. On a deeper level it represents the underlying and motivating fears in the life of the native: it governs the materialistic element in life, and in particular the physical limitations which the native is likely to experience. When Saturn is beneficially emphasized in a chart, it is usually an indication that the subject will be practical, patient, reliable, prudent and honest, if a little austere in his attitude to life. A badly placed Saturn tends towards excessive limitation or restriction, which manifests through a deep-seated fear of life. The subject tends to be emotionally cold or despondent, narrow in outlook, and subject to melancholia. In the melothesic man Saturn has rule over the knees, as well as over the entire skeletal frame, an expression of the cosmic fact that Saturn lends structure to life's forms. Saturnine types usually find expression on the physical plane through activities demanding control and organizational ability. For this reason they tend to make excellent accountants or agents, for they are particularly adapted for dealing in theories of finance, although they are often personally rather parsimonious and perhaps over-careful. On the social plane Saturn has rule over bureaucracy, yet another manifestation of the urge of Saturn to draw demarcations, to establish rigid structures and to exercise control over life.

Saturn Period   A term derived from modern esoteric astrology, relating to periods of cosmogenesis. Saturn is said to be the first of the planets, although this is almost a meaningless phrase, since at that early stage of cosmogenesis Saturn was more a state of being than a planet in any sense that we might use the word now. It is described in occult literature as being something like a 'warmth globe', at a time when there was as yet no central sun or planetary system. All potential for the future development of the solar system was contained in this Saturnine warmth globe, a state of being esoterically termed the 'Saturn Period'. This period, sometimes also called 'Old Saturn', was overseen by the hierarchy known as the Lords of Flame. See also MOON PERIOD and SUN PERIOD.

Saturn Revolution A term derived from modern esoteric astrology relating to cosmogenesis. It is said that the path or evolution in the development of the solar system, with its periods of activity and sleep (*pralaya*), must recapitulate, however briefly, the entire sequence of evolution up to that point. Since the cosmogenesis of our own system began in Saturn (see SATURN PERIOD), the Saturn Revolution is the first of these recapitulations.

Saturn Scheme The 'Saturn Scheme' and the 'Saturnine Chain' are terms derived specifically from the Theosophical cosmoconception linked with the SCHEME OF EVOLUTION and are not to be confused with the SATURN PERIOD of the evolutionary sequence.

Satva Sometimes *sattva* or *satwa*, one of the TRIGUNAS.

Satya Yuga A Sanskrit term for the Golden Age or KRITA YUGA.

Scala A term used in late-medieval astrology and occultism, the late Latin for 'ladder', and closely allied to the CALENDARIA MAGICA systems. The scalae give lists of correspondences on a numerological basis, although (unlike the calendaria) they use no symbols, signs or sigils. Figure 69 is a scala of septenaries recorded by the fifteenth-century occultist Agrippa. In the second line down we see the Hebraic and Latin names for the seven Archangels, in the line below the corresponding seven planets, and in the fourth block down we see the names of the corresponding birds, fishes, animals, metals and stones. The fifth block down gives the seven parts of the body in correspondence with the planets, as well as the planetary rule over seven parts of the face. The last block gives the seven regions of Inferno.

Scales A popular name for both zodiacal and constellational Libra.

Figure 69 *A list of scala correspondences according to the number seven (from Agrippa's* Occulta Philosophia, *1531)*

SCALA.

rchetypo	Ararita	אראריתא	
ndo intelligibili	צפקיאל Zaphkiel	צדקיאל Zadkiel	כמאל Camael	רפאל Raphael
ndo cœlesti	שבתאי Saturnus	צדק Iupiter	מאדים Mars	שמש Sol
ndo elementali	Vppupa Sepia Talpa Plumbum Onychinus	Aquila Delphinus Ceruus Stannum Sapphirus	Vultur Lucius Lupus Ferrū Adamas	Olor Vitul° marin⁹ Leo Aurum Carbūculus
iore mundo	Pes dexter Auris dextra	Caput Auris finiftra	Manus dexttra Narisdextra	Cor Oculꝰ dexter
do infernali	Gehēna גיהנם	Portę mortis וצל מות	Vmbra mortis שערי מות	Puteus interitus באר שהת

SEPTENARII

Affer Eheie אשר אהיה			Nomina dei septem literarum
האניאל Haniel	מיכאל Michaël	גבריאל Gabriel	Septem angeli qui adstāt ante faciem dei.
נוגה Venus	כוכב Mercurius	לבנה Luna	Septem Planetæ.
Columba Thimallus Hircus Cuprum Smaragdus	Ciconia Mugil Simia Argētū uiuū Achates	Noctua Aelurus Feles Argentum Cryftallus	Septem aues planetarum Septem pisces planetarum Septem animalia planetarum Septem metalla planetarum Septem lapides planetarum
Pudendum Naris finiftra	Manus finiftra Os	Pesfinifter (fter Oculus finiʾ	Septem membra integralia planetis diftributa. Septē foramina capitis planetis diftributa.
Lutum fecis טיט הין	Perditio אברון	Fouea שאול	Septē habitacula inferorum, quæ de fcribit Rabi Iofeph Caftilienfis cabalifta in Horto nucis.

191

Schema One of the most frequently used words in medieval astrology for an astrological chart, the Latin term really applying to the 'scheme of the heavens'.

Scheme of evolution According to the Theosophical cosmoconception there are ten separate schemes of evolution in our own solar system, these being the so-called Ten Chains (see GLOBE PERIOD), of which only the first seven have been definitely named (for the eighth, however, see ASTEROID SCHEME). See EARTH CHAIN, JUPITER SCHEME, NEPTUNE SCHEME, SATURN SCHEME, VENUS SCHEME and VULCAN SCHEME.

Schrack See SEVEN PROPERTIES.

Sciomancy A term derived from the Greek *skia* ('shadow') and *manteia* ('divination') and applied to the prediction of the future from commerce with the shades of the dead. This term is etymologically a more correct usage than 'NECROMANCY'.

Scorpio The name given to the eighth sign of the zodiac and sometimes to the zodiacal constellation SCORPIUS, through which association it has taken on certain of the occult attributes listed under this heading. The sigil for Scorpio ♏ is said by some to be a vestigial drawing of the male private parts, over which the sign has rule, but it is more likely that it is derived from a vestigial drawing of the severed half of a serpent's tail. Scorpio is the only zodiacal sign to have been accorded two quite different images – that of a scorpion and that of an EAGLE. The former is symbol of the unregenerative Scorpionic urge, while the latter symbolizes the regenerative nature. Scorpio is of the Water element and of the Fixed quality, the influence being magnetic, determined, secretive, shrewd, dignified, self-confident, masterful, sensitive and critical. The nature of Scorpio as it manifests in human beings is expressed in the many key words which have been attached to it by modern astrologers: regenerative, inspirational, tenacious, forceful, magnetic, emotional, penetrating, competitive, extremist, strong in desire – in a word, all those qualities which may be associated with a Water type expressing itself powerfully. In excess the Scorpionic nature may be described in terms which express its underlying cruelty, sense of violence and instinct for crime (esoterically, the desire to have something for nothing): rebellious, degenerate, suspicious, sarcastic, cruel, selfish, violent, indulgent and domineering. In modern astrological systems Scorpio is usually said to be ruled by the planet PLUTO, although in the traditional form it was accorded the rule of NEGATIVE MARS. It is said in modern terms to mark the exaltation of Uranus and the fall of the Moon.

Scorpius A zodiacal constellation which in antiquity was the largest of such asterisms, incorporating in its claws (the Greek *chelae*) what is now our separate asterism of Libra. Scorpius is linked with the TAROT arcanum called in the English system 'The House of God' (which was one of the names for a hospital), despite the fact that in the atout the tower which symbolizes this house appears to have been struck by lightning.

Scrying In a specialist occult sense the term is applied to the act of examining the surface of a crystal, shiny stone or other reflective surface in search of spirits or visions which will reveal futurity. It is sometimes said that a scryer is a crystal gazer, but this is not quite true, for the crystal gazer will look only for visions or portents within the crystal, while the scryer seeks for spirits who will give him or her the required information about the past or the future. See also ACTINOBOLISM, COLLYRIE and VASSAGO.

Seal In a specialist occult sense a seal is one of the graphic symbols or SIGILS representing an occultly derived prophylactic force or VIRTUE. Just as in a nonspecialist sense an official seal might be stamped on a document as a sign of ratification, so a magical seal was often used to imprint a magical power into some materiality, such as a sheet of paper or a strip of metal, or even a magical gem. The seal, as a magical symbol, was supposed to be imbued with a secret power, beneficial or maleficient, depending upon how and when it was constructed, and upon the intentions of the magician or astrologer who used it (in connection with the use of seals, see CONJURATION). Ancient seals, often imbued with esoteric significance, have been recorded for planets, spirits (and demons), decans, zodiacal angels, rulers of the spheres and so on (Figure 70). It would seem that a knowledge of magical seals gave the same power over the realm of spirits as did knowledge of demonic names. This explains why so many of

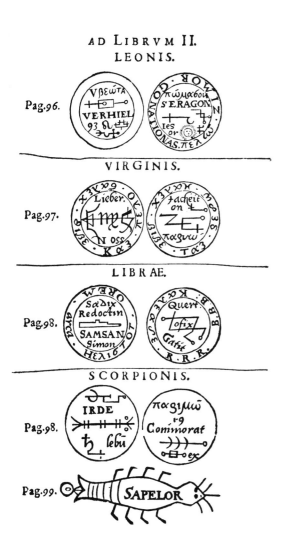

Figure 70   *A number of seals (front and back) for four signs of the zodiac (Leo to Scorpio) (sixteenth century, after Paracelsus)*

the seals are so frequently incorporated into amulets and talismans such as MAGIC STONES, in which the seal (usually astrological in nature) was a sign that a magical virtue had been imprinted into the jewel. See also DEVIL'S MARK.

Seal of Solomon   A name given to the six-pointed star constructed from two interpenetrating triangles (see Figure 77 under TALISMANIC MAGIC, marked 'Sacred Pentades'). The symbolism expressed in this figure is extremely rich: on one level it represents the triad of the macrocosm

interpenetrating the triad of the microcosm (wherein it becomes a symbolic duad). On another level it is seen as the interaction of the four elements, wherein it is a symbolic quaternary. Within the system of Rosicrucian symbolism the space within the central hexagon is seen as the repository for the invisible fifth element, the QUINTESSENCE, for which the seal is often offered as SIGIL.

Seance   A name given to an organized group of people who gather together under specific conditions for the purpose of investigating or experiencing supernormal or psychic manifestations. Sometimes such organized groups are called 'circles', a name derived from the fact that usually they will sit around a table (or on chairs arranged in a circle) in order to link hands, in the belief that this increases the psychic or 'magnetic' forces which encourage the sought manifestations. Generally seances are organized by those clairvoyants, mediums and spiritualists who have some familiarity with the manifestations of the lower levels of the ASTRAL plane and are therefore able to deal adequately with the lower evil forces and beings which attempt to manifest in seances.

There are very few rules for the conducting of a genuine seance – perhaps the two most important requirements are the presence of an experienced medium and a quiet, restful (usually darkened) room. The number of people in a seance may vary, but generally between six and twelve has been found to be the most satisfactory. Many leaders of spiritualist seances insist on establishing strong psychic currents by having all the participants join hands. Music and flowers have been found to help in making a conducive atmosphere, and in some cases perfumes are used. Experience has shown that the presence of more than one doubter or cynical sitter, or even one sitter who is afraid of spiritualistic phenomena, may be detrimental to the quality of the manifestations. Strong emotions – particularly the negative emotions of fear and distrust – are generally avoided, for they prevent the satisfactory development of manifestations and may even damage the sensitivity of the medium

Within the present context it should be pointed out that properly speaking seances do not fall into the realm of occultism. In many respects the tenets of spiritualism and the tenets of occultism are totally opposed – the two are merely united in the conviction that it is possible to contact spiritual beings, but they differ both in their explanation as to what these beings are and what they represent, as well as in their attitudes to the legitimacy of making such contact for ordinary purposes. Most spiritualists are firmly convinced that by means of seances they are making contact with the spirits of the dead. However, even the first of the great mediums, Andrew Jackson Davis, warned against this belief (see, for example, DIAKKA).

Spiritualist seances are really the continuation of the ancient art of SCIOMANCY, although they are often confused with the art of NECROMANCY. There is little new in their practices, save for terminology. As Waite says, 'It is only within recent times that the attempt to communicate with the dead has been elevated to the dignity of White Magic.'

Seats Another name for the THRONES.

Second death An occult term used in two different and (confusingly) related senses. First, to denote the gradual dissolution of the lower principles of man in KAMALOKA after the death of the physical body. When this is finalized the higher part of man (see TERNARY) is freed. The same term is also used to denote the shedding of the ETHERIC BODY after ordinary death. There is some disagreement as to how long this takes place after the physical death, but a period of three to four days is sometimes mentioned, while others equate it with the time of burial. Since this etheric death is only a stage of dying, there is a third death, which is the shedding of the ASTRAL BODY, sometimes called 'astral death', which usually occurs some years after the physical death.

Second hierarchy See CELESTIAL HIERARCHIES.

Second Race In the Theosophical cosmoconception the Second Root Race is the second of the human races, or streams of human evolution, sometimes called the Hyperborean race, which was said to largely occupy the long-disappeared northern continent named Plaksha. See SEVEN RACES.

Second ray In the esoteric system described by Bailey the second of the SEVEN RAYS of her Intuitional Astrology is called the 'ray of love-

wisdom' and is linked with the will to unify, to cause vision and is said to bring the power to perceive.

Second sight A term used to denote the power of CLAIRVOYANCE.

Secret Doctrine A term used in modern occultism to denote the esoteric teachings of antiquity. In modern ESOTERICISM, particularly in Theosophical circles, the term is usually a reference to the title of Blavatsky's book, *The Secret Doctrine*, which was first published in 1888 and which set out to present to non-esoteric circles the available doctrines of ancient esotericism. Blavatsky summarizes the three fundamental propositions established by the Secret Doctrine as: (a) an omnipresent, eternal, boundless and immutable principle upon which all speculation is impossible. Spirit (or consciousness) and matter are to be regarded as the two facets or aspects of this absolute (see GREAT BREATH). (b) The eternity of the universe *in toto* is a boundless plane, which is periodically the 'playground of numberless Universes incessantly manifesting and disappearing'. (c) The fundamental identity of all souls with the universal over-soul (Emerson's term), the latter being an aspect of the unknown root of (a) above. This identity involves the obligatory pilgrimage of every soul – a spark of the universal – through the cycle of incarnation in accordance with cyclic and karmic law (see therefore KARMA).

Secret scripts A large number of secret scripts and alphabets have survived from medieval times, a few of them being essentially bowdlerized versions of historic alphabets, of 'lost' languages such as RUNES, or of Europeanized systems of classical acrostics, Qabbalistic GEMATRIA, NOTARICON or TEMURAH. Some fifty alphabets relating to secret scripts have been recorded by Gettings; these include the *Scriptura coelestis* or Heavenly Script (Figure 71), and the Enochian (also called the Malachim) and the so-called *Transitus fluvii* (Crossing the River), which are recorded in Figure 72, by way of example. See also STEGANOGRAPHY.

Secundadeian Beings The name (originated by the Abbot Trithemius at the end of the fifteenth century, working from Arabian sources) is applied to an important group of spiritual beings

Scriptura Cœlestis

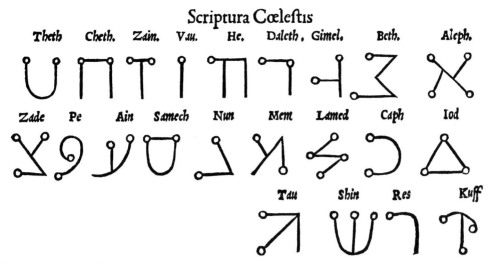

Figure 71 *An example of a secret script — Scriptura coelestis or the Heavenly Script — collected by Agrippa in the fifteenth century*

Figure 72 *Examples of secret steganographic scripts collected by Agrippa in the fifteenth century: the* Scriptura transitus fluvii *is the script now called Crossing the River, and the* Scriptura Malachim (top) *is now called the* Enochian

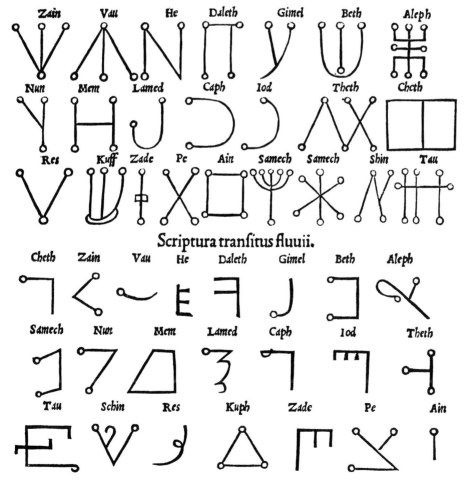

Scriptura tranſitus fluuii.

assigned rule over a sequence of repeated historical periods of 354 years' duration, sometimes called the 'Trithemian Periods'. Each of these beings is said to be of the rank of Archangel, although in respect to their historical charge over periods (rather than over races of people) they are really of the rank of ARCHAI. The names, along with many associations (including predictions relating to certain post-fifteenth-century rules), are derived from the Hebraic–Gnostic tradition and are linked with the planetary spheres rather than with the planets themselves. The names of the seven Secundadeians are OPHIEL, ZACHARIAL, SAMAEL, MICHAEL, ANAEL, RAPHAEL and GABRIEL, who rule the spheres in descending order from Saturn to Moon. Trithemius assigned the rule of solar Michael to our own epoch, which was said to have begun in 1881 (a variant interpretation of his figures gives 1882).

Seer   A name applied to someone with either SECOND SIGHT or INNER SIGHT, that is, someone with personally developed or atavistic spiritual vision.

Seere   One of the seventy-two SPIRITS OF SOLOMON. He is said to appear in the shape of a long-haired man, mounted on a winged horse.

Selenocentric chart   A horoscope chart computed for the solar system, presuming the Moon (Greek Selene) to be the centre of that system.

Self-haunting   See DWELLER ON THE THRESHOLD.

Semina   A Latin word meaning 'seeds' and used by Paracelsus to denote 'threshold objects' between the ideal and the real, between spirit and matter. From these semina comes all our knowledge and insight, for 'all things have a seed, and in the seed all things are enclosed'. It would appear that Paracelsus regards each seed as the repository of a single idea. The semina are sometimes described as 'little stars' – they have a power superior to anything on the material plane. In the prematerial state they are often linked with the *Simplicia formalia* of the SIMPLICIA MATERIA of Mercury, Sulphur and Salt.

Semi-sextile   A beneficial ASPECT of 30 degrees, the two aspecting points being separated by an arc equivalent to one sign of the zodiac.

Semi-square   A difficult ASPECT of 45 degrees, the two aspecting points being separated by the equivalent arc of one and a half signs of the zodiac.

Senary   See SIX.

Senators   According to the magician Michael Scot (who wrote in the thirteenth century), there are seven senators or rulers of the seven spheres, named Orphymel, Tingra, Dapnael, Kabura, Asinor, Tascar and Boel. These are to be distinguished from the seven planetary spirits, which in later times are called the 'Olympic Spirits' or 'PLANETARY ANGELS', whom Scot called 'rectors'.

Sentient Body   A term given by Steiner (in German, *Empfindungsleib*) for the ASTRAL BODY; sometimes the 'Soul Body' (in German, *Seelenleib*).

Sentient Soul   A name originated by Steiner to denote the soul, in so far as this is united with the ASTRAL BODY. Within Steiner's view of the nature of man it is the soul which gives knowledge permanence and duration. See also SENTIENT BODY.

Senzar   Sometimes Senzart, a name given to the secret sacerdotal language, said by Blavatsky to have been the tongue in which the occult BOOK OF DYZAN was written.

Separ   One of the names for VEPAR.

Sephirah   A Hebraic term usually taken to mean 'emanation of Deity'. See also SEPHIROTH.

Sephiroth   The plural of 'Sephirah', the ten emanations of Deity expressed in the figure of the SEPHIROTHIC TREE. In sequence of emanation, see KETHER, CHOKMAH, BINAH, CHESED, GERUBAH, TIPHERETH, NETZACH, HOD, YESOD and MALKUTH. See also QABBALA.

Sephirothic Tree   The name given by the Qabbalists to a graphic presentation of what is in effect a three-dimensional image of the spiritual world. This Tree penetrates like a ladder through four worlds (ATZILUTH, BRIAH, YETZIRAH and ASSIAH), stretching from the material realm of the earth plane to the highest level of spirituality available to man, beyond which spirituality must

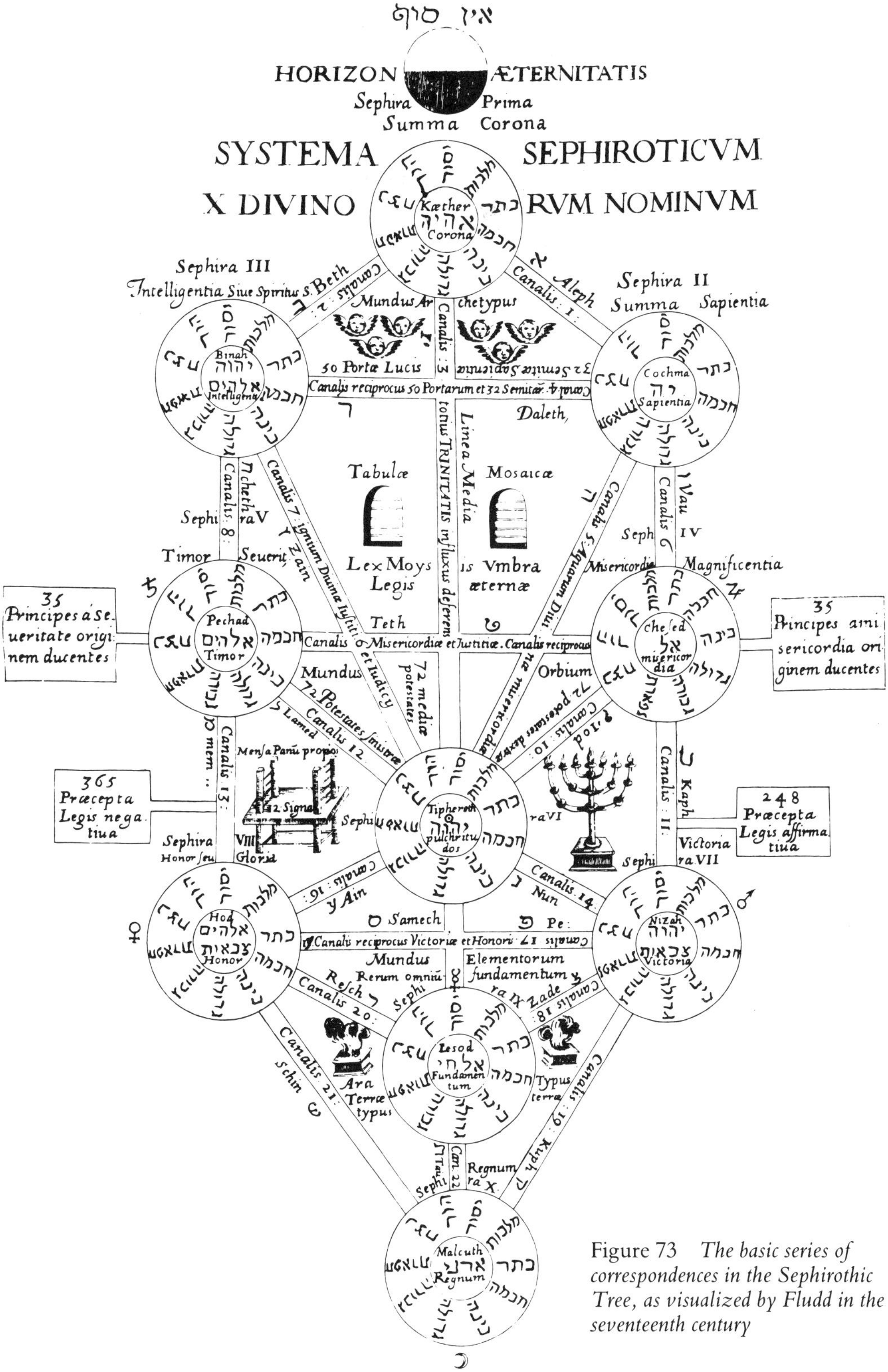

Figure 73   *The basic series of correspondences in the Sephirothic Tree, as visualized by Fludd in the seventeenth century*

Table 23

Sephirah	Meaning	God or angel ruler	in World of	Planet
KETHER	Crown	Ahih (but see KETHER)	Atziluth	*Primum mobile*
		Metatron	Briah	
		Chioth ha Qodesh	Yetzirah	
		Ain Soph	Assiah	
CHOKMAH	Wisdom	Jehovah (Yawe)	Atziluth	Zodiac
		Ratziel	Briah	
		Cherubim	Yetzirah	
		Zodiacal beings	Assiah	
BINAH	Understanding	Yawe Elohim	Atziluth	Saturn
		Zaphkiel	Briah	
		Aralim	Yetzirah	
		Thrones	Assiah	
DAATH and the ABYSS				
CHESED	Mercy	El	Atziluth	Jupiter
		Zadkiel	Briah	
		Chasmalim	Yetzirah	
		Dominions	Assiah	
GEBURAH	Severity	Elohim Gibor	Atziluth	Mars
		Khamael	Briah	
		Seraphim	Yetzirah	
		Dynamis	Assiah	
TIPHERETH	Beauty	Eloah va Daath	Atziluth	Sun
		Michael (Mikel)	Briah	
		Malachim	Yetzirah	
		Exsusiai	Assiah	
NETZACH	Victory	Yawe Sabaoth	Atziluth	Venus
		Hamiel (Auriel)	Briah	
		Elohim	Yetzirah	
		Archai	Assiah	
HOD	Splendour	Elohim Sabaoth	Atziluth	Mercury
		Raphael	Briah	
		Beni-Elohim	Yetzirah	
		Archangels	Assiah	
YESOD	Foundation	Shaddai el Chaiim	Atziluth	Moon
		Gabriel	Briah	
		Aishim	Yetzirah	
		Angels	Assiah	
MALKUTH	The Kingdom	Adonai Malakh	Atziluth	Earth
		Sandalphon	Briah	
		Cherubim	Yetzirah	
		Man	Assiah	

be defined almost in terms of negatives (see in this context SECRET DOCTRINE). The tree itself is complex, as Figure 73 indicates, but the penetration through the four realms may be simplified in terms of names and angelic rulerships as in Table 23. This table sets out for each Sephirah the Hebraic or Qabbalistic name, its reasonable translation into English, the name of the GOD-ASPECT or spiritual ruler in the four worlds in which each finds expression, and the planet with which it is linked by most occultists. For a study of individual functions, see the particular entries as indicated in this table.

Septenary See SEVEN.

Seraphim A term of much disputed etymology, although of Hebraic origin where it is linked both with 'serpent' (*ShRPM*) and 'burning' (*ShRP*). It is used to denote the celestial creatures described in Isaiah, 6, 2, as beings with a human form and three pairs of wings. Within the occult tradition they are linked with the Ophanim, serpent beings associated with the four fixed signs of the zodiac, and thus with the four Evangelists of the Christian tradition (although see also CHERUBIM). The Seraphim are sometimes called 'Spirits of Love', and in some occult systems are named as the rulers of the zodiac.

Serpent fire   See KUNDALINI.

Sesquiquadrate   An ASPECT of 135 degrees.

Seven   Perhaps the most powerful of all numbers, the 7 stands for the complete man, as a union of the lower ternary (of physical, etheric and astral), and the higher ternary (of Atma, Buddhi and Manas) united by the fulcrum of the Ego: 3 + 1 + 3 = 7. This is why it is called the 'hermetic number', the 'complete temple' (the human being in the sacred place of the world). For all the structure of its form, the 7 is called the 'closed number': it is said to be a reservoir, filled with water, without an outlet; to be the highest and most spiritual of numbers. It is the mystic element within septenaries which has preserved the idea of the seven planets, the seven days of the week and all the magical sevens which are found in the occult realm (see, for example, CALENDRIA MAGICA). It is the number of the good life: the four Cardinal virtues and the three theological virtues combine (4 + 3 = 7) to make this the perfect number of philosophers and moral men. It is linked with the letter G, and with extremes of action, love and intellectual acumen. With such a power in the sound it is not a restful or peaceful number, for all its holiness: like the number 1 it stands alone, often against the world. In this respect it is a creative number, for the creative man or woman must separate from the world to bring down divinity to earth. The numerological adage that '7 is creative' rests on the addition (1 + 6 = 7) which is another way of saying that the isolated monad (1) relates to the Venus impulse (6) to bring down to earth the heavenly order (7). All art is involved with the spiritualization of the material realm – that is, with adding the trinity to the material elements (3 + 4 = 7). The Hebraic equivalent is Zayin. Seven is the number of the earth in the spring and summer, when the Earth-forces are dormant. See NUMBERS.

Seven ages   In popular astrology the term is usually applied to the various doctrines relating to the division of the life of man into septenaries (see CLIMACTERICS). In a specialist sense the term is sometimes applied to the seven historic ages governed by the SECUNDADEIAN BEINGS, the so-called Trithemian Periods. In its popular sense the division is in terms of the seven planetary ages, following a sequence from the first sphere of the Moon through to the sphere of Saturn, to each sequence of which is attached a definite number of years (see PLANETARY AGES). A list of the traditional seven ages gives the Moon up to the age of 4, Mercury from 4 to 14, Venus from 14 to 24, Sun from 24 to 43, Mars from 43 to 58, Jupiter from 58 to 70, and Saturn to all the years afterwards. There are, however, several such periodicities. Several attempts have been made to link these planetary ages with the list poetically set out by Shakespeare in *As You Like It*, but it is more likely the poet had in mind one of the several sources from Proclus, who does not give periodicities (these no doubt being taken for granted) but only the planetary rulerships.

Seven creative spirits   A European esoteric term for the DHYAN-CHOHANS.

Seven cosmical elements   In the esoteric lore there are said to be seven elements, only four of which are visible, these being the traditional Earth, Air, Fire and Water (see ELEMENTS). The fifth element, or QUINTESSENCE, is said to be semi-material and is already visible to certain individuals, but the other two (unnamed, but linked with Atma and Buddhi) will not become visible until some remote future. The seven elements are said to be conditional modifications and aspects of the one element, the source of AKASHA itself.

Seven elements   See SEVEN COSMICAL ELEMENTS.

Seven planetary spirits   See OLYMPIC SPIRITS.

Seven properties   A term derived from the esoteric astrology of the German mystic Boehme, and sometimes called the 'seven forms' or the 'seven working properties' (the German original term being *wirkende Eigenschafte*). The seven forms are linked with the seven planets, although it is the principles behind the planets which interest Boehme in his esoteric account of the effects produced by their individual working, their polarities and their balance. The first form is that of Saturn, which is a harsh and hardening principle, a centripetal force, 'indrawing and compacting about its chosen centre'; it is Saturn which draws and fixes. The second form is Mercury (Mercurius), which strives for freedom against the restraint imposed by Saturn; it is separative and centrifugal, in eternal flight from fixity. Its role is seen in the thinking mind, in 'divisive analysis'. The third form is Mars, which results from the opposition of the first two and may be likened to a turning wheel, which itself represents a fusion of the centripetal and the centrifugal impulses; it is the 'turning wheel of desire'. This is the ternary of fire, which bursts forth into action into the fourth form, which is that of the Sun. Boehme likens this solar bursting to the crack of lightning, which is the explosion of spirit into time; it is sometimes called the 'Schrack'. The attainment of desire in this Sun form brings its own joy and harmony, which is the fifth form, that of Venus. This form is active and harmony-producing, from the resolution of conflict to the 'mirage-paradise of misplaced hopes'. From this develops the sixth form, the fuller self-perception and understanding which is characteristic of Jupiter. The seventh form, that of the Moon, is anticlimactic, yet is involved with 'final production of concrete realization'. A relationship is established between this seventh and the first form, with the result that the seven properties work cyclically.

Seven Races In the Theosophical cosmo-conception the Seven Races are the seven streams of human evolution, four of which have run their course in the present GLOBE PERIOD, the fifth of which is still in progress (see FIFTH RACE) and two of which are to be developed in the future. See FIRST RACE, SECOND RACE, THIRD RACE and FOURTH RACE. See ROOT RACES.

Seven rays In the esoteric astrological system of Intuitional Astrology described by Bailey, a series of seven rays are outlined, each originating in the constellation of Ursa Major (although besides being individually linked with the major seven stars of this asterism, they are also associated with the Pleiades and the fixed star Sirius) and thence transmitted to our solar system by means

of three 'constellations', which are the zodiacal signs, and by a conventional system of planetary rulers paralleled by an unconventional system of rulers, called respectively the 'orthodox' and the 'esoteric' (see RAY).

The rays set out in terms of planetary influences by Morrish are discussed under SEVEN RAY-TYPES and must not be confused with the Bailey system. The seven rays especially linked with the theosophical astrology are also not to be confused with those of the Intuitional Astrology. The former are in fact rays emanating from the seven planetary spirits or angels. Strictly speaking, these rays directly influence the seven spiritual bodies of man, the first three corresponding to the three as yet undeveloped in ordinary man (Atma, Buddhi and Manas), the last four corresponding to the personality and the so-called bridge which enables a reciprocal action between the higher and lower ternaries of man's being (see TERNARY). These septenaries are associated with eight planets (the Sun overlooking each of the seven rays).

Seven ray-types In his syncretic system of astrology Morrish sets out what he calls the 'seven ray-types', seemingly derived from a system of occultism which might easily be confused (in nomenclature at least) with the SEVEN RAYS of Bailey or of the Theosophical system. The first ray is that of Saturn, 'ruler by means of set forms of obedience to established authority'. The second ray is that of Venus, the 'philanthropist'. The third ray is that of Mercury, the 'adaptable type – the active mental organizer'. The fourth ray is that of the Earth, the 'artist' who is 'able to create material forms expressing spiritual values'. The fifth ray is that of Jupiter, the 'scientist or philosopher' who is to be distinguished from the Saturn-type scientist, the 'materialist' who works with set forms, with a tendency to suppression. The fifth ray-type is an idealist 'expressing itself expansively'. The sixth ray is that of Mars, the 'devotee–fanatic', the 'object-worshipper', the 'militant religious and partisan'. Morrish notes that while the Venusian type works for the group, the Martian type tries to force others to do so. The seventh ray is that of Uranus, the 'occultist', the 'research worker and electrician' who is at the same time the 'reformer'.

Seventh ray In the esoteric system described by Bailey the seventh of the SEVEN RAYS is called the 'ray of ceremonial order' and is linked with the will to express and with the principle of order. See also SEVEN RAY-TYPES.

Seventh ray-type The seventh of the SEVEN RAY-TYPES, associated with the planet Uranus.

Sextile An ASPECT of 60 degrees, generally regarded as a beneficial influence.

Sha In Chinese cosmology the maleficent though impersonal force which moves in straight lines and is connected with the system of FENG-SHUI. The *sha* forces may be warded off, or deflected, by judicious building.

Shaddai See YESOD.

Shade A name given in occultism to an astral copy of a deceased entity, usually that of a human, possessing most of the pre-mortem characteristics, but divorced from all the Ego life of that human. Such shades are little more than soulless bundles of the lowest qualities of the previous living entity, but may be confused with the entity itself. In popular use the word is applied to all types of ghosts. See also KLIPPOTH.

Shadow body A name used in modern occultism for a wide variety of different (though related) spiritual bodies. In spiritualistic circles the term is often used as being synonymous with the DOUBLE. In popular occult circles it is used as being synonymous with the ETHERIC BODY, and in some circles as synonymous with the DWELLER ON THE THRESHOLD, which is visualized as a sort of demonic shadow. A full survey of spiritual bodies, along with many of the ancient terminologies, is given by Mead.

Shadow Self See DWELLER ON THE THRESHOLD.

Shadowy arc See DESCENDING ARC.

Shamali See THIRD RACE.

Shamayim One of the names given to the first of the seven heavens of the Qabbalists, ruled by GABRIEL.

Shamballa Sometimes S'ambhala or Shambhala, a term with two seemingly unrelated meanings. In the Theosophical cosmoconception (rooted in Vedic esotericism) Shamballa is said to be a place presently located in an oasis in the Gobi Desert, the 'spiritual pole of the earth'; although widely quoted as 'factual', this may be one of Blavatsky's clever jokes or occult blinds. The place is at all events said to be the dwelling of high INITIATES, as of the undying Lords of Venus, the Sons of Fire, and those who taught primitive man. Unfortunately the esoteric aspect of this Shamballa has been extericized out of all recognition in popular occultism.

The same term 'Shamballa' is used with more caution and precision by the esotericist Bailey, who described it as 'that major centre of our planetary life', locating it in our solar system and placing it under the 'control' of the fixed star Polaris, as playing a part of the sequence of projection of the SEVEN RAYS. In another context she locates Shamballa 'where the Will of God is focused' on our planet.

Shamsheil Name given to one of the GRIGORI, exalted beings of the Hebraic tradition who taught men the signs of the Sun and (probably) the nature of the zodiac.

Shani The Sanskrit word for the planet Saturn, as used in Hindu astrology.

Shax One of the seventy-two SPIRITS OF SOLOMON. He is said to appear in the form of a bird, and will procure for the magician deafness, dumbness and blindness in enemies.

Shedu See GENIUS.

Shekinah A Hebraic term used in the QABBALA as a name for the last Sephirah, that of Earth, called MALKUTH. In Jewish esotericism it is the veil of the Absolute (the AIN SOPH), and in exoteric thought the cloud of glory on the mercy seat of the Holy of Holies.

Shells A term used in modern occultism, translated from Qabbalism, for the empty phantoms of the dead (that is, empty of life or of egohood); see KLIPPOTH. Very often the so-called spirits of seances are nothing other than shells, the opposite of spirits. See also DWELLER ON THE THRESHOLD.

Sheol A Hebraic name for the equivalent of Hell/Purgatory: a state or region of fixity and inactivity. The Sheol-ob is one who consults with phantasmic SHELLS, a so-called necromancer. See OB.

Shipton prophecies A general name given to a number of different prophecies attached to the name of Ursula Shipton, the first batch of which were published early in the seventeenth century, although in fact relating only to events already fulfilled. A later series, published in the nineteenth century, were also *post rem* (including such things as the 'motorcar', and the 'end of the world for 1881'). These were published fraudulently by Charles Hindley. The prophecies attached to the name Shipton (who almost certainly did not exist) are still being published by the popular press – the Hindley 'end of the world' date has been suitably altered to read 1991!

Shoftiel The name of one of the Angels of Punishment, 'the judge of God'.

Shukra The Sanskrit word for the planet Venus, as used in Hindu astrology.

Sibylline Books Prophetic books of the ancient Roman world, said to have been written in hexameter, containing a secret language or acrostic, and preserved in the Capitol at Rome, later in the Palatine. The important texts (supposedly written on palm leaves) – notably the series written by the Cumean Sybil – are lost, and the ones claimed to be still in existence are almost certainly (early) forgeries.

Siddhis A Sanskrit term (see also IDDHI) for the supranormal psychic faculties in man. The word is used in the plural because there are two forms of *siddhi* – one which is of a coarse nature (sometimes linked with atavistic clairvoyance) and one which is of a higher nature, the result of disciplined training, as might arise from the correct practice of YOGA.

Sidereal The term 'sidereal', meaning 'pertaining to the stars', is derived from the genitive form of the Latin *sidus* ('star'), *sideris*.

Sidereal Body The Astroeides is sometimes called the 'Sidereal Body', although the word means 'starlike'. See ASTRAL BODY and SUBTLE BODY.

Sidereal light See ASTRAL LIGHT.

Sigil The name given to a graphic symbol of an occult, alchemical, astrological or otherwise magical designation. The sigil for the planet Jupiter, for example, is now ♃; in the thirteenth century it was ♃. The sigils and SIGNS of the zodiac are often confused: the sigil for the sign Aries, for example, is ♈, while the sigil for the sign Virgo is ♍.

Sign A sign of the zodiac is a 30-degree arc, resulting from the division of the ecliptic into twelve equal parts as shown schematically in Figure 74. The signs are often confused with the constellations. However, a constellation is a pattern of stars, sometimes called an asterism, which need not be contained within a 30-degree arc in the skies. Although twelve of the constellations have similar names to the signs of the zodiac, there is little or no relationship between them beyond the name (see Figure 54 under MODERN ZODIAC).

Signatures One of the important concepts in medieval magic is the notion that everything on the material plane has a corresponding planetary or celestial influence in the higher realm. It is further maintained that occult vision permits someone especially trained in such matters to 'see', from the form of a material object or entity, what this influence (or nexus of influences) is. The influence, stamped on the material plane, in a form which may be 'read' by someone proficient in the occult script, is called the 'signature'. A knowledge of what the signature of a material thing is may be regarded as the first step in almost any alchemical, astrological or magico-therapeutic practice. This notion is expressed in all the important occult systems, from astrology to Qabbalism. In astrology it is normal to trace the signature, imprinted on every physical object, to the planets or to the zodiacal signs; in some cases it is also possible to trace such signatures to one of the four elements. Thus the dog might well be traced to the planet Mars, perhaps to the sign Aries (depending upon what kind of a dog it is), and to the Fire element, because of its inner nature. This example belies the complexity of the doctrine of signatures, however, by suggesting that it is always easy to determine under what signature a being or object in the material world may be, which is far from the case. For example

Figure 74 *A schematic presentation of the signs of the zodiac (from a Shepherd's Calendar of the early sixteenth century)*

(to remain within the canine realm), the guard dog is linked with the zodiacal sign Cancer, for reasons which are too complex to set out here, but which are ultimately linked with mythologies connected with fixed stars. For this reason the very long lists of 'correspondences' determined by the doctrine of signatures is often confusing and even irritating to one of a modern cast of mind, which usually seeks for causal relations of a more obvious kind. The signatures of astrology have influenced those used practically in alchemy, magic and even in certain of the modern holistic medicines, though there are important differences between various systems, especially so in connection with the signatures of planets and signs reflected in the plant kingdom. The tradition of signatures in Qabbalism is perhaps less complex, for fascinating and creative lines of influence may be traced from the lowest realm of MALKUTH, where the elemental natures find expression, through to the highest godhead beyond the twig-ends of KETHER.

Silent Watchers A term used by modern Theosophists for the supremely developed spirits who, since they are omniscient in human terms, have accepted the role of helping the evolution of man by means of compassion and secret aid.

Silver cord A name given to the spiritual tie which links together the physical body with its spiritual counterparts, especially with the ETHERIC BODY. It is said that the silver cord remains firmly attached during the whole period of a lifetime and dissolves only at death. It is possible that the term was derived from Ecclesiastes, 12, 6. The medieval occultists called it *Nodus*, sometimes *Nodus coelestis*. See in particular ASTRAL BODY and PISCES.

Simplicia Materia A name given to the THREE PRINCIPLES of Mercury, Sulphur and Salt in their role as prematerializing SEMINA. Mercury is that which enlivens; Sulphur is that which promotes growth; and Salt is that which keeps form together by giving firmness. The *Simplicia formalia*, being the 'form' or 'ideal' of the *Materia*, are closer to spirit than to matter, however, and must be thought of as the seminal natures of the three principles.

203

Simurgh A fabulous Iranian composite creature, part lion, part peacock, part griffin and part dog.

Six Within the form of the 6 is the conflict of the open form of the top and the enclosed form of its base, an altercation of open and closed, of motion and rest – dualities which are expressed in the occult tradition as the conflict between virtue and vice. Choice is expressed in the esoteric symbolism of the PYTHAGOREAN LETTER which is the Y, a symbol of the triad, which in this number is 3 doubled ($3 + 3 = 6$). This is why the number 6 is said to stand for either good or evil and to exhibit all the signs of oppositions within its frame. The numerologist Hogenraad says of this number that it is 'a dreamer of dreams' who is 'apt to be indifferent to others'. This is so because the resolution of the tensions in its basic duality may only be found in the spiritual realm. If this resolution is not experienced in the spiritual (where dreams are to be found), then it will lead inevitably to isolation. The individual becomes trapped in the space of zero (the enclosed space may be either the quintessence (5) or a monadic (1) prison (5, or 6−1)) in the lower part of the figure. It is probably better to remain 'open' in the top half of the figure, to 'build castles in the air', than to remain in such a prison. If 6 responds to the lower half, then it is bound to become caught up in itself and will therefore be indifferent to others: one is constantly faced with the destiny of 6 to be either good or bad. The number is linked with Venus in astrological circles, with the Hebraic Vau, and with the letter F. The so-called NUPTIAL NUMBER of 60 reduces to 6. Six is sometimes called the 'number of animating principle' – it is the number of the earth in the autumn and winter, when the earth forces are most active. The senary is sometimes called the symbol of the 'physical man', while the septenary is sometimes called the 'spiritual man'. The oldest of the occult symbols, the swastika, is ascribed the number 6. See NUMBERS.

Skotograph A photograph, or negative image, usually of psychic phenomena, produced without a camera. See SPIRIT PHOTOGRAPHY.

Sky-walker See KESHARA.

Slate writing A name given to a curious procedure in the SEANCE rooms, whereby two operators (one of them a medium) would each hold two corners of an ordinary slate board under the seance table, with a slate pencil pressed between the slate and the underside of the table. The spirit agency is sometimes claimed to write on the slate by means of what has been called the 'direct method', without a human agency. When the medium or an amanuensis writes, it is sometimes called the 'indirect method'.

Sleepers See LIVING DEAD.

Sleeping dead See SOUL.

Smaragdine tablet See TABULA SMARAGDINA.

Sod A Hebraic term for a 'mystery' or 'arcanum'. The *sodales* of the Roman world were the initiated members of the colleges of priests. The Sodalian Oath was a sacred oath of initiation.

Solas Sometimes Stolas, one of the seventy-two SPIRITS OF SOLOMON. He is said to appear in the form of a black raven. He is learned in astrology and in the magical powers of plants and stones.

Solomon's Seal See SEAL OF SOLOMON.

Soma A Sanskrit name for the Moon and for the god of the Moon (who dwells in the lunar realm of Soma-loka), as well as for the juice of a plant used to induce trance, although some occultists say that this is the ambrosial drink of the gods. Others say that the soma is at once a plant and an angel.

Somapa A class of lunar PITRIS.

Son See SON OF WOMAN.

Son of woman In occultism this term is used to indicate one of the lower degrees of initiation, the term 'woman' referring to Nature. The 'Son of Man' applies to a higher initiation, the term 'man' being linked with the human soul. The 'Son of Gods' applies to initiation into the cosmogonic sciences, while in occultism 'Son of God' applies to an initiation into the supreme science.

Soniferous ether See AKASHA.

Sons of Life A modern name for the ANGELS. See SPIRITUAL HIERARCHIES.

Sons of Light See WHITE MAGIC.

Sons of Twilight A modern name for the ANGELS. See SPIRITUAL HIERARCHIES.

Soothsayer One who predicts the future. Originally the term was derived from the Old English word for 'truth' and meant 'one who speaks the truth'.

Sophia The name given originally to the Gnostic aeon of wisdom, the downfall of whom gave rise to the material world. Accounts of the fall of Sophia vary: in one version it is through pride, in another through her wish to emulate the Father by producing children without conjugal intercourse. According to the Gnostic *Pistis Sophia*, she is seduced by a demon named Authades, who issued a ray of light which Sophia confused with an emanation of the Father. In this way she is enticed into the Chaos below the aeonic PLEROMA, where she is imprisoned.

Sorcerer Strictly speaking, the word means 'one who casts lots', derived from the latin *sortiarius* (see SORTES). In modern times the word is used to denote a magician (properly speaking a black magician) or one who practises witchcraft.

Sortes The ancient equivalent of 'sortilege', or divination by lots, of which there were very many types. For example, the *Sortes sanctorum* used as a divinatory method by the medieval clergy consisted of random opening of Holy Writ, the words revealed taken to indicate response to questions posed prior to the ritual. The sortes of divination are not to be confused with the Sortes (Greek *klipoi*) of astrology, long defunct, the equivalent of the modern PARS. See DIVINATION.

Sortilege Divination by lots. See SORTES.

Sosol In certain GRIMOIRES the name given to the governor of the zodiacal sign Scorpio.

Sothis period Sometimes the Sothic period, a term derived from the Egyptian chronology (Sothis being the name for the fixed star Sirius). It is a period of 1460 years which has been linked with the periodicity of the benu bird or PHOENIX.

Soul In modern times the word 'soul' is often confused with 'spirit', but in all ancient esoteric systems the distinction was very clear: soul was the mediator between spirit and matter, and man was viewed as a triune being with physical body and eternal spirit connected for the duration of a lifetime by 'soul'. The *psyche* of the Greeks and the *nephesh* ('breath of life') of the Hebrews both connote this connection, even though the terms are often translated as 'vital principles', 'life force' and so on. In modern esotericism the soul is that which connects the physical body with the upper triune (see TERNARY), and may be said to consist of the ETHERIC BODY and the ASTRAL BODY, both of which are eventually dissolved after death. Some systems place the Ego as part of the mediating soul. In other words, while the human SPIRIT is eternal (and may seek reincarnate life), the soul itself is not, even though it does have a longer term of existence that the physical body. The 'living dead' or the 'sleeping dead' of esoteric lore are those in whom soul is not yet sufficiently activated, as a result of which they lack true humanity – the benefits afforded such a soul with the human MONAD have not yet accrued. These are sometimes called the 'soulless beings', not to be confused with 'lost souls'. The lost souls of esoteric lore are those (relatively few) individuals who, through a series of reincarnations, have so involuted as to have lost contact with their monad. The soulless are those who still have the potential of spiritual life before them, while lost souls have in the course of lifetimes severed the possibility of wholesome evolution. The Hebraic RUACH is the spirit which rests on the NEPHESH soul.

Soul beings The four classes of ELEMENTALS, often wrongly called 'elemental spirits', are generally regarded by occultists to be elemental soul beings, since the very quality they lack is that of spirit, in that they do not have the Ego, or even the Ego potential, which is part of the human constitution. In the occult tradition the four classes are linked with the four elements (hence their generic name). The GNOMES are the Earth beings, the SALAMANDERS are the Fire beings, the SYLPHS are the Air beings and the UNDINES are the Water beings.

Soul Body A name used in modern occultism for the ASTRAL BODY. See SENTIENT BODY.

Soul numbers A series of numbers linked with the platonic theory of harmonics and DESCENT OF THE SOUL which figured in later numerological theories connected with occultism and astrology. The numbers are 1, 2, 3, 4, 8, 9 and 27, but the argument as to their mystical natures is beyond the compass of the present treatment. The first four correspond to the point, line, plane and solid. These are called the 'boundary numbers of the soul' and, in relation to the cycle of descent and reascent of the soul into and out of matter, were adopted in many astrological schemas of an esoteric kind. The remaining three are derived from these by additions and simple multiplication.

Soulless being See APAP and SOUL.

Souls of fire A name given to the Aishim of Qabbalism. See YESOD.

Spagyric A term coined from the Greek *spao* ('divide') and *ageiro* ('unite'), and applied to the processes underlying the alchemical art. ALCHEMY is indeed sometimes called the 'spagyric art'.

Spagyric artists A name for alchemists; see VULCAN.

Speculation In a strictly astrological and occult context Paracelsus defines 'speculation' as an activity arising from the stars 'which are concerned about man'. From the larger context of his writings we may assume that the term is intended to denote the relationship that exists between what we would now call the 'archetype' (which Paracelsus variously called the 'Archeus' or the 'heavens') and human thinking. Hence Paracelsus speaks of a speculating man as one having his imagination united with heaven, and 'heaven operates so within him that more is discovered than would seem possible by merely human methods'. The Latin equivalent term was fairly close to 'contemplation': in Latin a *specula* was a watch tower, from which one might examine

Figure 75 *A witch casting a spell (after Jan van der Velde, 1624)*

both the world below and the world of stars. Phantasy appears to have been a sort of uncontrolled speculation, for according to Paracelsus it is the 'speculation of a fool'.

Spell A word from the Old English *spel* ('speech') and applied to the idea of a magical word or binding power which may be spoken or written down. Just as the word 'CHARM' was originally involved with the idea of song, so a spell was something which arose from the spoken word, as an incantation or a formula of power. The idea is that the spoken phrase puts into a single verbal charge of energy the wishes of the magician – whether evil or beneficient. This charge of energy could be transmitted to a parchment or paper by means of symbols (Figure 75). This accounts for the reason why all the best instructions for magical invocations and spells are so precise about how the wishes should be nurtured and intensified during the construction of magical formulas and conjuration. In fact, the writing of a serious spell or the inscribing of a TALISMAN or AMULETS requires an almost infinite patience: at every stage there is required a ritual of invocation to named spirits, with names such as are found only in the GRIMOIRES. There exist complex rituals for the preparation of paper, pen, ink and even inkstands, before the inscription of the spell may usefully be undertaken. The rules are usually extremely detailed: the parchment must be 'virgin' or 'unborn' (that is, uterine), the pen must be a quill pulled from the third feather of the right wing of a male gosling; the ink must be made from the right wing of the exorcised living bat or pigeon and so on. In some extreme cases the manufacture of spells requires animal sacrifice and thus merges into the questionable area of BLACK MAGIC. See also SYMPATHETIC MAGIC.

Sperm of the World See MAGNESIA.

Sphere of Democritus A name applied to an ancient (probably Hellenistic) system of prognostication by means of numbers, only peripherally linked with prediction by means of OMINA.

Sphere of Heaven The Stellatum or Coelum (but see also EIGHTH SPHERE) in the Ptolemaic system, the sphere in which dwell the beings and orbs of the fixed stars. In the medieval cosmoconception the sphere was said to be the dwelling of the CHERUBIM, ruled by the spiritual being Ophaniel and linked with the image of a dove.

Sphere of the Primum mobile Sometimes called the *Primum movens* ('first mover') in the Ptolemaic system, this is the sphere which was supposed to give motion to all the other spheres which it enclosed. In the medieval cosmoconception the sphere was said to be the dwelling of the SERAPHIM, ruled by the spiritual being METATRON, and often linked with the image of a leopard.

Spheres The early Greek and Roman cosmoconception postulated that the seven planets (which included the luminaries) were carried around the central Earth in a series of spheres. The body of the planet, often called the 'planetary orb' in later European systems, was carried along by the movement of that sphere – a movement transmitted to it ultimately by the SPHERE OF THE PRIMUM MOBILE. Because seven planets are described in the Ptolemaic system (which is itself an extension of the Aristotelian system) it is generally believed that there were only seven planetary spheres carrying the planetary orbs; however, this is far from the truth. The need to unite the Aristotelian dictum that planets move in perfect circles with the observable movement of these bodies required a most sophisticated system of epicycles and deferent circles and involved a complex series of spheres within spheres. By the sixteenth century, shortly before the Ptolemaic model broke down under its own weight of complexity, a model existed which postulated the existence of as many as seventy-nine spheres. By the time Dante was putting the Arabian astrology into poetic imagery a working model had been constructed with only twenty-seven spheres. The idea that it was the Earth itself which revolved, rather than the vast concentrics of spheres, was suggested in Greek times, but was mooted in Europe in the thirteenth century by the Franciscan monk Francois de Meyronnes.

Under the impress of the theory of the CELESTIAL HIERARCHIES, derived from the sixth-century theology of Dionysius, a system of spiritual beings, with named rulers, were established around the theory of the spheres.

One important difference between the modern heliocentric system and the late-medieval system inherited by astrology was the sequence of the planets: it was believed that Venus was nearer to

Table 24

Number	Planet	Hierarchy	Ruler	Spirit	Symbol
1	Moon	Angels	Gabriel	Phul	Ox
2	Mercury	Archangels	Raphael	Ophiel	Serpent
3	Venus	Archai	Haniel	Hagiel	Man
4	Sun	Exsusiai	Michael	Och	Lion
5	Mars	Dynamis	Samael	Phaleg	Horse
6	Jupiter	Dominions	Zadkiel	Befor	Eagle
7	Saturn	Thrones	Zaphkiel	Avatron	Serpent

the Sun, so that in most of the models of our system prior to the seventeenth century the sequence of the spheres was presented in the order set out in Table 24. The lists give the main names of each of the seven planetary spheres, the corresponding number, the name of the celestial hierarchy, the personal name of the spirit ruler and associated daimon-spirit, and the image derived from medieval symbolism.

Spherical descent See DESCENT OF THE SOUL.

Spherical regulators See INTELLIGENCY.

Spica A binary fixed star, the alpha of constellation Virgo, set in the ear of corn held by this female figure. Its symbolic importance is just about equivalent to its astrological importance, for the Christian astrologers linked Virgo with the Virgin Mary, and the Spica (ear of corn) in the arms of the asterism with Jesus, held in the arms of his virgin mother. This imagery may be traced back to the Egyptian ISIS (see, for example, STELLA MARIS), a goddess linked with the constellation and sign VIRGO. A few Greek temples (including that ancient wonder at Ephesus, later the site for a cult of the Virgin Mary) were also orientated towards Spica.

Spirit This word is used in occult texts to denote a wide variety of different concepts. A spirit is usually a disembodied being – a celestial spirit (such as an ANGEL) is a good spirit, while a DEMON is an evil spirit, or at least one not concerned overtly with the evolution of man. The word 'spirit' is often misused to denote the SOUL BEINGS in the term 'elemental spirits'. Equally, the shells, elementaries, diakka, phantoms, spooks and other discarnate entities of seances are sometimes called 'spirits', as, for example, in the term SPIRIT PHOTOGRAPHY. The word is also used to denote the 'human spirit', and in this use it is sometimes applied to distinguish the eternal indestructible part of man (esoterically the EGO or the TERNARY) from the soul which connects this with the material body or sheath. All too frequently, however, 'spirit' is confused with 'SOUL'. In esotericism the ternary of Atma, Buddhi and Manas is properly speaking the 'spirit' of man. As Blavatsky says, spirit 'belongs directly to Universal Consciousness' and is 'its homogeneous and unadulterated emanation'.

Spirit husband See INCUBUS.

Spirit Man A name given by Steiner (in the German, *Geistmensch*) to the highest of the human spiritual ternary, the ATMA.

Spirit photography The technique of recording on film the manifestation of spirit beings was first developed in the United States of America round about the middle of the last century by William Hudson. Pictures were first taken of spirits invisible to the photographer, then later clairvoyantly visible to the photographer or to a medium present at the photographic session. Later techniques of photography permitted extensive records of manifestations in seances to be recorded, often by means of flash techniques which proved ultimately destructive to the seances. Images of complete materializations of spirits, of partial materializations and of related phenomena are certainly more frequently obtained than is generally realized. Genuine mediumship, beset as always by extensive fraudulent practice, resulted in highly sophisticated techniques of spirit photography, which, by the end of the century, was the subject of intensive scientific investigation. Perhaps the most famous of late-nineteenth-century spirits to be photographed in a materialized form was Katie King, who manifested through the mediumship of

Florence Cook and was minutely studied by Sir William Crookes. She was often photographed with this scientist, who wrote: 'Photography was inadequate to depict the perfect beauty of Katie's face, as words are powerless to describe her charm of manner. . . .' The development of genuine spirit photography into the arcane areas described by Constable has almost been obfuscated by the many fraudulent practices; genuine attempts and fraud have been partly chronicled by Gettings. See also CHEMICOGRAPH, PSYCHOGRAPH, RADIOGRAPH and SKOTOGRAPH.

Spirit Self   The name given by Steiner (in the German, *Geistselbst*) to the lowest of the human ternary, the MANAS.

Spiritism   A name originally applied to the nineteenth-century French version of SPIRITUALISM as propounded by Rivail ('Allan Kardec') which involved a view of reincarnation that was not adopted universally – particularly in English and American spiritualist circles.

Spiritoid   A term coined by Boirac for messages apparently from a spiritual source but in fact originating in the subsonsious mind.

Spirits of Form   One of the modern names for the EXSUSIAI.

Spirits of Harmonies   One of the names given by Steiner (in German, *Geister der Harmonien*), with a suggested correct translation of the plural form, 'Spirits of the Cosmic Harmonies'. These beings are sometimes called 'Spirits of Harmony'.

Spirits of Love   One of the modern names for the SERAPHIM.

Spirits of Movement   One of the modern names for the DYNAMIS.

Spirits of Personality   One of the modern names for the ARCHAI.

Spirits of Revolution of Time   See ARCHAI.

Spirits of Solomon   These are the seventy-two spirits or demons listed in the *Lemegeton*, the grimoire attributed (quite spuriously) to King Solomon. Very many such demon lists exist, however, in both manuscript form and in printed books, and many of the seventy-two demons appear in these. In the *Lemegeton* each of the

demons is described in the (usually frightful) form in which it is accustomed to appear before the conjurer, and the specific reason for his conjuration is also given. Thus, AGARES is said to appear in the form of a sage, riding a crocodile and carrying a hawk. His particular function is to bring back those who have run away and to provide knowledge of foreign tongues; at the request of the conjurer, he will also cause earthquakes. Usually the appearances of the conjured spirits are ghastly, but they may be commanded to adopt a human shape. Only one demon, GOMORY, appears in the form of a woman;

Figure 76   *The sigils for (from top to bottom) the demons Bifrons, Vepar, Bune, Zagan, an alternative for Bune, and Naberius, from the seventy-two sigils recorded in the demonological* Book of Solomon *(from a sixteenth-century manuscript in the British Museum)*

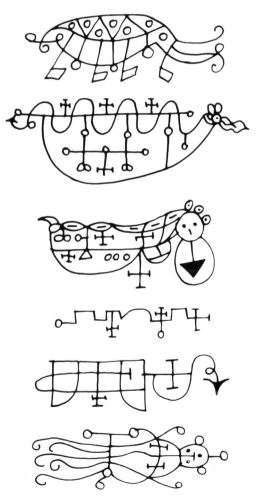

ASTORETH and PROCEL, on the other hand, will appear in the guise of angels. BELIAL is unique in this list as being the only one to demand sacrifices. VINE is unique because he is the only spirit who will reveal to the magician the names or identities of other sorcerers and witches. The spirits of Solomon are especially well known in the grimoire tradition because of the sigils (or seals) which have been attached to their names; examples of these may be seen in Figure 76, where the sigils for BIFRONS, VEPAR, BUNE, ZAGAN, an alternative for Bune, and the sigil for NABERIUS are given. Many demons of this class will confer the power of invisibility on the conjurer and will teach the secrets of the earth, such as the medicinal values of plants, herbs and stones as, for example, the demon SOLAS. Some are conjured for their specific abilities; for example, MALPAS for his ability to build or make by supernatural means, GAMGYN for his power to bring back the souls of the dead for interrogation (he is, along with MURMUR, the most famous of the necromantic spirits); PHOENIX is specialized in teaching poetry and letters; SABNACK in the curing of war wounds and in advising on fortifications and so on. Vepar is the demon concerned with the sea, and may be invoked to cause storms and to bring disasters, shipwrecks and death by drowning; this may explain why the sigil for Vepar (see Figure 76) so closely resembles the drawing of a ship. Many of the spirits will also teach the art of astrology, but ORIAS is unique in that he will teach the art without the conjurer having to follow tiresome studies – he will be granted knowledge of the complex art 'in an instant'. As the information in Table 25 indicates, however, some demons have more than one specialization. The list under 'Tongues' refers to those who teach either foreign or secret languages and the Language of the Birds (which is nothing other than the esoteric tongue). The list under 'Love' is related mainly to love between the sexes and often involves carnal love and, as in the case of SYNTRY, power over lust – this latter demon being able to compel any woman to appear nude before the conjurer. The list under 'Wealth' includes the secrets of alchemical transmutation of base metal into gold. The list under 'Knowledge' includes all those studies which will give power over men, as well as occult studies. The list under 'Treasure' includes those demons specialized in obtaining hidden treasures for the conjurer. Many spirits will grant demonic FAMILIARS when these are demanded, but the demons listed under 'Familiars' are specialist in this art. Again, almost all the demons have (or at least, pretend to have) knowledge of futurity, and of the past; the list under 'Future' names only those specially conjured for such knowledge. The table would suggest that the four main demands made of demons by the conjurers are connected with knowledge of futurity, the power over knowledge (and hidden treasure), and the command over love and lust.

See also ALLOCEN, ANDREALPHUS, ANDROMALIUS, BAETL, BATHIN, BERITH, BIFRONS, BOFI, BUER, DANTALIAN, DECARABIA, FLAUROS, FOCALOR, FURCAS, HALPAS, LERAJIE, MALPAS, MARBAS, MARCHOSIAS, MORAX, NABERIUS, OSE, PAIMON, SABNACK, SEERE, SOLAS, VALAC, VEPAR, VUEL, ZAGAN.

Spirits of Will One of the modern names for the THRONES.

Spirits of Wisdom One of the modern names given to the KYRIOTETES.

Table 25

Tongues	Love	Wealth	Knowledge	Treasure	Familiars	Future
Agares	Amon	Berith	Aini	Amy	Amduscias	Amon
Bune	Beleth	Bune	Asmoday	Asmoday	Amy	Astaroth
Caim	Furfur	Gomory	Baal	Barbatos	Morax	Balam
Forneus	Gaap	Hagenti	Buer	Cimeries	Paimon	Barbatos
Ronobe	Gomory	Raum	Ose	Eligor	Shax	Botis
	Saleos	Zagan	Paimon	Foras		Caim
	Syntry		Procel	Gaap		Glasyalabolas
	Vual		Purson	Shax		Gusion
	Zepar		Valefor			Ipos
			Vapula			Purson
						Raum
						Vassago

Table 26

Greek name	Sphere	Medieval Latin	Modern
Seraphim	Stellatum	Seraphim	Spirits of Love
Cherubim	Zodiac	Cherubim	Spirits of Harmonies
Thrones	Saturn	Thrones	Spirits of Will
Kyriotetes	Jupiter	Dominions	Spirits of Wisdom
Dynamis	Mars	Mights, Virtues	Spirits of Movement
Exsusiai	Sun	Powers	Spirits of Form
Archai	Venus	Principalities	Spirits of Personality
Archangeloi	Mercury	Archangels	Fire-Spirits
Angeloi	Moon	Angels	Sons of Life (Twilight)

Spiritual bilocation A term used in certain occult circles to denote the faculty of an individual to separate his higher bodies, such as the ASTRAL BODY, from the lower and to travel consciously, so that while his physical body remains in one part of the world his higher consciousness may be contemporaneously present in another part of the world.

Spiritual Hierarchies The name sometimes used to denote the CELESTIAL HIERARCHIES, in which the traditional nomenclature is given. In modern esotericism a system of names derived from the Theosophic tradition has been proposed by Steiner. This is now. widely used in occult circles. A comparative list is given in Table 26.

Spiritual Soul One of the names for the BUDDHI, and used by Steiner to denote that part of the soul which is connected with the ATMA, which develops through the development or transformation of the physical body. See SPIRIT MAN.

Spiritual Sun See ESOTERIC SUN.

Spirituale One of the *entia* of Paracelsus. This corresponds to the EGO body of Man. See ENS.

Spiritualism In the truest sense of the word this term applies to a doctrine which affirms that everything material in the universe is vitalized by a universal spirit – that, indeed, the material is itself symbol of a realm spiritual. However, in its commonly accepted meaning 'spiritualism' is a term applied to a body of teachings and practices involved with mediumistic communication with the supposed spirits of the dead (see SEANCE) or with psychic entities of a non-material nature,

such as POLTERGEISTS, MATERIALIZATIONS and the like. Blavatsky points out that such activities as seek to 'materialize' the spiritual lead to 'the degredation of the human and the divine souls. Believers in such communications are simply dishonouring the dead and performing constant sacrilege.' Naturally Blavatsky is presenting the occultist point of view, and the truth is that occultism and spiritualism are basically opposed in their aims and philosophies. Spiritualism in its modern practices is actually an extension of the ancient SCIOMANCY, although it is often wrongly linked with NECROMANCY.

Splanchnomancy A term derived from the Greek *splanchna* ('inner parts'), and now used to refer to a method of predicting the future similar to that used by the Etruscans (see HARUSPEX), who foretold the future from the inspection of the warm and palpitating entrails of victims.

Spleen chakra See SVADHISHTHANA.

Spodomancy Divination from the appearance of cinders in fires, originally from the cinders and remains in fires on sacrificial altars.

Spook A general term for a ghost or apparition. See SHADE.

Square An aspect of 90 degrees. Since planets (or nodal points) separated by 90 degrees must be in signs which are opposed in their elemental natures, it is clear that such planets must find themselves working inharmoniously.

Star calendar zodiac A zodiac of constellations of unequal length, originally specified approximately in its present form by Vreede and

Schultz in 1929, and slightly corrected *circa* 1972, but based loosely on indications given by Steiner in 1912 in his own star calendar (*Sternkalender*) of that year, which reverted to an astronomical zodiac of unequal divisions.

Star daemon   An esoteric name for the human being.

Star of Bethlehem   Name given to the so-called star followed by the Wise Men from the East, mentioned in chapter 2 of the Gospel according to St Matthew. While most occultists are aware that the star was actually a unique astral light, there have been many attempts by historians and astrologers to identify the star in ordinary astronomical terms. Fulcanelli echoes the esoteric tradition when he says quite bluntly that this was not an ordinary star of the heavens, but a certain 'virtue and power' which had merely taken on the form of a star. See MAGIAN.

Star of Mary   See STELLA MARIS.

Star of the Sea   See STELLA MARIS.

Stareomancy   A variant spelling of 'stereomancy', a term derived from the Greek *stereos* ('solid') and *manteia* (divination) and applied to a method of predicting the future from the elements. While obscure in reference to a particular form of divination, it may be applied to what Agrippa called the 'four famous kinds of divination' which use the four elements – GEOMANCY (Earth), HYDROMANCY (Water), AEROMANCY (Air) and PYROMANCY (Fire).

Starry Cup   A term derived from Macrobius and usually claimed to relate to the constellation Crater, though Macrobius himself says that his 'mystic secret' of the Starry Cup is placed between Cancer and Leo, and refers the idea of the cup to the Bacchic intoxication 'first experienced by souls in their descent by the influx of matter into them'. This account is clearly linked with the idea of the GATE OF BIRTH, located in Cancer.

Steganography   A term (perhaps originated by the esotericist Trithemius) from the Greek *steganos* ('hidden') and *graphein* ('to write'), to denote a system of secret writing based on the substitution of letters of the alphabet within a system of simple rules. See also SECRET SCRIPTS.

Stella maris   Latin term usually translated as 'Star of the Sea', and sometimes applied directly to the Virgin Mary, although more properly to the star which is associated with the Virgin Mary (most often depicted on her dress or upon her mapharion). This star may be traced back to the prototype of early Marian symbolism, the Egyptian Isis who was also called Star of the Sea, though some authorities identify it with the fixed star Sirius. Astrologically the star on the clothing of Mary is derived from the fixed star SPICA, the lucida of Virgo, which was, of course, also associated with Isis and Mary.

Stellar music   See MUSIC OF THE SPHERES.

Stellatum   One of the several names given to the sphere of fixed stars in the cosmoconception derived from the Aristotelian system. This was at one time believed to be the sphere of the *Primum mobile*, which imparted motion to the planetary spheres. Beyond the Stellatum the universe itself ended. It seems that within the early cosmoconceptions there was no precise distinction made between the zodiac and the realm of the fixed stars. See SPHERES OF HEAVEN.

Sternomancy   A method of divination, of obscure form, said to be derived from the consultation of the area of the body occupied by the sternum.

Sthula sarira   The name for the physical body in oriental occultism. See SARIRA.

Stoicheiomancy   A term presumed to be derived from the Greek *staicheiomanticoi* ('those who cast horoscopes'), but applied to a method of divining by the random opening of a book, such as Virgil or the Bible, and taking the first paragraph on the page as an answer to an already formulated question.

Stolisomancy   An ancient form of divination, apparently based on the chance accident of dress.

Strix   See VAMPIRE.

Subterraneans   See INFERNAL HIERARCHIES.

Subtle Body   A term used specifically by Mead in his study of the origins, in both pagan and Christian sources, of the ideas connected with the AUGOEIDES, a spiritual body which he maintained had been misunderstood in modern occult circles. In this study Mead reintroduced many ancient terminologies into the mainstream of modern occultism. These terms included his new definition of the Augoeides, which was the 'form of splendour', sometimes called the 'Astroeides' (the 'starlike' body). Mead insisted that the Augoeides was a spiritual body joined to the physical by a light-spark at a point in or near the head, rather than being a sort of aura around the physical body as is generally supposed. Another term is the 'Helioedes' (the 'Sunlike' body), which appears to be the original Augoeides when working in connection with pure reasoning; when not so working it appears to have been called the 'Aetherial Body' (in Greek, *aitherion*).

One of the most important terms relating to the Subtle Body is 'Perfect Body', a term sometimes given to the quintessential 'Resurrectional Body' of the early Christians. This Perfect Body does not appear to have been a sort of 'reborn body in the flesh' (as the idea of 'resurrection' was translated in later times) but rather a Subtle Body which was gradually developed in the ATMAN) as a result of the perfecting of the forces inherent within the physical body; it was indeed the spiritually 'perfected body' rather than the 'perfect body'. This view of the Resurrectional Body (or of the Perfect Body) in no way militated against the Christian view of the Resurrection of Christ, but simply maintained that the forces inherent within the physical body would eventually resurrect, or be transformed anew, to make an altogether more spiritual element available to man. The term suggests rather that the truly cosmic nature of the Resurrection was misunderstood in later times and (to judge from the terminologies used and from the texts available) was certainly understood in a different way in early Christian circles. Mead himself, although seemingly reluctant to give definitions, appears to call this Perfect Body the 'Radiant Body', linking it specifically with the pagan stream of early Gnostic and Neo-Platonic schools. The Christian version of this body was the 'Resurrectional Body', of course, and one notes that this Subtle Body was 'materialized' into a resurrected fleshly body in the third century, by Tertullian, in a view which was opposed (on spiritual grounds) by Origen, who saw the Resurrection Body (of Christ, and eventually of all developed men) as being of a supernal spiritual nature, and not of a carnal or fleshly nature at all.

Succubus A demon in the form of a woman, who seeks to have carnal intercourse with men. See INCUBUS.

Sukra A Sanskrit name for the planet Venus.

Sukshma sarira A Sanskrit term sometimes translated as 'dream body', a name given to the immaterial bodies of the gods.

Sulphur In alchemy a name used to veil the forces of the will in man. See THREE PRINCIPLES.

Summerland The name given by the American clairvoyant Davis to a spiritual region of great beauty and civilized life which is inhabited by human beings after the physical death. It seems to be a materialistic vision of DEVACHAN.

Sun In astrology the solar body is termed a 'planet' simple because the traditions and nomenclatures attached to it were established during the time when the majority of astrological systems were geocentric. In the alchemico-esoteric system of Boehme the Sun is the fourth form of the SEVEN PROPERTIES, the creative burst of lightning flash which is said by some commentators to be the explosion of spirit into time (an excellent description of the solar activity, from an occult point of view). The sigil for the Sun ☉ is sometimes said to represent the circle of spirit containing the central seed or nascent soul, although this sigil cannot be traced back in an astrological context beyond the fifteenth century. In ancient times the sigil ☉ was (as a hieroglyphic) an Egyptian determinative for 'god', and in early Christian symbolism was used as a sigil and glyph for Christ. The late-medieval sigil for the Sun was the Greek form ♂ .

The Sun has rule over zodiacal Leo, is exalted in Aries and has its fall in Libra. It represents the conscious element in the native and is usually studied as providing an index of the creative self-expression of the personality. An emphatic Sun in a chart is usually an indication of creative or artistic ability, as of a physical dignity and self-reliance, and often of a generous, affectionate and commanding nature. A badly placed Sun tends towards excess, so that the native is often showy, ostentatious, overconfident, egotistical and selfish. Traditionally the Sun rules the heart of the melothesic man, and is also connected with the blood, even though it is the opposite sign Aquarius that properly rules the circulation of the blood. The Sun is a useful index of how the vital forces work through the physical body; this is because spiritual (as well as physical) energies are derived ultimately from the Sun. The solar type is one who finds such energies easily and is able to transmit them for the benefit of those around within the immediate environment. He or she is therefore often involved with activities demanding exertion and authority, even with creative enterprises on a large scale, as well as with outlets associated with the FIFTH HOUSE. Solar types seek positions where power, dignity and responsibility may be combined. They make good executives and, while generous, are not always good accountants or even very careful with money (especially the money of other people). The metal of the Sun is gold, the ruling Archangel is Michael. See TIPHERETH.

Sun forces A term which originated in the esoteric astrology favoured by Stein, based upon a specific cosmic interpretation of the dualism which pervades all occultism. Stein pictures the fundamental contrast underlying phenomena as the working of the dual Sun forces and the MOON FORCES: the former radiate and liberate, while the latter concentrate and wither. In fact, Stein appears to use the terms as modern equivalents for the power of ORMUZD (the modern name for which is often given as 'LUCIFER') and Angramainyu (the modern name for which is often given as 'AHRIMAN'), derived from the ancient dualism of Zoroastrianism.

Sun Period A term which has nothing to do with the cycle of the Sun, or indeed with any SOLAR PERIOD. As a specialist term it is derived from modern esoteric astrology, relating to cosmogenesis. The Sun is said to be the second of the planetary states in the genesis of our world; it was initially a gaseous ball of warm light, from which the present solar system eventually evolved. This early period was overseen by the hierarchy of CHERUBIM. The Sun Period is sometimes called 'Old Sun'. See MOON PERIOD and SATURN PERIOD.

Sun Revolution A term derived from modern esoteric astrology and relating to cosmogenesis (see SUN PERIOD). It is said that the path of evolution of our present solar system, with its

periods of activity and *pralaya* (sleep), as indeed the growth of every organic being, must recapitulate, however briefly, the entire sequence of evolution. Since the first stage of the cosmogenesis of our present system began in Saturn (see SATURN PERIOD) and reached its second stage in the Sun Period, the term 'Sun Revolution' pertains to the second of these recapitulations, which is essentially one of 'warmth–light'.

Sun sign The sign of the zodiac in which the sun is placed at a specific moment, or in a particular horoscope chart.

Sunya A Sanskrit term (sometimes *shunya*) usually translated in esoteric literature as meaning 'illusion' and applied to the dreamlike and shadowy existence of the objective universe. The *sunyata* is the nothingness of the universe. Unfortunately the same term also means the 'space of heaven' and 'ether'.

Supernatural Ilech An esoteric name for the invisible influence which links the material realm with the stellar realm, but see ILECH.

Sura A general Sanskrit term for the gods, but see also ASURAS.

Surya A Sanskrit word for the Sun, as used in Hindu astrology.

Sushumna See BRAHMARANDHRA.

Sutratman A Sanskrit compound meaning approximately 'thread of self' or 'thread of spirit'. The *sutratman* is the thread of consciousness which runs through all the various principles which constitute the human being, and which holds together the digest of all experiences within the numerous incarnations granted to man. See also PRANA.

Svadhishthana The six-rayed CHAKRA between the Root chakra and the Navel chakra, and located approximately over the spleen of the human body.

Svati Name given to the thirteenth of the Hindu NAKSHATRAS.

Sweat-born A name given by nineteenth-century Theosophists to a previous race of man, the second and third of the ROOT RACES, already atavistic by the time of LEMURIA. They were born not through the union of separate sexes but by a sort of fissiparous creative act of a single individual.

Sycomancy   Divination by means of the leaves of the fig tree. Questions are written on leaves and the rate of drying of the leaf is interpreted in terms of the questions proposed.

Sydonay   One of the names for ASMODAY.

Sylphs   The class of ELEMENTALS linked with Air. They correspond to the Nenuphars of esoteric lore, while in the astrological correspondences of the CALENDARIA MAGICA they are often called 'Aerei'.

Symbol   The term 'symbol' is used very loosely in occult circles to cover such different concepts as IMAGES, SIGILS and SEALS. In a strictly occult sense, however, a symbol is something which stands for or represents something else. However, a true symbol is intended to be more than merely a representative, for it should in some way act as a sort of commentary on the nature of that thing. Perhaps the most useful definition is that provided by the historian Haase, who writes of the symbol as being 'essentially purposive' in that 'it points to some Higher Order for whose characteristics it is a kind of abbreviation'. The true nature of symbolism is perhaps most profoundly expressed in the Egyptian *medu-neters*, which the Greeks called 'hieroglyphics' ('secret writings'). Each hieroglyphic had at least three related meanings: one was strictly spiritual, being linked with the equivalent of our archetypes; one was linked with the potential of the thing symbolized; and a third was linked with the hitherto unrealized potential of the thing in itself. In addition to these united triadic meanings, the symbol was intensified by the name ascribed to it, which (in Egyptian symbolism at least) was associated with a spiritual cosmic language which would now be regarded as purely magical.

Such an ancient view of symbolism – set out by de Lubicz – is to some extent still preserved in esoteric circles, but has been largely lost to modern thought, so that the union which once existed between the image, sigil, seal and sign (which found a single form in hieroglyphics) has been subject to fissiparous tendencies. The result is that, while each word has obviously a common

ideological reference, each now refers to a different system of symbolizing – the image through representation, the sigil through graphic symbolism, the seal through magical and numerologically originated symbols, and signs through a (formerly) numious symbolism.

Sympathetic magic   A special form of MAGIC involved with exercising an influence upon a being or entity at a distance through the medium of some object which is in some way representative of that entity. The most common form of sympathetic magic is that in which the sorcerer manufactures an image of a person, in wax or clay or some easily worked material, and then treats this image (sometimes called a 'POPPET') in a destructive way in order to bring about the illness or demise of the person it represents (see WAX IMAGE). The aim of sympathetic magic is not always the demise or illness of an individual or creature, although in almost all cases the magician seeks to exercise power over the subject. Indeed, one of the most frequently used rituals is that designed to obtain the sexual favours of another, involving complex SPELLS and images (models or photographs) of the sexual object.

In sympathetic magic few things are more potent, more representative of the 'whole', than the name of the thing. It is for this reason that the magician who knows the secret name of a spirit or demon is said to have real power over that being. It is for this reason also that a magician must name the clay or waxen poppet with the same name of the person he wishes to influence or harm, before his magic spell is cast. The occultist Fludd calls the force used in sympathetic magic 'MUMIA', a word he probably took from Paracelsus. He seems to have believed that this mumia might be found in blood and that it could be drawn out with a magnet, thence to be projected into external material objects to make poppets or other images. There are many names used for this power of magic, however – there is the *mana* of the Kahuna, the *waken* of the Sioux Indians, the *orenda* of the Iroquois, and so on.

Sympathetic magic is intimately bound up with the concept of the EVIL EYE. Thus the cowrie shell, which so resembles the human eye, is often strung to make necklaces which will (by virtue of the sympathetic force) avert the evil eye. Many charms are constructed on the principle that the drawing or resemblance of an eye will turn back the *jettatura* on sympathetic grounds. The doctrine of SIGNATURES is also embedded in concepts of sympathetic powers and magic.

See also MAGIC NAILS.

Sympathy   In its specialist astrological sense this term appears to have two separate applications. The word is used to denote that force, subtle influence or spiritual empathy which links all things in union within the CHAIN OF BEING. The same term is used also to describe individual relationships between creatures and things: all sublunary things are visualized as being either 'in sympathy' or 'in antipathy', depending upon the elemental, planetary and zodiacal forces involved. Thus a dog (under the rulership of Mars) would not be 'in sympathy' with a cat (under the rulerships of Venus), and so on.

Synastry   A term used to denote that branch of ASTROLOGY which deals with the study of agreements and disagreements reflected in pairs of charts cast for two people (or in charts cast for groups of people).

Synchronicity   A term popularized by C. G. Jung, who sought to designate a psychic parallelism between events which cannot be related causally. The parallelism, or connectedness, between such non-causally related events and happenings he dubbed 'synchronistic'. The word explains nothing, of course, but initiates a sort of spiritual causality, the laws of which are unknown. The origin of the word is partly derived from Jung's acquaintance with the I CHING, the true nature of which he failed to appreciate fully. In the Western tradition it is believed that the *I Ching* works as a divinatory method by the random fall of sticks and coins, within a fixed ritual. It appears, therefore, to be non-causal. However, the Chinese themselves insist that the working of the oracle is not in any sense involved with synchronisms, but is operated by spiritual beings; it is therefore a divinatory technique involving animistic causality.

Sytry   One of the SPIRITS OF SOLOMON, said to appear in the winged body of a human, though with the head of a variety of different wild animals. He is said to have the power to make any woman display herself naked before the conjuring magician.

Syzygy   A term derived from the Greek meaning 'a yoking together' and used most especially of the conjunction between the Sun and Moon.

The twentieth letter of the alphabet, associated with the Hebraic TAU and given the numerical value of 400. It is significant that our modern T is a modification of the earlier X, the 'foundation framework of construction', as Blavatsky puts it. When the T and the S are combined into one sigil, they are said to represent the healing Mercury or the CADUCEUS
. The numerological reduction of 400 (T) and 60 (S) gives 1 (460 = 4 + 6 + 0 = 10 = 1). The reduction of the magical 10 to the individuality of 1 is symbolic of the Mercurial healing power, which seeks always to reintegrate the individuality into the healing embrace of the cosmos (see TEN), that he or she may emerge once again as a separate and healed individuality.

Table turning   A popular method of consulting spiritual agencies in SEANCES. Those present in such a gathering will rest their fingertips on the top of a small table, their fingers touching to form a chain or circle. Under certain circumstances the table will begin to move – to rotate, turn or even rise completely from the ground. The direction of movement (towards letters of the alphabet on the table or in agreed response to questions) is taken as being oracular. See also ECTENIC FORCE.

Tabula Smaragdina   The occult name ('Emerald Tablet') given by occultists to an alchemical tablet which was said to contain twelve cryptic hermetic statements. It is claimed that the sayings were engraved on a plate of emerald held in the hands of the dead body of Hermes TRISMEGISTUS. The tablet itself is lost, and the oldest certain reference to it which has survived is of the eighth century AD.

Tactile metagnomy   A term used by Sudry to denote PSYCHOMETRY.

T'ai Chi symbol   See YIN AND YANG.

Taijasi   A Sanskrit term etymologically linked with *tejas* (see TATTVA) and used to denote the thought body (*manasa rupa*) as well as the stars.

Talisman   A word said to be derived from the Arabian *tilism* ('magic image') and applied to specially prepared objects – of stone, metal, wood, parchment and so on – inscribed with magical drawings, sigils or characters. See CHARM and TALISMANIC MAGIC.

Talismanic magic   From the very earliest times the various astrological SIGILS, SEALS and IMAGES have been engraved or stamped on metal or pottery talismans to make portable charms; a large number of these have survived in artefacts and in magical images (see TALISMAN). A complex procedure was supposed to attend the production of the genuine talisman: not only had it to be made under the correct astrological conditions (under the appropriate planetary hour and so on), but it had to be manufactured in the metal or gem related to the planetary or stellar forces being evoked in the charm. Wherever possible many of the more potent images, sigils, symbols and

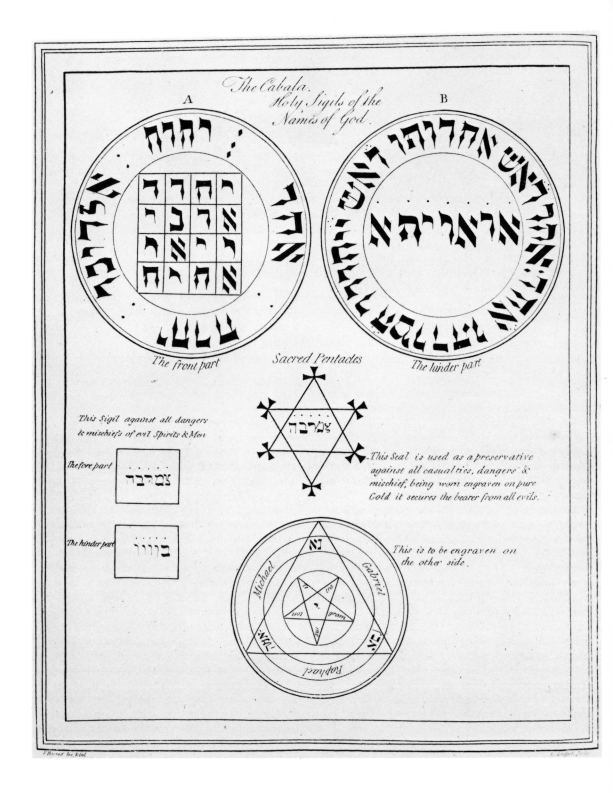

Figure 77   *A selection of Qabbalistic talismans, evoking the names of God (after Barrett)*

Figure 78 *Three talismans – the first Christian (using the Chi Rho symbol), the second occult (using sigils of the zodiac and the inverted pentagram linked with Venus), and the third Qabbalistic (after Agrippa)*

names were combined into one talismanic form. The result is that there are literally thousands of medieval manuscripts dealing with the art of talismanic magic which, in one form or another, is linked with traditional methods of astrology (Figure 77). A complex art of talismanic symbolism has been attached both to constellations and to fixed stars (in connection with the latter, see FIFTEEN STARS). The talismanic use of seals, sigils and images relating to the decans was highly complex and at times resulted in the most interesting symbols (Figure 78). The use of zodiacal and planetary sigils and images for talismanic ends is almost in itself a chapter in the history of astrology, but very many of the medieval astrological manuscripts touch in one way or another on the magical power or significance of the basic sigils, as the writings of Agrippa (mainly eclectic) confirm. Peter of Abano was one of the most influential astrologers to adapt the Christian symbolism to zodiacal and planetary sigils and images. For specific examples of talismanic bases, see PENTAGRAM, PENTALPHA, SEAL OF SOLOMON and TETRACTYS.

Tamas A Sanskrit term for the lowest of the TRIGUNAS. It represents the quality of inertia, darkness and ignorance.

Tanha A Pali word meaning 'thirst' and applied to that thirst for the world which brings the disincarnate MONAD, or Ego, back into reincarnation. Occultists see this as more than merely a thirst to live in the physical plane, but rather as a thirst for the freedom to work out karmic responsibilities which reincarnation affords.

Tantra A Sanskrit term meaning literally 'rule' or 'ritual', but applied mainly in respect of the worship of the power of SAKTI.

Tap One of the many versions of GAAP.

Taphos The name given to the sarcophagus of the INITIATION Mysteries.

Taphthartharath Name given by Agrippa (quoting ancient Qabbalistic sources) to the DAEMON of Saturn, for whom he gives the magical number 2080, which is a multiple of the number of Mercury (8) and the linear addition of the Mercurial MAGIC SQUARE. See also TIRIEL.

Tarot A set of cards used for the purpose of divination, the name probably derived from the name of the Italian card game Tarocchi. A full pack consists of seventy-eight cards, twenty-two of which are picture cards called 'atouts' or the 'Major Arcana', and fifty-six being the 'Minor Arcana', which resemble in some respects ordinary playing cards. The connection between the Major and Minor is at best a tenuous one, and generally it is the Major set which is used for divination. The atouts each consists of a picture of a deeply symbolic nature (Figure 79), in which the colours, forms, graphic devices and iconographic allusions combine to stimulate the mind of the clairvoyant using the cards. The numerical order of the Major Arcana and their equivalent names in English, French and Italian are set out in Table 27 (p. 221). The original designs are of uncertain provenance, although almost certainly earlier than the sixteenth century and probably from an

THE WORLD

THE MOON

JUDGEMENT

THE FOOL

Figure 79   *Four major arcana of the Marseilles pack: 'The World', 'The Moon', 'Judgement' and 'The Fool' – the zero card*

LA·LUNE

IL BAGATTEL.

Figure 80   *Three examples of different atouts: 'The Moon' card to the left is French, late eighteenth century; the central card is a specialist atout from a French pack, also eighteenth century; the card to the right is Italian, printed in the nineteenth century*

Table 27

Card	English	French	Italian
1	The Juggler	Le Bateleur	Il Bagatto
2	The Lady Pope	La Papesse	La Papessa
3	The Empress	L'Impératrice	La Imperatrice
4	The Emperor	L'Empereur	L'Imperatore
5	The Pope	Le Pape	Il Papa
6	The Lovers	L'Amoureux	L'Amore
7	The Chariot	Le Chariot	La Carozza
8	Justice	La Justice	La Giustizia
9	The Hermit	L'Hermite	L'Eremita
10	The Wheel of Fortune	La Roue de Fortune	La Ruota
11	Strength	La Force	La Forza
12	The Hanging Man	Le Pendu	L'Impicato
13	(An untitled image of death)		
14	Temperance	La Tempérance	La Temperanza
15	The Devil	Le Diable	Il Diavolo
16	The House of God	La Maison Dieu	La Torre
17	The Star	L'Etoile	La Stella
18	The Moon	La Lune	La Luna
19	The Sun	Le Soleil	Il Sole
20	Judgement	Le Jugement	Il Giudizio
21	The World	Le Monde	Il Mondo
	The Fool	Le Mat	Il Pazzo

Italian source. The majority of modern designs are not the product of an esoteric lore, as were the originals, but mainly a result of individual imagination and fantasy. In modern times the atouts of the French Marseilles pack (sometimes called the Grimaud pack) approximate most closely to the intentions of the original designers. The last card, sometimes called the zero card, is the only one not numbered in the sequence.

The three Tarot cards in Figure 80 illustrate interesting aspects of the rich tradition of symbolism which has been built around this pack. The French 'Moon' card to the left shows the astrological strain of symbolism, for the image of the crayfish in the waters below the Moon is a reference to the zodiacal sign Cancer (ruled by the Moon). In early forms of astrology the image for Cancer was more often that of a crayfish than a crab. The central card belongs to a rather special set used for divination – one might easily assume that this picture is a reference to the zodiacal sign Scorpio, but in fact it is an image of the constellation Scorpius, which carries a different set of occult associations to the corresponding zodiacal sign. The Italian card to the right has a Hebraic letter, Aleph, at the top. This reminds us that from relatively early times the sequence of twenty-two cards was associated with the sequence of twenty-two letters of the Hebraic alphabet, according to a complex theory of numerological symbolism.

Tat In occult contexts this word has two different meanings. First, it is a Sanskrit-derived word meaning 'that', which is reference to the unnamed principle from which the cosmos arose. It is contrasted with *idam* ('this'), which refers to the creations of this principle. Secondly, 'tat' may refer to an Egyptian symbol or AMULET which consists of an upright with four crosspieces, representing (it is said) the four principles of the human quaternary.

Tattva Sometimes *tattwa*, a Sanskrit word introduced into Western occultism by the Theosophists, and meaning approximately 'measure' or 'frequency of vibration' with reference to the nature of the original substance underlying the universe. The *tattvas* have their correspondence on each of the planes of existence: the *prithivi* is that of the physical plane, the *apas* that of the astral plane, and the *tejas* of the mental plane. These have been linked with the European elements of Earth, Water and Fire respectively. In the Sankhya system there are listed as many as twenty-five *tattvas*; however, within the

European occult system the term is usually restricted to the three, though sometimes they are linked with a sevenfold system, in reference to the lower three of the human quaternary and the higher TERNARY.

Tau   The name given to the T cross, sometimes described as the earliest of the Christian crosses. In fact, its form is that of an early Egyptian AMULET, to be distinguished from the *Crux ansata*. See ANKH.

Taurus   The name of the second sign of the zodiac, the celestial Bull. As a sign Taurus corresponds neither in location nor significance with the constellation of the same name, which is linked by Qabbalists with the first letter of the Hebraic alphabet, Aleph (itself derived from a vestigial drawing of an oxhead), and with the TAROT arcanum of 'The Juggler', which as the zero card stands at either the end or the beginning of the sequence. In occultism the sign was associated with the first-born solar gods and is linked graphically with the letter A. This connection with beginnings (of the alphabet and of the Tarot sequence) is linked esoterically with the idea that at the beginning of Western civilization (*c.* 4000 BC) the sign marked the beginning of the zodiac, with the vernal equinox falling in the first degrees of Taurus, with the lucida of Taurus (Aldebaran) as fiducial. The SIGIL for Taurus ♉ is said by some to be a drawing of the head and horns of the bull, with which image Taurus is associated. However, in the esoteric tradition it has been suggested that this is a vestigial drawing of the larynx, with the Eustachian tubes, linking the idea of speech with the idea of listening. This is sometimes used as an explanation as to why the image of the bull is at times linked with Christ, for within both Taurus and Christ are contained the idea of the Logos or Word, as well as the idea of sacrifice. The bull was regarded as a symbol of the procreative power, and hence of the Logos. Blavatsky suggests that the horns of the sigil represent the horns on the head of Isis: 'Ancient mystics saw the ansated cross, in the horns of Taurus (the upper portion of the Hebrew Aleph) pushing away the Dragon and Christians connected the sign and constellation with Christ. . . . The Egyptians called it "the interpreter of the divine voice".'

Taurus is of the EARTH ELEMENT and of the Fixed quality, the influence being constructive, strong-willed, conservative, slow, practical and sensuous. The nature of Taurus, as it manifests in human beings, is expressed in the many key words which have been attached to it by modern astrologers: practical, slow, heavy, possessive, conservative, intractable, relentless – in a word, all those qualities which may be associated with an Earth type expressing itself with determination. In excess the Taurean nature may be described in terms which express an underlying inertia, curiously married with a sort of magmatic violence which erupts when the subject is goaded: overbearing, deeply jealous, fixed in attitude, tyrannical, coarse, gluttonous, repetitive, selfish and unexpectedly violent or cruel. Taurus is ruled by the planet Venus, which accounts for the fact that so many Taureans are fair in form and are also frequently associated with a beautiful or rich voice. The sign marks the exaltation of the Moon and (according to some modern schemas) the fall of Uranus. In common with the other three fixed signs of the zodiac, Taurus is linked with the imagery of the TETRAMORPH and specifically with the Evangelist Luke.

Teacher   See MAHATMA.

Tejas   See TATTVA.

Telegram   A word used in an occult context by Andrew Jackson Davis with regard to communications with higher levels of being: 'A telegram from a person in the Summerland is a pulsation (in my case) on the left temple imparting words inwardly to the mind.'

Telekinesis   A term used to denote the supposed faculty of moving material objects by means of thought or some invisible and unusual agency. An APPORT is made telekinetically.

Telepathy   A term used to denote direct understanding between minds without resort to written, verbal or physical means of communication.

Tellurism   An alternative name for ANIMAL MAGNETISM.

Temperaments   The Grecian medical theory of HUMOURS which so radically influenced the development of occult ideas was based on a fundamental tetrad which linked bodily fluids with certain mental dispositions, the so-called tempers or temperaments. These temperaments

Table 28

Temperament	Element	Zodiacal signs
Phlegmatic	Water	Cancer, Scorpio, Pisces
Melancholic	Earth	Taurus, Virgo, Capricorn
Choleric	Fire	Aries, Leo, Sagittarius
Sanguine	Air	Gemini, Libra, Aquarius

were distinguished eventually as the CHOLERIC, MELANCHOLIC, PHLEGMATIC and SANGUINE, the etymologies for which are in each case derived from a corresponding Greek term for the humour. This tetrad of temperaments was linked to the tetrad of ELEMENTS, and was accordingly reflected in the structure of the zodiac, as indicated in the schema set out in Table 28.

Temurah A Hebraic term meaning 'change' and used to denote one of the interpretative methods of Qabbalistic manipulative techniques with verbal analogies. Words and letters are subjected to change by the substitution of one letter for another, or by the changing of the orders of letters in words, according to definite principles. This substitution (or permutation) of letters in words gives new words which, by analogic inference, are regarded as being linked with the original word. The same term is also used to denote methods of constructing alphabetic codes by means of artificial correspondences; for example, by folding the alphabet so that the lower and upper letters may be regarded as interchangeable:

A B C D E F G H I J K L M
N O P Q R S T U V W X Y Z
or
M L K J I H G F E D C B A
N O P Q R S T U V W X Y Z

A code might be constructed using each of these series alternately: for example, the code '*grnhins*' would read '*temurah*'.

Temurah is sometimes confused with GEMATRIA and NOTARICON.

Ten The most mystic of all the NUMBERS for it is the sum of the magic SEVEN and the holy THREE, while its form in Western script points to the two contrasts in the created universe – the expansive direct of the single upright, which links heaven with earth, and the eternity of the circle, which points to spiritual matters. The single unit or monad of the upright is linked with the individuation principle of the human being, with the Ego, which sets him apart from the universe as a whole – see therefore ONE. The circle is symbolic of the spiritual realm, which seeks to enclose all created forms, without distinction of individuality – see therefore TWO. What is important about the 1 and the 0 in the figure 10 is the space between them, the space which separates the unique Ego of the upright 1 (the 'I' in English) from the rest of the universe, the zero beyond the I. The importance of this space makes the figure 10 into a triad (upright 1, space and zero); hence the 10 links with 3 in its form, as much as in its relationship with the 7. This 3 will combine with the 1 of the figure 10 to make FOUR. The 10 divides in on itself (since it consists of two figures) to produce FIVE. The 3 will multiply by the duality of its form to give SIX, and so on. This is why in occult terms it may be said that within the 10 lie all created things and the secrets of such things. Part of its magic is that, while within its form all things are contained, it reduces back to 1, constantly moving in from the periphery back to the centre, and then out again to form the 10. Many of the deeper levels of occult sigils are linked with the interplay of the upright and the zero, and with the connotations of numerology which this interplay carries with it.

Tenth Heaven Name given to the outer of the SPHERES, which was regarded as being totally motionless, the dwelling of God and his ministering angels. It was sometimes called the 'Empyrean', although this term (at least after the medieval period) was sometimes used of all the spheres beyond the lunar sphere (see, however, Figure 86 under ZODIAC). In the early diagrammatic and literary accounts of the spheres there was no tenth sphere, no Tenth Heaven, the ninth sphere being the *Primum mobile*. Eventually, however, perhaps for theological reasons, the *Primum movens* was separated from the Ninth Heaven, at one time the Stellatum, to become a distinct sphere beyond it. The classification of the basic spheres (in the outer limits, at least) therefore depends upon context and upon the period under review.

Tenth Hierarchy A name sometimes given to man, who dwells at the lowest level of the hierarchies, below the Ninth Hierarchy of the angels.

Tenth sphere See TENTH HEAVEN.

Table 29

Higher ternary	Lower ternary	Complete man	Quaternary	Religious image
Atma		Atman		Spirit
Buddhi		Buddhi		Spirit
Manas		Manas		Spirit
		Ego	Ego	Soul
	Astral	Astral	Astral	Soul
	Etheric	Etheric	Etheric	Soul
	Physical	Physical	Physical	Body

Tephillim   A Hebraic term for a special
AMULET consisting of a written charm (or prayer)
enclosed within a leather case. See also
PHYLACTERY.

Tephramancy   Divination from the ashes of
victims burned in sacrificial fires. Some define it as
'divination by means of sacrificial flames', which
is to say that it is a subdivision of PYROMANCY.

Teraphim   A word used to denote small idols
or figures used as TALISMANS, although in
esoteric contexts the Hebraic word also refers to
serpent images.

Ternary   When the term ternary is used in a
spiritual context there are usually two ternaries in
mind – the lower and the higher. The lower
ternary consists of the Physical, Etheric and Astral
bodies. The higher ternary consists of Atma,
Buddhi and Manas. Forming a link between these
two, the chain between Heaven and earth, is the
Ego. This is why in some cases the term 'quaternary' is used to describe the lower part of man,
which includes the Ego and the lower ternary.
Sometimes the ternary of body, soul and spirit is
also recognized in the religious image of man, as
set out in Table 29, although the relationship of
the Ego to the soul gives rise to various different
structures.

In an alchemical context the word 'ternary' is
sometimes used to point to the THREE
PRINCIPLES (see, however, TERNARY OF FIRE).
See also MONAD.

Ternary of fire   A term derived from Boehme's
esoteric astrology and linked with his SEVEN
PROPERTIES. It is the expression of the first three
principles (the planets Saturn, Mercury and
Mars), which is a ternary harmonized by the Sun.
This triad, sometimes called the 'ternary of
desire', is balanced against the ternary of light, as

set out in the schema below. The entire schema
points to the deepest esoteric insights into the
nature of the septenary being of man.

Saturn	Mercury	Mars	Sun	Venus	Jupiter	Moon
Fire				Light		

Ternary of light   See TERNARY OF FIRE.

Terrene body   See ORPHIC DESCENT OF THE
SOUL.

Tetaktys   One of the forms of TETRACTYS.

Tetractys   The name of God in four letters and a
word used to denote the binding oath of the
Pythagoreans. It is also a name given to a symbolic arrangement of ten points which has in one
way or another been incorporated into occult
symbolism, especially so in regard to numerological symbolism (see NUMBERS). While the
tetractys is usually traced back to the Pythagorean
school, the best exoteric treatment of its symbolism is found in Philo Judaeus, who treats it as
merely a matter of numerical sequence, as one of
the numerical triangles, which have a significance
mainly in regard to their corresponding numerical
squares. The schema below sets out the graphic
implications of the tetractys and explains why the
numbers are sometimes called 'triangles' and
'squares':

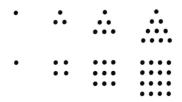

The philosophy of the septenary colours the
second of this series, which represents the four
physical elements and the spiritual triad. In

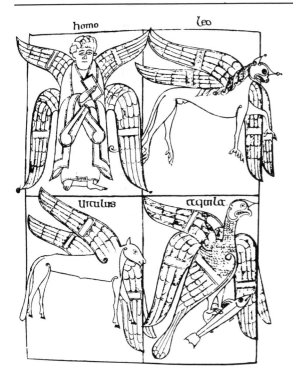

Figure 81 *Tetramorph: the four symbols of the Evangelists, derived from zodiacal imagery (drawing after an illuminated page in the ninth-century* Book of Armagh *in Trinity College, Dublin)*

esoteric terms the 4 of the square represents the union of the physical, Etheric, Astral and Ego bodies of man, while the 3 of the triangle represents the spiritual ternary (ATMAN, BUDDHI and MANAS) which man is required to develop in future incarnations.

This septenary, here applied only to man as the microcosm, may, of course, be used of other realms. The learned Kircher shows that the tetractys is to be understood in regard to the Qabbalistic numerology attached to the tetrad of the word 'IHVH' ('Jehovah'), of which the corresponding numbers are given below:

•	1	H = 10
••	2	VH = 15
•••	3	HVH = 21
••••	4	IHVH = 26

The total by means of this association of numbers is 72 – the magical number of the tetractys and one of the most pure of astrological symbolic numbers. This magical 72 is linked with the pulse rate of the human blood (the microcosmic 72) and with the fact that in 72 years the sun retrogrades

due to PRECESSION exactly 1 degree (the macrocosmic 72). As Blavatsky says, the tetractys 'has a very mystic and varied significance'. It is sometimes called the 'tetrad' or the 'mystic tetrad'.

Tetragrammaton The name of God in four letters: IHVH in the English version of the Hebraic Yod, He, Vau, He. Although generally pronounced 'Jehovah', the true pronunciation is unknown. See also TETRACTYS.

Tetramorph A term derived from the Greek, meaning 'of a fourfold form', and applied by occultists to a composite figure which unites in a single form the images of the four Fixed signs of the zodiac – Aquarius, Leo, Taurus and Scorpio – which are themselves linked with the four elements. The so-called Christian tetramorphs are actually four separate figures combining imagery related to the (pagan) four Fixed signs and associated by Christian apologists with the imagery in the Bible in Revelation, 4, 6–8, and Ezekiel, 1, 5–10, an imagery which is in any case derived from ancient pre-Christian astrological concepts. Figure 81 illustrates the Christian tradition for the four Evangelists. The figure marked 'homo' is the image of St Matthew, itself derived from the Air sign Aquarius, the waterbearer, figured as a human being with wings. The sacred book in his hands is the Christianized version of the water pot of the pagan figure, both urn and book being bearers of spiritual energy, the latter linked with the Logos or Word. The image marked 'leo' is the lion of St Mark, derived from the Fire sign Leo. The creature named 'vitulus' (the Latin for a young bull) is derived from the Earth sign Taurus and linked with St Luke. St John is linked with the Water sign Scorpio, symbolized by the 'aquila' or eagle, which holds in its talons a fish, almost certainly a symbol for Christ, whose story is recorded by the four Evangelists. The wings in the figure symbolize the Water rather than the Air element as they are associated with the eagle of Scorpio, the symbol of the regenerate Scorpionic nature (see EAGLE).

Blavatsky, in her esoteric treatment of the tetramorphs, points out that the 'man' of the Ezekiel symbolism was originally a dragon in Gnostic circles, especially with the Ophites, where the associations were in any case directly linked with four of the seven Archangels: the lion with Michael, the bull with Uriel, the eagle with

Gabriel and the dragon with Raphael. Something of this tradition still survives in esoteric symbolism.

Thanatism A term derived from the Greek *thanatos* ('death') and used to denote the belief that after death the human soul (the Ego or monad in esoteric terms) ceases to exist. It is, of course, a proposition entirely unacceptable to occultists.

Thanatomania A term derived from the same root as THANATISM and applied to the belief that one is fated to die as a result of certain evil influences. See, for example, the induced death wish of the DEATH PRAYER.

Tharana A Sanskrit term often translated as meaning 'mesmerism' or 'self-hypnosis', but derived from a word meaning 'to brush away' and applied to the idea of brushing away demons or bad influences; hence, a kind of EXORCISM.

Tharmas See FOUR ZOAS.

Thaumaturgy A term from the Greek words *thauma* ('wonder') and *theurgia* ('divine work'), usually translated as 'miracle working'.

Thaumiel A name given to the adversary of METATRON in the Sephirah KETHER.

Thema In early astrology a term used to denote a horoscope. The *Thema mundi* was the horoscope (of which there are several versions) for the creation of the world. See also SCHEMA.

Theolithos See LAPIS.

Theomancy A word from the Greek meaning 'divination through the gods' or 'divination by means of oracles'.

Theopneusty Divine inspiration.

Theopoea A Greek word used to denote the art of imbuing such inanimate objects as statues with life to permit speech or movement. Theopoea was practised widely in Roman temples, especially as a divinatory method, or in the service of ORACLES.

Theosophia A Greek word meaning 'divine wisdom' (from *theos* and *sophia* – 'god' and 'wisdom'). See THEOSOPHY.

Theosophy A term from the Greek THEOSOPHIA and in modern times applied to a corpus of knowledge received from the ancient Mysteries. In modern occultism the term 'Theosophists' is usually applied to the members of the Theosophical Society (founded New York, 1875), to the precisely formulated tenets of the revealed Mystery wisdom in the works of Blavatsky, and sometimes (though wrongly) to members of its schisms such as Anthroposophists. However, in earlier times the word was used of the followers and propounders of a wide variety of different esoteric systems, all more or less connected with the Secret Doctrine or with Mystery wisdom. The Alexandrian Neo-Platonists were called 'theosophists', as were many of the medieval alchemists and Qabbalists, as well as such individuals as Paracelsus and Boehme.

Theriomancy A term derived from the Greek *therio* ('wild beast') and *manteia* ('divination') and applied to a method of predicting the future from the movement of animals. The Romans in particular were fond of divining from the movement and direction taken by a liberated hare.

Theurgy A term from the Greek *theourgia*, usually translated as meaning 'sorcery' and originally applied to a Gnostic system of magic relating to the communication with angelic beings such as planetary spirits. Theurgists are those (usually trained in temples or esoteric schools) with the knowledge of the complex rules of CEREMONIAL MAGIC sufficient to make such communication efficacious. In modern use the term is frequently employed to distinguish white magic (theurgy) from the goety of black magic.

Third death See SECOND DEATH.

Third Eye A name given in occultism to the Brow CHAKRA, the AJNA of the oriental occultists. The term is radically misunderstood and misapplied in popular occultism, however. See also EYE OF DANGMA. The specialist in oriental chakric lore, Avalon, called the Third Eye the *Jnanachaksha*.

Third Heaven Usually this term is used synonymously with the third sphere within the concentrics of the spheres, which in the medieval occult cosmoconception was the sphere of Venus, associated in the Christian hierarchy with the ARCHAI. In the days when the sequence of the spheres was promulgated it was believed that Venus was nearer to the Sun than Mercury.

Third Hierarchy See CELESTIAL HIER-ARCHIES.

Third Race In the Theosophical cosmoconception the Third Root Race is the third of the seven human races, or streams of human evolution, sometimes called the Lemurian Race, which was said to occupy the almost completely lost continent of LEMURIA (or Shamali, as it was sometimes called), which covered approximately the present Pacific area. During this Root Race the separation of humanity into the two sexes took place. Lemuria is said to have perished before the beginning of the Eocene Age, and it was the last subrace of this epoch which is supposed to have left behind the famous gigantic statues in Easter Island (or at least their prototypes).

Third sphere See THIRD HEAVEN.

Thoth See TRISMEGISTUS.

Thought form An occult term originated by Leadbeater or Besant towards the end of the last century in connection with their clairvoyant researches. They teach that every thought issued by a human being gives rise to two effects: first, there is a vibration, which has the spiritual effect of reduplicating itself in other humans and thereby influencing their own thinking. Secondly, there is a distinct thought form, which is described as a spiritual force ensouled in the ELEMENTAL ESSENCE. This thought form is visible to a clairvoyant vision on the ASTRAL plane, and Leadbeater developed a technique of producing painted images of representative forms to show their appearance to the non-clairvoyant. In particular, he produced images of the appearance of musical forms on the astral plane (these had an influence on the development of modern abstract art, as Ringbom has shown). Other occultists describe thought forms mainly in terms of the colours which are associated with particular states of being, and in terms of the clarity of outline of the form, which reflects the precision of thought. The very fact that the occultists admit that thought forms are conditioned by emotional attitudes suggests that, rather than being pure thought forms, they are really 'emotion forms'. Annie Besant called thought

forms 'Astro-mental images', intending to show that they are secondary forms, derived from the MANAS, but existing on the astral level.

Thread soul A translation of the Sanskrit SUTRATMA.

Three With 3 we find a breath of release from the development of the 1 into a 2, by which a relationship had been established $(1 + 2 = 3)$. In a sense 3 stands for that relationship itself, which is, from an occult point of view, a separate entity which arises from the meeting and merging of two people or of two separate entities. This is why 3 is sometimes called the 'Cosmic Breath', the 'Lucky Number', and why it is obviously linked with the human TERNARY, as indeed with all ternaries in the world and spiritual realm. In some systems it is regarded as the equivalent of the Hebraic Gimel. The figure 3 is called a scattered figure, for its two half-loops do not contain, as does the 0, so that it tends to be prodigal of its powers and forces. It is Mercurial and therefore androgyne in its direction and inclinations, containing within it the male 1 and the female 2 (see ANDROGYNE). Being Mercurial it is intellectual, and is linked with the sign Virgo, which makes it a healer, and this explains why the 3 is said to be the principal number of expression and to be a teacher. Three is the number of light. It combines with 4, which is the number of life, to make 7, the septenary of union. Three is the number of fruitful Earth, linked with the Greek Gaia, who is the goddess of the Earth and who is associated with the third letter of the Hebraic and Greek alphabet. However, the Earth in autumn and winter is associated with the number 6, and in spring and summer with the number 7 (a sort of reversal or mirror image of the Greek gamma). See NUMBERS.

Three Fires A name given to the human TERNARY of Atma, Buddhi and Manas.

Three principles Essentially an alchemical doctrine (put into open script by Paracelsus and developed by Boehme) linked with a fundamentally important spiritual triad. The triad consists of MERCURY, SULPHUR and SALT, which are visualized as psychological processes in man. In simple terms, Salt represents the spiritual tendency towards inertness – human thinking is an example of the salt process. Sulphur represents

Figure 82 *An alchemical image, sometimes called Mercurius, of the three principles in man. The three heads are the lunar (linked with the lower will element), the solar (linked with the consciousness of thinking) and the unifying Mercury (note how this head has the horns and lower cross of the standard sigil for Mercury)*

the spiritual tendency towards movement – the will life of man is an example of the sulphur process. It is Mercury which unites these two polar opposites: within the microcosm Mercury represents the realm of emotions. Mercury makes itself noticeable by the acidity and penetrating power that it lends to fluids. The emotional life of man reconciles the dark will forces (Sulphur) and the death-producing thought processes (Salt), yet none of the three principles may act without the conditioning influence of the other two. Since Mercury also participates in the spiritual septenary of the planets, it is its mediating principle

228

(which reconciles the two separate images of the macrocosm and the microcosm – the triadic with the septenary) in both the alchemical and occult esoteric systems. Sometimes the three principles are linked with the spiritual ternary – Mercury is spirit, Sulphur is soul and Salt is body. Mercury, as the *Vinculum animae*, links Sulphur to Salt. The three are sometimes together called 'Mercurius', for Mercury is seen as the unifying element which pulls together in harmony the other two, as in the alchemical image of Figure 82: the three heads between them represent the three principles, expressed as Sun, Moon and Mercury. The solar element is linked with thinking, the Moon with the will life, and Mercury with the unifying life of the emotions. See also SEMINA.

Threshold   See DWELLER ON THE THRESHOLD.

Throat chakra   See VISUDDHA.

Thrones   The third in descending order of the CELESTIAL HIERARCHIES, so named by Dionysius the Areopagite. The Thrones, sometimes called variously 'Throni', 'Troni' or 'Seats', are the rulers over the sphere of Saturn and are said by occultists to have responsibility for the flow of time itself. Their appearance, unlike that of the celestial beings above them in rank (the SERAPHIM and the CHERUBIM), has received scant attention. They are often symbolized in Christian art by the attribute of a pair of scales (a sign of their role in divine justice), and while they have six wings (like those of higher rank) they often are distinguished by a yellow stone – perhaps a topaz – on their breasts. The Thrones are sometimes called the 'Spirit of Will' in modern esotericism.

Thumos   The Greek term for the 'astral' according to some occultists, for the 'etheric' according to others. The word means 'passion' or 'desire'. For the related *thumikon*, see ORPHIC DESCENT OF THE SOUL.

Tiphereth   The name of the sixth Sephirah of the Qabbalistic SEPHIROTHIC TREE, meaning 'beauty'. It is the central heart of the Tree, as befits a Sephirah linked with the Sun of our own solar system. It is the central pivot of existence, the purpose and centre of the human being. In the lowest World of Expression (ASSIAH) it is connected with the solar power, and with all its dynamic life force. In the World of Formation

(YETZIRAH) it is ruled by the angelic order of Malachim, the controllers who provide and maintain conditions suitable for life (the equivalent of the EXSUSIAI). In the World of Creation (BRIAH) the Archangel of Tiphereth is MICHAEL, who holds together the solar powers and struggles against the principle of evil. In the World of Origins (ATZILUTH) the ruler is Eloah va Daath, the God-aspect which has been translated as 'omniscient one', who rests at the centre of the pivotal centripetal and centrifugal movement of that world.

Tiriel Name given by Agrippa (quoting ancient Qabbalistic sources) to the INTELLIGENCY of Mercury. He gives the magical number of Tiriel as 260, which is the linear sum of the MAGIC SQUARE of Mercury.

Togarini An Adversary of the ARCHANGELS OF THE SEPHIROTH.

Touching Touching is a semi-magical procedure linked with SYMPATHETIC MAGIC, the idea being that by the laying-on of hands an invisible though therapeutic energy is passed between two individuals, or from one individual to an object.

Toxotes One of the Greek names, meaning 'archer', for the zodiacal sign and constellation Sagittarius. It is one of the terms used by Ptolemy.

Trance The subjective experience of being in a trance state is connected with an expansion of consciousness, of liberation from the confines of the physical sheath, and frequently the sense of 'self' is experienced a little above and behind the physical head. A characteristic of trance is that the person in such a state is more receptive to the working of the spiritual realm. Indeed, certain trance states are encouraged mainly as a preparation to that invasion of spiritual entities which is called 'POSSESSION'. In extreme states of trance the 'self' is quite free to leave the body entirely. There are numerous occult techniques directed at placing a person in a state of trance – which is to say, in a state of awareness which is different from the normal. The most common forms of trance in Western cultures arise from HYPNOSIS which is often used for seeming therapeutic purposes, or from mediumship, which is intended to prepare a somatic relationship which will enable discarnate beings freely to use the physical body of the medium. In the majority of oriental techniques the whole purpose of trance is similarly directed towards making contact with spirits. As one Malayan shaman remarked, 'You cannot see spirits unless you are in trance, then you can move freely among them.' This level of trance is clearly linked with SPIRITUAL BILOCATION. Trance is induced in primitive cultures in a variety of simple ways, although most methods involve establishing an abnormal rhythm within the body. Control of breathing is probably the most frequently used technique, although repetitive noises, such as drumbeats, the utterance of mantras and prayers, or even the rhythms of music, dancing, fasting and so on are also efficacious. Drugs also appear to play a part in certain shaministic trance techniques. The distinction between trance and meditation is largely a question of consciousness: the person who meditates does not intensify his consciousness with the aim of allowing spirits to take control of his physical body; indeed, he is usually concerned with making contact with higher levels of consciousness within his own spiritual organism. However, in some cases – as, for example, in temple dancing or in dervish dancing – the distinction between trance and meditation is blurred.

Transcendental magic This popular term is rather misleading, for it does not refer to the transcendental purposes underlying religious and mystical praxes, whereby the spark of divinity in man seeks for union with God. The term should really be 'practical magic', for its aim is the transcendence of the ordinary limits of the physical plane, by means of theurgy, in order to communicate with spirits (both good and bad) in the belief that such spirits will grant aid. See MAGIC.

Transitus fluvii A name given to one of the Qabbalistic systems of STEGANOGRAPHY, sometimes called 'Passing the River', or 'Crossing the River'. See Figure 72 under SECRET SCRIPTS.

Transmigration See METEMPSYCHOSIS and REINCARNATION.

Transmutation In ALCHEMY the term is used to denote the end of the Great Work, by which the base metals (that is, the lower and darker parts of man) are changed into gold (that is, into a higher form).

Table 30

Trigram	Chinese name	Associations			
☰	Ch'ien	Creative	Strong	Heavenly	Father
☷	K'un	Receptive	Yielding	Earthly	Mother
☳	Chen	Arousing	Inciting	Thunder	First son
☵	K'an	Abysmal	Dangerous	Water	Second son
☶	Ken	Keeping still	Resting	Mountain	Third son
☴	Sun	Gentle	Penetrating	Wind	First daughter
☲	Li	Clinging	Light-giving	Fire	Second daughter
☱	Tui	Joyful	Bubbling	Lake	Third daughter

Transpluto Name given to one of the HYPOTHETICAL PLANETS.

Trarames A name used in early alchemical documents to denote invisible spirits who make noises and throw things; perhaps these were the POLTERGEISTS of later spiritualism.

Treta Yuga Sometimes the Trita Yuga, the Silver Age of Hindu chronology, a periodicity of 1,296,000 years (see, however, YUGA). The period given includes the 'twilights' or *sandhya* and *sandhyansa*, which are 300 divine years each.

Triad See TERNARY.

Trifertes See SALAMANDER.

Trigram A name given to a triple combination of YIN and YANG lines in the Chinese divinatory system of the I CHING. A series of eight trigrams may be constructed from these polar opposites; each of these trigrams is regarded as a cosmic force and is accorded a set of associations. When two pairs of trigrams are brought together in union, they form a HEXAGRAM, which contains within it two NUCLEAR TRIGRAMS. The names and the main associations of the trigrams are set out in Table 30.

Trigunas A Sanskrit term for the three qualities of matter: *satva* is that of quiescence, *rajas* that of desire, and *tamas* that of stagnation. They correspond to the three QUALITIES of European astrology, and it is quite possible to trace a similarity between the *trigunas* and the alchemical THREE PRINCIPLES.

Trine In astrology a name for an ASPECT maintained by two or more planets so placed that they are separated by one third of the zodiac, which is to say by an arc of 120 degrees. This aspect is regarded as being wholly beneficial.

Trishna A Sanskrit term meaning approximately 'thirst' and applied to the fifth Nidana, or cause of existence, in Buddhist terminology. This is the 'thirst for existence' which calls the human entity back into the physical plane.

Trismegistus Sometimes Hermes Trismegistus, Mercurius or simply Hermes, the name of a legendary INITIATE (or possibly a school of initiates, or even a succession of initiates) identified with the Egyptian Mysteries through the name Thoth (approximately the Egyptian equivalent of Hermes). He is the supposed author of the HERMETIC CANON. Evidence suggests that the term 'Trismegistus' ('thrice great', and possibly a reference to his triune rank as philosopher, priest and king) was not used until about the second century AD, and prior to that the Grecian *megas* (exoterically said to mean 'great') was repeated three times in reference to the personage.

Tristitia 'Sadness', a name given to one of the sixteen figures of GEOMANCY.

Trita Yuga See TRETA YUGA.

Trithemian Periods See SECUNDADEIAN BEINGS.

Triune star See APOCALYPTIC STAR.

Tropical zodiac The ZODIAC is often called the 'tropical zodiac' because it is defined in terms of the tropics, being centred on the path of the Sun. Often the term is used to distinguish the true zodiac from the constellations, which are really a series of asterisms which include among them twelve names used in the zodiac proper.

However, these two so-called zodiacs are often confused.

Trulli symbols In the Italian town of Alberobello and the surrounding Pulian region are a number of conically roofed houses, locally called *trulli*. Many of these have painted upon their roofs a variety of Christian, astrological and occult symbols. It is not certain when the practice of painting such occult and Christian symbols was adopted, although there is some evidence for it going back to the sixteenth century. They were probably painted for prophylactic purposes.

Truphit An esoteric alchemical term, said by Paracelsus to be the principle in every metal which is capable of development. It is the secret virtue of every mineral.

Trutine of Hermes See HERMETIC RULE.

Tual In certain methods of ceremonial magic, Tual is named as the governor of the zodiacal sign Taurus.

Tula The Sanskrit name for zodiacal Libra, but see also CITRA. Sometimes the word is given in European texts as 'Tulam'.

Tulam Se TULA.

Turpicular See AMULET.

Twelve creative hierarchies According to esoteric astrological lore the twelve creative hierarchies are spiritual beings who participate, or have participated, in the cosmogenesis of our planetary system. Each rank of hierarchy has been linked with one of the twelve signs of the zodiac. The first two are not named, although linked with Aries and Taurus. Heindel, who has most of his occultism from Steiner, says that they 'have passed beyond the ken of anyone on Earth'. Gemini is linked with the SERAPHIM, who oversaw the creative phase of the MOON PERIOD. Cancer is linked with the CHERUBIM, who oversaw the creative phase of the SUN PERIOD. Leo is linked with the group of exalted beings known in esotericism as the Lords of Flame, who oversaw the creative phase of the SATURN PERIOD, which inaugurated the cosmogenesis of our present system. The remaining seven hierarchies are called the Lords of Wisdom, Lords of Individuality, Lords of Form, Lords of Mind, the ARCHANGELS, the ANGELS and the VIRGIN SPIRITS.

Twilight A name used in modern occultism for PRALAYA. The 'spirits of twilight' are the ANGELS. See YUGA.

Two The number 2 is the equivalent of Beth or B in most systems, and is said to be feminine and receptive. It is essentially the mother nature and is linked with words suggesting deep incarnation, derived from the Sanskrit term *maya*, such as 'matter', 'material', 'manifestation' and the like. For all that it is the 'eternal womanhood' (in Goethe's phrase), it is also earthy and fiery, as well as the moulding matrix, marking the union of spirit with matter, as though the maternal receptivity of this number has conceived in its womb the isolation of the monadic 1. It is the number of beauty and love, but with a penchant for instability in affairs of love, arising no doubt from the duality in which it is immersed. The number 2 represents the element of choice in life (see PYTHAGOREAN LETTER) and the attraction (or repulsion) between the sexes. See NUMBERS.

Typtology A modern term used to denote the art of communicating with spirits by means of RAPPING, or by systems of agreed codes, as, for example, in the arrangements of alphabets in TABLE TURNING. The simplest typtological means of communication is to take a single sound (or rap) as a positive response to a question, a double sound (or rap) as a negative response; supposed communication with spiritual agencies is maintained by means of questions.

Tzadkiel Name given by the Qabbalists to the Archangel working within the realm of Briah in the Jupiterian Sephirah of CHESED. He is the Zadkiel of Western occultism, which links him with the sphere of Jupiter.

Tzaphkiel A variant spelling of ZAPHKIEL.

Tzelem A Hebraic term used in occult literature as meaning 'image' or 'shadow' and applied to both the human shadow and to the ASTRAL BODY.

Tziruph Sometimes (wrongly) Ziruph, a Hebraic term applied to a set of permutations of letters intended to reveal analogies. See also TEMURA.

U

The twenty-first letter of the alphabet. According to Blavatsky, the Qabbalists regard the letter U as being the equivalent of 3 × 7, holy numbers, whose product (21) reduces to 3. It is said to symbolize the twenty-one days necessary for the transmutation of base matter into silver, being the completion (in astrological terms) of the full sequence of aspects – a square, trine, opposition, trine and square. In medieval documentation the U is regarded as being the equivalent of the V, although their numerical values differ.

Uhane In KAHUNA magic the conscious mind of man. The term is also used to indicate the ghost or spirit of a dead person, which has the ability to talk or cry (the Polynesian roots *ha* and *ne* mean 'to talk in a low voice'). Such a *uhane* might be used in the DEATH PRAYER.

Umbilical chakra See MANIPURA.

Umbilicomancy See OMPHALOMANCY.

Umbra The Latin for 'shadow', sometimes used to denote a ghost, probably originally the ASTRAL DOUBLE.

Unctions The name given in some occult circles to the annointing oils used in certain magical praxes. In the witchcraft literature the word is also used for the flying salve used by witches as a body oil to enable them to fly to the Sabbat. Such unctions were demonic oils, said to be made from the boiled bodies of sacrificed infants and so on. See COLLYRIE.

Undines The name for the water fairies, whose dwelling is really on the astral plane, where they remain invisible to ordinary sight. Clairvoyants describe them as having bodies of a pulsating, iridescent light; they appear to be wingless, diminutive and delicate creatures, with a form somewhat resembling the human. In the medieval tradition they are often called 'nympha'. See ELEMENTALS.

Unguents In witchcraft the name given to magical salves used to promote magical effects. The most frequently used unguent (if the witchcraft records are to be believed) was that supposedly made from human fat and used by witches to enable them to transvect (see SABBAT).

Unhipili In KAHUNA magic the unconscious part of man. See UHANE.

Universal fluid See ANIMAL MAGNETISM.

Universal Quintessence A specialist term used in ALCHEMY in connection with the manufacture of the spagyric LAPIS.

Universal Solvent See ALCHEMY.

Universal Spirit See ATMA.

Uragas A Sanskrit term for the serpent NAGAS of Patala (Hell).

Urania One of the nine Muses of classical mythology, assigned in Roman times to rule over astronomy and astrology, her symbol being the staff pointing to the globe. The symbol is often interpreted as an esoteric allegory, for the staff is straight and the globe is circular, and they both may be taken as reference to the astrological (Aristotelian) doctrine that bodies in the supralunar spheres move in perfect circles, while those in the sublunar spheres (which, of course, include the Earth) move in straight lines. The symbolism addresses itself to the fact that astrology is concerned with the earthly as much as with the celestial. The word 'Urania' is often applied in modern times to the whole realm of astrology, though when so used it is often in a pejorative sense.

Uranus In astrology Uranus was the first of the extra-Saturnine planets to be discovered (1781), and was first called *Georgium sidus* after the reigning George III of England, and sometimes Herschel after its discoverer. Astrologers regard the planet as marking disruptive changes, revolutions and unconventional behaviour. In modern astrology Uranus is usually said to rule the sign Aquarius, having displaced Saturn from that role.

Uriel The name given to the Archangel specifically charged with care of the Earth. He is the being who makes from the healing forces of Raphael the power of human thinking, which is passed over to Michael, who makes of it human activity. In Milton's *Paradise Lost* he is said to be the 'sharpest-sighted spirit of all in heaven'. See ARCHANGELS.

Urizen See FOUR ZOAS.

Urthona See FOUR ZOAS.

Usanas A Sanskrit name for the planet Venus.

Uzza An angel who sided with Azrael to oppose the creation of man.

The twenty-second letter of the alphabet. Although the V is often regarded as being the equivalent of U, the numerical values and origins differ considerably, the Hebraic Vau being linked with the number SIX. Other systems equate it with 21 and its reduction 3 – see, for example, U, and the 'double U' (2 × 3) which is W. In the Roman system of numbering it represents the 5, of course, though this does not appear to be occultly derived.

Vahana A Sanskrit word for a 'vehicle' or 'receptacle' and applied to the different physical and spiritual bodies of man.

Valac One of the seventy-two SPIRITS OF SOLOMON, appearing as a small boy riding a dragon.

Valefor One of the seventy-two SPIRITS OF SOLOMON, appearing in the conjuration rites as a lion or a composite animal.

Vampire A name given to the dead body of a human which is inhabited, or galvanized into life, by a demon or an elementary. In popular lore the vampire is pictured as issuing from its coffin at night with a view to sucking the blood of humans in order to maintain its own half life. The name is probably derived from the Magyar *vampir*, which means much the same as the English and is linked with the Lithuanian *wempti* ('to drink') in reference to the unwholesome diet of the creature.

While traditions concerning the vampire vary from locality to locality, there appears to be a worldwide insistence that vampires exist, and there is a general agreement that a vampire may be 'constructed' (if that is the term) only from the body of a man who previously led an immoral life. A special belief is that a vampire is the offspring of a witch and a werewolf. In certain traditions vampires are compounded from the bodies of those who in life practised black magic, in others from the bodies of suicides (a belief which has in certain areas led to the mutilation of

suicides to render their potential vampirism ineffective). In such ideas we see the roots of the custom of burying suicides at crossroads, sometimes transfixed with a stake. So prevalent was this practice, indeed, that it was made illegal in England as late as 1824. Summers regards 'any profanation of a dead body' (including necrophagy and necrophilia) as vampirism, but his definition is not widely accepted. The whole definition of vampirism rests on the idea of POSSESSION of a dead body by an evil spirit. The original use of the word NECROMANCY was involved with such possession, of course, but a dead body raised for means of prediction was not a vampire, in the sense that it did not seek human blood for nourishment.

While the vampire has been reported in most centuries, the concept seems to have taken strongest hold over Europe during the eighteenth century. Calmet spoke of it as being rife in mid-Europe during the whole of that century, although the word was not introduced into the English language until 1700–1730. The romantic novelists of the nineteenth century extended the popular imagination in this field and endowed the vampire with many qualities which even the popular occult tradition had been loath to invest it. Bram Stoker's *Dracula* of 1897 rightly remains the classic in this field. The Latin term *strix* was used to mean 'vampire', although it originally meant 'screech owl', and this may be rooted in a connection drawn between LILITH and the owl. Sometimes indeed the vampire is said to change into a bat in order to get from one place to another.

Vapula One of the seventy-two SPIRITS OF SOLOMON, appearing in the form of a winged lion, something along the lines of the symbol for St Mark.

Vassago One of the seventy-two SPIRITS OF SOLOMON, conjured especially because of his knowledge of past and future events.

Vehicle of Life A term given by Blavatsky as relating to septenary man, namely the four elemental principles and the spiritual ternary.

Veneni One of the occult *entia* or body forces of Paracelsus (see ENS). This is the force which pertains to the ETHERIC BODY and is said to govern the mysterious alchemy of the body in its ability to transform foods, air and impressions into forces which may spiritualize the soul life of man. The word *veneni* is etymologically linked with 'poisons' and the choice of this term would suggest that the etheric is seen both as a receptacle for poisons (such as evil thoughts, low-grade emotions and so on) and as a cleanser of such poisons.

Venus The planet in orbit around the Sun at a mean distance of about 67 million miles, with a periodicity of about 244 days. In the esoteric system of Boehme, Venus is the receptive force of the solar éclat, the fifth form, which represents the attainment of desire, which brings its own joy and harmony, in the sequence of the SEVEN PROPERTIES. For Qabbalistic associations, see NETZACH. It is traditionally termed the 'planet of love', and is indeed a useful indicator of how the subject loves the world and all its rich manifestations. It governs also the higher emotions and the general refinement of the individual. The sigil for Venus ♀, which has been adapted to denote the feminine principle in modern times, is explained as representing the circle of spirit (which contains all spiritual potential) lifted by the cross of materiality, suggesting that the Venusian nature may be regarded as equivalent to a refined or redeemed earthly quality. It is indeed sometimes described as 'the twin sister of the Earth' by esotericists. Venus has rule over zodiacal Taurus and Libra. Astronomers tell us that the peculiar brilliance of Venus is due to the reflective power of the atmosphere of clouds in which the body is sheathed. This may link with the esoteric tradition which makes Venus the ruler of the physical body, by virtue of its connection with the ETHERIC forces in which the physical is

sheathed. In astrology Venus represents the spiritual side of the native as manifest in his physical life, and it is an index of the ability of the subject to enjoy beauty and to cooperate with others. A Venus which is emphasized in a chart, through an essential dignity, is usually a sign of physical beauty and of the fact that the native will be in some way creative. Such a well-placed Venus also makes for great popularity with the opposite sex, as well as for a harmonious emotional life. A badly placed Venus tends to restrict in some way the urge towards cooperation with others, and the native may be impractical, lazy or opportunist. Venus is exalted in Pisces and has its fall in Libra. Traditionally the planet rules the small of the back (but see MELOTHESIC MAN), as well as the entire shape of the physical body.

Venus Period The name given in esoteric astrology to a future condition of our present Earth, beyond the future development of the JUPITER PERIOD, yet prior to the final VULCAN PERIOD, when humanity will attain to objective, self-conscious, creative being.

Venus Scheme 'Venus Scheme' and 'Venusian Chain' are terms derived from the Theosophical SCHEME OF EVOLUTION and claimed to relate to the most advanced of the planetary forms.

Vepar One of the seventy-two SPIRITS OF SOLOMON, conjured especially because of his dominion of matters of the sea: he appears in the form of a mermaid, and his sigil (Figure 76 under SPIRITS OF SOLOMON) somewhat resembles an ancient boat. He will bring about storms, death by drowning and similar disasters.

Vesperus The name (with the variant Vesper) given by Roman and medieval astrologers to the planet Venus when the Evening Star visible after the setting of the sun. See also LUCIFER.

Vetala A Sanskrit term for an elementary or ghost. *Vetala siddhi* is the black magic by means of which power is obtained over the living, through unwholesome ceremonies practised over dead bodies.

Via 'Way' or 'Road', a name given to one of the sixteen figures of GEOMANCY.

Vicakha The Sanskrit name for constellation Scorpio, but see VRISHIKAM.

Vices See VIRTUES AND VICES.

Vidya   A Sanskrit term sometimes translated as meaning 'occult science'.

Vinculum animae   See THREE PRINCIPLES.

Vine   One of the seventy-two SPIRITS OF SOLOMON, appearing in the form of a lion or monster. His special power is to bring about destruction and to inform the magician of the (secret) names of other sorcerers and witches.

Virgin   Name given to both zodiacal Virgo and to the Virgo constellation.

Virgin spirits   One of the esoteric names given to present-day humanity, viewed as one of the TWELVE CREATIVE HIERARCHIES.

Virgin's Milk   See ALCHEMICAL MERCURY.

Virgo   The sixth sign of the zodiac. It corresponds neither in location nor significance with the asterism of the same name, which is linked by the Qabbalists with the Hebraic Gimel and with the TAROT arcanum 'The Empress'. The sigil for the sign ♍ is said to have been a contracted drawing of the severed serpent, from which the sigils for Scorpio and Virgo are said by certain occultists to have evolved, and the fact is that even the Egyptian demotic scripts appear to carry such an association. The link with the head of a serpent postulated in this theory is interesting, for Virgo is indeed a sign deeply committed to the intellectual process. The sigil has also been derived (imaginatively, as it happens) from the merged letters MV (*Maria virgo*) as part of the important Marian symbolism assciated with the sign and constellation. Virgo is of the Earth element and of the Mutable quality, the influence being discriminative, quiet, exacting, nervous, shrewd and methodical. The nature of Virgo as it manifests in human beings is dignified, clever, intelligent, nervous (although often good under pressure), graceful, mentally alert, gentle – in a word, all those qualities which may be associated with an Earth type expressing itself in the spiritual realm of mentality. In excess the Virgoan nature may be described in terms which express its underlying critical nature, the key words being: carping, hypercritical, bookish, shrewish and backbiting. Virgo is traditionally ruled by Mercury and marks the fall of Venus.

Virtue   In a specialist astrological sense the term applied to a hidden power within all sublunary things, a power which proceeds from the stars. It has many names in occultism, alchemy and astrology (see, for example, ETHERIC, ILECH, QUINTESSENCE and YLIADUS). To some extent this idea is still contained in the modern use of the term in its general sense, the 'human virtue' being an inner quality proceeding from an image of the celestial or ideal man (the Latin *vir* means 'man'). The practice of TALISMANIC MAGIC, so important a branch of medieval occultism, was based on the idea that it was possible to inject a celestial or planetary virtue into an amulet, which would then contain a beneficial or protective power derived from that virtue.

Virtues   See VIRTUTES.

Virtues and vices   In the medieval tradition the seven virtues and vices were linked with the seven planets in a variety of systems, and these frequently appear in medieval astrological symbolism in paintings and sculpture. The correspondences in Table 31 are fairly standard in occult literature.

Virtutes   A name given to the incorporeal spiritual beings of the series of CELESTIAL HIERARCHIES established by Dionysius the Areopagite. Strictly speaking they should be linked with the EXSUSIAI, as rulers of the sphere of the Sun – the medieval legends confirm this by linking the Virtues, as they are sometimes

Table 31

Planet	Virtue	Vice	Symbol (vice)	Part of man
Sun	Hope	Indolence	Ass	Life force (spirit)
Moon	Chastity	Envy	Dog	Psychic forces (soul)
Mercury	Wisdom	Gluttony	Pig	Intellect (mind)
Venus	Love	Lust	Bear	Divinity in man
Mars	Courage	Wrath	Wolf	Bestial lower element
Jupiter	Faith	Pride	Peacock	Higher aspirations
Saturn	Prudence	Covetousness	Hedgehog	Physical body

called, with the divine mystery of the Eucharist, for in the esoteric lore Christ is linked with the solar sphere. However, the Virtutes have been wrongly equated with the ARCHAI (for example, by St Gregory), which would give them rule over Venus. The rule of the Archai over Venus and of the Virtutes over the Sun is beyond dispute in astrological lore, however.

Visudhha   Name given to the CHAKRA located near the throat. It is described as having sixteen spokes, symbolized as a sixteen-leaved lotus. Its function is to receive the violet-blue ray from the Spleen chakra, and to transform this in order to influence the vocal chords and hearing apparatus of the human being. When fully developed in a human being it promotes the astral equivalent of hearing.

Vital body   In medieval terminology the vital body was the 'living body'. This term was not used to denote the living physical body, but the higher spiritual body which maintained the physical body in life; it was therefore the equivalent of the ETHERIC BODY.

Vitality globule   This is a term applied to certain effects in the sky, resulting from the entry of PRANA from the solar realms into the atmosphere. These brilliant gyrating specks may sometimes be seen in the atmosphere (especially on a clear day) oscillating freely in vast quantities. As a pranic source, a globule suffers no change until it is absorbed by a living creature. The globule is sometimes called the 'etheric globule' or the '*prana* globule'.

Viwan   A Sanskrit name for a sort of balloon or vehicle of the air which was used by the inhabitants of ATLANTIS.

Voel   In certain forms of ceremonial magic the name is given to the governor of zodiacal Leo.

Vril   A term used by Bulwer-Lytton to denote one of the awesome powers which would be available to mankind in future times. The word (like several of Bulwer-Lytton's adaptations and mistranslations of occult terminologies) was adopted widely in Theosophical circles, especially in connection with its destructive power. Bulwer-Lytton wrote his romance *The Coming Race* in 1871, and his Vril, for all its terrible power, had the potential for supporting a very refined degree of social life – it was the misuse of the power which made it destructive. Blavatsky says that

this Vril is the same as the terrible sidereal force used by the Atlanteans, called MASH-MAK.

Vrishabham   One of the Sanskrit terms for the zodiacal Gemini, as used in Hindu astrology.

Vrishikam   The Sanskrit name for zodiacal Scorpio, but see also VICAKHA.

Vual   Sometimes called the 'Egyptian demon', Vual appears on a camel, speaking in what is taken to be ancient Egyptian tongues. He is one of the seventy-two SPIRITS OF SOLOMON.

Vui   The Melanesian term for a spirit, clearly distinguished from a ghost, which is called a *tindalo*. The *vui* has a life of its own, is possessed of more intelligence than ordinary man, and has a wider knowledge of things hidden to those living in physical bodies.

Vulcan   The term has several applications in astrology. It was a name given to one of the intramercurial HYPOTHETICAL PLANETS. The Vulcan described by Bailey in her system of Intuitional Astrology is actually one of the SACRED PLANETS and is connected especially with the first ray. The term Vulcan is also used to veil an esoteric astrological doctrine; it is one of the names applied to a planetary state which is supposed to represent the future embodiment of our Earth (see VULCAN PERIOD). The Vulcanic art or the Vulcanico-magical art is ALCHEMY, for Vulcan was the ancient god of fire and forges, and alchemy was the art of the fire philosophers or spagyric artists.

Vulcan Period   A term used in esoteric astrology to denote a future (and in some respects final) condition of our present Earth, marking an evolution of humanity to the highest spiritual consciousness. The term is used only in esoteric astrology, and has nothing to do with any of the hypotheticals linked under VULCAN.

Vulcan Scheme   'Vulcan Scheme' and 'Vulcanian Chain' are terms derived from considerations set out under the Theosophical SCHEME OF EVOLUTION, not to be confused with the hypotheticals listed under VULCAN. It is claimed that the Vulcan Scheme relates to a CHAIN which will produce entities at a lower level than those of the present EARTH CHAIN.

Vulkanus   Name given to one of the HYPOTHETICAL PLANETS, said to relate to power and strength.

The twenty-third letter of the alphabet. There is no Hebraic equivalent and so there is no widely accepted numerological value placed upon it. In occultism the W is regarded as being a double V (rather than a double U) and is linked with the idea of celestial waters, the old name for the etheric forces. Perhaps this explains many of the early Christian uses of the symbol ᴡ which has been linked with the initial letters of *Ave Maria* and with the N of *Nike* ('victory'). The numerological association of W with SIX probably derives from the link between V and 3 ($2 \times 3 = 6$). See also the letter x.

Waken See SYMPATHETIC MAGIC.

Warlock A male witch, the word probably coming from the Old english *waerloga*, a 'deceiver' or 'oath-breaker'. See WITCH.

Warmth ether See ETHERIC.

Warmth globe See SATURN PERIOD.

Water element In ALCHEMY the term 'water' relates to something other than the familiar liquid. The *Aqua celestina*, for example, is 'Mercurial water', while *Aqua celestis* is probably nothing other than rectified wine. In contrast, however, the *Aqua permanens* of Paracelsus is the MERCURY OF THE PHILOSOPHERS, sometimes also called the water of the Sun and Moon. The esoteric water element is far removed from the fluidic water of the modern chemists, although suitable analogies between the material fluid and the spiritual principle are often found in the popular treatments of the elements. In astrology Water finds expression in the zodiac through the WATER TRIPLICITY; it is the element most deeply concerned with reflection, sensitivity and fluidity. Water is esoterically an 'impressionable' principle, the important aspect of this tradition revolving around the idea (more fully expressed in alchemical than in astrological texts) that Water, to operate in accordance with its true

nature, needs to be contained and thus given form. This is why among some of the Greek philosophers Water was the 'first principle' from which form arose, the 'potentiality' of form (in the medieval tradition the first principle was actually the element of Fire). This partly explains the esoteric connection drawn between the dry Moon and Water, for the Moon is that which gives growth and change to form.

Water signs These are the zodiacal signs Cancer, Scorpio and Pisces. See WATER TRIPLICITY.

Water triplicity This is the group of signs linked with the WATER ELEMENT, manifesting different aspects of the PHLEGMATIC temperament: Cancer, Scorpio and Pisces. Water may be

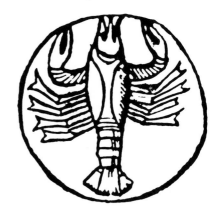

seen in three different forms: Cancer is water as a fluid – changeable, tending to reflect the colours of the sky and landscape around; Scorpio is frozen water, a shield of ice beneath which is a depth unknown; Pisces is vaporous water, almost a dematerialized state of being, often out of touch with (hovering over) the physical realm. Each of the Water signs are extremely emotional and are often described as 'their own worst enemies' or 'victims of circumstances'. Since the Water triplicity is concerned with the spiritual element in life, with the dissolving of boundaries, each of the signs reflects an aspect of this in the world.

Waters of Space   See OURANOS.

Wax image   A name given to one of the products of witchcraft – a model in wax, sometimes called a 'POPPET', of a person or creature who is to be psychically attacked by means of some form of SYMPATHETIC MAGIC. The black magician, warlock or witch will make an image in wax (or clay) of the person or animal he wishes to harm or kill and, after various invocations to demons, will mutilate the image, either by melting it or by sticking into it pins, knives or nails. The idea is that whatever is done to the image will be enacted, through demonic agencies, on the living person of which the poppet is a model.

Summers, in writing about the magician John of Nottingham, who had been hired to kill Edward II and some of his courtiers by thrusting pins into images, says, 'this is certainly one of the oldest and most universal of spells'. In this particular case we may assume that the punishment inflicted on the poppet of Richard de Sowe (one of Edward's courtiers) must have been extreme, for the living man's suffering was such that one of Nottingham's henchmen was so horrified that he turned informant in order to stop the operation.

Kings appear to have been an especially favoured target for this kind of sympathetic magic: a group of witches was burned in 968 for attempting the life of King Duffus by slowly melting his waxen image, while the famous Berwick witch trials of 1590 revealed that the technique used against James VI was that of the melted waxen image. One of the most scandalous conspiracies against a pope was that organized by Giacinto Centini, who tried to murder Urban VIII by mutilating his waxen model.

Instructions for the manufacture of images are contained in some of the texts on ritual magic:

special hours and days (astrological considerations) must be reserved for the act and magical characters must be drawn. In some cases such sigils must be traced on strips of skin taken from the body of a frog or toad ritually killed by the operator. The waxen image (containing the spells in hollows in its body) must then be suspended by one of the hairs of the operator in a cavern, at midnight, while magical incantations are recited. After incense has been burned, the image must be buried in a deal box. In a theological text Eusebius speaks of poppets being made from pulverized lizards and the roots of rue. It is evident from such instructions that the whole art is diabolic, and properly belongs to BLACK MAGIC.

Werewolf   Name given to a man who is (permanently or temporarily) changed into the form of a wolf – a form of lycanthropy which belongs more to popular folk myth than to occultism.

White Eagle   Sometimes used by modern astrologers as a term for zodiacal Scorpio. There is also an important initiate–teacher of this name. See EAGLE.

White fire   A term used by Qabbalists to denote the Ain Soph (see AIN).

White magic   The name given to the magic practised by those of the Right-Hand Path, a magic which is concerned with furthering the evolution of the world and of man. The term is usually employed to distinguish this branch of magic from BLACK MAGIC. Originally the term was used of those magicians or initiates or priests (all sometimes called 'white magicians') who employed beneficient spirits (as opposed to demons); however, in the late medieval period it was often equated with those who practised what is now called NATURAL MAGIC. See also MAGIC.

White magicians   See WHITE MAGIC.

White Magnesia   See MAGNESIA.

Wind raising   A witch, or even a white magician, was said to have the ability to raise winds, either by invoking demons towards this end, or by the use of such devices as the WITCH KNOT (Figure 83). The charge of wind raising was the chief one brought in 1590 against the North Berwick witches, who were alleged to have raised

Figure 83   *Witches raising a storm to cause a shipwreck (after Olaus Magnus)*

a storm to wreck the fleet bringing James VI and Ann of Denmark to Scotland. Witches were also supposed to have the ability to becalm ships, by stopping winds.

Wise Men   See INITIATES and MAGIAN.

Witch   The term is from the Anglo-Saxon *wicca* ('one who practises sorcery'), related to the Germanic *wissen* ('to know') and *wikken* ('to divine'). Technically, a witch is one given to the service of the Devil, and it is usual to consider anyone who has entered into a PACT as either a witch or a warlock. However, the witch trials that were so formative of popular beliefs about witchcraft appear to have based many of their judgments on the doctrine that someone might be a witch not only without the direct influence of the Devil but even unwittingly (that is 'unconsciously' in modern terminology). One of the most comprehensive definitions of the acts stemming from witchcraft is that contained in the famous Bull of Pope Innocent VIII of 1484 which prefaced the MALLEUS MALEFICARUM (see WITCHCRAFT). A shorter definition from this book is 'one who attempts to induce the fallen angels to work evil wonders'. Bodin's famous definition of a witch is 'one who by commerce and close confederacy with the Devil has a deliberate and very determined intention of attaining his own selfish ends.' In such words we see laid bare the very basis of BLACK MAGIC, which is essentially the use of cosmic powers for selfish purposes. There may be no doubt, however, that the majority of people who were hanged or burned for practising witchcraft were far from being witches in any of these technical senses, and at the height of the anti-witch fervour it was clear that virtually any socially unacceptable individual might be dunned as a witch and killed – usually after considerable torture. Reginald Scot's description of the typical witch might bear this out: 'women which be commonly old, lame, blear-eied, pale, fowle, and full of wrinkles; poore, sullen, superstitious, and papists; or such as knowe no religion: in whose drousie minds the divell hath goten a fine seat. . . .' This poor creature is a far cry from the energetic heretics who raised the idea of the witchcraft purges in the minds of priests during the early fifteenth century. See Figure 84 and SABBAT.

Witch knot   Name given to a cord tied in elaborate loops, sometimes with feathers inserted in the knots or in the rope strands. These cords were prepared and used for many different purposes, though the underlying idea was that they might be used by a witch to 'bind' into the

Figure 84 (right):   The Witches, *an engraving by Albrecht Dürer (private collection)*

240

ABOMINATION DES SORCIERS

Est il rien qui soit plus damnable,
Ny plus digne du feu d'enfer,
Que cette engeance abominable
Des ministres de Lucifer?

Ils tirent de leurs noirs mysteres
L'horreur, la hayne le debat,
Et font de sanglans caracteres
Dans leur execrable Sabat.

C'est la que ces maudites ames
Se vont preparer leur tourment;
Et qu'elles attisent les flammes,
Qui bruslent eternellement.

knot certain diabolic powers. Olaus Mangus, who calls them *Nodi magici*, records that they were used by wizards to bind winds and might be stored on board ship against such time as when the vessel was becalmed; the untying of the knots would raise winds. The knots are sometimes called 'witch ladders'.

Witch ladder   See WITCH KNOT.

Witch Sabbath   See SABBAT.

Witchcraft   Belief in witchcraft arises basically from the notion that the Devil or his demons cannot wreak havoc in the world save through human agency, therefore the Devil seeks to bind into his service (by both treachery and pact) humans who will do this for him; the basis of witchcraft is a PACT. The technical definition of the WITCH and warlock is that given in the Bull of Pope Innocent VIII of 1484:

Many persons of both sexes, unmindful of their own salvation and straying from the Catholic Faith, have abandoned themselves to devils, incubi and succubi, and by their incantations, spells, conjurations and other accursed charms and crafts, enormities and horrid offences, have slain infants yet in the mother's womb, as also the offspring of cattle, have blasted the produce of the earth, the grapes of the vine, the fruits of trees, nay, men and women, beasts of burthen, herd-beasts, as well as animals of other kinds, vineyards, orchards, meadows, pastureland, corn, wheat, and all other cereals; these wretches furthermore afflict and torment men and women, beasts of burthen, herd-beasts, as well as animals of other kind, with terrible and piteous pains and sore diseases, both internal and external; they hinder men from performing the sexual act and women from conceiving, whence husbands cannot know their wives nor wives receive their husbands; over and above this they blasphemously renounce the Faith which is theirs by the Sacrament of Baptism, and at the instigation of the Enemy of Mankind they do not shrink from committing and perpetrating the foulest abominations and filthiest excesses to the deadly peril of their own souls, whereby they outrage Divine Majesty and are a cause of scandal and danger to the very many.

The images of witchcraft were designed to foster this idea of bestial creatures surrounded by diabolic agencies (Figure 85). We see therefore that witchcraft is based on what may be described as POSSESSION, since the witch is supposed to be

Figure 85 (left):   The Evils of Witchcraft *by Jasper (eighteenth century)*

(temporarily or permanently) under the control of the Devil himself (see SABBAT).

While teachings concerning the nature of witchcraft, both as an international conspiracy and as ritual Devil worship, have gained popularity in modern times, it is certain that a few individuals professed to be witches, and a few practised the black magical arts which are associated with witchcraft. Occultists have no hesitation in affirming that witchcraft, in its widest sense as the practice of 'one in close and deliberate confederacy with the Devil', has always existed in all parts of the world and is by no means unknown today. The main question is whether the various attributes of witchcraft will bear close examination. A careful study of the numerous indictments brought against witches leads one to the same doubting despair as Reginald Scot, who fought so valiantly to suppress the 'witchcraft delusion' without at the same time denying the efficacy of evil spirits:

The fables of Witchcraft have taken so fast hold and deepe root in the heart of man, that fewe or non can (nowadaies) with patience indure the hand and correction of God. . . . Such faithlesse people (I saie) are also persuaded, that neither haile nor snowe, thunder nor lightening, raine nor tempestuous winds come from the heavens at the commandment of God: but are raised by the cunning and power of witches and conjurers; insomuch as a clap of thunder, or a gale of wind is no sooner heard, but either they run to ring bells, or crie out to burne witches. . . . But if all the divels in hell were dead, and all the witches in England were burnt or hanged; I warrant you we should not faile to have raine, haile and tempests, as now we have; according to the appointment and will of God.

The conflict revealed here runs deep, for the dualism inherent in Christianity was never fully resolved. The dualism permitted not merely the actions of a god, but also the actions of the demons, yet set no really clear standards for judging which effects came from which source. Linguistic and theological arguments insisted that actions of demons were possible 'only with the permission of God', but these delicacies of argument escaped most minds and were rarely used in order to free the condemned from flame or rope.

Occultism is rooted in a belief not only in the existence of God and of demons, but also in the idea that demons may be used by human beings and (a far more dangerous practice) that human beings may be used by demons – this is the true witchcraft. While few occultists would support Summers in the vast generalizations through which he found it possible to link the 'dark fraternities' of late medieval heresy with modern anarchism, the Third International and Bolshevism, all serious occultists will affirm the reality of witchcraft.

Witchfinder During the WITCHCRAFT trials in Europe it was established legal procedure for specially appointed (or even self-appointed) individuals to find or discover witches and warlocks and bring them to trial. As fees were usually paid for such discoveries, the role of witchfinder was often highly lucrative. The most famous English witchfinder, the so-called Witchfinder General, was Mathew Hopkins, who in fourteen months (from 1645) had several hundred witches hanged – over a hundred at Bury St Edmunds alone. His equally notorious pricker (see PRICKING) was John Stearne.

Witchmark See PRICKING.

Wizard A male sorcerer, probably from the same root as WITCH.

World of Creation The third world, the 'soul world', of the Qabbalistic system of the SEPHIROTHIC TREE. See BRIAH.

World of Expression The lowest world in the Qabbalistic system of the SEPHIROTHIC TREE, the physical world. See ASSIAH.

World of Formation The mental world in the Qabbalistic system of the SEPHIROTHIC TREE, which links the World of Creation (Briah) with the World of Expression (Assiah). See YETZIRAH.

World of Origins The highest, 'spirit world' of the four worlds in the Qabbalistic system of the SEPHIROTHIC TREE. See ATZILUTH.

World spheres See OPHANIM.

World-mother One of the names given to the power of KUNDALINI, especially in Theosophical texts.

Wraith One of the many names given by occultists to the form taken by the ETHERIC DOUBLE when the magnetic cord has snapped, and it is thus loosening from the physical body. See also DOUBLE.

The twenty-fourth letter of the alphabet. As Blavatsky points out, the number which stands in mathematics for an unknown quantity also stands in occultism for the perfect number, which is 10, the old symbol of the individual facing the cosmic ZERO. This notion is represented in the Roman use of the X to represent the number 10. In fact, the origin of the X as the 'unknown factor' has nothing to do with occultism – it came by way of Arabian mathematics, the word *shei* meaning 'thing' or 'something', being transcribed as *xei*. The esotericism of the form X is properly linked with the symbolism of the cross and therefore with the sacrifice of the Logos. This symbolism is extended to consider the natures of the two letters alphabetically arranged on either side of X – that is, the W, with its association with spiritual victory, and the Y, the Pythagorean letter of choice. By symbolic extension, these two letters are linked with the two crosses on either side on the Cross of Golgotha.

Xylomancy Divination by means of wood. The Chinese system of the I CHING, which depends for its operation on the manipulation of stocks (or stalks), may be said to be a form of xylomancy. This sophisticated art or science may be contrasted with the popular form of divination by means of thrown sticks, the random patterns of which are regarded as lending clues to futurity. Again, augury derived from the manner in which wood burns (a form of PYROMANCY) is also said to be a xylomantic art.

The twenty-fifth letter of the alphabet. The so-called Samian letter, representative of the choice between good and evil which bifurcates every single path of virtue. See also the letter X. The Hebraic equivalent of Yod is apportioned the number TEN, as for example in the numerology of the tetragrammaton, which gives the mystical number 26:

$$Yod \quad He \quad Vau \quad He$$
$$10 + 5 + 6 + 5 = 26$$

See also NUMBERS.

Yaksha A Sanskrit term for a kind of demon. They are probably elementaries, although Blavatsky writes that clairvoyants see them descend on men 'open to the reception of such influences, like a fiery comet or a shooting star'.

Yama See YOGA.

Yang See YIN AND YANG.

Yatra A Sanskrit term used to denote the Hindu form of military astrology, specialized in determining suitable comets for such things as attack and defence in war.

Yatus Sometimes *yatukdhanas*, the Sanskrit name for theriomorphic demons; they are said by esotericists to be human passions.

Yawe One of the numerous spellings for 'Jehovah', which according to the occult glosses is derived from a compound of words linked with the idea of the united male–female. Be that as it may, the word 'Yawe', which was not to be spoken (see KETHER), is said to have been compounded by the scribes from the consonantal 'JHVH' (the sacred TETRAGRAMMATON) with the vowels from 'Adonai', that this sacred name might be pronounced in place of the unspeakable one. Only later, in non-Hebraic communities, was this blind confused with the real name, to give the sounds expressed in the many variations of Jehovah.

Years of the Gods See DIVINE YEARS.

Yesod The name given to a Sephirah in the SEPHIROTHIC TREE of the Qabbalists, usually translated as meaning 'foundation'. After a remarkable and sensitive analysis of the lunar expressions of Yesod through the four worlds, Gray comes to the conclusion that the concern of this Sephirah is 'essentially that of causing life'. In the World of Expression, the realm of ASSIAH, Yesod is reflected in the Moon and in lunar qualities. The Moon in this sense is a sort of mirror of the solar truth, so that what human beings meet in Yesod is (in the words of Gray) 'not untruth so much as truth adapted to our abilities of understanding'; this points to the occult truth that Yesod is the realm of symbols. In the World of Formations (YETZIRAH) this Sephirah is linked with the angelic order of the Aishim, the Souls of Fire, who are concerned with the fecundation which resides in the life forms of our world. In this area of Yesod one becomes aware of the distinction between the solar life beyond and the lunar light within. In the World of Creation, which is that of BRIAH, the lunar realm of Yesod is directed by the Archangel GABRIEL, the Angel of the Annunciation, and hence linked with the lunar mysteries of incarnation and birth, which is the theme of this Sephirah. In the highest realm of ATZILUTH, the World of Origins, the Sephirah is under the Supreme Lords of Life, the so-called Shaddai el Chaiim of the Qabbalists, who are concerned with the rightful and harmonious union of souls.

Yetzirah The World of Formation or formative world of the Sephirothic Tree, governed by the formators or CELESTIAL HIERARCHIES. It is approximately the 'mental world' of Western occultism. For the specific rulerships of the Formators, see SEPHIROTHIC TREE.

Yin and Yang Two of the most important principles in Chinese thought, incorporated into Western occultism mainly through the influence of the *Book of Changes*, the I CHING, which is rooted in the concept of the altercation between the cosmic powers of yin and yang. Yin and yang are root principles which are said to form the very basis of the world order, their struggle being said to lie at the root of all phenomena. Yin is feminine and is linked with the earth forces, with the feminine or maternal element, with the fructification of the earth, with darkness and shadow, and with all that receives; the origin of the word is said to be in the meaning 'something overcast' or 'something in shadow'. In this cosmic symbolism yin is partly supplemented by, and partly opposed by, the power of yang, which is masculine or paternal, is linked with celestial forces, with creative forces, with light and brilliance, and with all that is active and giving; sinologists suggest that the word originally meant approximately 'something shone upon' or 'bright'.

In relation to the *I Ching* text, yin is represented as a broken line, while yang is represented as a single unbroken line. Combinations of these lines, in sequences of three, make up the TRIGRAMS. When the trigrams are ranged in pairs they make the six-lined figures of the HEXAGRAMS. The combinations of pairs of trigrams in hexagrams result in sixty-four figures, the study of whch constitutes the commentaries and interpretations of what is now called the *Book of Changes*.

The cosmic alternation between yin and yang has been represented in the diagram known in the West as the T'ai Chi symbol: ☯. The white area is the light yang, which contains within it a seed of yin, while the black area is the dark yin, which contains within it a seed of yang. Thus each of the primal powers in the universe is seen as containing within it the seeds of its own opposite, as a result of which everything changes into its own opposite manifestation. The diagram is to be considered as being in motion, rotating upon its own centre, as symbol of the endless cycle of change which lies at the root of being.

Y King Sometimes *Y-Kim*, an archaic Western equivalent for the I CHING.

Yliadus A Paracelsian term used to denote an invisible spirit or agency within the human body (and indeed within the FOUR ELEMENTS). It is sometimes spelled 'Yliadum' or 'Yleidus' and perhaps linked with the ILIASTER. Paracelsus possibly coined this term, and he certainly claims that it is 'elemental air'; it seems indeed to be the equivalent of the medieval *Ens veneni*, of the modern ETHERIC, a subtle essence which responds to planetary and stellar influences, and which, when obstructed in its flow through the physical body, induces illness and disease. In this connection see the etymology of the related 'VENENI'.

Yoga A term derived from the Sanskrit to denote a variety of techniques devoted to arriving at union with the divine–spiritual ground of the world, or to a lesser extent at ecstatic states or a clear perception of truth. The word originally meant approximately 'conjunction' or 'union', the union sought by such practices being with the divine–spiritual in man and the cosmos. In India, where the schools of Yoga are most widely studied in modern times, it is one of the six schools of philosophy (*darsanas*) ascribed to the sage Patanjali. There are several different forms of yogic practice and discipline. Hatha-Yoga is concerned with the development of the physical body, by means of disciplines or postures, to reach into higher states. Bhakti-Yoga is a form concerned with development by means of devotion or affection. Raja-Yoga, generally regarded as being the highest and most spiritual of the methods, is concerned with development by means of psychic disciplines and the concentration of thought. Since Yoga is properly concerned with inner disciplines and with states of consciousness, it is worth observing that there are eight stages recorded in the esoteric realm of

247

Yoga. That of forbearance or restraint is called Yama. That of religious observations (fasting, prayers, etc.) is called Niyama. That by means of physical postures is alled Asana (from a verbal root *as* meaning 'to sit quietly'). That by means of the regulation of breathing is called Pranayama. That by means of the withdrawal of consciousness from the bodily sheath is called Pratyahara. That by means of mental concentration, steadiness and resolution is called Dharana. That by means of the total gathering of consciousness into union with the divine spirit is called Samadhi, a word meaning approximately 'to direct towards'.

Yuga In the Hindu chronology, which has had some influence on modern esoteric thought, the *yuga* is a 'world age', a thousandth part of a KALPA. Each *yuga* is preceded by a twilight period (*sandhya*) and terminated by a twilight period (*sandhyansa*), and the four yugic periods (together called a *mahayuga* – which also incorporates the twilights) are named KRITA YUGA, TRETA YUGA, DWAPARA YUGA and KALI YUGA. The periods are expressed in divine years and in the mortal years of ordinary time: the divine year is equal to 360 mortal years. The Krita is 4800 divine years or 1,728,000 mortal years. The Treta is 3600 divine years or 1,296,000 mortal years. The Dwapara is 2400 divine years or 864,000 mortal years. The Kali Yuga is 1200 divine years or 432,000 mortal years. In spite of such reliable figures, one still finds certain writers maintaining that mankind entered the present age, which is that of the Kali Yuga, at the death of Krishna (*c.* 3102 BC) and that this age thereore ended in 1898 (or thereabouts). However, the Hindu tradition insists that the world is still in the Kali Yuga.

Yugic periods See YUGA.

Z

The last letter of the alphabet. In some occult texts the Z alone, or with a vertical line through it, stands for Jupiter, presumably from the Grecian 'Zeus'. Significantly the Hebraic equivalent, Zayin, is said to represent a sceptre. The numerological link between Z and SEVEN is derived from the association of this number with the Hebraic Zayin.

Zachariel The name given to the SECUNDADEIAN BEING who is the ruler of the sphere of Jupiter.

Zadakiel A variant for ZADKIEL.

Zadkiel One of the more important names given to the spiritual being ruling the sphere of Jupiter, the name meaning 'righteousness of God'.

Zagan One of the seventy-two SPIRITS OF SOLOMON, appearing to the magician in the form of a winged bull. He is especially adept in alchemy.

Zaleos One of the names of SALEOS.

Zaphkiel In Qabbalism this Archangel is the creative force working in the Saturnine sphere of BRIAH. His name is usually translated as meaning 'beholder of God' or 'watcher of God', and he is described as the 'Eye' by which the necessary contact with wisdom is maintained by man in order to permit him to make decisions sensibly. He is said to be the chief of the THRONES. He is sometimes called Iophiel, although Fludd puts this Archangel over the Cherubim, and thus beyond the sphere of Saturn.

Zazel The name given by Agrippa (quoting ancient Qabbalistic sources) to the DAEMON of Saturn, for whom he gives the magical number 45. See AGIEL.

Zepar One of the seventy-two SPIRITS OF SOLOMON, raised because he can bring any woman to love any man.

Zero It is the great zero of 0, which defines the world and God. In ordinary life one might draw a zero and think that one is enclosing a small space within a circle of line – the numerologist however knows that in drawing such a circle he is defining the whole cosmos beyond it. The space inside is a mirror image of the whole vastness of space. One draws a zero, 0, and in so doing one describes the zodiac on the edge of space and time. This is why the 0 is called the womb from which all other numbers proceed – indeed, from which all life emanates. The monadic 1 confronts the whole world of 0 to make the number 10, a symbol of the individual facing up to his own destiny or karma, and defining himself as an upright man (Blavatsky gives the figure 10 precisely as a symbol for the upright knowing man!). Yet the man is an occult symbol himself, and the number 10 is the Wheel of Fortune (see TAROT), which carries him as an isolated monad between the alpha and omega space of 9 (1 + 9 = 10). This figure, by necessary reduction, leads back only to the monadic 1 (1 + 0 = 1), and the human being stands alone on the Wheel of Fortune, which is life. So a philosophy is constructed around the relationship which the nine numbers hold to this strange zero of 0 – it is at once a zero of nothingness and the great circle of the Stellatum which embraces all.

Another example will throw more light on this claim. As we see in the entry for N, this letter is linked with the image of a fish, and is equated with the number 50; this is to say that the 5 defines itself by confronting the zero of the world and the perfect circle of God (what Eckhart called the 'quintessential nothingness'). This is $5 + 0 = 5$, so that 50 reduces to 5, the number of the Quintessence, the sacred ETHERIC. The etheric has at all times been pictured as a sea, as waters, the 'virgin waters', and the like, so we should not be surprised to find a fish swiming in such a spiritual sea (sometimes called 'Nun'). This fish is of course the Christ, the 'Ichthus' of the early Christians. The image of the pentagram, such as we see in the MORNING STAR (Figure 55), is in this context the crucified Christ.

We see from these examples that the zero has the power to carry an individual number out into the speculative realm of thought itself, out into the cosmos which it represents, yet, by virtue of its intrinsic nature when the two figures are subjected to reduction, the number is again dropped back from the cosmos into its own isolated significance. Thus, the 50 of N carries us out into Christian speculations on the nature Christ, and the Piscean symbolism of the fish, but, on reduction to 5, drops us back into the pentacle symbol and the five wounds of Christ. See NUMBERS.

Zervana Akarana   The name of an ancient Persian primal god, variously translated as meaning 'without limit of time' or 'duration in a circle', although obviously pointing to an eternal existence beyond the time barrier of the sphere of Saturn. This primal Zervan is interesting to occultists, since images used to depict him combine the symbolism of the so-called TETRAMORPHS into one figure.

Zeugon   A Greek term, sometimes romanized as Zugon, meaning 'beam of a balance', and used to denote both zodiacal and constellational Libra.

Zeus   The name given to a HYPOTHETICAL PLANET.

Ziruph   See TZIRUPH.

Zoa   See FOUR ZOAS.

Zodiac   Properly speaking, the belt centred on the ecliptic, divided into twelve arcs of 30 degrees and called the 'signs of the zodiac' and named as in the sequence set out in Table 32. Confusion has arisen because of the similarity of the names used to denote the signs of the zodiac and the twelve asterisms of the Stellatum, which are included among the fourteen or so which extend into the zodiacal belt. Figure 87 shows a standard zodiac image of twelve equal arcs, while Figure 25 under CONSTELLATION ZODIAC shows a standard modern division of the asterisms into unequal arcs

Figure 86 (right):   *An early sixteenth-century wood engraving of the Ptolemaic divisions of the heavens with a traditional zodiacal belt. Note the terminology of the upper spheres: the 'primum mobile', the 'Crystalline [Heavens]' and the 'Firmament', which was the sphere of the fixed stars, the ancient Stellatum*

Table 32

Sign	Abbreviation	Sigil	Greek	Sanskrit
Aries	AR	♈	Krios	Mesham
Taurus	TA	♉	Tauros	Vrisha
Gemini	GE	♊	Didemoi	Mithuna
Cancer	CN	♋	Karkinos	Karkata
Leo	LE	♌	Leon	Simha
Virgo	VG	♍	Parthenos	Kanya
Libra	LB	♎	Zugos	Tula
Scorpio	SC	♏	Skorpios	Vrischika
Sagittarius	SG	♐	Toxotes	Dhanus
Capricorn	CP	♑	Aigokeros	Makara
Aquarius	AQ	♒	Hydroxous	Kumbha
Pisces	PI	♓	Ichthues	Mina

PRIMVM MOBILE
CRISTALLINE
FIRMAMENT

FIER
AER
YEARTH

CŒLIFER ATLAS

Hic canet errantē Lunam, Solisq; labores
Arcturūq;,pluuiasq; hyad.gēinosq; triões

ID.

Figure 87   *The tropical zodiac of equal-arc divisions. The images of the zodiac are set within the central circle, while the corresponding sigils for the zodiac are contained in the outer ring*

with similar names – these latter are properly the zodiacal constellations. The zodiac is properly the *zodiacus*, a Latin term derived from the Greek *zodion*, itself etymologically connected with the word *zoon*, which is difficult of translation, but which (as Smith has shown) is certainly linked with the idea of life or with living beings. The popular derivations insist that the Greek zodiac was a circle of animals (which is simply not true), so that the ancient series of twelve images within a zodiacal belt (Figure 86) was often called the 'Animal Zodiac' or the 'Twelve Animals' and so on. These images, which must not be confused with the SIGNS of the zodiac, were almost certainly derived from the equivalent constellational asterisms, with which they are all too often equated. Esotericists insist that this zodiac (the original *zodiacus*) was really a circle of living beings – a concept which, of course, links with the living beings of the biblical Ezekiel, associated with the CHERUBIM as the beings who dwell outside time.

Zodiacal age   See PRECESSION.

Zodiacal angels   As with the ZODIACAL SPIRITS, there is much confusion as to the

nomenclature and roles of the zodiacal angels, and this confusion is at least as old as Agrippa. However, it is the name list preserved by Agrippa which has been absorbed into modern astrology, to the extent that the names are still important, even if the specific functions of the angels are now confused:

AR	– Malchidiel	GE	– Ambriel
LE	– Verchiel	LB	– Zuriel
SG	– Adnachiel	AQ	– Gabiel
TA	– Asmodel	CN	– Muriel
VG	– Hamaliel	SC	– Barbiel
CP	– Hanael	PI	– Barchiel

The Archangels are sometimes wrongly called 'zodiacal angels' – these are MICHAEL, RAPHAEL, GABRIEL and URIEL, respectively of the elemental regions of Fire, Air, Water and Earth.

Zodiacal man   See MELOTHESIC MAN.

Zodiacal spirits   In the esoteric tradition the true zodiacal spirits are variously the CHERUBIM and the SERAPHIM, depending upon the system of hierarchies used. However, the term is often in modern times misused for any of the spirits associated with the individual signs of the zodiac (for example, Ausiel as zodiacal spirit or governor of zodiacal Aquarius). Such names go back to the time when it was believed that the planetary motions were imparted and regulated by spiritual beings. Even by the time of Agrippa, when the last fragments of the esoteric tradition relating to spirits were being put into print, there was much confusion as to the spiritual beings, the ZODIACAL ANGELS, the SECUNDADEIAN BEINGS, the PLANETARY ANGELS and even the whole range of CELESTIAL HIERARCHIES being confused in name and operation.

Zodiacus   A Latin term for the tropical zodiac, used to distinguish this from the CONSTELLATIONAL ZODIAC (Figure 25).

Zodiacus vitae   The Latin for 'zodiac of life', sometimes applied to the idea that the various signs of the zodiac symbolize (in their progression from Aries to Pisces) sequential eras or periods which may be related analogously to the life of mankind, individual humans, mythopoetic legends and so on.

Zohar One of the basic texts of the Jewish Qabbalistic system, the *Sepher ha Zohar* (*Book of Splendour*), comprising a vast collection of treatises from widely different sources and of a composite nature. While much of the text is very ancient, it was probably compiled in its present form by Rabbi Moses de Leon in the fourteenth century. The mystical and occult speculations within the text are complex but of the highest spiritual order, incorporating Platonic, Gnostic and Manichean sources, as well as strains of apocalyptic literature, marked dualism, concepts of metempsychosis and legends from the rabbinic tradition.

Zophkiel See ZAPHKIEL.

Zugos One of the Greek names for the sign and constellation Libra. An earlier term, *Chelon ton Skorpion* ('Claws of the Scorpion') points to a time when the constellation was regarded as being a part of the SCORPIUS asterism.

Bibliography

The following book list is by no means a complete bibliography of texts dealing with occult terminologies – it is merely a list of authors mentioned in the preceding text. In view of the availability of numerous modern reprints of out-of-copyright occult texts, I have sought not to confuse the reader by including the names of publishers, deeming it sufficient to give only the year of publication of the edition which I consulted in my own reading, and wherever possible giving foreign titles in English translations when I know these to be available. The classical texts I have listed only by author and title.

Addey   J. Addey, *Astrology Reborn*, 1971.

Agrippa   Agrippa von Nettesheim, *Occulta Philosophia*, 1531. But see also NOWOTNY.

Allen   P. M. Allen, *A Christian Rosenkreutz Anthology*, 1968.

Apuleius   Apuleius, *The Golden Ass*.

Arenson   A. Arenson, *Leitfaden Durch 50 Vortragszyklen Rudolf Steiner*, 1972 edn.

Arnaldus   Arnaldus of Villanova. See NOWOTNY.

Arpentigny   C. S. D'Arpentigny, *La Chirognomie*. . . . But see E. H. Allen, *The Science of the Hand*.

Augustine   St Augustine, *The City of God*.

Bach   H. I. Bach, *C. J. Jung on Synchronicity*, 1953.

Bailey   A. Bailey, *A Treatise on the Seven Rays: Vol. III – Esoteric Astrology; A Treatise on White Magic*, 1934; *A Treatise on Cosmic Fire*, 1970 edn.

Barrett   F. Barrett, *The Magus, or Celestial Intelligencer*, 1801.

Berry   A. Berry, *Porhyry's Work against the Christians*, 1933.

Besant   A. Besant (and C. W. Leadbeater), *Thought-Forms*.

Binsfeld   P. Binsfeld, 'Commentarius de Maleficis' to *Tractatus de confessionibus*, 1589. But see also ROBBINS.

Blake   W. Blake. See S. F. Damon, *A Blake Dictionary*, 1965.

Blavatsky   H. P. Blavatsky, *Isis Unveiled*, 1877; *The Secret Doctrine*, 1888; *Theosophical Glossary*, 1892.

Bodin   J. Bodin, *Daemonomania*, 1580.

Boehme   J. Boehme, *The Three Principles*. See also W. Law, *The Works of Jacob Behmen the Teutonic Theosopher*, 1764.

Boirac   E. Boirac, *La Psychologie Inconnu*, 1915. See also *The Psychology of the Future*, 1918.

Bond   F. B. Bond, *The Gates of Remembrance*. See also W. W. Kenawell, *The Quest at Glastonbury*.

Bozzano   E. Bozzano, 'Dei Fenomeni Premonitori', in *Luce e Ombra*, 1914.

Buchanan   H. R. Buchanan, *Manual of Psychometry*, 1889.

Bulwer-Lytton   E. G. Bulwer-Lytton, *The Coming Race*, 1871.

Butler   H. E. Butler, *Solar Biology*, 1920 edn.

Calmet   A. Calmet, *The Phantom World*, 1850 trans.

Carus   G. C. Carus, *Ueber Grund und Bedeutung der verschiedenen Formen der Hand in vershieden Personen*, 1846.

Cavendish   R. Cavendish, *The Black Arts*.

Collin   R. Collin (R. C. Smith), *The Theory of Celestial Influences*, 1971 edn.

Conches   William of Conches, *Philosophicarum et Astronomicarum*, 1531.

Constable   T. J. Constable, *The Cosmic Pulse of Life*, 1976.

Cook   Florence Cook. See PODMORE.

Cornell   H. L. Cornell, *Encyclopaedia of Medical Astrology*, 1972 edn.

Crookes   W. Crookes, *Researches in the Phenomena of Spiritualism*, 1926 edn.

Crowley   'Master Therion' (A. Crowley), *Magick in Theory and Practice*, 1963 edn.

Dante   Dante Alighieri, *The Divine Comedy*. See E. Moore, *Studies in Dante. Third Series – Miscellaneous Essays*, 1968 edn.

D'Arpentigny   C. S. D'Arpentigny, *The Science of the Hand*, trans. by E. H. Allen, 1886.

Davis   A. J. Davis, *The Diakka, and their Earthly Victims . . .*, 1873; *Penetralia*, 1850.

Davison   *Dictionary of Angels, including the Fallen Angels*.

Dee   J. Dee, *Monas Hieroglyphica*, 1558.

Delporte   E. Delporte, *Atlas Celeste*, 1930.

Dorneus   G. Dorneus, *Dictionarum Theophrasti Paracelsi*, 1574.

Elworthy   F. T. Elworthy, *The Evil Eye*, 1895.

Feerhov   F. Feerhov, *Kursus der praktischen Astrologie*, 1912.

Fludd   W. Fludd, *Utriusque Cosmi . . . Historia . . .*, 1617.

Fodor   N. Fodor, *Encyclopaedia of Psychic Science*, 1966 edn.

Gardner   E. L. Gardner, *Fairies*.

Gaule   J. Gaule, *Mysmantia*, 1652.

Gettings   F. Gettings, *Dictionary of Occult, Hermetic and Alchemical Sigils*, 1981; *The Hidden Art*, 1979; *Dictionary of Astrology*, 1986.

Grasshoff   C. L. Grasshoff (Max Heindel), *The Rosicrucian Cosmo-conception*, 1909 edn.

Gray   W. G. Gray, *The Latter of Lights (or Qabalah Renovata)*, 1971.

Gurdjieff   See OUSPENSKY.

Gurney   E. Gurney *et al.*, *Phantasms of the Living*, 1886.

Harrison   C. J. Harrison, *The Transcendental Universe*, 1893.

Haase   R. Haase, 'Kepler's Harmonics . . .', in *Vistas in Astronomy*, vol. 18, 1975.

Heindel   M. Heindel, *The Rosicrucian Cosmo-conception*, 1937 edn.

Hoult   P. Hoult, *A Dictionary of Some Theosophical Terms*, 1910.

Hudson   William Hudson. See GETTINGS.

Huxley   A. Huxley, *The Perennial Philosophy*.

Iamblichus   T. Taylor (trans.), *Theurgia, or the Mysteries of the Egyptians, Chaldeans, and Assyrians*, 1895.

Jensen   H. Jensen, *Sign, Symbol and Script*, 1970.

Jones   M. E. Jones, *Occult Philosophy: an Introduction, the Major Concepts and a Glossary*, 1971.

Jung   C. G. Jung. See R. Wilhelm, *The I Ching or Book of Changes*, with foreword by Jung, 1951. In connection with synchronicity, see BACH.

Kardec   A. Kardec, *The Book of Spirits*, 1898 trans.

Kircher   A. Kircher, *Oedipus Aegyptiacus, hoc est universalis doctrinae hieglyphicae instauratio*, 1652/55.

Kramer   See SPRENGER.

Leadbeater   C. W. Leadbeater, *The Chakras*, 1927; *The Inner Life*, 1910; *The Astral Plane*.

Leo   A. Leo, *Alan Leo's Dictionary of Astrology*, 1929.

Levi   'Eliphas Levi' (L. A. Constant), *Transcendental Magic*, 1871.

Long   M. F. Long, *The Secret Science behind Miracles*, 1954 edn.

Lovejoy   A. O. Lovejoy, *The Great Chain of Being*, 1964 edn.

Lubicz   R. A. Schwaller de Lubicz, *The Temple is Man: The Secrets of Ancient Egypt*, 1977.

Maclagan   R. C. Maclagan, *Evil Eye in the Western Highlands*.

Macrobius   A. T. Macrobius, *Commentarii in Somnium Scipionis*. See T. Whittaker, *Macrobius, or Philosophy, Science and Letters in the Year 400*, 1923.

Magnus   See OLAUS.

Maltwood   K. E. Maltwood, *Itinerary of 'The Somerset Giants'*, 1946.

Mead   G. R. S. Mead, *The Doctrine of the Subtle Body in Western Tradition*, 1919.

Mesmer   F. A. Mesmer. See G. Frankau, *Mesmerism by Doctor Mesmer (1779)*, 1948.

Michaelis   S. Michaelis, *A Discourse of Spirits*, 1613 trans.

Morrish   L. F. Morrish, *Outline of Astro-Psychology*, 1952.

Myers   F. W. H. Myers, *Human Personality and its Survival of Bodily Death*, 1903 edn.

Nostradamus   M. de Nostradame, *Les Centuries de Michel Nostradamus*, 1555. But see also J. Laver, *Nostradamus*, 1946.

Nowotny   K. A. Nowotny, *De Occulta Philosophia: Agrippa ab Nettesheym*, 1967.

O'Brien   M. J. O'Brien, *Prophecy of St Malachy*, 1897.

Olaus   Olaus Magnus, *A Compendious History of the Goths, Swedes, and Vandals*, 1658 trans.

Origen   See MEAD.

Ouspensky   P. D. Ouspensky, *A New Model of the Universe*, 1931.

Ovid   *Metamorphoses*.

Pagan   I. M. Pagan, *From Pioneer to Poet*, 1911 edn. *Racial Cleavage, or the Seven Ages of Man*, 1937.

Paracelsus   See A. E. Waite, *The Hermetic and Alchemical Writings of . . . Paracelsus the Great*, 1894.

Petarius   D. Petarius, *Uranologion*, 1630.

Philalethes   E. Philalethes, *The Fame and Confession of the Fraternity of R: Rc:*, 1652. But see also ALLEN and PARACELSUS.

Plancy, de   J. A. S. Collin de Plancy, *Dictionnaire Infernal*, 1818 edn.

Podmore   F. Podmore, *Modern Spiritualism: a History and a Criticism*, 1902.

Porphyry   See BERRY.

Powell   A. E. Powell, *The Causal Body and the Ego*, 1928; *The Etheric Double*.

Psellus   M. Psellus, *De Operatione Daemonum Dialogus*, 1615.

Ptolemy   C. Ptolemeus, *Tetrabiblos*, ed. and trans. by F. E. Robbins, 1914.

Purucker   G. de Purucker, *Occult Glossary: a Compendium of Oriental and Theosophical Terms*, 1972.

Ram   See GETTINGS, 1986.

Reichenbach   K. L. von Reichenbach, *Les phénomènes odiques*, 1907.

Ringbom   S. Ringbom, *The Sounding Cosmos*, 1970.

Robbins   R. H. Robbins, *The Encyclopaedia of Witchcraft and Demonology*, 1959.

Schultz   J. Schultz, *Rhythmen der Sterne*, 1963.

Schussler   *The Biodynamic Cell-Salts*.

Scot   R. Scot, *The Discoverie of Witchcraft*, 1886 edn.

Sendivogius   M. Sendivogius, *A New Chymical Dictionary*, 1674.

Spence   L. Spence, *An Encyclopaedia of Occultism*, 1960.

Sprenger   J. Sprenger and H. Kramer, *Malleus Maleficarum*, 1486.

Stebbing   L. Stebbing, *A Dictionary of the Occult Sciences*, no date.

Steiner   R. Steiner, *Occult Science – an Outline*, 1914; *Man in the Light of Occultism, Theosophy and Philosophy*, 1945 edn; *Reincarnation and Karma: Their Significance in Modern Culture*, 1960 edn.

Sudre   R. Sudre, *Treatise on Parapsychology*, 1960 edn.

Summers   M. Summers, *The Geography of Witchcraft*, 1927.

Swedenborg   E. Swedenborg, *De Coelo et de Inferno*, 1850 edn.

Tertullian   See MEAD.

Thierens   A. E. Thierens, *Elements of Esoteric Astrology*, 1931.

Thury   J. Thury, *Les Tables Tournantes . . .* , 1855.

Trachtenberg   J. Trachtenberg, *Jewish Magic and Superstition*, 1939 edn.

Trismegistus   See the Editors of the Shrine of Wisdom, *The Divine Pymander of Hermes Trismegistus*, 1955 edn.

Trithemius   J. Trithemius, *De Septem Secundadeis . . .* , 1520.

Thompson   R. C. Thompson, *Semitic Magic, Its Origins and Development*, 1908.

Varley   J. Varley. See A. T. Story, *James Holmes and John Varley*, 1894.

Wachsmuth   G. Wachsmuth, *Etheric Formative Forces*, 1932, *Reincarnation as a Phenomenon of Metamorphosis*, 1937.

Waite   A. E. Waite. See PARACELSUS.

Walker   E. D. Walker, *Reincarnation: a Study of Forgotten Truth*, 1952.

Wierius   J. Weiher, *De Praestigiis Daemonum*, 1563.